Higher **BIOLOGY**
for CfE

D1513646

Writing Team:

James Torrance

James Fullarton

Clare Marsh

James Simms

Caroline Stevenson

Diagrams by **James Torrance**

HODDER GIBSON
AN HACHETTE UK COMPANY

The publishers would like to thank the following for permission to reproduce copyright material:

Photo credits
p.1 (background) and Unit 1 running head image © 2010 Steve Allen/Brand X Pictures/photolibrary.com; p.1 (inset left) © april21st – Fotolia, (inset centre) © Dr Keith Wheeler/Science Photo Library, (inset right) James Torrance; p.9 © Science Source/Science Photo Library; p.25 © april21st – Fotolia; p.31 Image prepared by Eric Martz from 7tim using Jmol (MolviZ.Org); p.32 © PHOTOTAKE Inc./Alamy; p.46 (left) © Dr Keith Wheeler/Science Photo Library, (right) © M.I. Walker/Science Photo Library; p.50 © Deco Images II/Alamy; p.51 © Cindee Madison and Susan Landau, UC Berkeley; p.54 © James King-Holmes/Science Photo Library; p.59 James Torrance; p.74 © Aurora Photos/Alamy; p.78 © Scott Camazine/Alamy; p.79 © Medical-on-Line/Alamy; p.81 (top) © Németh János 1995-2005/Fotolia.com, (bottom) James Torrance; p.90 (left) © NeverHome – Fotolia, (centre) © David Hosking/Alamy, (right) © Miguel Castro/Science Photo Library; p.92 © surub – Fotolia; p.98 © Ingram Publishing Limited; p.113 (background) and Unit 2 running head image © Loren Rodgers – Fotolia; p.113 (inset left) © Natural Visions/Alamy, (inset centre) © Dennis Kunkel Microscopy, Inc/Visuals Unlimited, Inc., (inset right) © Dennis Kunkel Microscopy, Inc./Visuals Unlimited/Corbis; p.117 © CNRI/Science Photo Library; p.118 © PHOTOTAKE Inc./Alamy; p.132 © Michael J. Gregory, Ph.D./Clinton Community College; p.154 © Orlando Florin Rosu – Fotolia; p.163 © Norbert Wu/Minden Pictures/FLPA; p.164 © Caro/Alamy; p.173 (top left) © outdoorsman – Fotolia, (top right) © EcoView – Fotolia, (bottom) © feathercollector – Fotolia; p.176 © Mangiarotti/Rex Features; p.177 (left) © Natural Visions/Alamy, (right) © FLPA/Linda Lewis; p.178 © Steve Byland – Fotolia; p.179 © FLPA/John Holmes; p.180 © Mark Parisi, permission granted for use. www.offthemark.com; p.186 © Dennis Kunkel Microscopy, Inc/Visuals Unlimited, Inc.; p.189 (top) © David Scharf/Science Faction/Corbis, (bottom) © Dr Jeremy Burgess/Science Photo Library; p.198 © Dennis Kunkel Microscopy, Inc./Visuals Unlimited/Corbis; p.225 (background) and Unit 3 running head image © pro6x7 – Fotolia; p.225 (inset left) © Anna – Fotolia, (inset centre) © Jef Meul/Minden Pictures/FLPA RM, (inset right) © Oceans-Image/Photoshot; pp.241, 242, 246, 247 (all) James Torrance; p.26 © Nigel Cattlin/Alamy; p.255 (top) © Image used with permission from the Plant and Soil Sciences eLibrary at http://passel.unl.edu, hosted by the Institute of Agriculture and Natural Resources at the University of Nebraska-Lincoln, (bottom) © Anna – Fotolia; p.256 © Margo Harrison – Fotolia; p.258 © Image used with permission from the Plant and Soil Sciences eLibrary at http://passel.unl.edu, hosted by the Institute of Agriculture and Natural Resources at the University of Nebraska-Lincoln; p.261 (top) © FLPA/Nigel Cattlin, (bottom) James Torrance; p.267 © The Natural History Museum/Alamy; p.268 © FLPA/Nigel Cattlin; p.269 © xalanx – Fotolia; p.270 James Torrance; p.276 © FLPA/ – Nigel Cattlin; p.279 © FLPA/Nigel Cattlin; p.280 (top left) © Science VU/J. R. Adams/Visuals Unlimited, Inc., (top right) © dragonraj – Fotolia, (bottom) © FLPA/Nigel Cattlin; p.283 (top) © levo – Fotolia, (bottom) © Eye Ubiquitous/Rex Features; p.284 © Image Source/Raphye Alexius/Getty Images; p.285 (top) © blickwinkel/Alamy, (bottom) © Shaun Finch – Coyote-Photography.co.uk/Alamy; p.288 © Shannon Wheeler/www.tmcm.com; p.291 (left) © FLPA/Ron Boardman/Life Science Image, (right) © Albert Mans/FN/Minden/FLPA RM; p.294 © Oxford Scientific/Getty Images; p.298 © Ron Sanford/Corbis; p.305 © Juniors Bildarchiv/Alamy; p.306 (top left) © Jef Meul/Minden Pictures/FLPA RM, (top right) © FLPA/imagebroker/ROM, (bottom) © FLPA/Jurgen & Christine Sohns; p.308 © Herbert Kehrer/Imagebroker/FLPA RF; p.311 (top) © Cyril Ruoso/Minden Pictures/FLPA RM, (bottom) © Frans Lanting/FLPA; p.312 © Cyril Ruoso/Minden Pictures/FLPA; p.316 © Punch Limited; p.319 © Oceans-Image/Photoshot; p.328 (top) James Torrance (bottom) © John Bracegirdle/Alamy; p.329 (top) ©Claudio Bacinello/Photographic Visions/http://www.photographersdirect.com, (bottom) © Michael Krabs/Imagebroker/FLPA.

Acknowledgements
The authors and publisher would like to extend grateful thanks to Jim Stafford for assistance offered at manuscript stage of this book, as well as for futher guidance and editorial advice during the production process.

Every effort has been made to trace all copyright holders, but if any have been inadvertently overlooked the Publishers will be pleased to make the necessary arrangements at the first opportunity.

Although every effort has been made to ensure that website addresses are correct at time of going to press, Hodder Gibson cannot be held responsible for the content of any website mentioned in this book. It is sometimes possible to find a relocated web page by typing in the address of the home page for a website in the URL window of your browser.

Hachette UK's policy is to use papers that are natural, renewable and recyclable products and made from wood grown in sustainable forests. The logging and manufacturing processes are expected to conform to the environmental regulations of the country of origin.

Whilst every effort has been made to check the instructions of the practical work in this book, it is still the duty and legal obligation of schools to carry out their own risk assessments.

Orders: please contact Bookpoint Ltd, 130 Park Drive, Abingdon, Oxon OX14 4SE. Telephone: (44) 01235 827720. Fax: (44) 01235 400454. Lines are open 9.00–5.00, Monday to Saturday, with a 24-hour message answering service. Visit our website at www.hoddereducation.co.uk. Hodder Gibson can be contacted direct on: Tel: 0141 848 1609; Fax: 0141 889 6315; email: hoddergibson@hodder.co.uk

© James Torrance, James Fullarton, Clare Marsh, James Simms, Caroline Stevenson 2012
First published in 2012 by
Hodder Gibson, an imprint of Hodder Education,
An Hachette UK Company
2a Christie Street
Paisley PA1 1NB

Without Answers
Impression number   5 4
Year   2015
ISBN: 978 1444 158632

With Answers
Impression number   5 4
Year   2015
ISBN: 978 1444 167542

Cover photo © Andy Rouse/naturepl.com
Illustrations by James Torrance
Typeset in Minion Pro 11pt by Fakenham Prepress Solutions, Fakenham, Norfolk NR21 8NN
Printed in Italy by Printer Trento S.r.l.

A catalogue record for this title is available from the British Library

Contents

The book you are holding is from a second (or subsequent) printing of this title. In this version, a short section on positive and negative controls has been added on page 141, there is a new case study on page 165 and an additional Testing Your Knowledge box on page 218. Furthermore, the Chapter/Section names and page numbers above have also been amended from the first printing. These changes have been made to be in line with amendments that were made to the ordering of the Higher syllabus in summer 2014.

Preface

This book has been written to act as a valuable resource for pupils studying Higher Grade Biology. It provides a **core text** which adheres closely to the SQA syllabus for *Higher Biology (revised)* introduced in 2014. Each section of the book matches a unit of the revised syllabus; each chapter corresponds to a content area. In addition to the core text, the book contains a variety of special features:

Suggested Learning Activities

Within each chapter there is an appropriate selection of suggested learning activities exactly as laid down in the SQA Course Support Notes. They take the form of *Case Studies*, *Case Histories*, *Related Topics*, *Research Topics*, *Related Activities* and *Investigations*. These non-essential activities are highlighted throughout in yellow for easy identification. They do not form part of the basic mandatory course content needed when preparing for the final exam but are intended to aid understanding and to support research tasks during course work.

Practical Activity and Report

An assignment designed to match the required performance criteria and provide students with the opportunity to write a *Scientific Report* which includes description of procedure, recording of results, drawing of conclusions and evaluation of procedure. This report satisfies the requirements of a mandatory part of SQA assessment.

Testing Your Knowledge

Key questions incorporated into the text of every chapter and designed to continuously assess *Knowledge and Understanding*. These are especially useful as homework and as instruments of diagnostic assessment to check that full understanding of course content has been achieved.

What You Should Know

Summaries of key facts and concepts as *'Cloze' Tests* accompanied by appropriate word banks. These feature at regular intervals throughout the book and provide an excellent source of material for consolidation and revision prior to the SQA examination.

Applying Your Knowledge and Skills

A variety of questions at the end of each unit designed to give students practice in exam questions and foster the development of *Skills of Scientific Experimentation, Investigation and Enquiry* (in other words, selection of relevant information, presentation of information, processing of information, planning experimental procedure, evaluating, drawing valid conclusions and making predictions and generalisations). These questions are especially useful as extensions to class work and as homework.

Updates and syllabus changes: important note to teachers and students from the publisher

This book covers all course arrangements for Revised Higher and CfE Higher, but does not attempt to give advice on any 'added value assessments' or 'open assignments' that may form part of a final grade in the CfE version of Higher Biology (2015 onwards).

Please remember that syllabus arrangements change from time to time. We make every effort to update our textbooks as soon as possible when this happens, but – especially if you are using an old copy of this book – it is always advisable to check whether there have been any alterations to the arrangements since this book was printed. You can check the latest arrangements at the SQA website (www.sqa.org.uk), and you can also check for any specific updates to this book at www.hoddereducation.co.uk/HigherScience.

We make every effort to ensure accuracy of content, but if you discover any mistakes please let us know as soon as possible – see contact details on back cover.

Unit **1**

DNA and the Genome

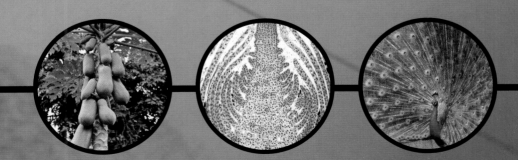

1 Structure of DNA

DNA (deoxyribonucleic acid) is a complex molecule present in all living cells. It stores genetic information in its sequence of bases which determines the organism's genotype and the structure of its proteins.

Structure of DNA

A molecule of DNA consists of two strands each composed of repeating units called **nucleotides**. Each DNA nucleotide consists of a molecule of **deoxyribose** sugar joined to a **phosphate** group and an organic **base**. Figure 1.1 shows the carbon skeleton of a molecule of deoxyribose. Figure 1.2 shows the four types of base present in DNA.

note
^3C = 3'carbon atom
^5C = 5'carbon atom

Figure 1.1 Deoxyribose

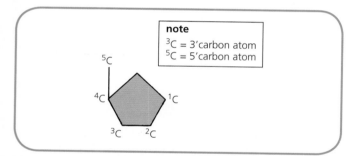

Figure 1.2 Four types of organic base

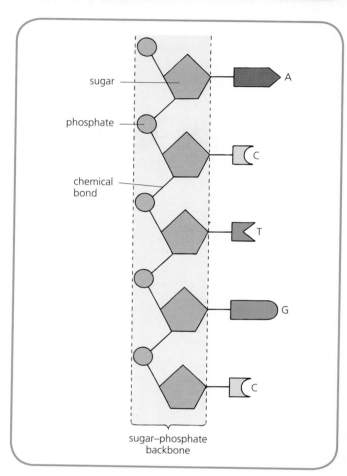

Figure 1.4 Sugar–phosphate backbone

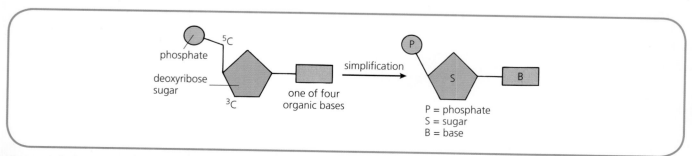

Figure 1.3 Structure of a DNA nucleotide

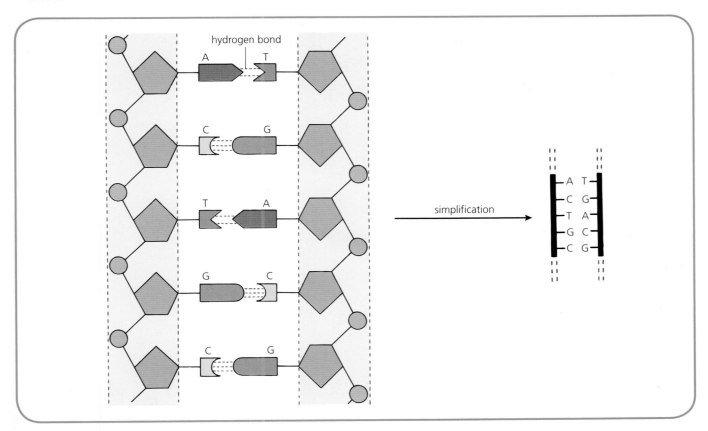

Figure 1.5 Base-pairing

Figure 1.3 shows how the deoxyribose molecule in a nucleotide has a base attached to its carbon 1 and a phosphate attached to its carbon 5. Since there are four types of base, there are four types of nucleotide.

Sugar–phosphate backbone

A chemical bond forms between the phosphate group of one nucleotide and the carbon 3 of the deoxyribose on another nucleotide (see Figure 1.4). By this means neighbouring nucleotides become joined together into a long permanent strand in which sugar molecules alternate with phosphate groups forming the DNA molecule's sugar–phosphate backbone.

Base-pairing

Two of these strands of nucleotides become joined together by hydrogen bonds forming between their bases (see Figure 1.5). However, the hydrogen bonds can be broken when it becomes necessary for the two strands to separate.

Each base can only join up with one other type of base: adenine (A) always bonds with thymine (T) and guanine (G) always bonds with cytosine (C). A–T and G–C are called base pairs.

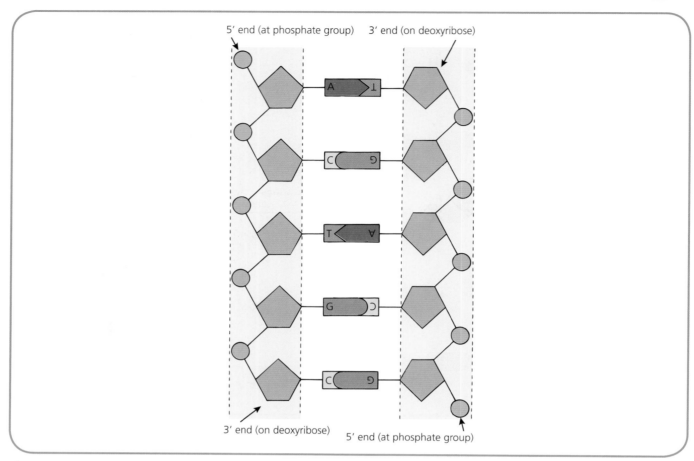

5′ end (at phosphate group)   3′ end (on deoxyribose)

3′ end (on deoxyribose)   5′ end (at phosphate group)

Figure 1.6 Antiparallel strands

Antiparallel strands

A DNA strand's **3′ end** on deoxyribose is distinct from its **5′ end** at a phosphate group. The chain is only able to 'grow' by adding nucleotides to its 3′ end. In Figure 1.6 the DNA strand on the left has its 3′ growing end at the bottom of the diagram and its 5′ end at the top. The reverse is true of its complementary strand on the right. This arrangement of the two strands with their sugar–phosphate backbones running in **opposite directions** is described as **antiparallel**. (For the sake of simplicity the letters in a diagram are normally all written the same way up.)

Double helix

In order for the base pairs to align with each other, the two strands in a DNA molecule take the form of a twisted coil called a **double helix** (see Figure 1.7) with the sugar–phosphate backbones on the outside and the base pairs on the inside. As a result a DNA molecule is like a spiral ladder in which the sugar–phosphate backbones form the uprights and the base pairs form the rungs.

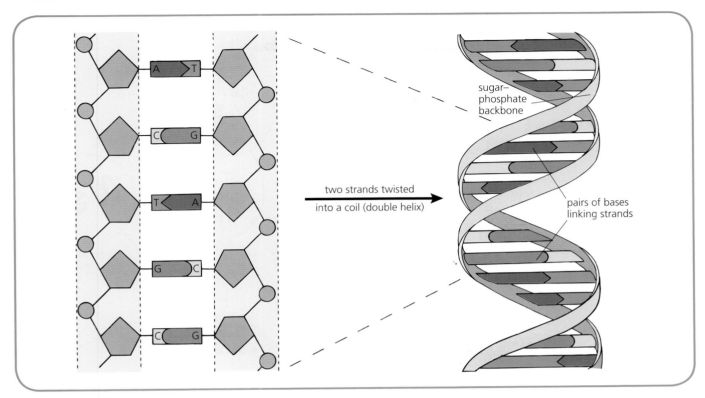

sugar–
phosphate
backbone

two strands twisted
into a coil (double helix)

pairs of bases
linking strands

Figure 1.7 Double helix

Case Study | Identity of genetic material

Proteins or DNA?

During the early part of the twentieth century, genes were known to be located on chromosomes and chromosomes to be composed of protein and DNA. However, scientists did not know for certain which of these two classes of molecule made up the genetic material.

Proteins vary greatly in structure and therefore it was widely believed at the time that they were the hereditary material. DNA, on the other hand, seemed to lack diversity. Therefore it was thought unlikely that DNA would be able to carry the vast quantity of genetic information needed for the transmission and expression of all the traits inherited by every species.

Bacterial transformation

In 1928 a scientist called Griffith was working with two strains of the bacterium *Streptococcus pneumoniae*.

Strain S caused pneumonia in mammals; strain R was harmless. Griffith used these two strains in the experiment shown in Figure 1.8.

From this experiment Griffith concluded that some chemical component had passed from dead S cells to live R cells. These live R cells had become **transformed** into live S cells. He called the chemical substance the **transforming principle** but he did not know which constituent of the bacterial cell was responsible.

Positive identification

The R cell/S cell line of enquiry was pursued by a team of scientists led by Avery. The team repeated Griffith's experiment and systematically isolated each constituent of the disease-causing strain of the bacterium. Over a period of 14 years they tested each substance for its ability to transform R cells to →

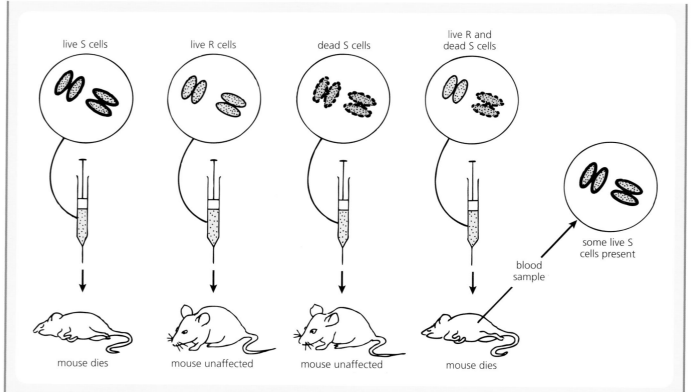

Figure 1.8 Bacterial transformation experiment

S cells. In 1944 they were able to report that without doubt only **DNA fragments** (and not proteins) were able to bring about this transformation. However, many scientists remained sceptical.

Compelling evidence

Background

A bacteriophage (phage for short) is a type of virus that attacks a bacterium and multiplies inside it. Figure 1.9 shows a bacteriophage which attacks

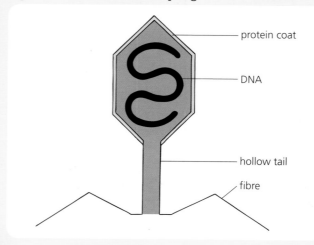

Figure 1.9 Bacteriophage virus

Escherichia coli bacteria. The virus' DNA strand is contained inside a protein coat from which a tail projects. The virus launches an attack by injecting its DNA into the bacterial host cell which then becomes a virus-producing factory (see Figure 1.10).

Phage experiments

In 1952 Hershey and Chase devised experiments to investigate whether the information needed to alter the host cell's biochemical machinery and make new viral particles resided in the original virus' DNA or in its protein coat.

Sulphur is found in protein but not in DNA. Therefore they labelled the protein coats of a group of phage particles by growing them in E. coli cells cultured in the presence of ^{35}S (a radioactive isotope of sulphur).

Phosphorus is found in DNA but not in protein. They labelled the DNA strands of a different group of phage particles by growing them in E. coli cells cultured in the presence of ^{32}P (a radioactive isotope of phosphorus).

Their experiments are shown in Figure 1.11. From these results it was concluded that the viral protein

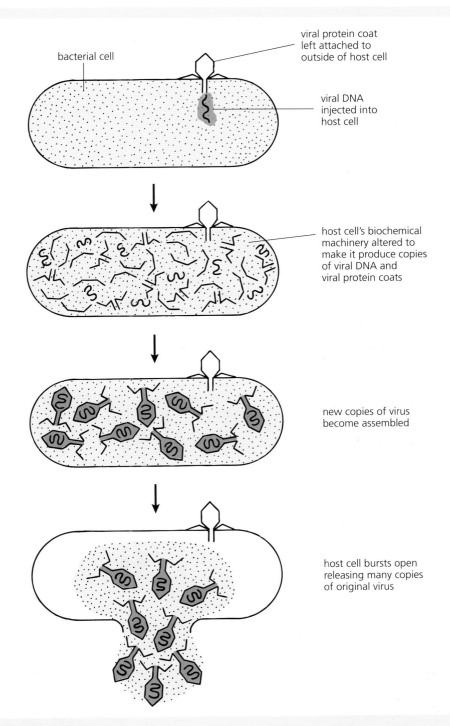

bacterial cell

viral protein coat
left attached to
outside of host cell

viral DNA
injected into
host cell

host cell's biochemical
machinery altered to
make it produce copies
of viral DNA and
viral protein coats

new copies of virus
become assembled

host cell bursts open
releasing many copies
of original virus

Figure 1.10 Multiplication of bacteriophage virus

(labelled with ^{35}S) did not enter the E. coli cells but that the viral DNA (labelled with ^{32}P) did enter the cells. Since the viral DNA was responsible for causing the host cell to produce new copies of the virus, this experiment provided compelling evidence to support the theory that **DNA** (and not protein) is the genetic material responsible for passing on hereditary information.

7

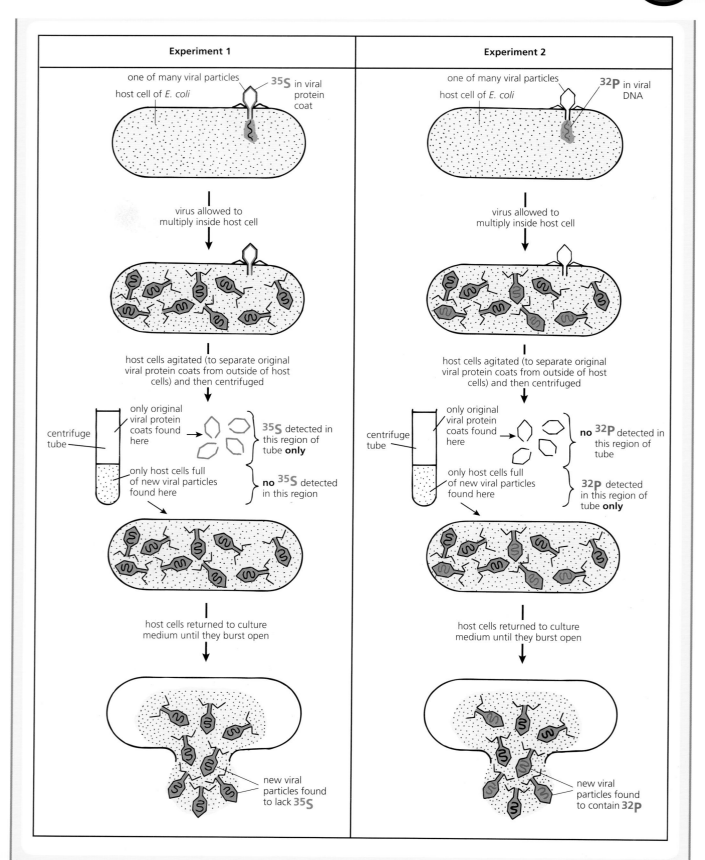

Figure 1.11 Phage experiments of Hershey and Chase

Establishing the structure of DNA

Once DNA was known for certain to be the genetic material, scientists became keen to establish the details of the molecule's three-dimensional structure.

Chemical analysis

In the late 1940s, Chargaff analysed the base composition of DNA extracted from a number of different species. He found that the quantities of the four bases were not all equal but that they always occurred in a **characteristic ratio** regardless of the source of the DNA. These findings, called Chargaff's rules, are summarised as follows:

The number of adenine bases = the number of thymine bases (i.e. A:T = 1:1).

The number of guanine bases = the number of cytosine bases (i.e. G:C = 1:1).

However, Chargaff's rules remained unexplained until the double helix was discovered.

X-ray crystallography

At around the time that Chargaff was carrying out chemical analysis of DNA, Wilkins and Franklin were employing **X-ray crystallography**. When X-rays are passed through a crystal of DNA, they become deflected (diffracted) into a **scatter pattern** which is determined by the arrangement of the atoms in the DNA molecule (see Figure 1.12).

When the scatter pattern of X-rays is recorded using a photographic plate, a **diffraction pattern** of spots is produced (see Figure 1.13). This reveals information which can be used to build up a **three-dimensional picture** of the molecules in the crystal. Wilkins and

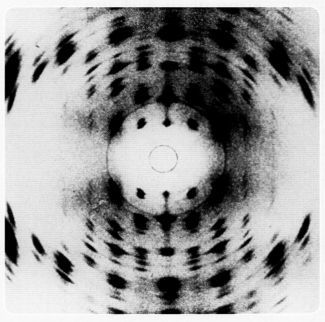

Figure 1.13 X-ray diffraction pattern of DNA

Franklin found that the X-ray diffraction patterns of DNA from different species (such as bull, trout and bacteria) were identical.

Formation of an evidence-based conclusion

From the X-ray diffraction patterns of DNA (produced by Wilkins and Franklin), Watson and Crick figured out that the DNA must be a long, thin molecule of constant diameter coiled in the form of a **helix**. In addition, the density of the arrangement of the atoms indicated to them that the DNA must be composed of **two strands**.

From Chargaff's rules they deduced that base A must be paired with T and base G with C. They figured that this could only be possible if DNA consisted of two strands held together by specific **pairing of bases**. Taking into account further information about distances between atoms and angles of bonds, Watson and Crick set about building a wire model of DNA and in 1953 were first to establish the three-dimensional **double helix** structure of DNA.

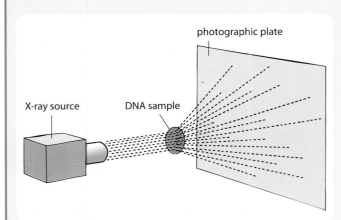

Figure 1.12 X-ray crystallography

Organisation of DNA in prokaryotes and eukaryotes

A molecule of DNA is double-stranded and can be **circular** or **linear** depending on the type of cell to which it belongs and on its location within the cell. Figure 1.14 compares a cell from a bacterium (a **prokaryote**) with a cell from a green plant (a type of **eukaryote**) with respect to the organisation of their DNA.

Some of a prokaryotic cell's DNA may be separate from the main circular chromosome in tiny rings called

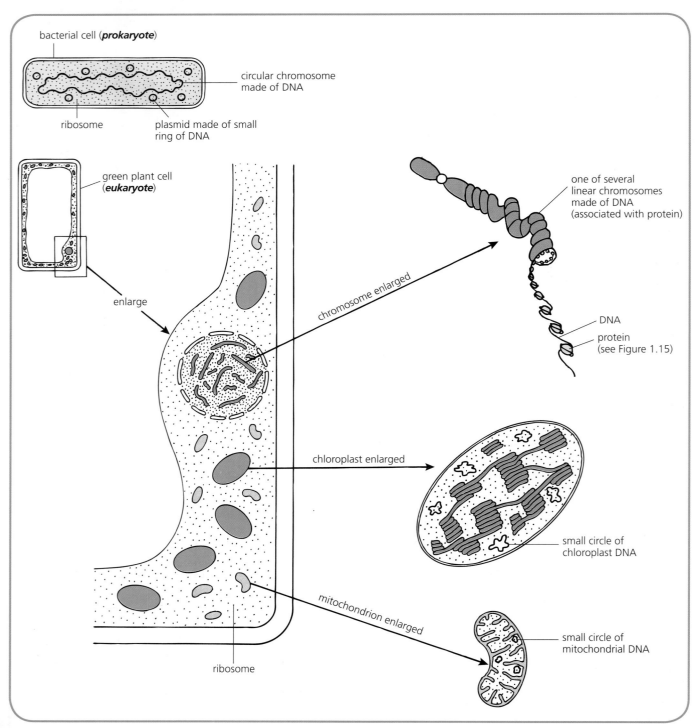

Figure 1.14 Prokaryotic cell and eukaryotic cell (not drawn to scale)

Characteristic	Prokaryotic cell	Eukaryotic cell
organism that has this type of cell	bacteria	fungi, green plants and animals
true nucleus bound by double membrane	absent	present
organisation of chromosomal DNA	composed of a ring of DNA associated with few or no proteins	composed of DNA in linear form associated with proteins
plasmids (each consisting of a small ring of DNA)	present in many types of bacterial cell	present in some yeasts; absent in plant and animal cells
chloroplasts (each containing several small circular chromosomes)	absent	present in green plant cells
mitochondria (each containing several small circular chromosomes)	absent	present
ribosomes	present	present

Table 1.1 Characteristics of prokaryotic and eukaryotic cells

plasmids. Not all of a eukaryotic cell's DNA is located in the nuclear chromosomes. Small **circles** of DNA are present in **chloroplasts** and **mitochondria**. The similarities and differences between the two types of cell are summarised in Table 1.1.

Arrangement of DNA in linear chromosomes

A strand of DNA is several thousand times longer than the length of the cell to which it belongs. Therefore it is essential that DNA molecules be organised in such a way that a chaotic tangle of strands in the nucleus is prevented. This is achieved by the molecules of DNA becoming **tightly coiled** and packaged around bundles of protein like beads on a string (see Figure 1.15). They are able to unwind again when required to do so.

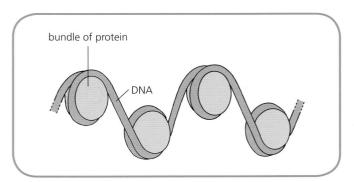

Figure 1.15 Structure of a linear chromosome

Related Activity

DNA gel electrophoresis

Gel electrophoresis is a technique used to separate electrically charged molecules that vary in size by subjecting them to an electric current which forces them to move through a sheet of gel. When the molecules are negatively charged, they move towards the positively charged end of the gel. However, they do not all move at the same rate. Smaller molecules move at a faster rate and are therefore found to have **moved further** than larger molecules in a given period of time.

A **restriction enzyme** (also see page 209, chapter 13) is used to prepare each DNA sample by cutting it at specific sites into smaller pieces of varying lengths characteristic of that type of DNA. Figure 1.16 illustrates the separation of three samples of DNA: sample C (from the crime scene), sample S1 (from suspect 1) and sample S2 (from suspect 2) using gel electrophoresis. From the results it is concluded that the DNA from suspect 2 matches the DNA from the crime scene.

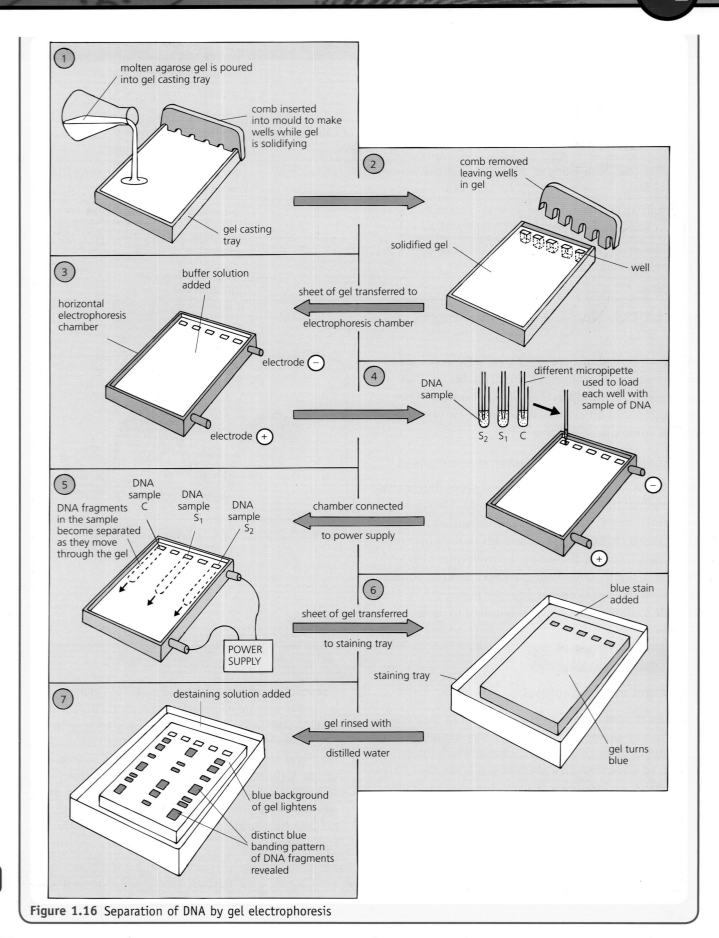

Figure 1.16 Separation of DNA by gel electrophoresis

Related Activity

DNA extraction from plant tissue

DNA can be isolated from cells as shown in Figure 1.17 for pea seeds. When kiwi fruit is used instead of peas, most of the white strands that form as a precipitate in the upper layer of cold ethanol are made of pectin (a complex carbohydrate) rather than DNA. Since the DNA is obscured by pectin, this result is described as a **false positive**.

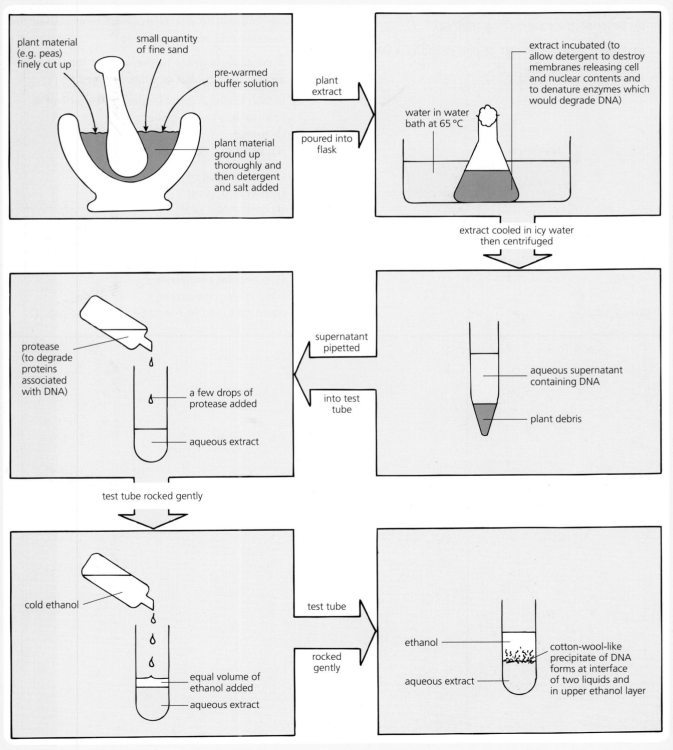

Figure 1.17 Isolation of DNA from plant tissue

Testing Your Knowledge

1 a) i) How many different types of base molecule are found in DNA?
   ii) Name each type. (3)

   b) Which type of bond forms between the bases of adjacent strands of a DNA molecule? (1)

   c) Describe the base-pairing rule. (1)

2 a) Figure 1.18 shows part of one strand of a DNA molecule.

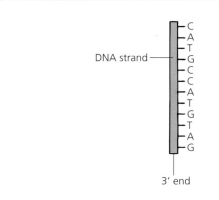

DNA strand —

C
A
T
G
C
C
A
T
G
T
A
G

3' end

Figure 1.18

   i) Redraw the strand and then draw the complementary strand alongside it.
   ii) Label the 3$'$ end and the 5$'$ end on each strand. (2)

   b) DNA consists of two strands whose backbones run in opposite directions. What term is used to describe this arrangement? (1)

3 a) What name is given to the twisted coil arrangement typical of a DNA molecule? (1)

   b) If DNA is like a spiral ladder, which part of it corresponds to the ladder's
   i) rungs;
   ii) uprights? (2)

4 a) Identify a type of
   i) prokaryotic cell
   ii) eukaryotic cell
   that contains plasmids.
   iii) What is a plasmid? (3)

   b) State where:
   i) a circular chromosome
   ii) a linear chromosome
   could be found in the same eukaryotic cell. (2)

2 Replication of DNA

DNA is a unique molecule because it is able to direct its own **replication** and reproduce itself exactly. The replication process is shown in a simple way in Figure 2.1.

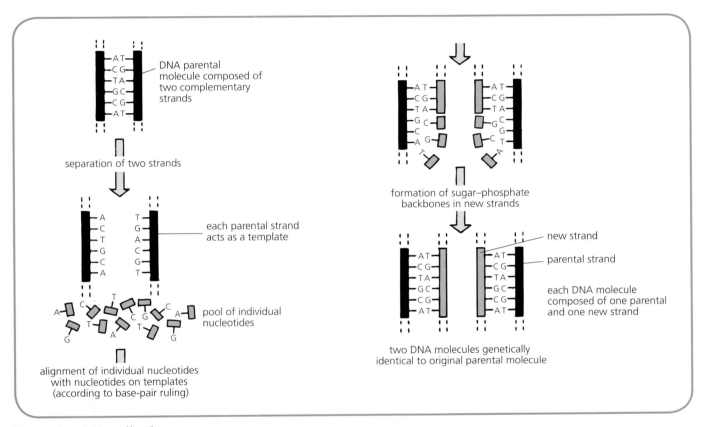

Figure 2.1 DNA replication

Case Study   **Establishing which theory of DNA replication is correct**

Watson and Crick accompanied their model of DNA with a theory for the way in which it could replicate. They predicted that the two strands would unwind and each act as a template for the new complementary strand. This would produce two identical DNA molecules each containing one 'parental' strand and one newly synthesised strand. This so-called **semi-conservative** replication remained a theory until put to the test by Meselson and Stahl.

Hypotheses

Figure 2.2 shows three different hypotheses, each of which could explain DNA replication.

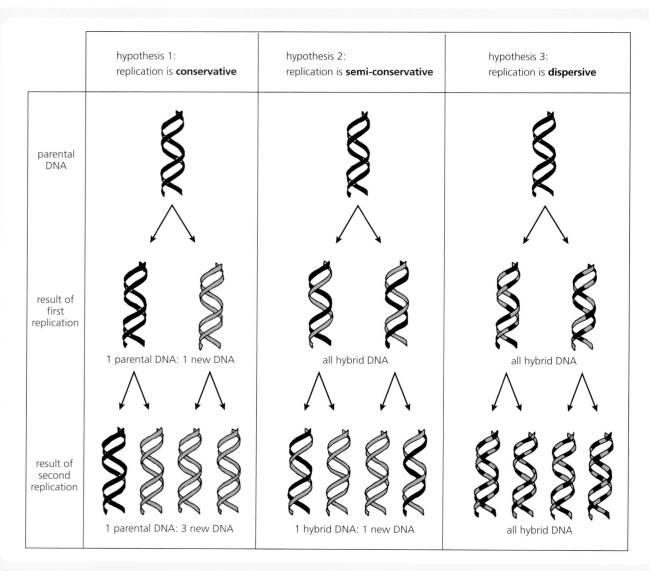

Figure 2.2 DNA replication hypotheses

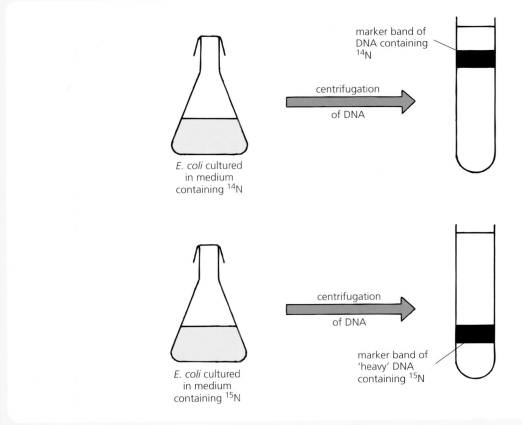

Figure 2.3 Labelling DNA with ^{14}N or ^{15}N

Testing the hypotheses

Background

When E. coli bacteria are cultured, they take up nitrogen from the surrounding medium and build it into DNA. They can be cultured for several generations in medium containing the common isotope of nitrogen (^{14}N) or the heavy isotope (^{15}N) as their only source of nitrogen. When DNA is extracted from each type of culture and centrifuged, the results shown in Figure 2.3 are obtained.

Putting the hypotheses to the test

Meselson and Stahl began with E. coli that had been grown for many generations in medium containing ^{15}N. They then cultured these bacteria in medium containing ^{14}N and sampled the culture after 20 minutes (the time needed by the bacteria to replicate DNA once). Figure 2.4 predicts the outcome of the experiment for each of the three hypotheses. Figure 2.5 shows the actual results of the experiment. From these results it is concluded that hypothesis 2 is supported and that the replication of DNA is **semi-conservative**.

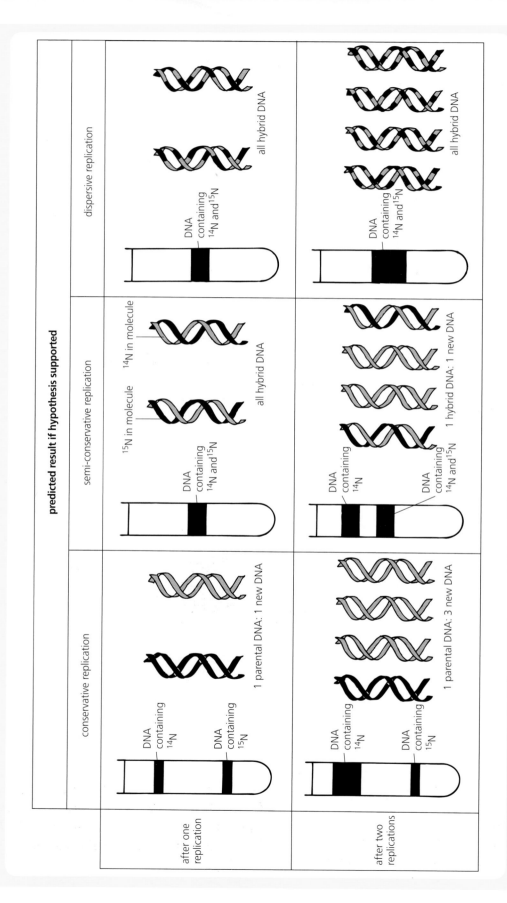

Figure 2.4 Predictions

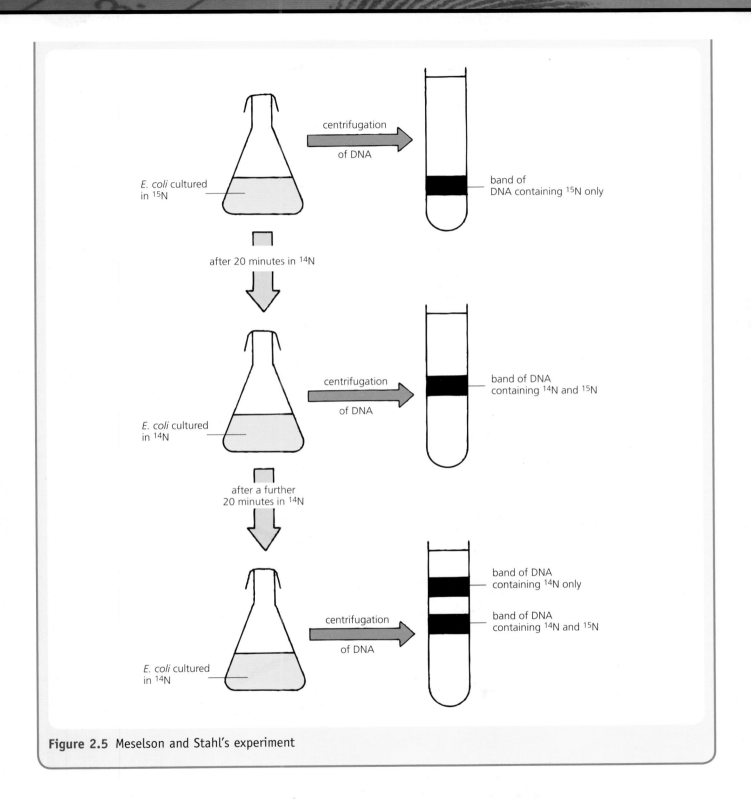

Figure 2.5 Meselson and Stahl's experiment

Enzyme control of DNA replication

DNA replication is a complex process involving many enzymes. It begins when a starting point on DNA is recognised. The DNA molecule unwinds and weak hydrogen bonds between base pairs break allowing the two strands to separate ('unzip'). These template strands become stabilised and expose their bases at a Y-shaped replication fork (see Figure 2.6).

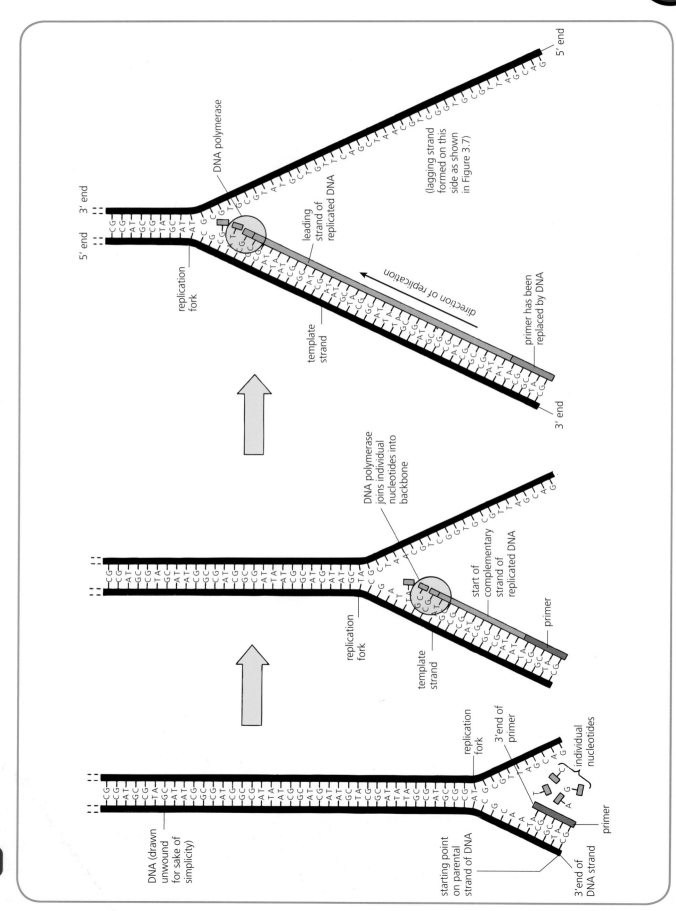

Figure 2.6 Formation of leading strand of replicated DNA

Formation of the leading DNA strand

The enzyme that controls the sugar–phosphate bonding of individual nucleotides into the new DNA strand is called **DNA polymerase**. This enzyme can only add nucleotides to a pre-existing chain. For it to begin to function, a **primer** must be present. This is a short sequence of nucleotides formed at the 3$^{/}$ end of the parental DNA strand about to be replicated as shown in Figure 2.6.

Once individual nucleotides have become aligned with their complementary partners on the template strand (by their bases following the base-pairing rules), they become bound to the 3$^{/}$ end of the primer and formation of the complementary DNA strand begins. Formation of sugar–phosphate bonding between the

primer and an individual nucleotide and between the individual nucleotides themselves is brought about by DNA polymerase. Replication of the parental DNA strand which has the 3$^{/}$ end is **continuous** and forms the **leading** strand of the replicated DNA.

Formation of the lagging DNA strand

DNA polymerase is only able to add nucleotides to the free 3$^{/}$ end of a growing strand. Therefore the DNA parental template strand which has the 5$^{/}$ end has to be replicated in fragments each starting at the 3$^{/}$ end of a primer as shown in Figure 2.7.

Each fragment must be primed as before to enable the DNA polymerase to bind individual nucleotides together. Once replication of a fragment is complete, its

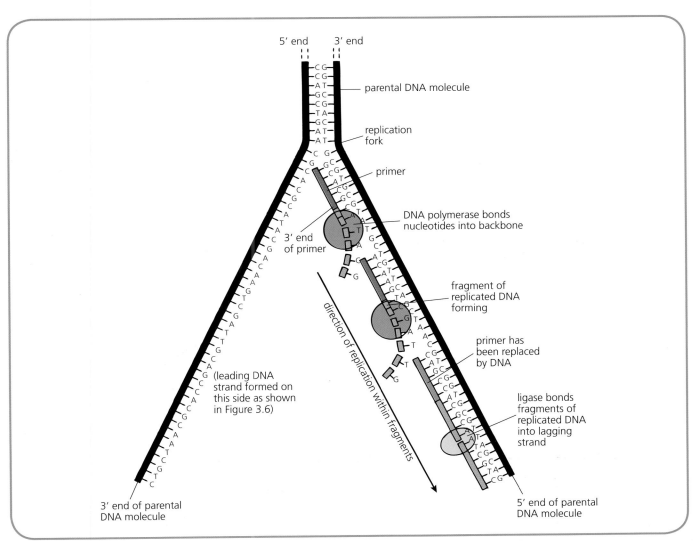

Figure 2.7 Formation of the lagging strand of replicated DNA

primer is replaced by DNA. Finally an enzyme called **ligase** joins the fragments together. The strand formed is called the **lagging** strand of replicated DNA and its formation is described as **discontinuous**.

Many replication forks

When a long chromosome (such as one from a mammalian cell) is being replicated, many replication forks operate simultaneously to ensure speedy copying of the lengthy DNA molecule (see Figure 2.8).

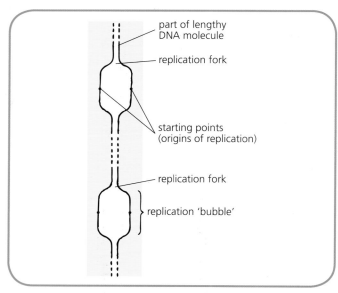

part of lengthy DNA molecule

replication fork

starting points (origins of replication)

replication fork

replication 'bubble'

Figure 2.8 Replication forks

Requirements for DNA replication

For DNA replication to occur, the nucleus must contain:

- DNA (to act as a template)
- primers
- a supply of the four types of DNA **nucleotide**
- the appropriate **enzymes** (such as DNA polymerase and ligase)
- a supply of ATP (for energy – see page 138).

Importance of DNA

DNA is the molecule of inheritance and it encodes the hereditary information in a **chemical language**. This takes the form of a sequence of organic bases, unique to each species, which makes up its **genotype**. DNA replication ensures that an exact copy of a species' genetic information is passed on from cell to cell during growth and from generation to generation during reproduction. Therefore DNA is essential for the continuation of life.

Polymerase chain reaction

The **polymerase chain reaction** (PCR) is a technique (see Figure 2.9) that can be used to create many copies of a piece of DNA *in vitro* (in other words, outside the body of an organism). This **amplification** of DNA involves the use of **primers**. In this case, each primer is a piece of single-stranded DNA complementary to a specific target sequence at the 3$^{/}$ end of the DNA strand to be replicated.

The DNA is heated to break the hydrogen bonds between base pairs and separate the two strands. Cooling allows each primer to bind to its target sequence. During the next step, heat-tolerant DNA polymerase adds nucleotides to the primers at the 3$^{/}$ end of the original DNA strands.

The first cycle of replication produces two identical molecules of DNA, the second cycle four identical molecules and so on giving an exponentially growing population of DNA molecules. By this means a tiny quantity of DNA can be greatly amplified and provide sufficient material for forensic purposes such as **DNA fingerprinting**. Further practical applications of PCR are given in the case study on page 24.

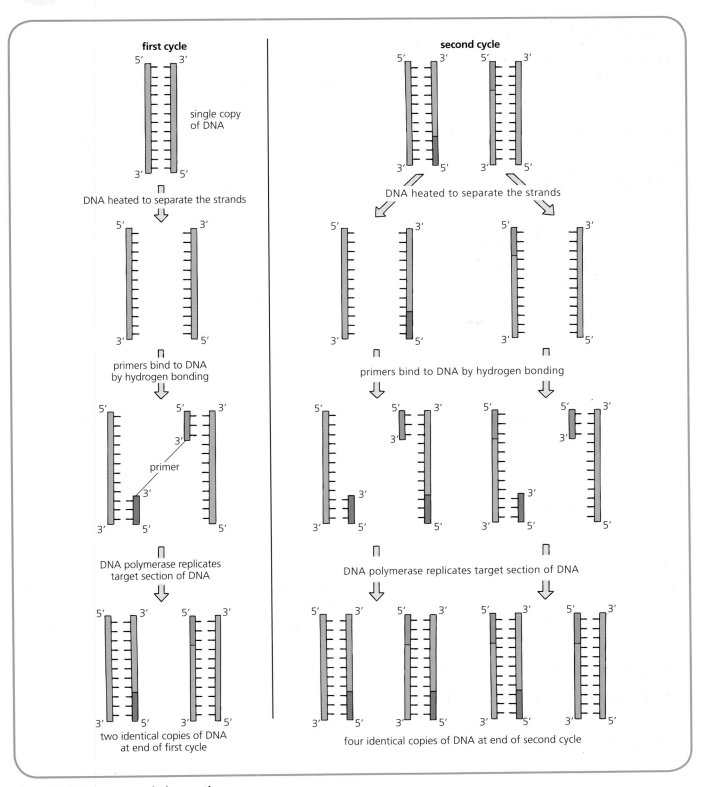

Figure 2.9 Polymerase chain reaction

Case Study | Use of PCR

PCR has been used to amplify DNA from many sources such as:

- blood, semen or tissue from a crime scene for DNA fingerprinting

- embryonic cells for prenatal diagnosis of genetic disorders (such as Duchenne muscular dystrophy)

- viruses

- preserved remains of extinct species (such as the woolly mammoth)

- chloroplasts for investigating plant evolution (also see page 24).

PCR depends on a process called **thermal cycling**. A cycle consists of three steps each carried out at a different temperature. The earliest designs of this technique used three water baths and normal DNA polymerase. The latter was destroyed during the heating step in the cycle and had to be replaced for use in the next cycle.

The following two important innovations enabled PCR to become automated:

- the isolation of **heat-tolerant** DNA polymerase from a species of bacterium native to hot springs

- the invention of the **thermal cycler**, a computerised heating machine able to control the repetitive temperature changes needed for PCR.

Figure 2.10 shows a simplified version of the steps carried out during thermal cycling in order to amplify DNA.

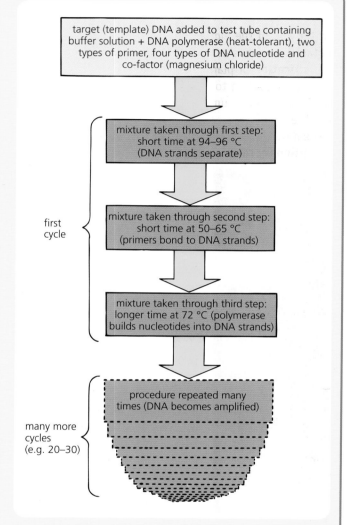

Figure 2.10 Amplification of DNA by thermal cycling

Related Topic

'Needles and haystacks'

Equally as impressive as the amplification of DNA by PCR is the **specificity** of the reaction. Each primer is a piece of single-stranded DNA synthesised as the exact complement of a short length of the DNA strand to which it is to become attached. This enables the primer to find 'the needle in the haystack'.

In other words it is able to locate, among many different sites, the specific target DNA sequence that is to be amplified. The process then goes on to produce millions or even billions of copies of the DNA. Therefore this amplification of DNA by PCR is sometimes described as being like 'a haystack from the needle'.

Related Topic

Investigating plant evolution using PCR

At the end of the eighteenth century the Swedish botanist Linnaeus carried out a comprehensive **classification** of plants by grouping them into families according to structural similarities such as leaf shape, petal number, seed type and presence or absence of a vascular system. However, Linnaeus' system does not always identify true underlying **evolutionary relationships**. This is because natural selection sometimes results in the development of similar structural adaptations by unrelated groups in response to environmental change.

Chloroplast (chloroplasmic) DNA

On average a green plant cell contains 10–100 chloroplasts and each of these contains 50–100 copies of **chloroplast DNA (cpDNA)**. cpDNA is ideal for evolutionary studies for the following reasons. It is inherited through egg cells and does not show variation resulting from recombination ('shuffling') of genetic material during gamete formation. However, it does show **mutations** that have occurred over time such as nucleotide insertions and deletions (also see page 60). Therefore cpDNA can be extracted from various types of green plant and compared for similarities and differences.

PCR

PCR is used to amplify the cpDNA. The cpDNA samples from a wide variety of plants can then be analysed using gel electrophoresis and their '**genetic fingerprints**' compared. From the results botanists are able to use this information to:

- group plants according to similarities and differences in their cpDNA

- infer evolutionary relationships

- construct a new family tree for flowering plants.

DNA evidence from molecular techniques indicates, for example, that the cabbage plant is a close relative of the tropical papaya plant (see Figure 2.11).

Figure 2.11 Papaya plant

Testing Your Knowledge

1. Decide whether each of the following statements is true or false and then use T or F to indicate your choice. Where a statement is false, give the word that should have been used in place of the word in bold print. (5)

   a) During DNA replication, each DNA parental strand acts as a **template**.

   b) A guanine base can only pair up with a **thymine** base.

   c) Complementary base pairs are held together by weak **antiparallel** bonds.

   d) Each new DNA molecule formed by replication contains one **parental** and one new strand.

   e) Many copies of a DNA sample can be synthesised using the **polymerase** chain reaction.

2. Figure 2.12 shows part of a DNA molecule undergoing replication. Match numbers 1–6 with the following statements. (6)

   a) DNA polymerase promotes formation of a fragment of the lagging strand of replicating DNA.

b) Parental double helix unwinds.

c) DNA polymerase bonds nucleotide to primer.

d) Ligase joins fragments into the lagging strand of replicating DNA.

e) DNA polymerase promotes formation of the leading strand of replicating DNA.

f) DNA molecule becomes stabilised as two template strands.

3 a) Name FOUR substances that must be present in a nucleus for DNA replication to occur. (4)

b) Briefly explain why DNA replication is important. (2)

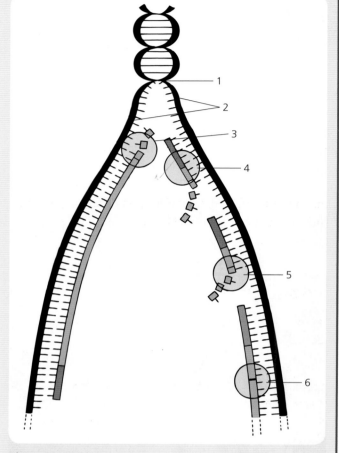

Figure 2.12

3 Control of gene expression

A cell's **genotype** (its genetic constitution) is determined by the sequence of the DNA bases in its genes (the genetic code). A cell's **phenotype** (its physical and chemical state) is determined by the proteins that are synthesised when the genes are expressed. Gene expression involves the processes of **transcription** and **translation** (discussed in this chapter). It is affected by environmental factors acting inside and outside the cell. Only a fraction of the genes in a cell are expressed.

Structure of proteins

All **proteins** contain the chemical elements carbon (C), hydrogen (H), oxygen (O) and nitrogen (N). Often they contain sulphur (S). Each protein is built up from a large number of subunits called **amino acids** of which there are 20 different types. The length of a protein molecule varies from many thousands of amino acids to just a few. Insulin, for example, contains only 51.

Related Activity

Separation and identification of amino acids using paper chromatography

Chromatography

Chromatography is a technique used to separate the components of a mixture which differ in their degree of solubility in the solvent. During ascending paper chromatography, the mixture is applied to absorbent paper. As the solvent passes up through the paper, it carries the components of the mixture up to different levels depending on their degree of solubility in the solvent (and the extent to which they are absorbed by the paper).

A strip of chromatography paper is prepared so that it fits the gas jar and the split stopper as shown in Figure 3.1. Plastic gloves are worn when handling the paper to prevent its contamination by amino acids from the skin. The solution of amino acids is spotted and dried repeatedly (see Figure 3.2). A small volume of solvent is added to the gas jar and the end of the paper is dipped into the solvent (see Figure 3.3).

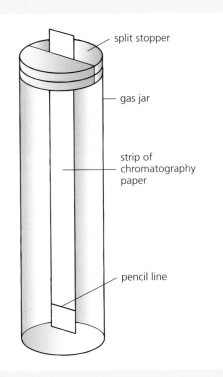

Figure 3.1 Preparing a strip of chromatography paper

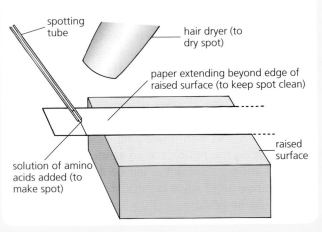

Figure 3.2 Spotting and drying

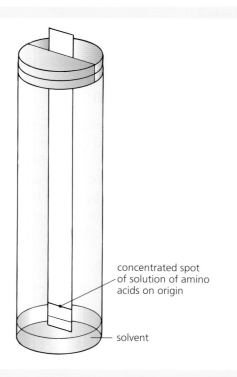

concentrated spot
of solution of amino
acids on origin

solvent

Figure 3.3 Running the chromatogram

The **chromatogram** is allowed to run until the solvent
has almost reached the top of the paper. A second
pencil line is drawn at the highest point reached
by the solvent (called the **solvent front**) and then
the strip is hung up to dry. The chromatogram is
developed in a fume cupboard using ninhydrin spray.
The amino acids show up as purple spots. The solvent
has carried the most soluble amino acids to the
highest position and so on down the paper to the
least soluble one.

Rf (relative front) value

Each amino acid separated by chromatography has
an **Rf value**. This is the ratio of the distance moved
by the amino acid front from the origin to the
distance moved by the solvent front from the origin.
It is normally expressed as a decimal fraction and
is constant for each amino acid provided that the
solvent and the type of paper strip used remain the
same each time.

Figure 3.4 shows a chromatogram with three spots
each indicating the position of an amino acid relative
to the solvent front which has moved 200 mm. Table
3.1 shows how an Rf value is calculated for each of
the three amino acids.

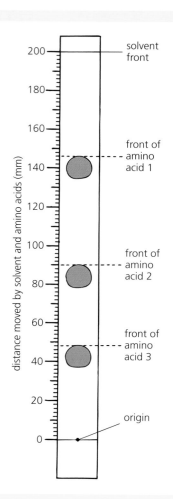

distance moved by solvent and amino acids (mm)

200 — solvent front

180 —

160 —

front of amino acid 1

140 —

120 —

100 —

front of amino acid 2

80 —

60 —

front of amino acid 3

40 —

20 —

origin

0 —

Figure 3.4 Chromatogram

Amino acid	Distance moved by amino acid's front (mm)	Rf value
1	146	146/200 = 0.73
2	90	90/200 = 0.45
3	48	48/200 = 0.24

Table 3.1 Rf calculations

Identification

The three amino acids can be identified by referring
to a table of known Rf values for amino acids in the
same solvent (see Table 3.2). Amino acid 1 is leucine,
amino acid 2 is tyrosine and amino acid 3 is aspartic
acid.

Amino acid	Abbreviation	Rf
histidine	his	0.11
glutamine	glun	0.13
lysine	lys	0.14
arginine	arg	0.20
aspartic acid	asp	0.24
glycine	gly	0.26
serine	ser	0.27
glutamic acid	glu	0.30
threonine	thr	0.35
alanine	ala	0.38
cysteine	cys	0.40
proline	pro	0.43
tyrosine	tyr	0.45
asparagine	aspn	0.50
methionine	met	0.55
valine	val	0.60
tryptophan	tryp	0.66
phenylalanine	phe	0.68
isoleucine	ileu	0.72
leucine	leu	0.73

Table 3.2 Rf values

Polypeptides

Amino acids become linked together into chains by chemical links called **peptide bonds**. Each chain is called a **polypeptide** and it normally consists of hundreds of amino acid molecules linked together. During the process of protein synthesis (see page 34), amino acids are joined together in a **specific order** which is determined by the sequence of bases on a portion of DNA. This sequence of amino acids determines the protein's ultimate structure and function.

Hydrogen bonds

Chemical links known as **hydrogen bonds** form between certain amino acids in a polypeptide chain causing the chain to become coiled or folded as shown in Figure 3.5.

Further linkages

During the folding process, different regions of the chain(s) come into contact with one another. This allows interaction between individual amino acids in one or more chains. It results in the formation of various types of cross-connection including **bridges** between **sulphur** atoms, attraction between positive and negative charges and further hydrogen bonding.

These cross-connections occur between amino acids in the same polypeptide chain and those on adjacent chains. They are important because they cause the molecule to adopt the final **three-dimensional structure** that it needs to carry out its specific function.

Some types of protein molecule are formed by several spiral-shaped polypeptide molecules becoming linked together in parallel when bonds form between them. This gives the protein molecule a rope-like structure.

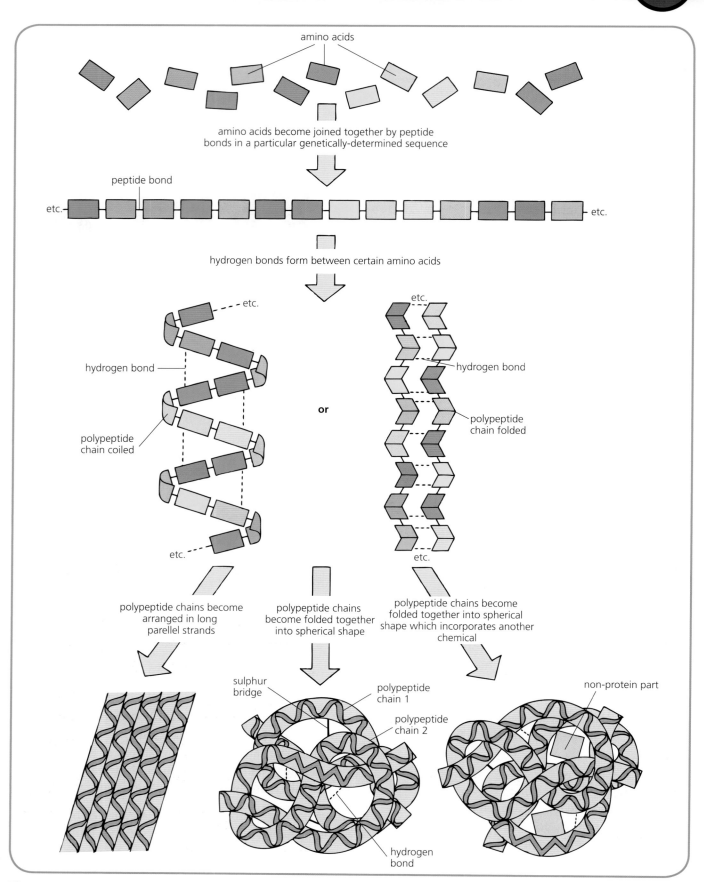

Figure 3.5 Structure of proteins

Other types of protein molecule consist of one or more polypeptide chains folded together into a roughly spherical shape like a tangled ball of string (see Figure 3.5). The exact form that the folding takes depends on the types of further linkage that form between amino acids on the same and adjacent chains. A computer-generated version of a protein molecule's three-dimensional structure is shown in Figure 3.6.

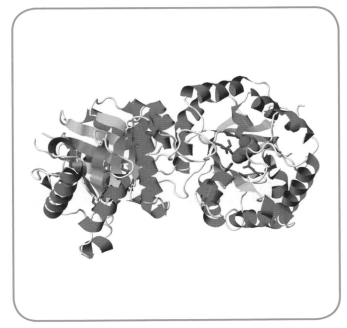

Figure 3.6 Protein molecule as visualised by Jmol software

Related Activity

Separation of fish proteins by agarose gel electrophoresis

Gel electrophoresis (also see page 11) is a technique used to separate electrically charged molecules by subjecting them to an electric current which forces them to move through a sheet of gel.

Eliminating two variable factors

The behaviour of a protein molecule during gel electrophoresis is affected by three variable factors: its shape, its size and its net electric charge. In this experiment variation in shape of the protein molecule and variation in electric charge (in other words, positive or negative) are eliminated by subjecting each protein sample to a negatively charged detergent, a session of heat treatment and a reducing agent. These processes give the molecule a uniformly negative charge and disrupt its hydrogen bonding and sulphur bridges. All the protein molecules become converted to one or more negatively charged linear polypeptides and therefore only vary in **size** (molecular weight).

The technique illustrated in Figure 1.16 on page 12 is used to separate the proteins present in extracts from four species of fish (W, X, Y and Z) and those in a standard sample of known proteins.

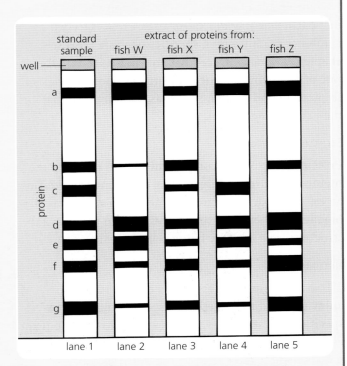

Figure 3.7 Banding results of gel electrophoresis

Identification of fish proteins

Figure 2.7 shows a gel with five lanes resulting from the electrophoresis process. The standard sample is known to contain the seven fish proteins listed in Table 2.3. The band nearest to the well in lane 1 represents the largest protein molecule which has moved the shortest distance (in other words, protein a). Similarly band b represents the next largest and so on to band g that has moved the furthest distance and must be the smallest. Comparison of each of lanes 2–5 with the standard reveals the identity of the proteins present in the extract from a particular species of fish.

Protein	Molecular weight (kDa)
a	210
b	107
c	90
d	42
e	35
f	30
g	5

Table 3.3 Proteins in standard sample

Functions of proteins

A vast variety of structures and shapes exists among proteins and as a result they are able to perform a wider range of functions than any other type of molecule in the body. Some are found in connective tissue, bone and muscle where their strong fibres provide support and allow movement. Other proteins are vital components of all living cells and play a variety of roles as follows.

Enzymes

Each molecule of **enzyme** is made of protein and folded in a particular way to expose an active surface which combines readily with a specific substrate (also see chapter 9). Since intracellular enzymes speed up the rate of biochemical processes such as photosynthesis, respiration and protein synthesis, they are essential for the maintenance of life.

Structural protein

Protein is one of two components which make up the **membrane** surrounding a living cell. Similarly it forms an essential part of all membranes possessed by a cell's organelles. Therefore this type of protein plays a vital structural role in every living cell.

Hormones

These are **chemical messengers** transported in an animal's blood to 'target' tissues where they exert a specific effect. Some hormones are made of protein and exert a regulatory effect on the animal's growth and metabolism. A few examples are given in Table 3.4.

Hormone	Secretory gland	Role of hormone
insulin	pancreas	regulates concentration of glucose in blood
anti-diuretic hormone	pituitary	controls water balance of human body
human growth hormone	pituitary	promotes growth of long bones

Table 3.4 Hormones composed of protein

Antibodies

Although Y-shaped rather than spherical, **antibodies** are also composed of protein (see Figure 3.8). They are made by white blood cells to defend the body against antigens.

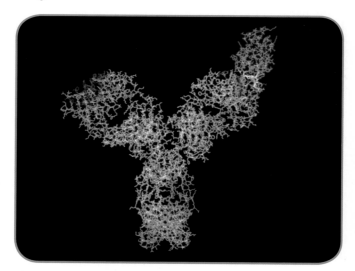

Figure 3.8 Antibody molecule

Associations with other chemicals

Some types of protein molecule are associated with non-protein chemicals (see Figure 3.5). A **glycoprotein** is composed of protein and carbohydrate. An example is mucus, the slimy viscous substance secreted by epithelial cells for protection and lubrication. **Haemoglobin** is the oxygen-transporting pigment in blood. It consists of protein associated with non-protein structures containing iron.

Testing Your Knowledge 1

1 a) How many different types of amino acid are known to occur in proteins? (1)

   b) What name is given to the chain formed when several amino acids become linked together? (1)

   c) What determines the order in which amino acids are joined together into a chain? (1)

   d) Describe TWO ways in which chains of amino acids can become arranged to form a protein. (2)

2 Decide whether each of the following statements is true or false and then use T or F to indicate your choice. Where a statement is false, give the word that should have been used in place of the word in bold print. (5)

   a) Amino acid molecules become linked by **hydrogen** bonds to form polypeptide chains.

   b) A chemical element always present in protein but absent from carbohydrates is **sulphur**.

   c) Folding of polypeptide chains to form a three-dimensional protein molecule results from **hydrogen** bonding.

   d) Insulin is a **hormone** that regulates blood sugar concentration.

   e) A glycoprotein such as mucus is composed of protein and **haemoglobin**.

Structure of RNA

The second type of nucleic acid is called **RNA** (ribonucleic acid). Each nucleotide in an RNA molecule is composed of a molecule of **ribose** sugar, an organic base and a phosphate group (see Figure 3.9). In RNA, the base **uracil (U)** replaces thymine found in DNA. Unlike DNA which consists of two strands, a molecule of RNA is a **single strand** as shown in Figure 3.10. The differences between RNA and DNA are summarised in Table 3.5.

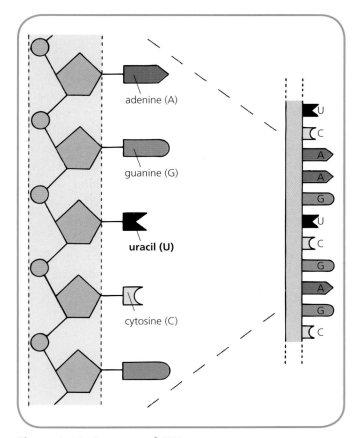

Figure 3.10 Structure of RNA

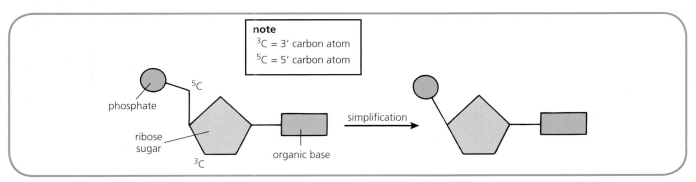

Figure 3.9 Structure of an RNA nucleotide

Characteristic	RNA	DNA
number of nucleotide strands present in one molecule	one	two
complementary base partner of adenine	uracil	thymine
sugar present in a nucleotide	ribose	deoxyribose

Table 3.5 Differences between RNA and DNA

Control of inherited characteristics

The sequence of bases along the DNA strands contains the **genetic instructions** which control an organism's inherited characteristics. These characteristics are the result of many biochemical processes controlled by enzymes which are made of protein. A protein's exact molecular structure, shape and ability to carry out its function all depend on the **sequence of its amino acids**. This critical order is determined by the order of the bases in the organism's DNA. By this means DNA controls the structure of enzymes and in doing so, determines the organism's inherited characteristics.

Genetic code

The information present in DNA takes the form of a molecular language called the **genetic code**. The sequence of bases along a DNA strand represents a sequence of 'codewords'. DNA possesses four different types of base. Proteins contain 20 different types of amino acid. If the bases are taken in groups of three then this gives 64 (4^3) different combinations (see Appendix 1). It is now known that each amino acid is coded for by one or more of these 64 **triplets** of bases. Thus a species' genetic information is encoded in its DNA with each strand bearing a series of base triplets arranged in a specific order for coding the particular proteins needed by that species.

Gene expression through protein synthesis

The genetic information for a particular polypeptide is carried on a section of DNA in the nucleus. However, the assembly of amino acids into a genetically determined sequence takes place in the cell's cytoplasm in tiny structures called **ribosomes**. Figure 3.11 gives an overview of gene expression through protein synthesis. A molecule of **mRNA** (messenger RNA) is formed (**transcribed**) from the appropriate section of the DNA strand and carries that information to ribosomes. There the mRNA meets **tRNA** (transfer RNA) and the genetic information is **translated** into protein.

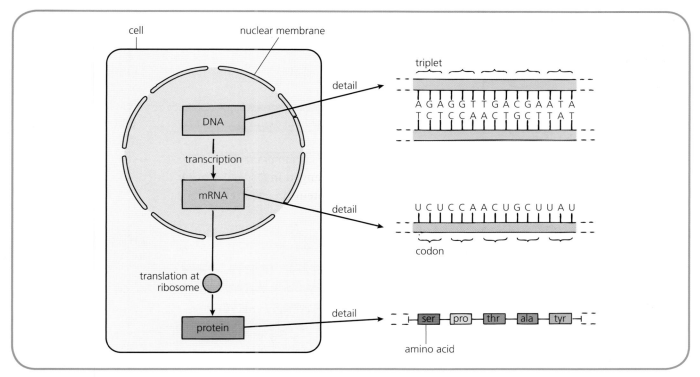

cell
nuclear membrane

DNA

transcription

mRNA

translation at ribosome

protein

detail

triplet

A G A G G T T G A C G A A T A
T C T C C A A C T G C T T A T

detail

U C U C C A A C U G C U U A U

codon

detail

ser — pro — thr — ala — tyr

amino acid

Figure 3.11 Overview of gene expression

Transcription

Transcription is the synthesis of mRNA from a section of DNA. A promoter is a region of DNA in a gene where transcription is initiated as shown in Figure 3.12 (where the DNA strand has been drawn uncoiled for the sake of simplicity).

RNA polymerase is the enzyme responsible for transcription. As it moves along the gene from the promoter, unwinding and opening up the DNA strand, it brings about the synthesis of an **mRNA** molecule. As a result of the base-pairing rule, the mRNA gets a nucleotide sequence complementary to one of the two DNA strands (the template strand) as shown in Figure 3.13.

RNA polymerase can only add nucleotides to the 3′ end of the growing mRNA molecule. The molecule elongates until a terminator sequence of nucleotides is reached on the DNA strand. The resultant mRNA strand which becomes separated from its DNA template is called a **primary transcript** of mRNA.

Modification of primary transcript

Normally the region of DNA transcribed to mRNA is about 8000 nucleotides long yet only about 1200 nucleotides are needed to code for an average-sized polypeptide chain. This is explained by the fact that in eukaryotes long stretches of DNA exist within a gene that do not play a part in the coding of the polypeptide. In addition these non-coding regions, called **introns**, are interspersed between the coding regions, called **exons**. Therefore the region in the primary transcript of mRNA responsible for coding the polypeptide is fragmented.

Splicing

Figure 3.14 shows how the introns are cut out and removed from the primary transcript of mRNA and the exons are **spliced** together to form mRNA with a continuous sequence of nucleotides. This mature transcript of mRNA passes out of the nucleus into the cytoplasm (see Figure 3.15) and moves on to the next stage of protein synthesis where it becomes translated into a sequence of amino acids.

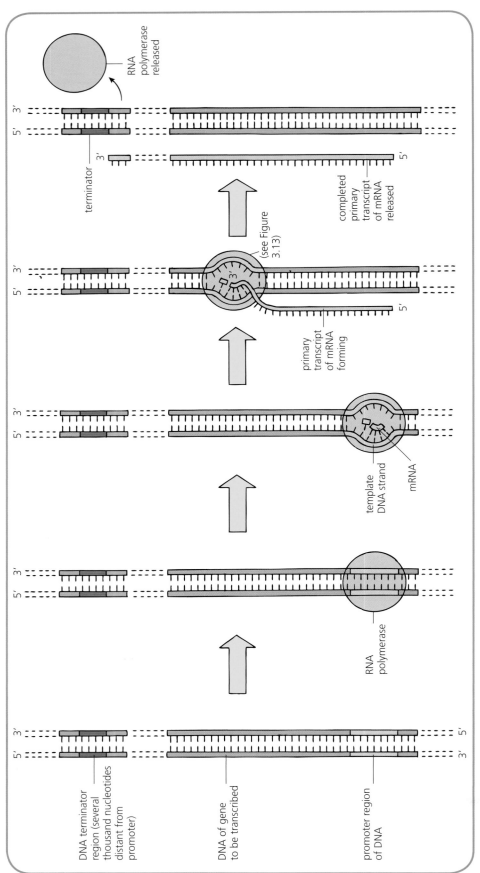

Figure 3.12 Transcription of mRNA

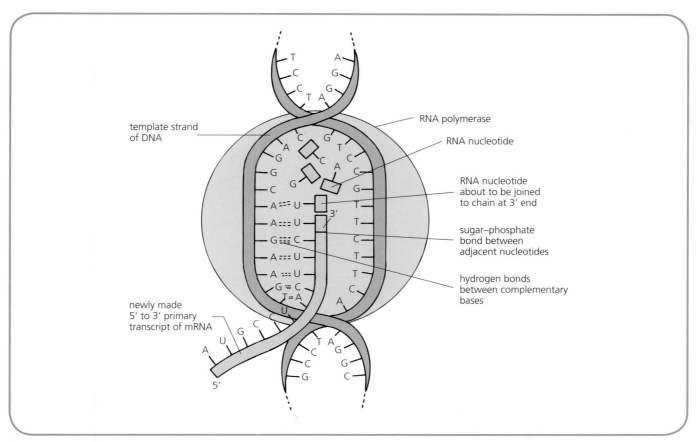

Figure 3.13 Detail of transcription

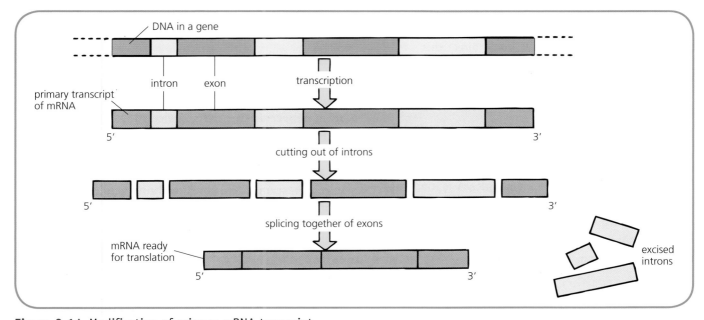

Figure 3.14 Modification of primary mRNA transcript

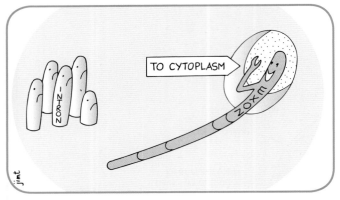

Figure 3.15 'Better luck next time, guys!'

Testing Your Knowledge 2

1. State THREE ways in which RNA and DNA differ in structure and chemical composition. (3)

2. a) In what way does the DNA of one species differ from that of another making each species unique? (1)

   b) How many bases in the genetic code correspond to one amino acid? (1)

   c) What name is given to the groups of bases that make up the genetic code? (1)

3. a) Draw a diagram of the mRNA strand that would be transcribed from section X of the DNA molecule shown in Figure 3.16. (2)

   b) Name the enzyme that would direct this process. (1)

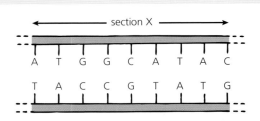

Figure 3.16

4. a) What is the difference between an *exon* and an *intron*?

   b) Which of these must be removed from the primary transcript of mRNA?

   c) By what process are they removed? (3)

Translation

Translation is the synthesis of **protein** as a polypeptide chain under the direction of **mRNA**. The genetic message carried by a molecule of mRNA is made up of a series of base triplets called **codons**. The codon is the **basic unit** of the genetic code. Each codon is complementary to a triplet of bases on the original template DNA strand.

Transfer RNA

A further type of RNA is found in the cell's cytoplasm. This is called **tRNA** (transfer RNA) and it is composed of a single strand of nucleotides. However, a molecule of tRNA has a three-dimensional structure because it is folded back on itself in such a way that hydrogen bonds

form between many of its nucleotide bases as shown in Figure 3.17. Each molecule of tRNA has only one particular triplet of bases exposed. This triplet is called an **anticodon**. It is complementary to an mRNA codon and corresponds to a specific amino acid carried by that tRNA at its **attachment site**.

Table 3.6 shows the relationship between mRNA's codons, tRNA's anticodons and the amino acids coded. Many different types of tRNA are present in a cell, one or more for each type of amino acid. Each tRNA picks up its appropriate amino acid molecule from the cytoplasm's amino acid pool at its site of attachment. The amino acid is then carried by the tRNA to a ribosome and added to the growing end of a polypeptide chain.

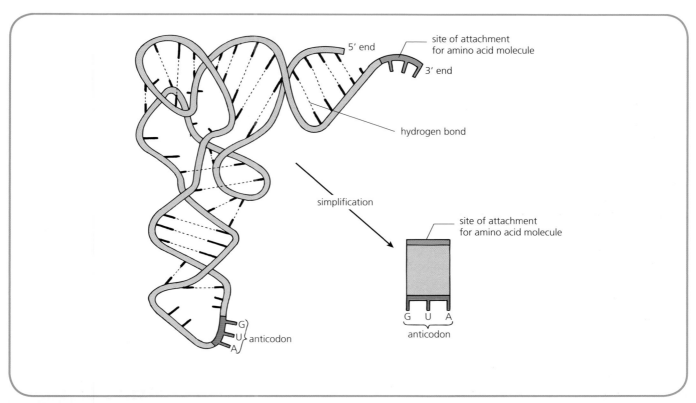

Figure 3.17 Structure of transfer RNA (tRNA)

Codon (mRNA)	Anti-codon (tRNA)	Amino acid	Codon (mRNA)	Anti-codon (tRNA)	Amino acid	Codon (mRNA)	Anti-codon (tRNA)	Amino acid	Codon (mRNA)	Anti-codon (tRNA)	Amino acid
UUU	AAA	} phe	UCU	AGA	} ser	UAU	AUA	} tyr	UGU	ACA	} cys
UUC	AAG		UCC	AGG		UAC	AUG		UGC	ACG	
UUA	AAU	} leu	UCA	AGU		UAA	AUU	STOP	UGA	ACU	STOP
UUG	AAC		UCG	AGC		UAG	AUC	STOP	UGG	ACC	tryp
CUU	GAA	} leu	CCU	GGA	} pro	CAU	GUA	} his	CGU	GCA	} arg
CUC	GAG		CCC	GGG		CAC	GUG		CGC	GCG	
CUA	GAU		CCA	GGU		CAA	GUU	} glun	CGA	GCU	
CUG	GAC		CCG	GGC		CAG	GUC		CGG	GCC	
AUU	UAA	} ileu	ACU	UGA	} thr	AAU	UUA	} aspn	AGU	UCA	} ser
AUC	UAG		ACC	UGG		AAC	UUG		AGC	UCG	
AUA	UAU		ACA	UGU		AAA	UUU	} lys	AGA	UCU	} arg
AUG	UAC	met or START	ACG	UGC		AAG	UUC		AGG	UCC	
GUU	CAA	} val	GCU	CGA	} ala	GAU	CUA	} asp	GGU	CCA	} gly
GUC	CAG		GCC	CGG		GAC	CUG		GGC	CCG	
GUA	CAU		GCA	CGU		GAA	CUU	} glu	GGA	CCU	
GUG	CAC		GCG	CGC		GAG	CUC		GGG	CCC	

Table 3.6 mRNA's codons, tRNA's anticodons and the amino acids coded

The mRNA codon AUG (complementary to tRNA anticodon UAC) is unusual in that it codes for methionine (met) *and* acts as the **start codon**. mRNA codons UAA, UAG and UGA do not code for amino acids but instead act as **stop codons**.

Ribosomes

Ribosomes are small, roughly spherical structures found in all cells. They contain ribosomal RNA (rRNA) and enzymes essential for protein synthesis. Many ribosomes are present in growing cells which need to produce large quantities of protein.

Binding sites

A ribosome's function is to bring tRNA molecules (bearing amino acids) into contact with mRNA. Ribosomes have one binding site for mRNA and three binding sites for tRNA as shown in Figure 3.18.

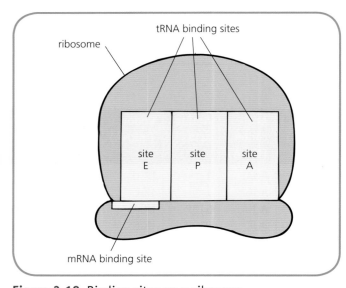

Figure 3.18 Binding sites on a ribosome

Of the tRNA binding sites:

- site P holds the tRNA carrying the growing polypeptide chain

- site A holds the tRNA carrying the next amino acid to be joined to the growing chain by a peptide bond

- site E discharges a tRNA from the ribosome once its amino acid has become part of the polypeptide chain.

Start and stop codons in action

Before translation can begin, a ribosome must bind to the 5$^/$ end of the mRNA template so that the mRNA's **start codon** (AUG) is in position at binding site P. Next a molecule of tRNA carrying its amino acid (methionine) becomes attached at site P by hydrogen bonds between its anticodon (UAC) and the start codon (see Figure 3.19).

The mRNA codon at site A recognises and then forms hydrogen bonds with the complementary anticodon on an appropriate tRNA molecule bearing its amino acid. When the first two amino acid molecules are adjacent to one another, they become joined by a **peptide bond**.

As the ribosome moves along one codon, the tRNA that was at site P is moved to site E and discharged from the ribosome to be reused. At the same time the tRNA that was at site A is moved to site P. The vacated site A becomes occupied by the next tRNA bearing its amino acid which becomes bonded to the growing peptide chain. The process is repeated many times allowing the mRNA to be translated into a complete **polypeptide chain**.

Eventually a **stop codon** (see Table 3.6) on the mRNA is reached. At this point, site A on the ribosome becomes occupied by a release factor which frees the polypeptide from the ribosome. The whole process needs energy from ATP (see chapter 10).

Polyribosome

A single molecule of mRNA is normally used to make many copies of the polypeptide. This **multiple translation** is achieved by several ribosomes becoming attached to the mRNA and translating its message at the same time. Such a string of ribosomes on the same mRNA molecule is called a **polyribosome** (see Figure 3.20).

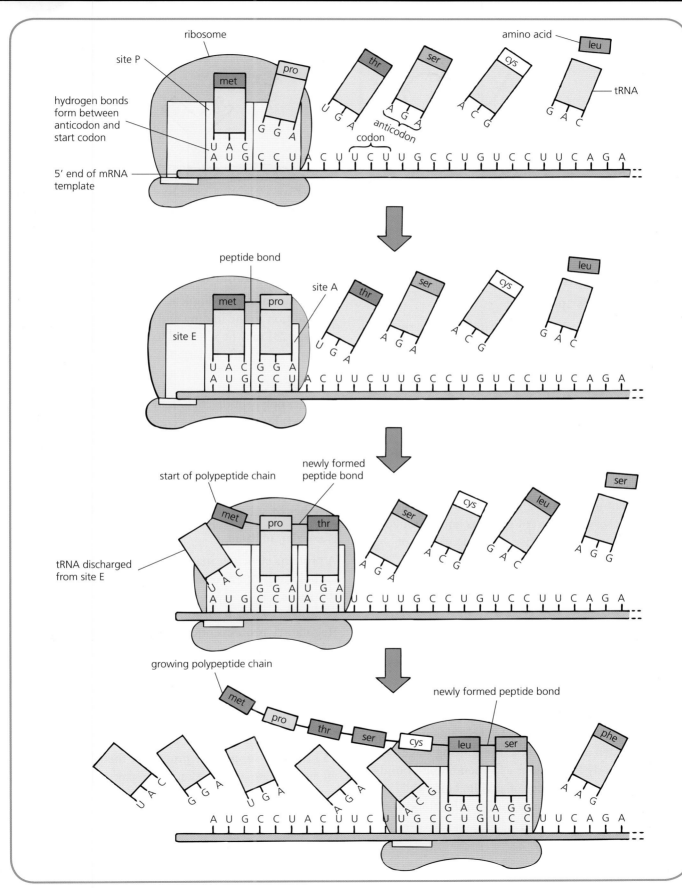

Figure 3.19 Translation of mRNA into polypeptide

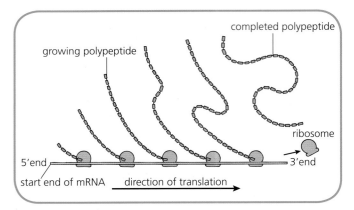

Figure 3.20 Polyribosome

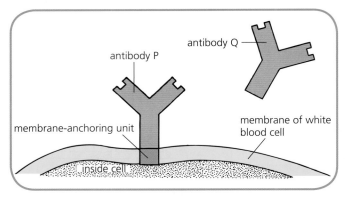

Figure 3.21 Products of alternative RNA splicing

One gene, many proteins

Alternative RNA splicing

Figure 3.14 on page 36 shows a primary transcript of mRNA being cut up and its exons being spliced together to form a molecule of mRNA ready for translation. This molecule of mRNA is not the only one that can be produced from that primary transcript. Depending on circumstances, **alternative segments of RNA** may be treated as the exons and introns. Therefore the same primary transcript has the potential to produce several mRNA molecules each with a different sequence of base triplets and each coding for a different polypeptide. In other words, one gene can code for several different proteins and a limited number of genes can give rise to a wide variety of proteins.

One gene, two antibodies – an example of alternative splicing

An antibody is a Y-shaped protein molecule (see Figure 3.8). The two antibody molecules (P and Q) shown in Figure 3.21 are coded for by the same gene yet they are different in structure. P possesses a membrane-anchoring unit coded for by an exon present in its mRNA. However, this membrane-anchoring unit is absent from Q because its mRNA lacks the necessary exon (discarded as an intron at the splicing stage). As a result, antibody P functions as a membrane-bound protein on the outer surface of a white blood cell whereas antibody Q operates freely in the bloodstream.

Post-translational modifications

Once translation is complete, further modification (in addition to the folding and coiling described on page 28) may be required to enable a protein to perform its specific function.

Cleavage

A single polypeptide chain may need to be cut (cleaved) by enzymes to become active. The protein **insulin**, for example, begins as a single polypeptide chain but requires its central section to be cut out by protease enzymes. This results in the formation of an active protein consisting of two polypeptide chains held together by sulphur bridges as shown in Figure 3.22.

Molecular addition

A protein's structure may be modified by adding a **carbohydrate** component or a **phosphate** group to it. **Mucus**, for example, is a glycoprotein consisting of protein to which carbohydrate has been added. **Regulatory proteins** often require the addition of a phosphate group to make them functional. **p53**, for example, is a regulatory protein that is normally inactive. However, in situations where a cell's DNA has become damaged, phosphate is added to p53. This process of phosphorylation (see page 140) makes inactive p53 change in structure and become **active p53 tumour-suppressor protein**. It then brings about an appropriate outcome such as repair of DNA or, in extreme cases, programmed cell death.

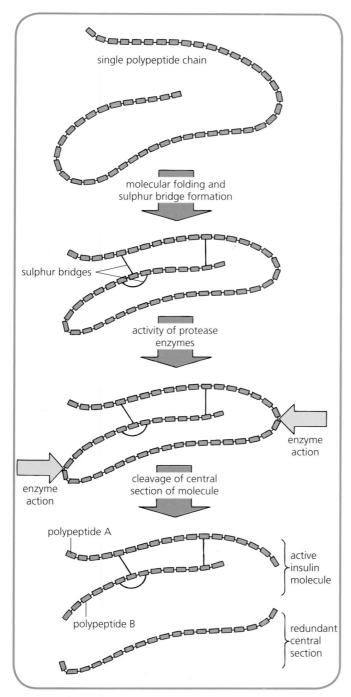

single polypeptide chain

molecular folding and
sulphur bridge formation

sulphur bridges

activity of protease
enzymes

enzyme
action

enzyme
action

cleavage of central
section of molecule

polypeptide A

active
insulin
molecule

polypeptide B

redundant
central
section

Figure 3.22 Post-translational modification by cleavage

Testing Your Knowledge 3

1 a) How many anticodons in a molecule of tRNA
are exposed? (1)

b) Each molecule of tRNA has a site of attachment
at one end. What becomes attached to this
site? (1)

2 a) What is a *ribosome*? (1)

b) i) How many tRNA binding sites are present on
a ribosome?
ii) To what does a tRNA's anticodon become
bound at one of these sites? (2)

c) What type of bond forms between adjacent
amino acids attached to tRNA molecules? (1)

d) What is the fate of a tRNA molecule once its
amino acid has been joined to the polypeptide
chain? (2)

3 Copy and complete Table 3.7. (2)

Stage of synthesis	Site in cell
formation of primary transcript of mRNA	
modification of primary transcript of mRNA	
collection of amino acid by tRNA	
formation of codon–anticodon links	

Table 3.7

4 Choose the correct answer from the underlined
choice for each of the following statements. (6)

a) The basic units of the genetic code present on
mRNA are called <u>anticodons/codons</u>.

b) The synthesis of mRNA from DNA is called
<u>transcription/translation</u>.

c) A non-coding region of mRNA is called an
<u>intron/exon</u>.

d) Protein synthesis occurs in a cell's <u>nucleus/
cytoplasm</u>.

e) Cleavage of the insulin polypeptide is an
example of <u>pre-/post-</u>translational modification.

f) To become functional some molecules of
regulatory proteins need the addition of
<u>phosphate/ribose</u> groups.

What You Should Know

Chapters 1–3

(See Table 3.8 for word bank.)

adenine	DNA polymerase	polypeptide
amino	eukaryotes	primary
amplified	exons	primer
anticodons	folded	protein
antiparallel	fragments	replication
backbone	genetic	ribose
bonds	guanine	ribosomes
chain	helix	RNA polymerase
codons	introns	splicing
coiled	ligase	starting
complementary	linear	thymine
cross-connections	modification	transcription
cycling	nucleotides	translation
cytosine	peptide	twenty
deoxyribose	plasmids	uracil

Table 3.8 Word bank for chapters 1–3

1 DNA consists of two strands twisted into a double _____. Each strand is composed of _____. Each nucleotide consists of _____ sugar, phosphate and one of four types of base (_____, thymine, _____ and cytosine).

2 Adenine always pairs with _____; guanine always pairs with _____.

3 Within each DNA strand neighbouring nucleotides are joined by chemical _____ into a sugar–phosphate _____. The backbones of complementary strands are _____ because they run in opposite directions.

4 Prokaryotes possess _____ and circular chromosomal DNA. _____ possess circular chromosomes in their mitochondria and chloroplasts, and _____ chromosomes made of tightly _____ DNA in their nucleus.

5 DNA is unique because it can direct its own _____. This begins by DNA unwinding and its two strands separating at a _____ point. A _____ forms beside the DNA strand with the 3/ end. Individual nucleotides aligned with _____

nucleotides on the DNA strand become joined into a new DNA strand by the enzyme _____.

6 The DNA strand with the 5/ end is replicated in _____ that are joined together by the enzyme _____.

7 DNA can be _____ by the polymerase _____ reaction using primers, heat-tolerant DNA polymerase and thermal _____.

8 Proteins consist of subunits called _____ acids of which there are _____ different types.

9 Amino acid molecules are joined together by _____ bonds to form polypeptides. Polypeptides are coiled and _____ to form protein molecules whose three-dimensional shape, which is maintained by _____ between amino acids, is directly related to its function.

10 RNA differs from DNA in that it is single-stranded, contains _____ (not deoxyribose) and has the base _____ in place of thymine.

11 DNA contains a species' _____ information as a coded language determined by the sequence of its bases arranged in triplets called _____. Expression of this information through _____ synthesis occurs in two stages when a gene is switched on.

12 The first stage, _____, begins when the enzyme _____ becomes attached to and moves along the DNA bringing about the synthesis of a _____ transcript of mRNA from individual RNA nucleotides. Primary RNA is cut and spliced to remove non-coding regions called _____ and bind together coding regions called _____.

13 The second stage, _____, occurs at _____ where codons on the mRNA strand match up with the _____ on tRNA molecules carrying amino acids. These become joined together by peptide bonds to form a _____ chain whose amino acid sequence reflects the code on the mRNA.

14 Alternative _____ of primary mRNA and post-translational _____ of protein structure enable a gene to be expressed as several proteins.

4 Cellular differentiation

A multicellular organism consists of a large number of cells. Rather than each cell carrying out every function for the maintenance of life, a **division of labour** occurs and most of the cells become differentiated. **Differentiation** is the process by which an unspecialised cell becomes altered and adapted to perform a special function as part of a permanent tissue.

Selective gene expression

Since all the cells in a multicellular organism have arisen from the zygote by repeated cell division, every cell possesses all the genes for constructing the whole organism. These genes all have the potential to become switched on and some of them are already switched on at this stage.

During differentiation:

● many genes remain switched on

● some genes that control characteristic features of this type of differentiated cell now become switched on

● some unnecessary genes now become switched off (otherwise they would be coding for proteins not required by this type of differentiated cell).

Growth and differentiation in multicellular plants

Meristems

In multicellular plants, growth is restricted to regions called **meristems**. A meristem is a group of unspecialised plant cells capable of dividing repeatedly throughout the life of the plant. Some of the cells formed remain meristematic and go on to produce new cells while others become differentiated.

Related Topic

Types of meristem

Apical meristems

An **apical meristem** is found at a root tip and at a shoot tip (apex). Increase in length of a root or shoot depends on both the formation of new cells by the apical meristem and the elongation of these new cells.

Figure 4.1 shows how growth occurs at a shoot apex. Each new cell formed by cell division in the meristem becomes elongated, vacuolated and finally differentiated. Some cells, for example, become specialised to form xylem vessels by developing into long hollow tubes supported by lignin; others become phloem tissue composed of sieve tubes and companion cells.

Figure 4.2 shows the apical meristem at a shoot tip. Figure 4.3 shows the apical meristem at a root tip, which is protected by a root cap but operates in the same way as a shoot tip.

Lateral meristem

Unlike an **annual** plant, a **perennial** plant such as a tree continues to grow and increase in size year after year. Therefore it needs more and more vascular tissue for additional support and transport of water. This new vascular tissue is produced by a **lateral meristem** inside the plant called **cambium**. Cambium takes the form of a continuous cylinder of meristematic cells which extends throughout the plant (see Figure 4.4). Each year it forms, on its inside, an annual ring of woody xylem. The number of rings possessed by a plant indicates its age.

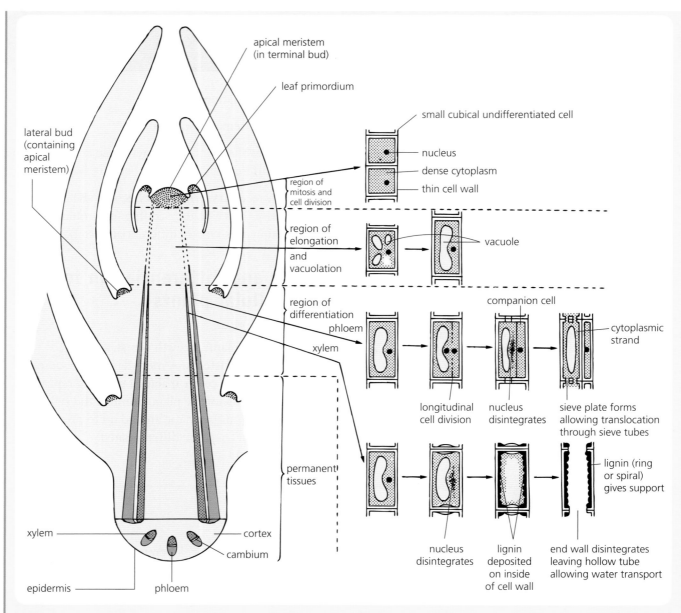

Figure 4.1 Growth at a stem apex

Figure 4.2 Apical meristem at shoot tip

Figure 4.3 Apical meristem at root tip

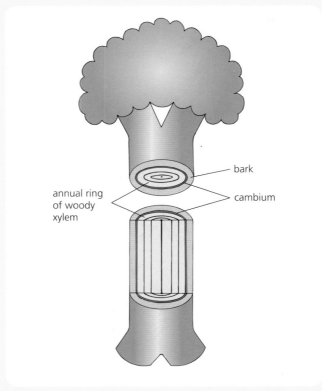

annual ring
of woody
xylem

bark

cambium

Figure 4.4 Lateral meristem

Related Topic

Tissue culture of plant material

Many types of plant cells are able to multiply and regenerate the whole plant. This ability is not restricted to meristematic cells. It also holds true for many types of differentiated cells whose switched-off genes are able to become switched on again by growth regulators.

Scientists are able to create a clone of a plant by employing **tissue-culturing** techniques. Tiny pieces of plant tissue are cut from the parent plant and grown on medium containing nutrients and growth regulators (plant hormones) in aseptic conditions (in other words, free of pathogens). The cells multiply and form a mass of undifferentiated cells called a **callus** (see Figure 4.5). In the presence of the correct balance of hormones in the growth medium, the callus tissue differentiates into plantlets with roots and shoots. When these plantlets are transferred to

potting compost, they develop into normal, complete plants. Thousands of genetically identical offspring can be obtained from a single plant by subdividing the calluses as they grow.

Applications

Tissue culturing of plants is used for many purposes including the following:

- production of clones of commercially important plants such as ornamentals (for example rose and orchid), crops (including pineapple and oil palm) and forests (for example pine trees)

- regeneration of transgenic plants following genetic modification of their cells

- multiplication of plants that have been cleared of pathogens, for use in horticulture and agriculture.

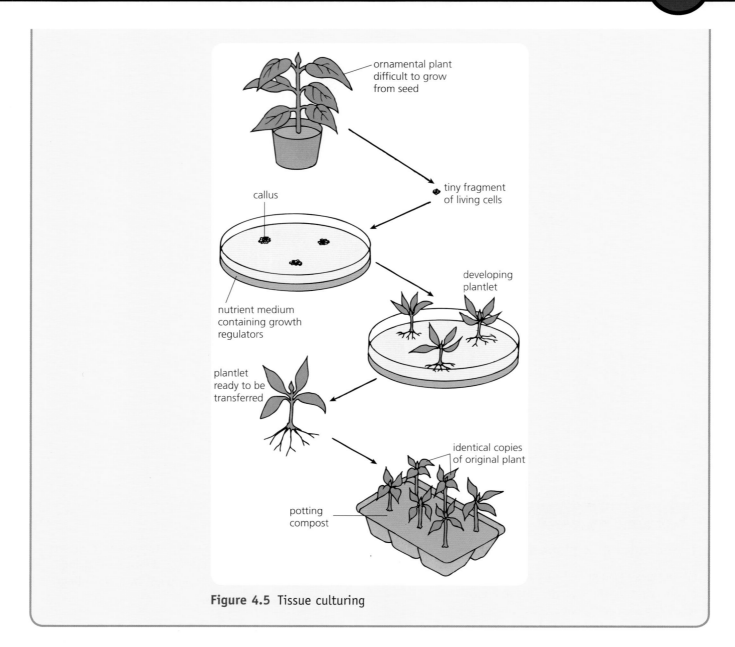

Figure 4.5 Tissue culturing

Growth and differentiation in multicellular animals

A multicellular animal such as a human being begins life as a fertilised egg (zygote) as shown in Figure 4.6. The zygote divides repeatedly by mitosis and cell division to form an embryo. Like the cells in an adult, each **embryonic cell** possesses all the genes for constructing the whole organism. However, unlike the adult, all the genes in cells at this early stage are still switched on or have the potential to become switched on.

As development proceeds, the cells undergo **differentiation** and become **specialised** in structure, making them perfectly adapted for carrying out a particular function. For example a motor neuron (see Figure 4.6) is a type of nerve cell which possesses an axon (a long insulated cytoplasmic extension). This

Once a cell becomes differentiated, it only expresses the genes that code for the proteins **specific** to the workings of that particular type of cell. For example, in a nerve cell, genes that code for the formation of neurotransmitter substances are switched on and continue to operate but those for mucus are switched off. The reverse is true of the genes in a goblet cell in the lining of the windpipe. Only a fraction of the genes in a specialised cell are expressed (for example 3–5% in a typical human cell).

Stem cells

Stem cells are unspecialised somatic cells that can:

- **reproduce** (self-renew) themselves by repeated mitosis and cell division while remaining undifferentiated

- **differentiate** into specialised cells when required to do so by the multicellular organism that possesses them.

Embryonic stem cells

A human **blastocyst** is an early embryo consisting of a ball of **embryonic stem cells** (see Figures 4.7 and 4.8). All of the genes in an embryonic cell have the potential to be switched on, therefore the cell is capable of differentiating into all of the cell types (more than 200) found in the human body. Such embryonic cells are described as being **pluripotent** (also see page 53).

Tissue (adult) stem cells

Tissue (adult) stem cells are found in locations such as skin and red bone marrow (see Figure 4.7). They have a much **narrower differentiation potential** than embryonic stem cells because many of their genes are already switched off. Therefore they only give rise to a limited range of cell types and are described as being **multipotent**. However, they are able to replenish continuously the supply of certain differentiated cells needed by the organism for growth, repair and renewal of tissues. Tissue stem cells in bone marrow, for example, give rise to red blood cells, platelets and various types of white blood cells.

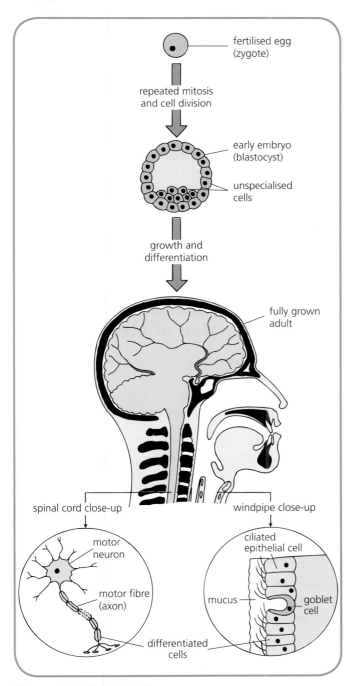

Figure 4.6 Differentiation

structure is ideally suited to the transmission of nerve impulses. Similarly the cells of the epithelial lining of the windpipe are perfectly suited to their job of sweeping dirty mucus up and away from the lungs.

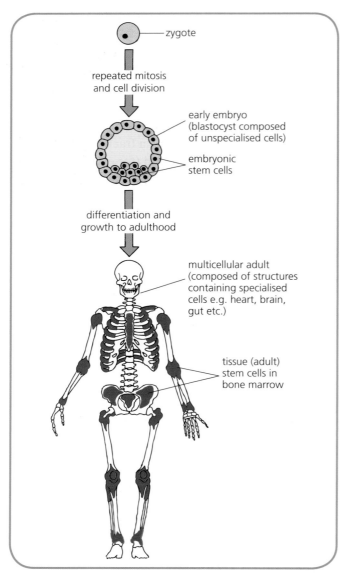

Figure 4.7 Two types of stem cells

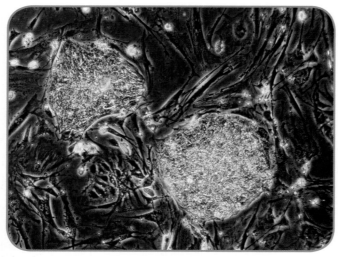

Figure 4.8 Embryonic stem cells

Research value of stem cells

Much of the research to date has been carried out using stem cells from mice and humans. Human stem cells can be grown in optimal culture conditions provided that certain growth factors are present. In the absence of these growth factors, the stem cells rapidly differentiate.

By investigating why stem cells continue to multiply in the presence of a certain chemical yet undergo differentiation in its absence, scientists are attempting to obtain a fuller understanding of cell processes such as growth and differentiation. It is hoped that this will lead in turn to a better understanding of gene regulation (including the molecular biology of cancer). Stem cells can also be used as **model cells** to study how diseases develop and to test new drugs.

Therapeutic value of stem cells

Tissue stem cells present in bone marrow and peripheral blood are routinely used in **bone marrow transplantation** to treat cancers of the blood (see Case study – Bone marrow transplantation).

In recent years scientists have shown that **corneal damage** by chemical burning can be treated successfully using stem cell tissue. This is grown from the patient's own stem cells located at the edge of the cornea. In most cases the person's eyesight is restored following grafting of the stem cell tissue of the healthy eye to the surface of the damaged eye.

Future therapeutic potential of stem cells

Recently, human embryonic stem cells grown on synthetic scaffolds have been used successfully to treat burn victims. The stem cell tissue provides a source of **temporary skin** while the patient is waiting for grafts of their own skin to develop.

Embryonic stem cells are able to differentiate into any type of cell in the body. Therefore they are believed to have the potential to provide treatments in the future for a wide range of disorders and degenerative conditions such as **diabetes, Parkinson's disease** and **Alzheimer's disease** (see Figure 4.9) that traditional medicine has been unable to cure. Already scientists have managed to generate nerve cells from embryonic stem cells in culture. It is hoped that this work will eventually be translated into effective therapies to treat neurological disorders such as multiple sclerosis. However, the use of embryonic stem cells raises questions of ethics (see page 52).

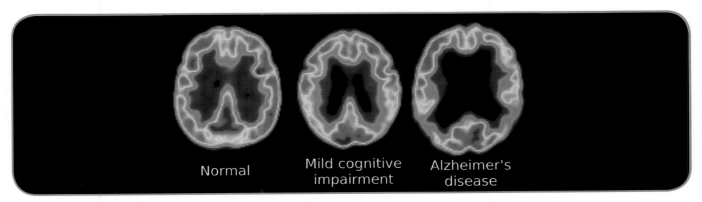

Figure 4.9 Brain scans

Case Study | Bone marrow transplantation

Leukaemia

Cancers of the blood such as **leukaemia** and **lymphoma** result from the uncontrolled proliferation of white blood cells. Treatment involves the destruction of the patient's own cancerous bone marrow cells by radiation or chemotherapy and their replacement with a '**bone marrow' transplant** of normal blood-forming stem cells.

HSCs

Stem cells that can multiply and differentiate into a variety of specialised blood cells are called haematopoietic stem cells (**HSCs**). HSCs are present in bone marrow, peripheral (circulating) blood and umbilical cord blood.

In the past the most common source of HSCs was bone marrow which was drawn from the donor using

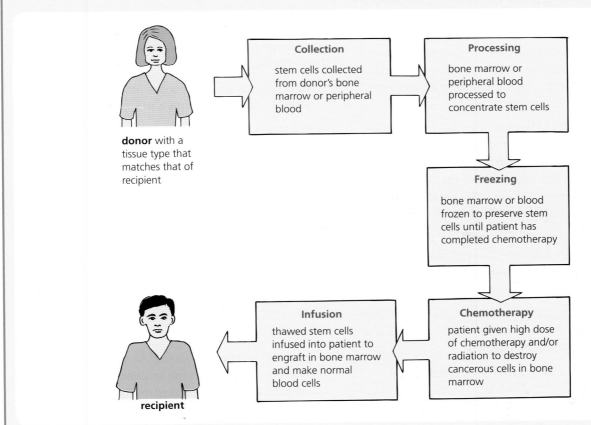

Figure 4.10 Bone marrow transplantation

a syringe. Most transplants now use HSCs obtained by harvesting them from the donor's **peripheral blood**. A few days before the harvest, the donor is injected with a chemical that coaxes additional HSCs to migrate from the marrow to the bloodstream. As a result up to 20% of the white cells collected in the sample are HSCs. This is at least double the number present in a bone marrow sample and its use normally leads to a speedier recovery by the patient.

Although umbilical cord blood is rich in HSCs, the volume of blood obtained is relatively small. Therefore its use in transplantation tends to be restricted to very small adults and children.

Figure 4.10 shows a simplified version of the procedure carried out during bone marrow transplantation.

Ethical issues

Ethics refers to the moral values and rules that ought to govern human conduct. The use of stem cells raises several **ethical issues**. For example the extraction of human embryonic stem cells to create a stem cell line (a continuous culture) for research purposes results in the destruction of the human embryo. Many people believe strongly that this practice is unethical. (See Case study – Embryonic stem cell debate.)

Ethical issues are also raised by the use of **induced pluripotent stem cells** (see Case study – Sources of stem cells) and by the use of **nuclear transfer techniques** (see Case study – Nuclear transfer technique).

Case Study   Embryonic stem cell debate

At present the creation of a human embryonic stem cell line using cells from a human embryo (of no more than 14 days) results in the destruction of the embryo. The ethical debate about the use of embryonic stem cells most commonly rests on the controversial question: 'Is a human embryo of less than two weeks a human *person?'*

People on one side of the debate believe that the embryo is definitely a human person and argue that fatally extracting stem cells from it constitutes murder. People on the other side of the debate feel certain that the embryo is not yet a person and believe that removing stem cells from it is morally acceptable.

The people who are against stem cell research using human embryos often support their case with the following claims.

- A human life begins when a sperm cell fuses with an egg cell and it is inviolable (in other words it is sacred and must not be harmed).

- A unique version of human DNA is created at conception.

- A fertilised egg is a human being with a soul.

- Stem cell research violates the sanctity of life.

The people who are in favour of stem cell research using human embryos often support their case with the following arguments.

- An embryo is not a person although it has the potential to develop into a person.

- At 14 days or less an embryo is not sentient (in other words it does not have a brain, a nervous system, consciousness or powers of sensation).

- The death of a very young embryo is not of serious moral concern when it has the potential to benefit humanity (particularly people whose daily lives are compromised by debilitating medical conditions).

- Abortion is legal in many countries including the UK. Destroying a 14-day-old embryo is far less objectionable to most people than terminating a fetus at 20 weeks.

- Stem cell research uses embryos that were generated for IVF (*in vitro* fertilisation) but were not used and would be destroyed as a matter of course.

Poss..

In the i..tions to the problem
embryon.
advances i. e ethical issues raised by the use of
technology (..lls may become less heated if
cells from **ampluripotent stem cell**
for their use. ..nd increased use of stem
..ee below) reduce the need

Case Study

Donated embryos

At present, patients undergo.. **cells**
may agree to donate any **extr..**
required for their treatment to ..
These very early embryos prove..
source of embryonic stem cells for.. nt
addition, **long-term cultures** origina..
cells isolated from donated embryos p..
further source of embryonic stem cells.

However, the number of human embryoni..
available for research remains limited and t..
restricts the ability of scientists to carry out re..
work in this important area.

Amniotic fluid

Scientists continue to search for new sources of stem..
cells. One of these is **amniotic fluid**. The stem cells
which it contains can be harvested from the fluid
removed from pregnant women for amniocentesis
tests (see Figure 4.11). The stem cells obtained are
capable of differentiating into many types of
specialised cells such as bone, muscle, nerve and
liver. One advantage of using stem cells from
amniotic fluid is that it does not involve the
destruction of a human embryo.

Induced pluripotent stem cells

A **totipotent** stem cell is one that is able to
differentiate into any cell type and is capable of

a..
tha..

Induc.. fluid
not true
example ..
genetically **pluripotent**
to switch sor.. **tem cell**
again. As a res.. ell types
used for resear.. ta.

amniotic fluid containing stem cells

fetus

uterus

Nuclear transfer technique

Case Study

This technique involves removing the nucleus from an egg (see Figure 4.12) and then replacing it with a nucleus from a donor cell. Some cells constructed in this way divide normally producing undifferentiated stem cells.

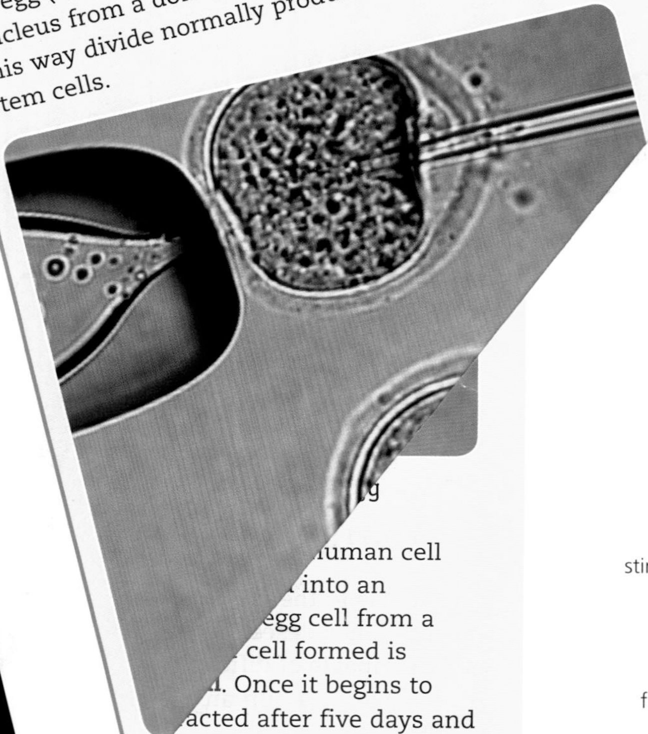

allow scientists to study the g̶n̶at disrupt the cells, observe how the dise̶... eventually develop new... disease process.

egg cell from animal (e.g. cow)

nucleus removed

enucleated cell

nucleus from human cell (e.g. skin) inserted

cytoplasmic hybrid cell

stimulation of cell division

further cell division

early embryo

hybrid embryonic stem cell

hybrid embryonic stem cells extracted to produce stem cell line for research

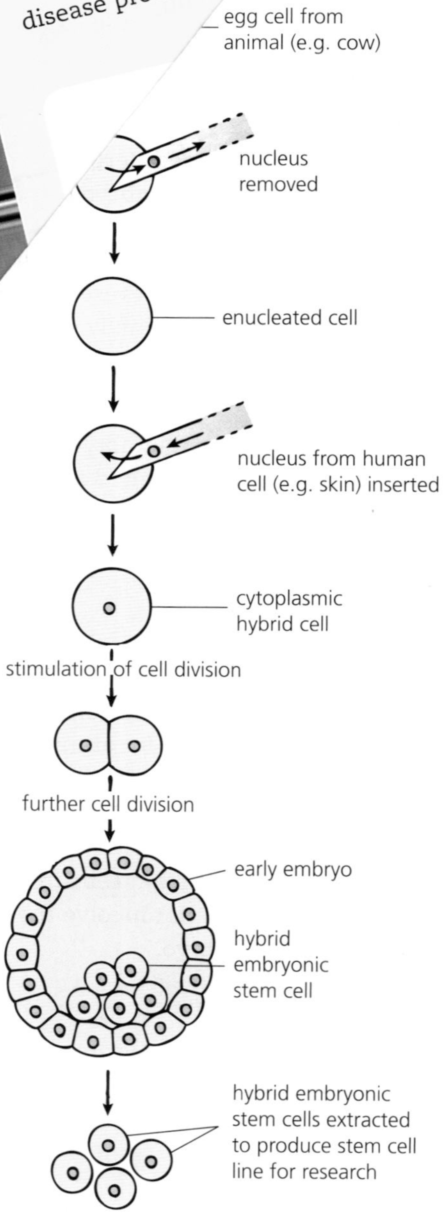

Figure 4.13 Nuclear transfer technique

...g

...uman cell ...into an ...egg cell from a ...cell formed is ...l. Once it begins to ...acted after five days and ..., they are not 100% human ...r therapeutic procedures.

...t it is unethical to mix materials ...with those of another species even ...s formed are used strictly for ...ses only. Other people support the ...f cytoplasmic hybrid cells because it ...lieve the shortage of human embryonic ...lls available for research. In addition, they ...out that the practice allows the nucleus from a ...eased human cell (for example from a patient ...uffering a degenerative disease or cancer) to be introduced into the enucleated animal egg. This may

Regulation

In the UK, the use of stem cells in research is carefully **regulated** by laws such as the *Human Fertilisation and Embryology Act* and the *Human Reproductive Cloning Act*. A licence from the *Human Fertilisation and Embryology Authority* must be obtained before research involving stem cells may be carried out. (Also see Case study – Regulation of stem cell research.)

The aim of this strict regulation is to ensure that the quality of the stem cells used and the safety of the procedures carried out are of the highest order and that abuses of the system are prevented.

Case Study | **Regulation of stem cell research**

The *Human Fertilisation and Embryology Authority* only grants a licence if it is satisfied that:

- the use of human embryos is necessary

- the purpose of the work is to increase knowledge about serious disease

- the knowledge obtained will be applied in the development of treatments for the serious disease.

Time limit

An **embryo** may be used up to 14 days after conception. Similarly, a **cytoplasmic hybrid cell** resulting from nuclear transfer (see page 53) may be grown in the laboratory for up to 14 days. During this time stem cells may be removed for research purposes.

Use of embryos beyond 14 days is against the law. They must be destroyed. Experts have chosen this time limit because it is the stage by which the embryo (as a blastocyst) normally becomes **implanted** in the uterus and begins to develop a nervous system.

Inter-species ban

It is illegal to place a human embryo in an animal such as a cow or to place an animal's embryo inside a human. Similarly it is against the law to allow a blastocyst from a cytoplasmic hybrid cell to develop within a human or an animal's body to enable it to grow.

Safeguards

A recent European directive entitled *Tissues and Cells* ensures that the following further safeguards apply to the use of stem cells now and in the future:

- safety and quality of stem cells is ensured

- donors are selected carefully

- transfer of stem cells from donor to recipient is tracked

- adverse effects (such as illness) following stem cell transplants are reported

- sources of all materials used are able to be traced.

Testing Your Knowledge

1 a) Define the term *differentiation*. (1)

   b) What is a *meristem*? (1)

2 a) In what way is a ciliated epithelial cell a good example of a specialised cell? (1)

   b) A goblet cell in the lining of the windpipe produces mucus but not insulin. Explain briefly how this specialisation is brought about with reference to genes. (2)

3 a) Give TWO characteristics of stem cells. (2)

   b) i) Name TWO types of stem cell found in humans.

   ii) For each type, identify ONE location where these cells could be found. (4)

   c) Which type of stem cell is capable of differentiating into all the types of cell that make up the organism to which it belongs? (1)

4 a) i) Name ONE medical condition that is routinely treated using tissue stem cells.
   ii) From where in the human body are these cells obtained? (2)

   b) Give an example of a medical condition that may be treated in the future using stem cells. (1)

c) Why can the stem cells used to treat the medical condition you gave as your answer to **a)** not be used to treat patients suffering from the condition you gave as your answer to **b)**? (2)

5 **a)** One definition of the word *ethical* is 'in accordance with principles that are morally correct'. Briefly explain why stem cell research using human embryos raises ethical issues. (2)

b) Why is it important that stem cell research is carefully regulated? (2)

5 Structure of the genome

Structure of the genome

An organism's **genome** consists of all the genetic information encoded in the DNA of a complete set of its chromosomes. **Genes** are sequences of DNA bases that **code** for protein. However, a genome is not made up exclusively of genes. In eukaryotes (but not prokaryotes) only a tiny proportion of the genome actually consists of genes. The remainder of the genome is composed of many lengthy sequences of DNA that do not code for protein.

Role of non-protein-coding sequences

The **non-protein-coding regions** of the genome often take the form of DNA sequences that are repeated thousands of times over. Although the functions of many of these still remain unknown, the roles played by some sequences are now known and are described below.

Regulation of transcription

RNA polymerase, the enzyme that drives transcription (see page 34), is unable to initiate the process on its own. It needs the assistance of **transcription factors**. Some of these are called **activators** and they are bound to non-coding **regulator** sequences of DNA, often at some distance from the coding genes (see Figure 5.1).

Bending of the DNA strand brings the regulator bearing its activators into contact with other transcription factors close to the promoter of the gene to be transcribed. A molecular complex now forms at the gene's promoter site and the process of transcription begins. By this means a sequence of DNA bases that does not code for protein **regulates** the transcription of a gene.

Protection

Some of a genome's repetitive DNA sequences make up a protective structure called a **telomere** at each end of a chromosome. It prevents the chromosome from becoming damaged by 'fraying' at its ends.

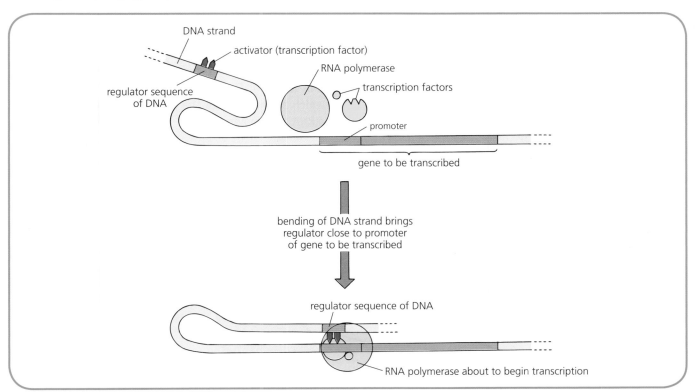

Figure 5.1 Regulation of transcription

Transcription of non-translated RNA

Genes code for mRNA whose sequence of bases is translated into protein (see page 37). However, some non-protein-coding sequences of DNA do code for forms of RNA other than mRNA. These types of RNA have specific functions but they are not translated into protein. (See Related topic – Non-translated forms of RNA.)

Related Topic

Non-translated forms of RNA

There are three types of RNA transcribed from DNA but not translated into protein as follows.

tRNA

The structure of a molecule of **transfer RNA (tRNA)** is shown in Figure 3.17 on page 39. Each single-stranded molecule folds up on itself following some pairing of bases. This gives a molecule with some regions of double-stranded RNA separated by some regions of unpaired RNA. Sometimes this is depicted as the clover leaf model of tRNA (see Figure 5.2).

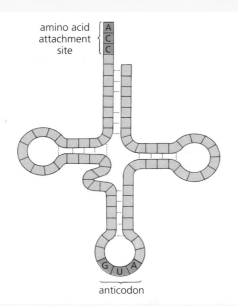

amino acid attachment site

A
C
C

anticodon

Figure 5.2 tRNA

Each tRNA molecule transports a specific amino acid molecule to a ribosome to be used during the translation process. However, the tRNA itself is not translated into protein.

rRNA

A **ribosome** consists of a large and a small subunit (see Figure 5.3). Each subunit consists of a complex of protein and **ribosomal RNA (rRNA)** molecules. The rRNA molecules are transcribed from non-protein-coding sequences of DNA and combine with protein to form a subunit in the nucleus. This is exported via a nuclear pore to be assembled with the other subunit into a ribosome in the cytoplasm.

The structure of a ribosome reflects its function in that it presents the **binding sites** needed by the molecules involved in translation of mRNA into protein. These sites enable molecules of amino acid to be added to the growing end of the polypeptide chain (see Figure 3.19 on page 41).

RNA fragments

Some of these **RNA fragments** are called small nuclear RNA (snRNA). They form complexes with proteins which are involved in the production of functional mRNA by removing introns from the primary transcript of mRNA.

Other types are called micro RNA (miRNA). On average they are only 22 nucleotides long yet they play an important role as post-transcriptional regulators which bring about the silencing of genes.

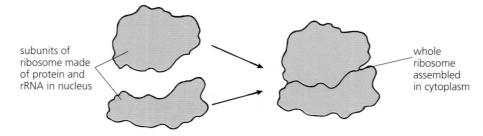

subunits of ribosome made of protein and rRNA in nucleus

whole ribosome assembled in cytoplasm

Figure 5.3 Ribosome structure

6 Mutations

Mutation

A **mutation** is a change in the structure or amount of an organism's genome. It varies in form from a tiny change in the DNA structure of a gene to a large-scale alteration in chromosome structure or number. A mutation may result in an altered protein or no protein being expressed. When a mutation produces a change in phenotype, the individual affected, such as the albino ivy plant shown in Figure 6.1, is called a **mutant**.

Frequency of mutation

In the absence of outside influences, gene mutations arise **spontaneously** and at **random** but only occur **rarely**. The mutation frequency of a gene is expressed as the number of mutations that occur at that gene site per million gametes. Mutation frequency varies from gene to gene and species to species as shown in Table 6.1.

Organism	Mutant characteristic	Mutation frequency (mutations at gene site/million gametes)	Chance of new mutation occurring
fruit fly	ebony body white eye	20 40	1 in 50 000 1 in 25 000
mouse	albino coat	10	1 in 100 000
human	haemophilia muscular dystrophy	5 80	1 in 200 000 1 in 12 500

Table 6.1 Mutation frequency

Figure 6.1 Mutant ivy plant

Germination rates of irradiated seeds

Mutation rate can be increased artificially by **mutagenic agents.** These include certain chemicals (such as mustard gas) and various types of radiation (including gamma rays, X-rays and UV light). The resultant mutations are described as **induced.**

The effect of radiation on germinating seeds is shown in Figure 6.2 where an increase in level of radiation is seen to bring about an increase in rate of mutation and a decrease in rate of germination.

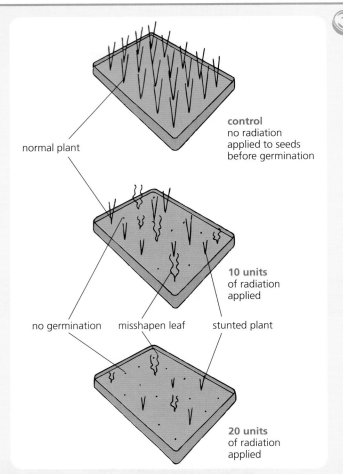

Figure 6.2 Effect of radiation on seeds

Point mutations

A point mutation involves a change in one of the base pairs in the DNA sequence of a single gene. A point mutation may occur within the protein-coding region of a gene or in one of the DNA sequences elsewhere on the chromosome that regulates the gene. Such a point mutation can alter the expression of the gene.

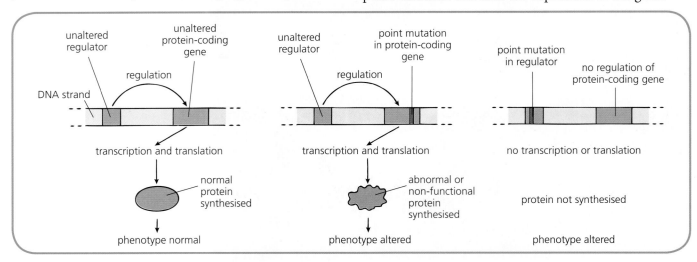

Figure 6.3 Possible effects of point mutations on gene expression

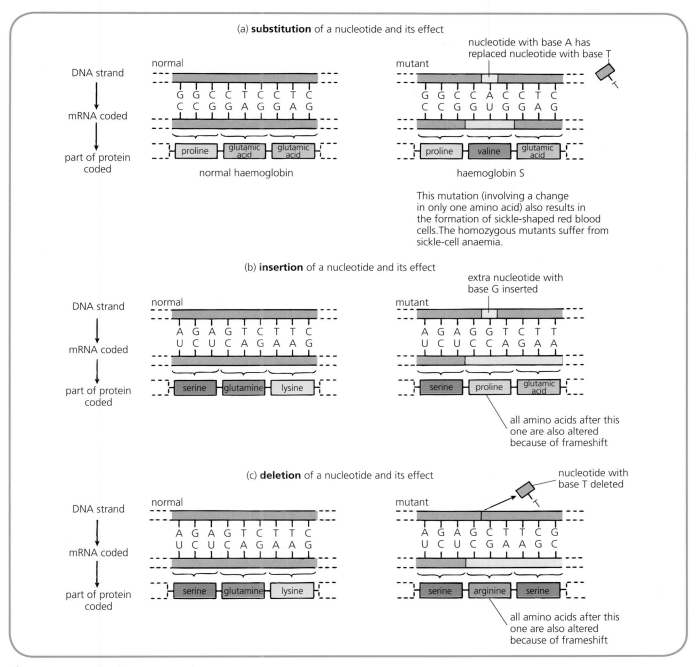

Figure 6.4 Types of point mutation

For example it may lead to a change in the protein that is synthesised and to an alteration in the organism's phenotype (see Figure 6.3).

Three types of point mutation are shown in Figure 6.4. A nucleotide is **substituted**, **inserted** or **deleted**. In each case this results in one or more codons for one or more amino acids becoming altered.

Impact on protein structure

For a protein to function properly it must have the correct sequence of amino acids. **Substitution** brings about only a **minor change** (one different amino acid) and the organism may be affected only slightly or not at all. However, if the substituted amino acid occurs at a critical position in the protein, then a major defect may arise (for example the formation of haemoglobin S and sickle-cell anaemia – see page 65).

Insertion and deletion both lead to a **major change** since each causes a large portion of the gene's DNA to be misread. The protein produced differs from normal protein by many amino acids and it is usually non-functional.

Related Activity

Investigating point mutations further

Point mutations can also be classified according to the effect that they have on the sequence of amino acids in the protein synthesised. Then they fall into five categories as follows.

Silent

As a result of a substitution, one base pair is altered. However, the codon that results is found to code for the same amino acid as before (see Figure 6.5). Therefore the protein synthesised is unaffected. This change in genome is called a **silent** mutation.

Neutral

The alteration of one base in a codon by a substitution results in a change from one amino acid to another with similar chemical properties (see Figure 6.5). Therefore there is little or no effect on the functioning of the protein synthesised. This change in genome is called a **neutral** mutation.

Missense

Following a substitution, the altered codon codes for an amino acid which still makes sense but not the original sense (see Figure 6.5). This change in genome is called a **missense** mutation.

Nonsense

As a result of a substitution, a codon that used to code for an amino acid becomes changed into one that acts as a **stop codon** (UAG, UAA or UGA). It causes protein synthesis to be halted prematurely (see Figure 6.5) and results in the formation of a polypeptide chain which is shorter than the normal one. This change in genome is called a **nonsense** mutation.

Frameshift

mRNA is read as a series of triplets (codons) during translation. Therefore if one base pair is **inserted** or **deleted** (see Figure 6.4) this affects the reading frame (triplet grouping) of the genetic code. It becomes shifted in a way that alters every subsequent codon and amino acid coded all along the remaining length of the gene. The protein formed is almost certain to be non-functional. This change in genome is called a **frameshift** mutation.

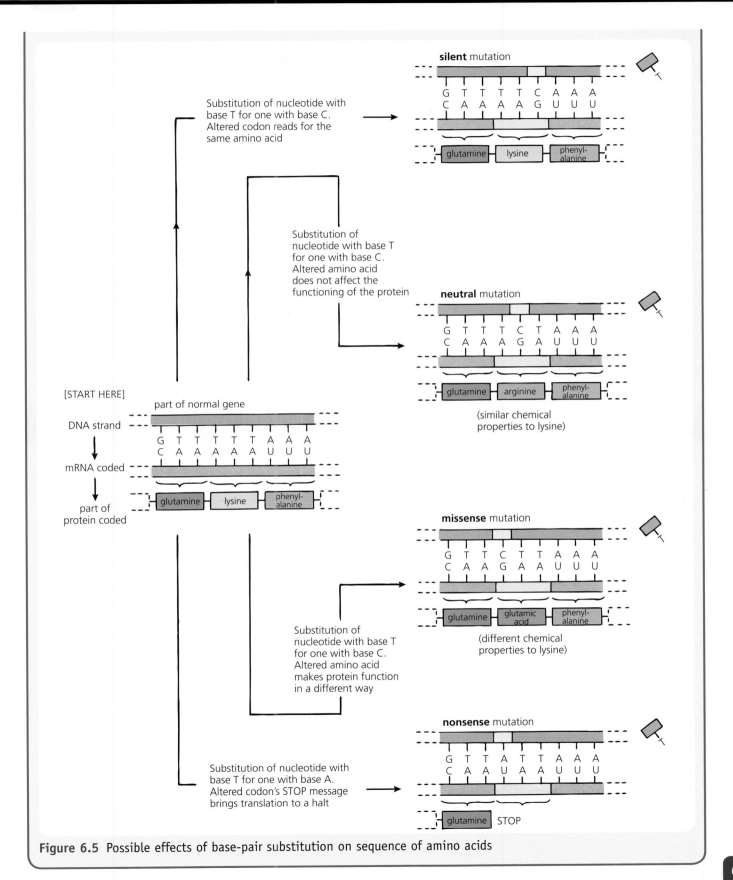

Figure 6.5 Possible effects of base-pair substitution on sequence of amino acids

Splice-site mutation

Figure 3.14 on page 36 shows a molecule of primary mRNA transcript undergoing modification by being spliced to remove introns and seal exons together. A **splice-site mutation** is one which substitutes, inserts or deletes one or more nucleotides at a site where introns are normally removed from the primary mRNA transcript.

If a mutated splice site is rendered non-functional in this way, one or more introns may be left in the modified mRNA. The mRNA may, in turn, be translated into an altered protein which does not function properly. Thalassemia, a type of anaemia that results from a defect in the synthesis of haemoglobin, is caused by a mutation at a splice site.

Inferior phenotype

Since most proteins are indispensable to the organism, most gene mutations produce an **inferior version** of the phenotype (see Table 6.2). If this results in the death of the mutant (an albino plant, for example, cannot photosynthesise) then the altered gene is said to be lethal.

Evolutionary importance of mutation

Mutation is the only source of **new variation**. Point mutations bring about changes in genes' DNA sequences and are therefore the means by which new alleles of genes arise. Without mutations, all organisms would be homozygous for all genes and no variation would exist.

Most mutations are harmful or even lethal. However, on very rare occasions there occurs by mutation a mutant allele which confers some **advantage** on the organism that receives it. Such mutant alleles, which are better than the originals, provide the alternative choices upon which natural selection can act. They are therefore the raw material of **evolution** (see chapter 7).

Organism	Characteristic controlled by normal gene	Mutant characteristic resulting from gene mutation
fruit fly	long wing grey body red eye	vestigial wing yellow body white eye
human	normal blood clotting secretion of normal mucus in lung normal haemoglobin and biconcave red blood cells	haemophilia secretion of abnormally thick mucus which blocks bronchioles (cystic fibrosis) haemoglobin S and sickle-shaped red blood cells (see Figure 6.7)
mouse	brown coat	white coat (albino) lacking melanin pigment
ivy	green leaves containing chlorophyll	albino leaves lacking chlorophyll (see Figure 6.1)

Table 6.2 Mutant characteristics

Research Topic | **Geographical variation in incidence of post-weaning lactose tolerance**

Lactose is a sugar present in milk. To be absorbed into the bloodstream it must first be digested to simple sugars (see Figure 6.6) by the enzyme **lactase** made by cells lining the small intestine. (The full scientific name of lactase is β-galactosidase – also see chapter 9.)

The gene that codes for lactase is active in these intestinal cells in babies when they are being fed milk. At the end of weaning, lactase production decreases by 90% or more among the members of human societies that consume few or no dairy products. However, it continues to be made after weaning by most members of societies that include many milk-based foodstuffs in their diet. The former societies are described as being **lactose intolerant**; the latter as **lactose tolerant** (lactase persistent).

Figure 6.6 Digestion of lactose

Historical background

Many thousands of years ago when humans were completely dependent on hunting and gathering as their methods of obtaining food, they were lactose intolerant in adulthood. The lactase-coding gene became switched off following weaning.

About 10 000 years ago some human societies began to practise agriculture by planting crops and herding and breeding animals. In addition to eating the meat of the animals that they domesticated, the people began to consume the milk and milk products such as cheese.

Lactose tolerance (lactase persistence) in adults evolved among the people in these societies following a **point mutation** that kept the lactase-coding gene switched on. Genetic studies show that several versions of the **mutated allele** for lactase persistence have arisen independently in different societies. They also suggest that the version most common among Europeans rose to a significant frequency about 7 500 years ago among Central European societies and then spread to other groups of Europeans that practised early forms of dairy farming.

Natural selection

Lactose tolerance (lactase persistence) among adults would have conferred an enormous **selective advantage** because it would have enabled people to consume an easily obtained, nourishing foodstuff throughout their lives without difficulty. Milk would also have acted as:

- an excellent substitute when other foods were scarce
- a reliable drink during periods of drought
- a rich source of calcium for healthy bones and teeth.

During the process of human evolution over several thousand years, **natural selection** has favoured post-weaning lactose tolerance among many European groups. Some of these show a very high incidence of the trait as shown in Table 6.3.

Human group	Post-weaning lactose tolerance (%)
Dutch	99
Danes	96
Swedes	94
British	91
Swiss	90
East European	85

Table 6.3 Groups with high lactose-tolerance levels

Hunter gatherers

In a few regions of the world, such as the Kalahari Desert in Africa, the remnants of Stone Age-type communities of **hunter gatherers** survive to this day. They are found to be 100% lactose intolerant. A high incidence of lactose intolerance is also found among people of some modern, developed societies (such as 98% intolerance in Thailand and 95% intolerance in China) where traditionally dairy products have barely featured in their diet. If the mutation for lactase persistence has arisen in these societies, it has not enjoyed a selective advantage.

Symptoms of intolerance

A lactose-intolerant adult who consumes dairy produce may suffer stomach cramps, nausea and acid reflux because the undigested lactose is acted upon by bacteria in the gut which release large volumes of gases such as methane.

Research Topic	Geographical variation in incidence of sickle-cell trait

Sickle-cell anaemia is a genetically transmitted disease of the blood. It is caused by the presence of abnormal **haemoglobin S** which occurs as a result of a **point mutation** (see Figure 6.4 on page 61). In the discussion that follows, H represents the allele for normal haemoglobin and S the allele for haemoglobin S.

The blood of people homozygous (SS) for the **mutant allele** contains haemoglobin S (which is inefficient at carrying oxygen) and **sickle-shaped** red blood cells (see Figure 6.7). These stick together, interfering with blood circulation. This causes severe anaemia, damage to vital organs and, in the majority of cases, death.

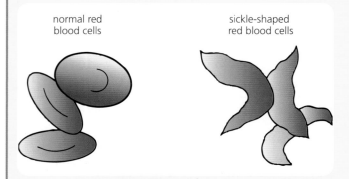

Figure 6.7 Two types of red blood cell

Alleles H and S are **co-dominant**. This means that they are both expressed in a person with the heterozygous genotype HS. The milder condition that results is known as **sickle-cell trait**. It is characterised by about one-third of the person's haemoglobin being type S. However, their red blood cells are normal and the slight anaemia that results does not prevent moderate activity.

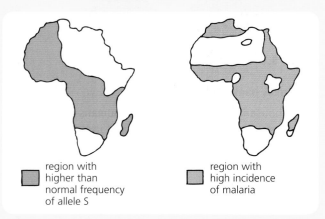

Figure 6.8 Correlation between allele S and malaria

Resistance to malaria

Allele S is rare in most populations since it is semi-lethal. However, in some parts of Africa, up to 40% of the population are genotype HS. Comparison of the two maps in Figure 6.8 shows that a correlation exists between incidence of **malaria** and high frequency of allele S. This is because sickle-cell-trait sufferers are **resistant** to malaria whereas people with normal haemoglobin are not. Thus in malarial regions, natural selection favours people with genotype HS over those with HH who may die during a serious outbreak of the disease (see Table 6.4). However, HS loses its selective advantage in non-malarial areas.

	Cross		
	HH × HH	**HH × HS**	**HS × HS**
Possible result in non-malarial region	HH, HH, HH, HH (100% of offspring survive)	HH, HH, HS, HS (100% of offspring survive)	HH, HS, HS, S̶S̶ (75% of offspring survive)
Possible result in malarial region affected by outbreak of the disease	H̶H̶, H̶H̶, H̶H̶, H̶H̶ (0% of offspring survive)	H̶H̶, H̶H̶, HS, HS (50% of offspring survive)	H̶H̶, HS, HS, S̶S̶ (50% of offspring survive)

Table 6.4 Selective advantage of sickle-cell trait

Testing Your Knowledge 1 (includes Chapter 5)

1 With the aid of an example, distinguish between the terms *mutant* and *mutation*. (2)

2 a) State TWO characteristics of mutant alleles with respect to their occurrence and frequency. (2)

b) i) Are all mutant alleles an inferior version of the original allele?
ii) Explain your answer. (2)

3 a) Identify THREE types of point mutation. (3)

b) i) Which of these is *least* likely to have a major impact on gene expression?
ii) Explain your answer. (2)

4 Decide whether each of the following statements is true or false and then use T or F to indicate your choice. Where a statement is false, give the word that should have been used in place of the word in bold print. (7)

a) The sum of the hereditary information encoded in an organism's DNA is called its **ribosome**.

b) A **gene** is a DNA sequence that codes via mRNA for a protein.

c) Most of the genome of a **prokaryote** is composed of DNA sequences that do not code for protein.

d) Some non-coding sequences regulate the process of **transcription**.

e) The function of many **coding** sequences of DNA remains unknown.

f) A mutation to a splice site may alter **pre**-transcriptional processing of mRNA.

g) A mutation to a regulatory sequence of DNA can alter the **expression** of a gene.

Chromosome structure mutations

This type of mutation involves the breakage of one or more chromosomes. A broken end of a chromosome is 'sticky' and it can join to another broken end. There are four different ways that this can happen and bring about a change in the **number** or **sequence** of the genes in a chromosome.

Deletion

The chromosome breaks in two places and the segment in between becomes detached (see Figures 6.9 and 6.10). The two ends then join up giving a shorter chromosome which **lacks** certain genes. **Deletion** normally has a drastic effect on the organism involved. In humans, for example, deletion of part of chromosome 5 leads to the *Cri du Chat* syndrome. The sufferer has severe learning difficulties and develops a small head with widely spaced eyes. (The condition is so-called because an infant sufferer's crying resembles that of a cat.)

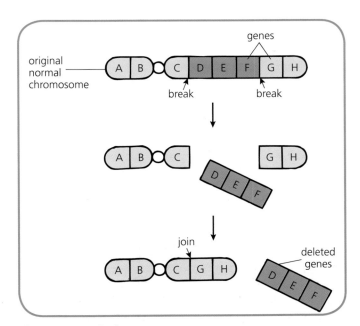

Figure 6.9 Deletion

Figure 6.10 'Look! Nessie's had a deletion.'

Duplication

A chromosome undergoes this type of change when a segment of genes (such as deleted genes from its matching partner) becomes attached to one end of the first chromosome or becomes inserted somewhere along its length as shown in Figure 6.11. This results in a set of genes being **repeated**.

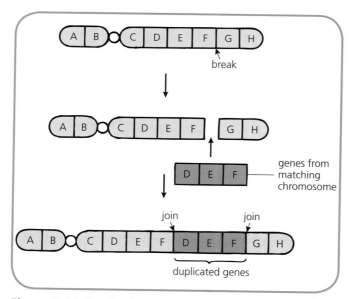

Figure 6.11 Duplication

Some **duplications** of genes may have a detrimental effect on the organism. For example the duplication of certain genes (called oncogenes) is a common cause of cancer. Other gene duplications may be of advantage to the species as follows.

Importance of gene duplication in evolution

Duplication of a gene produces a second copy that is free from selection pressure. It is thought that this extra copy can become altered without interfering with the original gene's function or affecting the organism in some harmful way.

This freedom allows the extra copy of the gene to undergo point mutations that produce **new DNA sequences**. One or more of these may confer some advantage on the organism thereby **increasing its fitness** and chance of survival. An example is found among some species of fish that live in Antarctic waters of −2 °C to 4 °C. In these animals a duplicate of a gene that codes for a digestive enzyme has mutated and now codes for a glycoprotein that acts as antifreeze in the fish's blood and body fluids.

Inversion

A chromosome undergoing **inversion** breaks in two places as shown in Figure 6.12. The segment between the two breaks turns round before joining up again. This brings about a **reversal** of the normal sequence of genes in the affected section of chromosome.

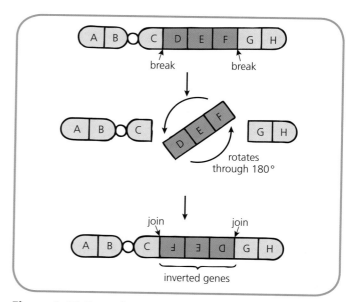

Figure 6.12 Inversion

When a chromosome which has undergone inversion meets its normal, non-mutated matching partner at gamete formation, the two have to form a complicated loop in order to pair up. This often results in the formation of **non-viable** gametes.

Translocation

This involves a section of one chromosome breaking off and becoming attached to another chromosome which is not its matching partner. Figure 6.13 shows two ways in which this may occur. **Translocation** usually leads to problems during pairing of chromosomes at gamete formation and results in the formation of **non-viable** gametes.

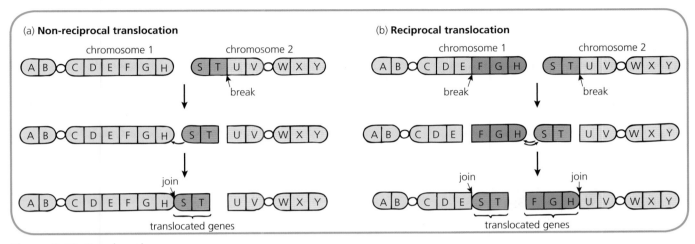

(a) **Non-reciprocal translocation**

(b) **Reciprocal translocation**

Figure 6.13 Translocation

Related Topic

Evidence for formation of human chromosome 2

All members of the great ape family have 24 pairs of chromosomes except human beings who have 23 pairs. When the chromosome complement of a human is compared to that of a chimpanzee (our closest relative), **human chromosome 2** is found to contain sections which correspond closely to sections of two different chromosomes in the chimpanzee (and to those of other apes such as the gorilla and orang-utan).

It is thought therefore that the common ancestor of the great apes had 24 pairs of chromosomes but, at some point in the evolution of humans, two of these ancestral chromosomes **fused** together (by a chromosomal mutation) to produce chromosome 2.

The evidence for this hypothesis is as follows:

- When laid end to end, chromosomes 2p and 2q from a great ape are found to possess an **identical banding** pattern (see Figure 6.14) and near identical DNA sequences to human chromosome 2.

- Human chromosome 2 possesses **a normal centromere** which lines up with the centromere of chromosome 2p from a great ape. In addition,

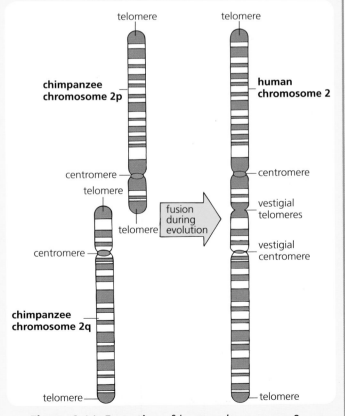

Figure 6.14 Formation of human chromosome 2

human chromosome 2 has the **remains of a centromere** equivalent to the centromere on chromosome 2q of a great ape. A chromosome normally only possesses one centromere.

- Human chromosome 2 has **vestigial telomeres** in its middle. A telomere is a region of repeated DNA sequences normally only found at the ends of a chromosome for its protection.

Gene duplication and alpha and beta globins in haemoglobin

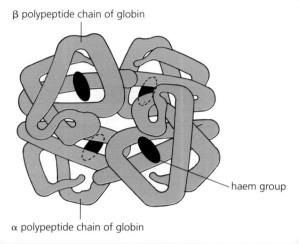

Figure 6.15 shows a molecule of **haemoglobin**, the oxygen-transporting pigment present in blood. It consists of four molecules of haem (an iron-containing compound) combined with four molecules of the polypeptide **globin**, two of which are type **alpha** (α) and two of which are type **beta** (β).

Multigene family

A **multigene family** is a set of related genes that have evolved from a common ancestor by **duplication**. The globin gene family is an example of a multigene family. In humans it is composed of seven α-like genes on chromosome 16 and six β-like genes on chromosome 11. It is thought that the original ancestral globin gene gave rise to both sides of the globin multigene family as shown in Figure 6.16.

Throughout the development of an individual human being, haemoglobin molecules each contain two

Figure 6.15 Haemoglobin molecule

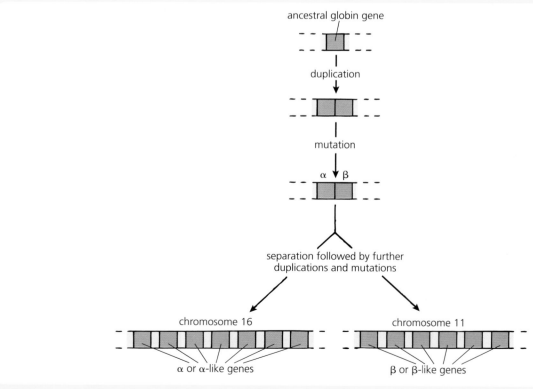

Figure 6.16 Evolution of globin multigene family

polypeptides coded for by genes on the α side of the family and two polypeptides coded for by genes on the β side of the family. However, different versions of α genes and β genes are expressed at different times to suit the developing organism's requirements. For example fetal haemoglobin contains globins that give it a higher affinity for oxygen than adult haemoglobin.

Polyploidy

An error may occur during gamete formation or cell division and all the matching chromosomes fail to separate. This results in a type of chromosome mutation where cells receive one or more **extra sets of chromosomes** (in other words, duplications of the whole genome). It is called **polyploidy**. Figure 6.17 shows how two types of polyploid cell (a **triploid** with three copies of the genome and a **tetraploid** with four copies) can arise from normal haploid and diploid cells.

Importance of polyploidy in evolution
Plants

It is estimated that at least 50% of plant species are polyploid. Genetic evidence suggests that millions of years ago an explosion in species diversity among flowering plants occurred following the **duplication of entire genomes** in their common ancestors. Polyploidy is certainly considered to have played an important role in the evolution of plants.

Related Topic

New species 'overnight'

Often a polyploid species arises from **more than one species**. A polyploid of this type contains copies of genomes derived from both parental species. *Spartina townsendii*, a species of grass plant, is thought to have evolved in this way as shown in Figure 6.18. The plant can be represented as AABB where A is a copy of the genome from parental species *Spartina maritima* (AA) and B a copy of the genome from the other parental species *Spartina alterniflora* (BB). Originally when a gamete containing genome A from species AA fused with a gamete containing genome B from species BB, a hybrid AB was produced. This plant was **sterile** because its chromosomes could not match up properly at gamete formation. However, it was able to survive by **asexual reproduction** until, eventually, another genetic error occurred during cell division producing the tetraploid *Spartina townsendii* (AABB). This species is fertile because its chromosomes can form pairs at gamete formation. Thus polyploidy is a method by which a new plant species can be produced 'overnight'.

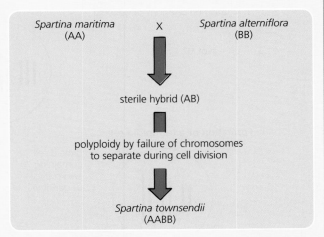

Figure 6.18 Formation of a new species by polyploidy

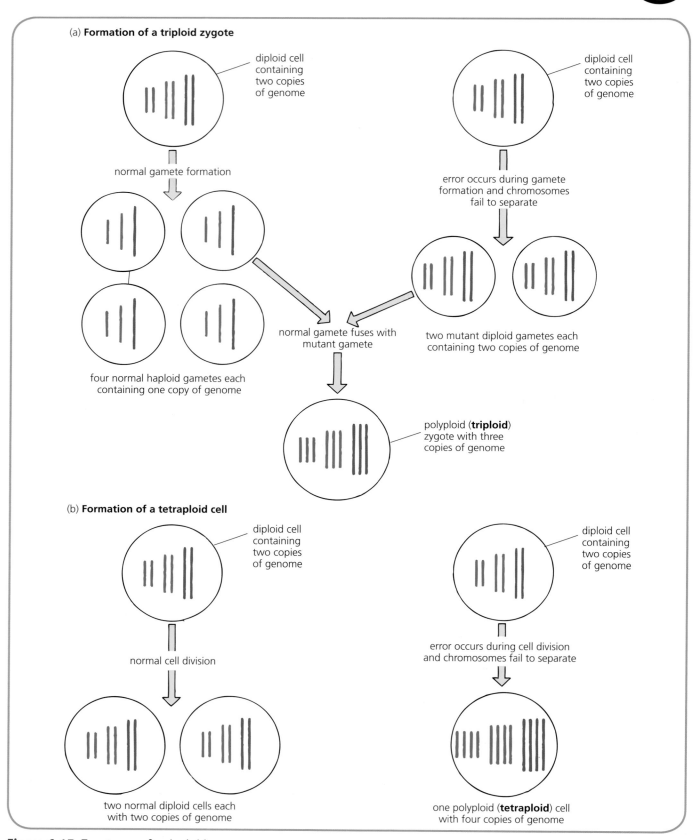

(a) **Formation of a triploid zygote**

diploid cell containing two copies of genome

diploid cell containing two copies of genome

normal gamete formation

error occurs during gamete formation and chromosomes fail to separate

normal gamete fuses with mutant gamete

two mutant diploid gametes each containing two copies of genome

four normal haploid gametes each containing one copy of genome

polyploid (**triploid**) zygote with three copies of genome

(b) **Formation of a tetraploid cell**

diploid cell containing two copies of genome

diploid cell containing two copies of genome

normal cell division

error occurs during cell division and chromosomes fail to separate

two normal diploid cells each with two copies of genome

one polyploid (**tetraploid**) cell with four copies of genome

Figure 6.17 Two types of polyploidy

Animals

Polyploidy is thought to have played a significant part in the evolution of the vertebrates (see Research Topic – Rarity of polyploidy in animals). However, animals are less well equipped to handle the 'sudden' increase in body size that normally accompanies polyploidy. In addition, dependence on asexual reproduction to survive for a long period as a sterile hybrid is not possible for many types of animal, especially more advanced species.

Economic importance of polyploidy

Polyploid plants are normally **larger** than their diploid relatives. This often includes increased seed and fruit size which is of economic importance. Many commercially developed crop plants, such as wheat, coffee, apples, tomatoes and strawberries (see Figure 6.19), are polyploid and therefore give bigger yields than their non-polyploid relatives.

Polyploid plants with an uneven number of sets of chromosomes are sterile. However, this is useful to humans because the affected plants produce **seedless** fruit (such as the banana). Where a polyploid plant has arisen from more than one species, it is often found to show an **increase in vigour**, **crop quality** and **resistance to disease** as a result of a combination of characteristics from both of its ancestors.

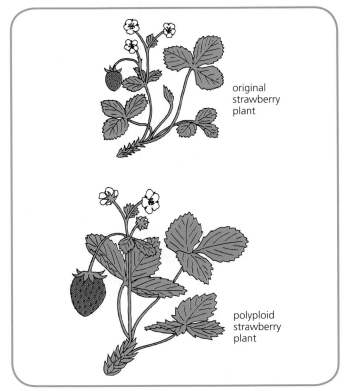

original strawberry plant

polyploid strawberry plant

Figure 6.19 Polyploidy in strawberry plants

Research Topic	**Polyploidy and origin of crop plants**

Many crop plants are polyploid. A few examples are given in Table 6.5.

Polyploid plants are often bigger and more robust than their diploid relatives. Therefore many of them have been selected by farmers as the parents of the next generation ever since breeding of crops began. As a result, many polyploid crop plants have enjoyed a selective advantage during the last 10 000 years.

Banana

Some crop plants, such as banana, are selected for the lack of seeds in their fruit. Bananas are **seedless** because the plant which produced them is a **sterile** hybrid. It originated from a cross between two species of wild banana. This produced a **triploid** (AAB) which cannot reproduce sexually because its chromosomes are unable to pair up correctly during gamete formation.

Ploidy	Number of copies of genome	Crop plant
triploid	3	banana, ginger
tetraploid	4	apple, potato (some varieties), cabbage
hexaploid	6	bread wheat, oat, kiwi fruit
octaploid	8	strawberry (some varieties), sugar cane

Table 6.5 Polyploid crop plants

Therefore banana plants have to be propagated asexually.

Potato

The potato plant is native to South America and many varieties exist, some of which are diploid, some triploid, some tetraploid and one that is pentaploid (five copies of genome). The species of potato grown worldwide is the **tetraploid** *Solanum tuberosum*.

Bread wheat

This important crop plant is thought to have evolved as shown in Figure 6.20. A cross between *Triticum monococcum* (AA) and a type of wild grass (BB) produced a sterile hybrid (AB). An error during cell division in AB resulted in fertile tetraploid *Triticum durum* (AABB). The process then repeated itself involving a second species of wild grass (CC) and another error during cell division resulting in fertile **hexaploid** *Triticum vulgare* (AABBCC) the modern bread wheat. (Note: Some of these species of wheat and its close relatives are also known by other scientific names.)

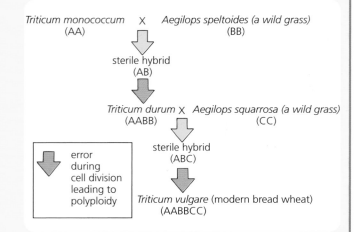

Figure 6.20 Evolution of modern bread wheat

Strawberry

There are more than 20 species of strawberry plant. They vary in ploidy number but most of them are diploid or **octaploid**. Broadly speaking, the larger the ploidy number, the larger and more robust the strawberries.

Research Topic	Rarity of polyploidy in animals

Polyploidy is rare among animals. However, it does exist among the 'lower' forms of animal life such as flatworms and leeches. In addition a few species of fish such as salmon and spined loach are tetraploid.

It is thought that during the evolution of early vertebrates from their invertebrate common ancestor, the whole genome underwent polyploidy by doubling on two separate occasions. In other words early vertebrates were probably **tetraploid** or even octaploid. The extra genes are thought to have undergone further mutations allowing the animals to increase the complexity of their anatomy and physiology to an enormous extent. This theory is supported by evidence from analyses of genomes and gene families. For example, some vertebrates possess four members of a multigene family in their genome whereas their distant invertebrate relatives have only one copy of the gene.

Mammals

Although some mammalian liver cells are polyploid, mammals whose bodies are completely polyploid almost

Figure 6.21 Plains viscacha rat

always fail to survive. An exception to this rule is the **plains viscacha rat** (see Figure 6.21), a rodent native to the desert scrubland of Argentina.

An error is thought to have occurred during chromosome separation and resulted in the doubling of the animal's chromosome number. Normally in mammals this would also result in a doubling of the sex chromosomes which would cause major reproductive problems. However, in this animal the extra set of sex chromosomes was somehow eliminated (probably by deletion). Its cells are about double the normal size and therefore the plains viscacha rat is significantly larger than its closest relative.

Testing Your Knowledge 2

1 a) i) What name is given to a change which involves a chromosome breaking in two places and a segment of genes dropping out?
   ii) Is this type of mutation likely to be beneficial or harmful to the organism affected?
   iii) Explain why. (3)

   b) i) Name the type of change which involves a chromosome breaking in two places and the affected length of genes becoming rotated through 180° before becoming reunited with the chromosome.
   ii) What effect does this change have on the sequence of the genes in the affected segment? (2)

2 a) i) What name is given to the type of chromosomal change which involves a segment of genes from one chromosome becoming inserted somewhere along the length of its matching partner?
   ii) Why might this mutation be of benefit to the organism affected? (2)

   b) i) Name the type of change which involves a section of one chromosome breaking off and joining onto another non-matching chromosome.
   ii) What effect does this change have on the number of genes present on each of the affected chromosomes? (2)

3 a) What is meant by the term *polyploidy*? (1)

   b) Explain how a polyploid plant such as banana containing three separate sets of chromosomes could have arisen. (2)

   c) State TWO ways in which polyploid plants can be of economic importance to farmers. (2)

What You Should Know

Chapters 4–6

(See Table 6.6 for word bank)

adult	genes	polyploid
advantage	genome	proteins
altered	insertion	random
crops	inverted	research
deleted	meristems	selection
differentiate	multicellular	specialised
differentiation	mutation	therapy
embryonic	nucleotide	transcription
evolution	phenotype	unspecialised
gene	point	variation

Table 6.6 Word bank for chapters 4–6

1 Regions of unspecialised cells in plants that are capable of cell division are called _____. The process by which an unspecialised cell becomes altered and adapted to perform a special function is called _____.

2 Cells produced in meristems differentiate into _____ cells. A specialised cell only expresses the _____ that code for proteins needed for the workings of that type of cell.

3 Stem cells are _____ cells that can reproduce themselves and _____ into specialised cells.

4 _____ stem cells are able to differentiate into all the cell types that make up a _____ organism. Tissue (_____) stem cells are only able to generate a limited range of cell types.

5 Stem cells are used in _____ to gain a better understanding of cell growth and gene regulation.

In the future several debilitating conditions may be treated successfully using stem cell _____.

6 The sum of all the genetic information encoded in an organism's DNA is called its _____.

7 A sequence of DNA that codes for a protein is defined as a _____. However, most of a eukaryote's genome is composed of DNA sequences that do not code for _____. Some of these regulate _____.

8 A _____ is a change in the structure or amount of an organism's genome. Spontaneous mutations occur infrequently and at _____. They can affect gene expression and lead to the synthesis of an _____ protein that changes the organism's _____.

9 A _____ mutation involves the substitution, _____ or deletion of a _____ in the DNA chain.

10 Point mutations are the source of the new _____ that provides the raw material for evolution. Very rarely a mutant allele arises that confers an _____ on an organism which is then favoured by natural _____.

11 A chromosome may undergo a structural mutation if one or more of its genes becomes duplicated, _____, translocated or _____. If a duplicated gene is further changed by a point mutation it may provide more raw material for _____.

12 Some errors that occur during cell division prevent the separation of chromosomes and result in the production of _____ cells with more than two copies of the genome. Many food _____ are polyploid.

7 Evolution

Evolution is the process of gradual change in the characteristics of a population of organisms that occurs over successive generations as a result of variations in the population's genome. These variations take the form of **changes** in the **frequencies** of certain **genetic sequences** (in other words, alleles of genes).

Evolution accounts for the origin of existing species from ancestors that lived long ago and were often very different from present-day species. It involves the processes of inheritance, selection, drift and speciation.

Inheritance

Vertical transfer of genetic material

Genetic sequences of DNA such as protein-coding genes are transferred **vertically** from parent down to offspring. This vertical inheritance may be the result of sexual or asexual reproduction.

In **sexual** reproduction the parents normally differ from one another genetically and produce offspring that vary further in their genetic make-up (see Figure 7.1). Vertical inheritance in humans is often represented as a family tree (see Figure 7.2).

In **asexual** reproduction a single parent with a certain genome produces offspring with exactly the same genome and no variation results among successive

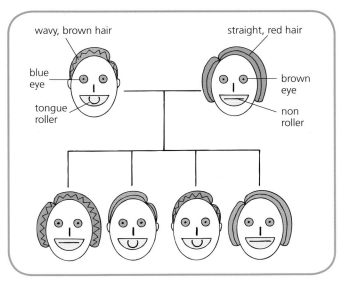

Figure 7.2 Vertical inheritance in a family tree

generations (see Figure 7.3). Vertical inheritance occurs among eukaryotes and prokaryotes.

Horizontal transfer of genetic material

In prokaryotes, genetic material can pass across from one cell to another **horizontally**. Therefore genetic sequences are not only handed down from one generation to the next by reproduction but are also exchanged among and between contemporary members of the population. The cells involved may not

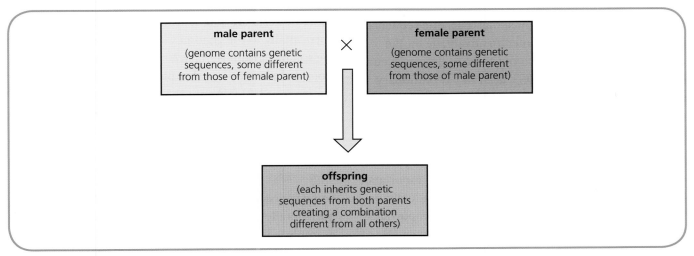

Figure 7.1 Vertical inheritance by sexual reproduction

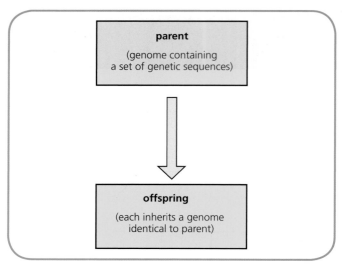

Figure 7.3 Vertical inheritance by asexual reproduction

even belong to the same species. This horizontal gene transfer can occur in one of several ways as described on pages 205–206.

Rapid evolutionary change in prokaryotes

It is thought that the rate of gene loss during genome replication and vertical inheritance was high during the very early stages of prokaryotic evolution. Experts believe that at the time this loss was compensated for by a high rate of **horizontal gene transfer** (HGT) which led to a rapid spread of new genetic sequences. These promoted the build up of larger genomes and allowed **rapid evolutionary change** to occur among early prokaryotes. After all, the acquisition of a beneficial gene from a neighbouring cell is a much faster method of obtaining it than waiting for it to evolve (if ever) by natural means.

However, there is no guarantee that a genetic sequence gained horizontally will confer an advantage on the recipient. In fact it may turn out to be useless or even harmful. For this reason HGT is a **risky** evolutionary strategy. By comparison, vertical inheritance is much **safer** because the genes that are passed on to successive generations have been tested and tried by the parent.

It is thought, therefore, that as organisms reached a certain level of multicellular complexity, the importance of gaining sequences by HGT decreased. Gradually, as the role of vertical inheritance increased in importance, distinct lineages began to emerge with their own sets of specific genes, eventually giving rise to the 'tree of life' (see Appendix 4).

MRSA

A significant amount of HGT still takes place in modern prokaryotes. An important example occurs among certain **bacteria** that exchange plasmids carrying the genes that confer **resistance to antibiotics** from one bacterial species to another.

This has resulted in the emergence of strains of bacteria resistant to several antibiotics. One of these, called **MRSA** (methicillin-resistant *Staphylococcus aureus*) is shown in Figure 7.4. It causes infections which are extremely difficult to cure and which sometimes prove to be fatal.

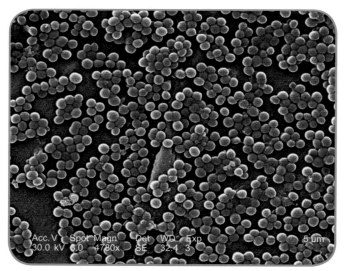

Figure 7.4 MRSA (methicillin-resistant *Staphylococcus aureus*)

Horizontal transfer of sequences into eukaryotes

From prokaryotes

Some bacteria are able to transfer genetic material horizontally to the genomes of eukaryotes. For example the soil bacterium *Agrobacterium tumefaciens* infects wounded plant cells with a plasmid which integrates a sequence of its DNA into the genome of the host plant cell. Genetic engineers use a harmless version of the plasmid as a vector to transfer desired genes into some types of crop plant to improve them (see page 261).

From viruses

Some **viruses** are able to transfer their DNA horizontally into the genome of their host cell. An example is herpes virus which causes cold sores. Initially it reproduces within the host cells and destroys many of them in the process. However, it is also able to integrate its DNA into the genome of other healthy cells and remain dormant as a **provirus** until the person's state of health drops to a low level. Under these circumstances the provirus leaves the host genome and initiates a new infection of blisters (see Figure 7.5). It is for this reason that herpes recurs throughout an infected person's life.

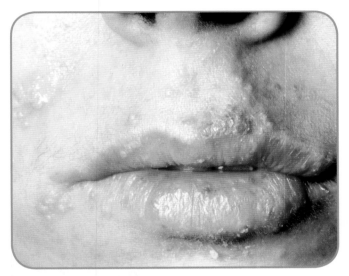

Figure 7.5 Cold sores

HIV (human immuno-deficiency virus), the virus responsible for AIDS (acquired immuno-deficiency syndrome), also succeeds in integrating a DNA provirus into the genome of host cells where it may remain dormant for many years before reproducing and destroying the cells.

Selection

Selection is the process by which the frequencies of some DNA sequences within a population increase because they are selected **for** and others decrease because they are selected **against**, in a non-random manner. It may take the form of **natural selection** or **sexual selection**.

Natural selection

In 1858 Charles Darwin and Alfred Wallace presented a joint paper suggesting that the main factor producing evolutionary change is **natural selection**. In *On the Origin of Species*, Darwin amplified his ideas as follows:

- Organisms tend to produce **more offspring** than the environment can support.

- A **struggle** for existence follows and many offspring die before reaching reproductive age because of factors such as lack of food, overcrowding and lack of resistance to disease.

- Members of a species show **variation** in all characteristics and much of this is inherited.

- Those offspring **better adapted** to the environment have a better chance of surviving, reproducing and passing on the favourable characteristics to their offspring.

- Those offspring **less well adapted** to the immediate environment die and fail to pass on the less favourable characteristics.

- This process is repeated generation after generation. The organisms best suited to the environment are naturally **selected** and eventually predominate in the population. This process is also called the **survival of the fittest**.

Thus **natural selection** is a non-random process that results in the **increase in frequency** among a population of organisms of those **genetic sequences** (such as certain alleles of genes) that confer an advantage on members of the population and help them to survive.

Evolution of resistant insects

DDT is a poisonous chemical which has been widely used against many insects. These include mosquitoes, which carry malaria and yellow fever, and insect pests which destroy crops. Within a few years of use, many **mutant** forms of insects **resistant** to the insecticide 'appeared'. These mutants are able to make an enzyme that renders the chemical harmless. They had not arisen in response to DDT. A tiny number of resistant mutants just happened to be present within the natural insect populations or arose later by a chance mutation.

When the spray was applied, the vast majority of non-resistant insects died and the resistant mutants suddenly enjoyed a **selective advantage** and multiplied (see Figure 7.6). Under such conditions natural selection may enable the mutants to eventually replace their wild-type relatives. This non-random increase in frequency of the gene for DDT resistance in the population increased the mosquito's chance of survival. Many new pesticides have been developed in recent

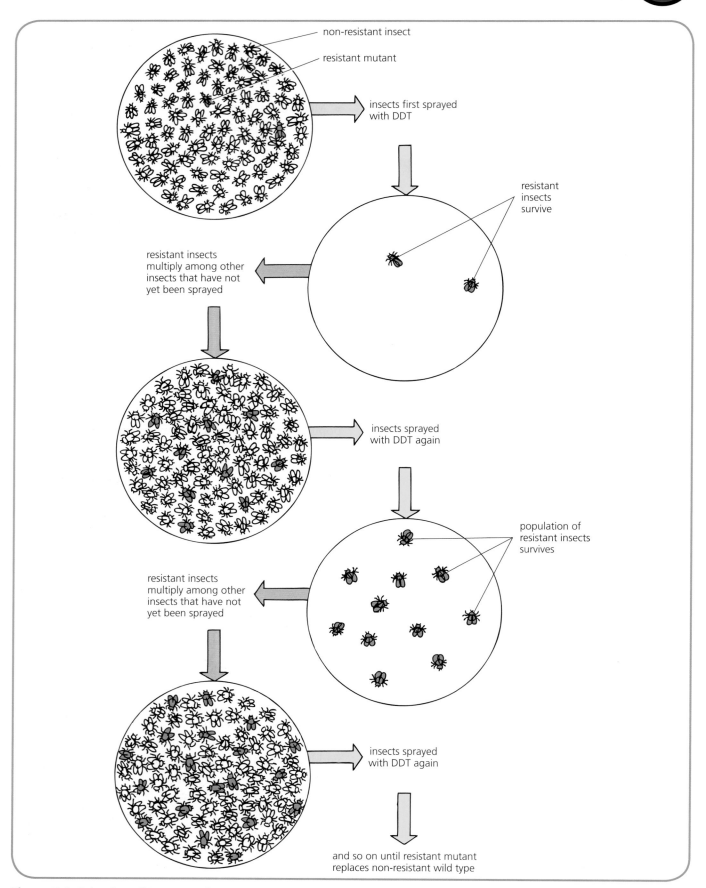

Figure 7.6 Selection of insects resistant to DDT

years but strains of pests resistant to these chemicals are now emerging.

Selection against deleterious sequences

Where a deleterious genetic sequence codes for an inferior version of a characteristic which leaves the individual poorly adapted to the environment, an affected individual will leave fewer than the average number of offspring. Since fewer and fewer copies of the deleterious sequence will be passed on to successive generations, a non-random **reduction** in its frequency will occur. It may even be eliminated from the population in time. A sequence that is **lethal** will disappear much more quickly than one that is less harmful since the selection pressure acting against a lethal allele will be of maximum strength.

Sexual selection

Sperm produced by male animals are much smaller and far more numerous than the eggs produced by females. Male animals have the resources to produce sufficient sperm to mate with very many females if the opportunities arise. On the other hand, females have to invest a large proportion of their resources to produce fewer eggs. They have little to gain by mating repeatedly with many partners; far better to be **selective** and choose one male of **high quality**. Therefore male animals often find themselves in competition for females.

Sexual selection is a non-random process that results in the **increase in frequency** of those **DNA sequences** that increase the reproductive success of the species. It operates in the following two ways.

Male-to-male competition

The males **compete** aggressively with one another for **territories** and **access** to females. This may depend on sheer physical size and strength such as that found among elephant seals who often inflict severe damage by biting their rivals during fights over territories.

It may also involve the use of 'weapons' such as the antlers on male deer used during the breeding season to engage in combat with their rivals (see Figure 7.7). By these means the smaller, weaker and less fierce males with the poorest weapons lose out. Only the largest, strongest and most aggressive males with the best weapons successfully mate with the females

and pass the alleles for these characteristics on to the next generation. In some animals this form of sexual selection is achieved by ritualised displays in place of real fighting (see page 307).

Figure 7.7 Male-to-male competition

Female choice

In some situations males are unable to control access to females. Then the onus falls on the female to select a male that she considers to be of high quality based on the traits that he displays. These take the form of 'ornaments' such as bright plumage in male birds. This reaches an extreme state in the peacock (male pea fowl) which possesses a set of very long display feathers.

Figure 7.8 A peacock's 'ornaments'

These can be raised to form a fan which displays dozens of shimmering 'eye spots' (see Figure 7.8).

For the female it is critical that she chooses a robust male who will father strong, healthy offspring with a **high survival rate**. She bases her choice of a suitable mate on the condition of his plumage and the quality of his display. Experimental evidence indicates that offspring sired by males with displays of the highest quality (in other words, the largest eye spots) show the highest rate of survival (see Figure 7.9). Many of these also inherit plumage with the best eye spots and in turn sire most of the next generation.

Male-to-male competition and female choice are both forms of **sexual selection**. This process results in the non-random increase in frequency of genetic sequences (alleles of genes) that increase the rate of successful reproduction among the members of a species.

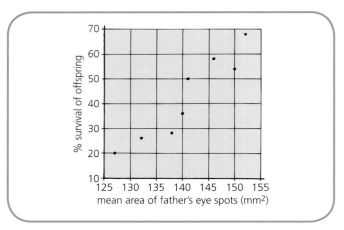

Figure 7.9 Effect of size of eye spots on survival

Related Topic

Investigating sexual selection in brine shrimps

The brine shrimp is an invertebrate animal. The males are about 8–14 mm long and the females are about 9–16 mm long. Males can be recognised by their **claspers** and females by their **brood pouch** containing eggs as shown in Figure 7.10.

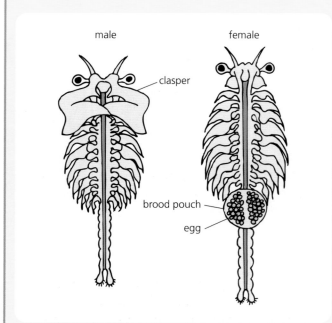

Figure 7.10 Brine shrimps

These animals use their limbs to sweep food such as algae and bacteria into their mouths as they propel themselves through the water. Mature animals swim together in **mating pairs** with the female in front and the male propelling her forward from behind. The male clasps his female partner for about 3 days to prevent her from mating with rival males.

This raises the question '*How do brine shrimps choose a mating partner?*' One hypothesis is that brine shrimps select and pair with larger mates rather than smaller ones. This can be tested by setting up the pair-choice experiment shown in Figure 7.11.

From the results it is concluded that the hypothesis is supported. During mate choice both sexes of brine shrimp are found to select larger mates in preference to smaller ones. It is of advantage to a male to mate with a larger female because she produces more eggs than the smaller one. Therefore he increases the chance of **passing his DNA** on to the next generation. It is of advantage to a female to select a large male with large claspers because he will clasp her securely and have the strength to propel her energetically through the water from which she can obtain a **rich supply of food** for her eggs.

Therefore in brine shrimps, sexual selection results in the non-random increase in frequency of the genetic sequences (alleles) responsible for large body size,

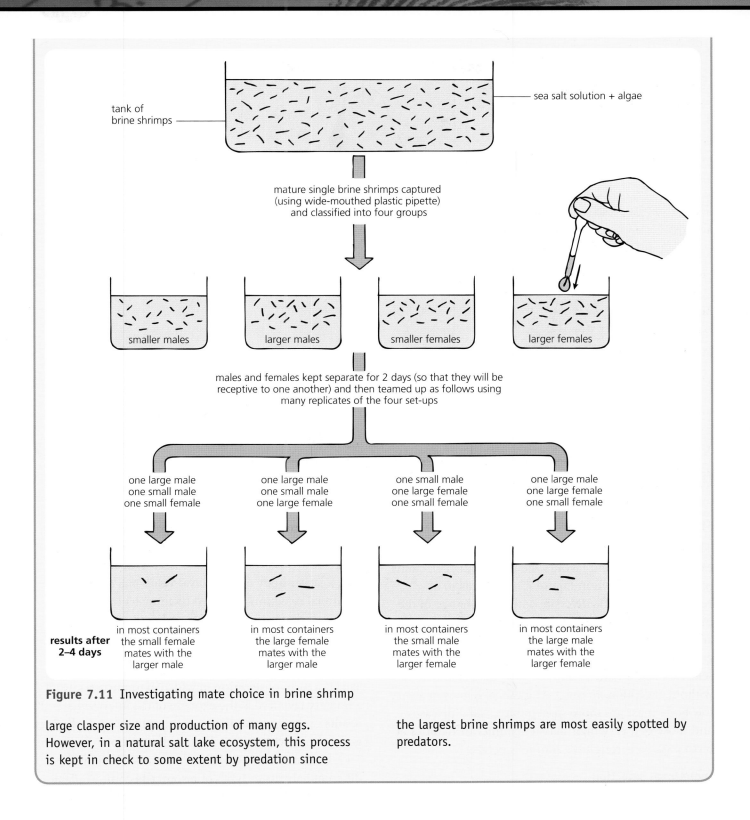

Figure 7.11 Investigating mate choice in brine shrimp

large clasper size and production of many eggs. However, in a natural salt lake ecosystem, this process is kept in check to some extent by predation since the largest brine shrimps are most easily spotted by predators.

Types of selection for a quantitative trait

A polygenic trait is controlled by the interaction of several genes. A characteristic of this type, such as seed mass, is quantitative. When the data for a large population are graphed, the result is a bell-shaped **normal distribution**. Natural selection can affect the frequency of a quantitative trait within a large population in any one of the following three ways.

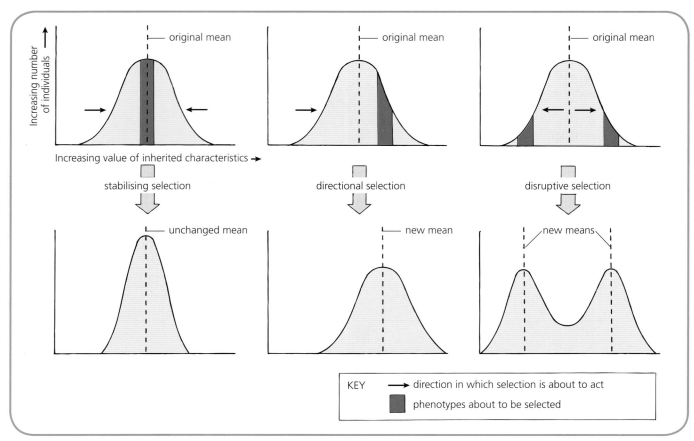

Figure 7.12 Three types of selection

Stabilising selection

This form of selection exerts its pressure against the extreme variants and favours the intermediate versions of the trait as shown in Figure 7.12. It leads to a **reduction** in genetic diversity without a change in the mean value. It operates in an unchanging environment and **maintains the status quo** for the best-adapted genotypes in the population. For example stabilising selection keeps natural human birth mass, almost without exception, in the 3–4 kg range. Babies of a very low body mass are more susceptible to fatal diseases and those of a very high mass encounter difficulties at birth passing through the mother's pelvis.

Directional selection

This type of selection is most common during a period of environmental change. It favours a version of the characteristic that was initially a less common form and results in a **progressive shift** in the population's mean value for the trait (see Figure 7.12). For example fossil evidence shows that European black bears increased, on average, in body size during each ice age. Since a larger body loses relatively less heat than a smaller one, a larger body is of survival value in a cold climate. **Artificial selection** practised by humans to improve strains of domesticated plants and animals is also a form of directional selection.

Disruptive selection

This is a form of selection in which extreme versions of a trait are favoured at the expense of the intermediates. It results in the population becoming split into **two distinct groups** each with its own mean value as shown in Figure 7.12. Under natural conditions it occurs when two different habitats or types of resource become available. It is considered to be the driving force behind **sympatric speciation** (see pages 89–90). Plant and animal breeding involving artificial selection of extremely large and extremely small varieties (for example breeds of dog) is also a form of disruptive selection.

Testing Your Knowledge 1

1 Figure 7.13 shows different directions of transfer of genetic material where P = prokaryotes, E = eukaryotes and V = viruses. Which of them are correct? (2)

2 **a)** What are thought to have been TWO benefits of a high rate of horizontal gene transfer during the early stages of prokaryotic evolution? (2)

   b) Briefly explain why horizontal gene transfer might prove to be a risky strategy. (1)

3 **a)** **i)** Within a breeding population, some organisms fail to reach reproductive age. Give TWO possible factors that could be responsible for their early death.

   ii) Other offspring do survive and reproduce on reaching adulthood. What name did Darwin give to this 'weeding out' process that promotes the survival of the fittest?

   iii) Define this process including in your answer the terms: *advantage, frequency, genetic sequences, population*. (5)

   b) **i)** Why is sexual selection of survival value to a population?

   ii) Identify TWO ways in which sexual selection may operate. (4)

4 Briefly explain the difference between *stabilising* selection and *disruptive* selection. (2)

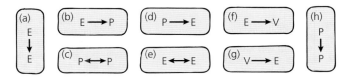

Figure 7.13

Genetic drift

The total of all the different genetic sequences (alleles of genes) present in a population is called the **gene pool**. In a large population the sample of alleles transmitted during reproduction is normally very large and fully representative of all the alleles present in the gene pool. Therefore, in the absence of environmental change or other unusual factors, the genetic composition of a large population tends to remain fairly **constant** from one generation to the next.

Genetic drift is the random increase or decrease in frequency of genetic sequences (alleles of genes) that occurs due to **sampling error**. This means that a non-representative sample of the alleles of the whole population is passed on. Small populations are particularly prone to genetic drift because the sample of alleles successfully transmitted to the next generation is normally relatively small and often not representative of the gene pool as a whole. Some alleles may be over-represented and others under-represented.

Therefore **wide fluctuations in gene frequencies** can occur simply by chance from one generation to the next.

By altering a small population's gene pool, random genetic drift creates the potential for **evolutionary change**. However, unlike natural selection, it normally fails to improve the population's ability to adapt to its environment. Genetic drift may even cause an allele to disappear completely from a small population thereby reducing genetic variation and driving the population towards **uniformity**.

Founder effect

The **founder effect** is a special case of genetic drift. It occurs when a small group of organisms (a **splinter group**) becomes isolated from the rest of the population and 'founds' a new population. The members of the splinter group possess a random sample of alleles which does not represent the alleles of the original population's gene pool in range and/or frequency.

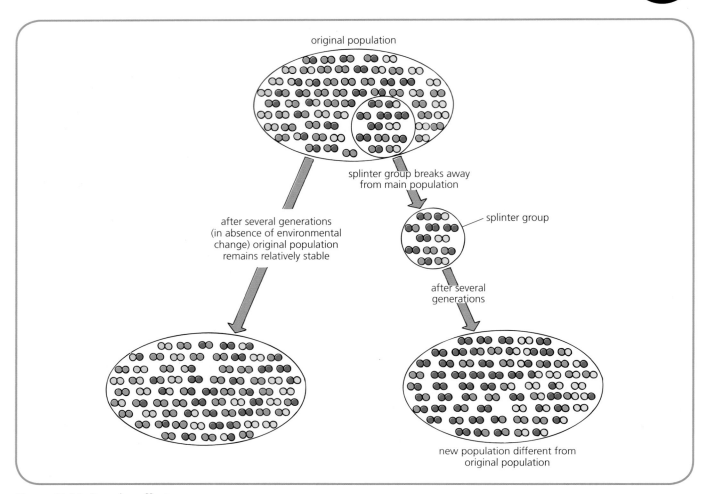

Figure 7.14 Founder effect

Figure 7.14 shows the founder effect in relation to the alleles of one gene. Each symbol represents a diploid organism which possesses two alleles of this gene. Among the members of the original population, four alleles of the gene are present. Among the members of the splinter group, only three of the alleles are present and they occur in frequencies **different** to those found in the original population. After several generations, the genetic make-up of the new population is very different to that of the original population and its members tend to become **distinctive**. In this example of the founder effect, only one gene was considered whereas in reality many alleles of many genes would probably be involved.

Blood groups

It is thought that North America was first populated by a small group of Asian people who migrated across the land bridge which is now the Bering Strait and became isolated from the rest of the human Mongoloid race. The **founder effect** is believed to account for the differences in the percentages of the population possessing certain blood groups as shown in Table 7.1. A similar alteration in a population's genetic make-up occurs as a result of the **bottleneck effect** (see page 324).

People	% population with blood group			
	A	B	AB	O
Chinese	31	28	7	34
Sioux Native Americans	7	2	0	91

Table 7.1 Founder effect on blood groups

Neutral mutations

When genomes of existing species are studied at molecular level, the vast majority of mutations that they possess are found to be **neutral** (for example GCC changed to GCA still codes for alanine – also see page 38). These molecular differences do not affect how well adapted the individual becomes to its environment and are therefore not subject to natural selection. However, they are affected by genetic drift. Therefore many geneticists believe that most of the changes that occur in the frequencies of these neutral genetic sequences are the result of random genetic drift acting as a mechanism of evolution.

Species and speciation

Species

A **species** is a group of organisms that are able to interbreed with one another and produce fertile offspring. They are genetically isolated and cannot produce viable, fertile offspring with members of other groups (in other words, different species). It is thought that there may be about 5–20 million different species on Earth at present. However, species are not constant, immutable units. Their number and kinds are always changing. At any given moment some will be enjoying a **stable relationship** with the environment, some will be moving towards **extinction** (see page 314) and others will be undergoing **speciation** (see page 88).

Research Topic | Definitions of a species

The definition of a species given in the text above is the most widely accepted one and is known as the **biological species concept**. However, it only refers to organisms capable of sexual reproduction and cannot be applied successfully to every situation. For example it is not possible to know whether certain types of extinct organisms, reconstructed from fossil evidence, were able to interbreed or not. In addition some living things (for example many unicellular organisms) only reproduce asexually, so no interbreeding is involved.

It is also true that some groups of related organisms are not completely isolated genetically and are capable of a limited amount of genetic exchange. For example in a 'ring' species (see page 92) interbreeding occurs between members of adjacent populations but not between members of non-adjacent populations. Several other species concepts have therefore been proposed to offer alternative solutions to the *'What is a species?'* problem.

Morphological species concept

A **morphological** species is a group of organisms that differs in **structure** from other populations. Recognition of different morphological species depends on the use of measurable **physical features** by which they differ. For example, a goose and a swan can be distinguished easily because only the swan has a very long neck.

Taxonomy is the branch of biology concerned with the classification of organisms based on structural similarities and differences. Taxonomists have used the morphological species concept for hundreds of years and have even applied it to fossils. However, in recent times the concept has been criticised for not taking genetic information into account. It is now known that some populations that resemble one another physically are genetically distinct while others that differ greatly in structure are closely related genetically.

Ecological species concept

This system defines a species on the basis of its **habitat** (where it lives) and its **ecological niche** (the use it makes of the resources available in its environment). For example two groups of organisms that appeared identical in structure would be regarded as two different **ecological** species if each was found only in a particular environment not inhabited by the other.

Genetic species concept

Techniques such as **genetic fingerprinting** are employed to compare the DNA of the organisms and find out if they are similar enough to be regarded as members of the same **genetic** species. However, members of the same species (such as human beings) vary in their genetic fingerprints so it is difficult to decide just how similar the genetic composition of two organisms should be to indicate that they belong to the same genetic species.

Phylogeny is the evolutionary history of a group of species. The ways in which they relate to one another and to a common ancestor are often presented as a **phylogenetic tree** (see page 102). A phylogenetic species is a group of organisms that share a **common** ancestor and belong to a lineage that is distinct from other phylogenetic lineages. The members of a phylogenetic species are subject to a unique set of selection pressures that unites them and sets them apart from other lineages in the phylogenetic tree.

Speciation

Speciation is the formation of new biological species. It is brought about by **evolution** as a result of isolation, mutation and selection. It occurs when circumstances arise that interrupt gene flow between two populations causing their gene pools to diverge. Two types of speciation are allopatric speciation and sympatric speciation.

Allopatric speciation

In **allopatric speciation**, gene flow between two (or more) populations is prevented by a **geographical barrier**. Some examples are given in Figure 7.15.

A simplified version of allopatric speciation is shown in Figure 7.16.

1 The members of a large population of a species occupy an environment. They share the same gene pool and interbreed freely.

2 The population becomes split into two completely

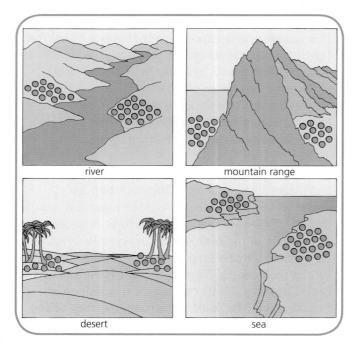

Figure 7.15 Geographical barriers

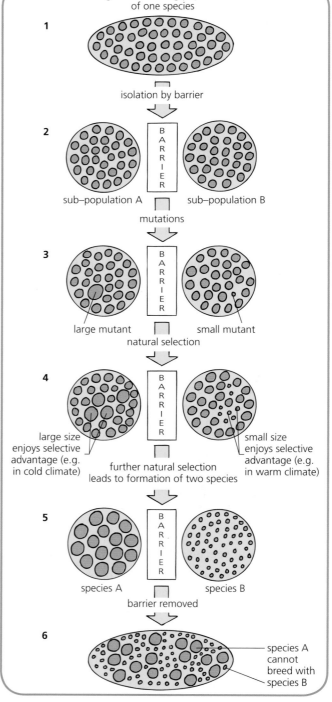

Figure 7.16 Allopatric speciation

isolated sub-populations by a **geographical barrier** which prevents interbreeding and gene exchange.

3 **Mutations** occur at random. Therefore most of the mutations that occur within one sub-population are different from those that occur within the other sub-population. This results in **new variation** arising within each group which is not shared by both groups.

4 The selection pressures acting on each sub-population are different depending on local conditions such as climate, predators and disease. **Natural selection** affects each sub-group in a different way by favouring those alleles which make the members of that sub-population best at exploiting their environment. If one of the populations is small, it may not possess the complete range of alleles. Therefore **genetic drift** may also play a role in the alteration of the group's gene frequencies.

5 Over a very, very long period of time, stages 3 and 4 cause the two gene pools to become so altered that the groups become genetically distinct and **isolated**.

6 If the barrier is removed, they are no longer able to interbreed since their chromosomes cannot make matching pairs. **Speciation** has occurred and two separate distinct species have evolved.

European wren

Figure 7.17 refers to three subspecies of the European wren. Geographical isolation from the original

mainland population and from one another has caused each island's wren population to take its own course of evolution. Although the populations have not been isolated for long enough to allow distinct species to

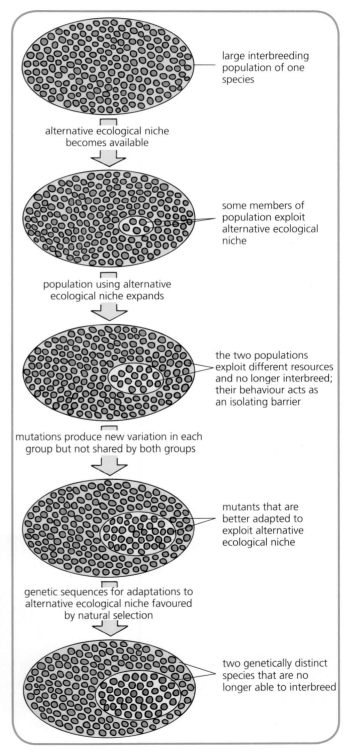

Figure 7.18 Sympatric speciation

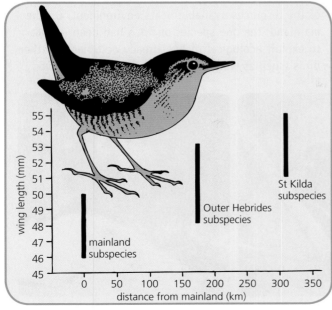

Figure 7.17 Subspecies of wren

arise, it is interesting to note that the subspecies on St Kilda (which is further from the mainland than the Hebrides) is already more different. Similarly four different subspecies of Orkney vole are found on four different islands in the Orkney group.

Sympatric speciation

In sympatric speciation, the two (or more) populations live in close proximity to one another in the same environment yet they become genetically isolated. This happens because gene flow between them is prevented by the presence of a behavioural or ecological barrier or by the occurrence of polyploidy in plants. Sympatric speciation is promoted by disruptive selection (see page 84). A simplified version of sympatric speciation is shown in Figure 7.18.

Fruit flies

A species of fruit fly is found in North America. It has evolved over a very long period of time. It lives on hawthorn trees and its larvae feed on the berries. About 200 years ago, settlers introduced a type of apple tree to North America. Some of the fruit flies soon began to exploit this new ecological niche and made use of the apples to feed their larvae.

The type of fruit tree where males search for mates and where females lay their eggs is normally the same as the type of fruit upon which the flies developed as larvae. This difference in behaviour has created an ecological barrier to gene flow between 'hawthorn' fruit flies and 'apple' fruit flies. Already some genetic differences have developed between the two groups and they are thought to have begun the process of sympatric speciation. Similarly many parasites that are specific to a certain host have arisen by sympatric speciation.

Polyploidy

A plant may undergo a type of mutation that produces a polyploid with one or more extra sets of chromosomes (see page 71). If the polyploid plant is unable to interbreed with the plant(s) that produced it, then it is genetically isolated and distinct from the parent(s) even though their ranges overlap. Thus a new species, the polyploid, has evolved 'overnight' by sympatric speciation.

Related Topic

Darwin's finches

In 1835 Darwin visited the Galapagos Islands which lie about 600 miles west of the South American mainland. He found them to be inhabited by many different species of finch which varied greatly in beak size and shape according to diet (see Figure 7.19). He also found that the mainland had only one species of finch. It is thought, therefore, that the islands

were originally colonised by a flock of the mainland species carried there by freak weather conditions.

An organism's ecological niche is the role that it plays within its ecosystem and the use that it makes of the resources available in its environment. On the mainland, the one species of finch had been unable to exploit ecological niches already occupied by other birds (such as woodpeckers and warblers). However,

Figure 7.19 Darwin's finches

the finches that arrived on the Galapagos found themselves in an environment lacking competitors and offering a wide range of unoccupied ecological niches. Reduced selection pressure enabled these finches to increase in number and occupy the islands.

It is thought that the finches underwent **allopatric** speciation with the sea acting as a geographical barrier. In addition, within populations living on the same island, it is probable that some groups underwent **sympatric** speciation by becoming adapted to suit, for example, a particular type of food available in an unoccupied ecological niche. Gradually many different species of finch evolved as shown in Figure 7.20.

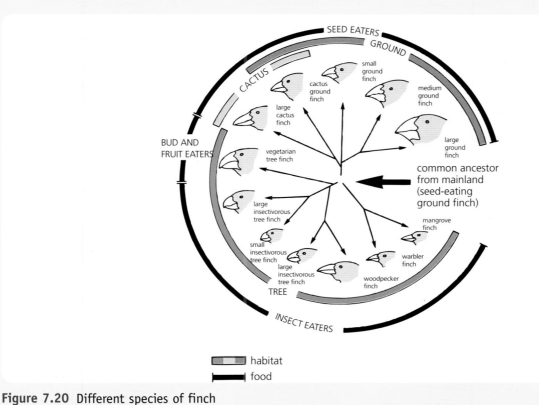

Figure 7.20 Different species of finch

Research Topic — London Underground mosquito

Culex pipiens is a species of mosquito that lives above ground in Europe and in many other parts of the world. It feeds by biting birds and sucking their blood. It is able to tolerate cold conditions in winter by 'hibernating'.

The London Underground mosquito is thought to have evolved from members of the above-ground species that moved below ground as a splinter group over 100 years ago when the tunnels for the Tube were being dug. Over the past century these mosquitoes have exploited their new ecological niche by breeding in pools of stagnant water in the tunnels and by feeding on rats and mice. They are also known to have bitten humans sheltering from air raids during the Second World War Blitz and in recent times to have 'molested' maintenance staff.

Therefore this type of mosquito has been named *Culex pipiens molestus*. It is cold intolerant because over time it has become adapted to the warm underground environment where it breeds all the year round.

Scientists have carried out tests to investigate whether the underground mosquito is genetically different from its above-ground relative. They have found that it is almost impossible to interbreed the two types of mosquito. The two strains possess several different frequencies of genetic sequences consistent with genetic drift and the founder effect. Therefore experts consider that the London Underground mosquito is well on its way to becoming a separate species by **allopatric speciation**.

Hybrid zones

A region may be occupied by several populations of an organism which vary in their ability to interbreed and which form **hybrid zones** as shown in Figure 7.21. Most biologists would regard these five closely related populations as belonging to the same 'ring' species because each population can interbreed with its immediate neighbour and form fertile hybrids. As a result genes are able to flow from A to E via B, C and D. However, if population B, C or D were to disappear then gene flow would be interrupted and A and E would become genetically isolated and form two distinct species.

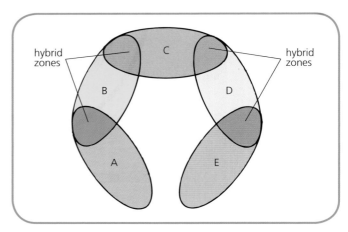

Figure 7.21 Hybrid zones of a 'ring' species

Related Topic

Carrion and hooded crows

The body of the **carrion** crow is completely black whereas that of the **hooded** crow is grey with a black hood, wings and tail (see Figure 7.22). The carrion crow is common throughout the UK; the hooded crow is largely restricted to northwest Scotland. It is there that a **hybrid zone** exists between the two types of crow.

Collaborative data gathered from hybrid zones in Scotland and other parts of Europe show that **successful interbreeding** occurs between the two types of crow and that fertile hybrids are often formed.

Figure 7.22 Hooded crow

Therefore, for many years the birds were considered to be geographical races of the same species. However, recent studies have shown that hybridisation is occurring far less frequently than expected and that the hybrids formed are **less vigorous** than their parents. In addition, slight **genetic differences** between the two types of crow indicate that they are at a very early stage of species divergence. For these reasons the carrion crow and the hooded crow are now regarded as becoming two distinct species.

Testing Your Knowledge 2

1 a) Why is a small population particularly prone to genetic drift? (2)

   b) All the cattle in Iceland are descendants of a small group taken there from Norway about a thousand years ago. The genetic make-up of present-day cattle in Iceland is found to be very different from that of their Norwegian relatives. Account for this difference. (3)

2 a) When a horse is crossed with a donkey, the result is a sterile animal called a mule.
      i) Do a mule's parents belong to the same species?
      ii) Explain your answer. (2)

   b) Define the term *speciation*. (1)

   c) Arrange the following stages into the correct order in which they would occur during allopatric speciation. (1)

   A isolation of gene pools

   B formation of new species

   C mutation

   D occupation of territory by one species with one gene pool

   E natural selection

3 a) **i)** Identify the type of speciation that involves geographical barriers.
      ii) Give TWO examples of geographical barriers. (2)

   b) Identify the type of speciation that involves behavioural or ecological barriers. (1)

8 Genomic sequencing

Genomics is the study of genomes. It involves determining the sequence of the nucleotide base molecules all the way along an organism's DNA (**genomic sequencing**) and then relating this genetic information about genes to their functions. Progress in this area has been accelerated by bioinformatics, making genomics one of the major scientific advances of recent years.

Bioinformatics is the name given to the fusion of molecular biology, statistical analysis and computer technology. This ever-advancing area now enables scientists to carry out rapid mapping and analysis of DNA sequences on a huge scale and then compare them. Information about genetic sequences that used to take years to unravel is now obtained in days or even hours. It can be used to investigate evolutionary biology, inheritance and personalised medicine.

Genomic sequencing

Use of restriction endonucleases

A **restriction endonuclease** is a type of enzyme that recognises a specific short sequence of DNA

nucleotides called a restriction site on a DNA strand (see page 210). It 'cuts' the DNA at this exact site all the way along the DNA strand. The restriction site recognised by one restriction endonuclease is different to that recognised by any other endonuclease.

Genome shotgun approach

The genome to be investigated is cut up into **fragments of DNA** using a restriction endonuclease. A further copy of the genome is cut up using a different endonuclease. Since these enzymes recognise different restriction sites on the DNA, they cut the genome at different points as shown in Figure 8.1.

Each DNA fragment produced is sequenced to establish the **order of its bases** (see Research topic – Sequencing DNA). This information is entered into a computer. Because of the way in which the DNA has been cut, many of the fragments overlap with one another. For example Figure 8.2 shows, in a simplified way, how the 'end' of fragment p overlaps with the 'start' of fragment q and the 'end' of fragment q overlaps with the 'start' of fragment r.

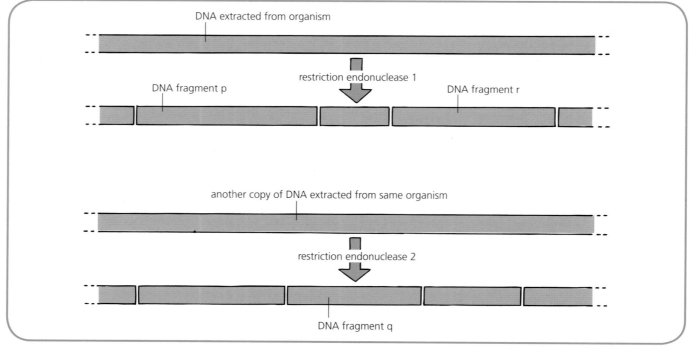

Figure 8.1 Cutting a genome using two different restriction endonucleases

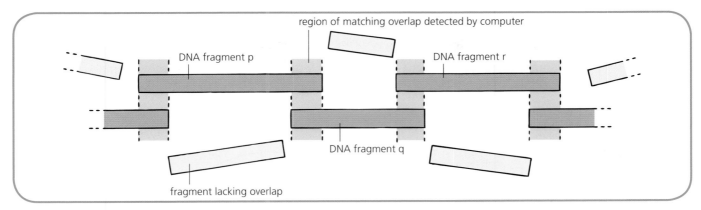

Figure 8.2 Overlapping DNA fragments

In this case the computer would recognise that the sequence of nucleotide bases at the 'end' of fragment p matches the sequence of nucleotide bases at the 'start' of fragment q and that the sequence of bases at the 'end' of q matches the sequence at the 'start' of r. It would therefore deduce that the fragments (and the order of their bases) run in the sequence p–q–r.

The computer analyses all the areas of overlap between the DNA fragments in a sample and is able to compile a **complete genome** based on these overlaps. Since each fragment has had its DNA sequenced, this procedure enables scientists to determine the sequence of bases for individual genes and for entire genomes.

Research Topic   Sequencing DNA

A portion of DNA with an unknown base sequence is chosen to be sequenced. Many copies of one of this DNA's strands (the template) are synthesised. Then, in order to make DNA strands that are complementary to these template strands, all the ingredients needed for synthesis are added to the preparation. These include DNA polymerase, primer and the four types of DNA nucleotide as shown in Figure 8.3. In addition the preparation receives a supply of **modified nucleotides** (ddA, ddT, ddG and ddC) each tagged with a different **fluorescent dye**.

Every so often during the synthesis process, a molecule of modified nucleotide just happens to be taken up instead of a normal one. However, when a modified nucleotide is incorporated into the new DNA strand, it brings the synthesis of that strand to a halt because a modified nucleotide does not allow any subsequent nucleotide to become bonded to it. Provided that the process is carried out on a large enough scale, the synthesis of a complementary strand will have been **stopped at every possible nucleotide position** along the DNA template.

The resultant mixture of DNA fragments of various lengths (each with its modified nucleotide and its unique fluorescent tag) is separated using **electrophoresis**. In this process the smallest (shortest) fragments travel the furthest distance. The identity and sequence of nucleotides (as indicated by their fluorescent dyes) is then read for the complementary DNA using this separation. From this information the sequence of the bases in the original DNA can be deduced.

This process has been automated by linking the detection of the four fluorescent dyes to a computer. As these are monitored, the computer, working as an **automated sequence analyser**, processes the information and rapidly displays the sequence of bases in the DNA sample as a series of peaks (see Figure 8.4).

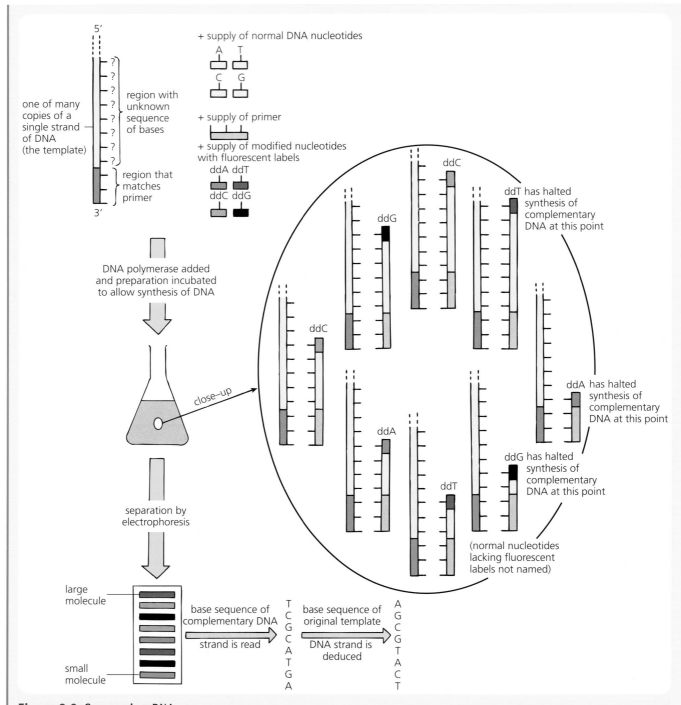

Figure 8.3 Sequencing DNA

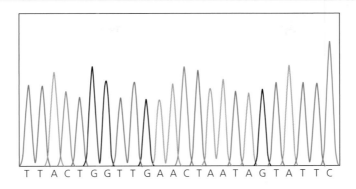

Figure 8.4 Printout from DNA sequence analyser

Genomics

A milestone in human history was reached in 2003 when the DNA sequence of the **human genome** was completed. It is based on the combined genome of a small number of donors and is regarded as the reference genome. It was sequenced using the **shotgun method**.

In addition to sequencing the human genome, part of the project's remit was to determine the nucleotide sequence of the genome of a range of other species. Many have now been sequenced and they include the following.

- A large number of **viruses** and many **bacteria**, most of which are disease-causing agents. A few of these species of pathogenic bacteria are given in Table 8.1.

- Many **pest species** such as the type of mosquito that acts as a vector for malaria and the unicellular organism (*Plasmodium*) that causes malaria.

- Species called **model organisms** (see Table 8.2) that are important for research because they possess genes equivalent to genes in humans responsible for inherited diseases and disorders. Therefore they may provide understanding of the malfunctioning of these genes and even lead the way to the development of new treatments.

Species of pathogenic bacterium	Number in single (haploid) genome		Disease or disorder caused
	Base pairs	Genes	
Chlamydia trachomatis	1 042 519	936	sexually-transmitted disease
Rickettsia prowazekii	1 111 523	834	typhus
Treponema pallidum	1 138 011	1 039	syphilis
Campylobacter jejuni	1 641 481	1 708	food poisoning
Helicobacter pylori	1 667 867	1 589	stomach ulcers
Neisseria meningitidis	2 272 351	2 221	meningitis
Propionibacterium acnes	2 560 265	2 333	acne
Vibrio cholerae	4 033 460	3 890	cholera
Mycobacterium tuberculosis	4 411 532	3 959	tuberculosis

Table 8.1 Genomes of pathogenic bacteria

Model organism	Number in single (haploid) genome		Notes
	Base pairs	Genes	
Escherichia coli	4 639 221	4 377	Bacterium that is an important model for molecular biology, genetics and biotechnology.
Saccharomyces cerevisiae	12 495 682	5 770	Unicellular yeast that has many genes in common with humans therefore it has potential for research as a model for eukaryotes.
Caenorhabditis elegans	100 258 171	c. 20 500	Tiny multicellular worm that acts as a simple model for multicellular organisms in the study of genetics and molecular aspects of development, nerve functioning and ageing.
Arabidopsis thaliana	115 409 949	c. 28 000	Small flowering plant that acts as a model for other plants in the study of genetics and molecular aspects of plant development.
Drosophila melanogaster	122 653 977	c. 17 000	Fruit fly that has many genes in common with those that cause disease in humans therefore it is useful in research programmes.
Mus musculus	3.4×10^9	c. 23 000	Mouse that possesses many genes present in humans. Useful information obtained using 'knock-out' mice where a gene is deleted or replaced with a mutant allele to investigate the effect.

(c. = approximately)

Table 8.2 Genomes of model organisms

Research Topic — Importance of *Fugu* genome

The genome of *Fugu rubripes*, the pufferfish (see Figure 6.5), has been sequenced completely. Its genome is one of the smallest found among the vertebrates. It is more than seven times smaller than that of humans yet its gene number is higher than that of humans (see Table 8.3).

The *Fugu* genome has a higher density of genes because it possesses **fewer introns** and very **little repetitive DNA**. By comparison the human genome is gene-sparse. The difference between the two is the result of a high rate of **deletion** in the chromosomes of *Fugu* which is largely confined to the intron regions of DNA.

Figure 8.5 Pufferfish

Organism		Genome size (Mb)	Approximate number of protein-coding genes
Scientific name	Common name		
Fugu rubripes	pufferfish	393	31 000
Rattus norvegicus	rat	2 750	30 200
Homo sapiens	human	2 900	20 000

Note: 1 megabase (Mb) = 1×10^6 bases

Table 8.3 Genomes of three vertebrates

The genome of *Fugu* is important because:

- many of its protein-coding genes and regulatory gene sequences are equivalent to those in the human genome

- the compact nature of its DNA makes it easier for

scientists to locate the genes and their regulatory sequences for study.

It is likely that decoding the functions of *Fugu*'s genes will in turn increase the understanding of the functions of many human genes.

Comparative genomics

This branch of genomics compares the sequenced genomes of:

- members of different species – for example disease-causing micro-organisms – to investigate whether they have important genetic sequences in common

- members of the same species – for example the harmless strain of *E. coli* with the strain that causes serious food poisoning to discover which genetic sequences cause illness

- cancerous cells and normal cells from the same individual to try to discover the specific 'driver' mutations that cause a healthy cell to divide uncontrollably and form a tumour.

Differences in genome

A variation in DNA sequence that affects a single base pair in a DNA chain is called a **single nucleotide polymorphism (SNP)**. SNPs are one of the ways in which genomes are found to differ from one another. For example the DNA of two people might differ by

the SNP shown in Figure 8.6. This difference has arisen as a result of a point mutation where one base pair has been **substituted** for another.

The use of bioinformatics has enabled scientists to catalogue more than a million SNPs and specify their exact locations in the human genome. They believe that this SNP map will help them to identify and understand the workings of genes associated with diseases. Therefore SNPs are regarded as a valuable tool in research and may aid the development of future treatments for genetic disorders.

Similarities in genome

In addition to displaying significant differences, a close comparison of genomes often reveals important similarities. For example they may show a high level of **conservation**. This means that the same or very similar DNA sequences are present in the genomes. Much of the genome is found to be highly conserved in a wide variety of organisms and across species boundaries. Among the most **highly conserved genetic sequences** are those that code for the active sites of essential enzymes and have been positively selected over time.

Humans and whales are very distant relatives. Their evolutionary paths diverged about a hundred million years ago. However, when their genomes are compared, the base sequences of many of their genes are found to be very similar. Figure 8.7 compares a section of the male-determining gene in both species. Apart from four point mutations, the sequence of DNA bases that they received from their common ancestor has been accurately conserved over evolutionary time.

Highly conserved DNA sequences can be used in comparisons of genomes of two groups to find out how **close** or **distant** their relationship is. The greater the number of conserved DNA sequences that their genomes have in common, the more closely related the two groups that possess them.

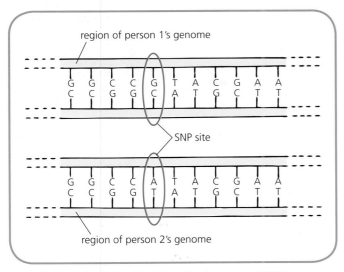

Figure 8.6 Single nucleotide polymorphism (SNP)

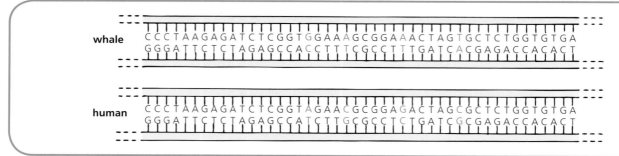

Figure 8.7 Part of male sex-determining gene in two species

Related Topic

Shared genes

Certain biochemical processes, such as respiration, occur in all living things. These processes require **similar genes** to code for the functional enzymes that operate the basic metabolic pathways involved. Therefore, although two organisms such as yeast and human may appear very different in structure, they have much in common at a cellular level and have many shared genes. Around 33% of yeast's genes have survived millions of years of evolutionary change and are conserved in the human genome.

Caenorhabditis elegans is a tiny transparent nematode worm. An adult's body consists of 959 cells of which 302 are nerve cells. *C. elegans* was the first multicellular eukaryote to have its entire genome sequenced. It possesses about 20 500 genes of which about 19 000 are protein-coding. Humans possess about 20 000 protein-coding genes and share approximately 7000 of these with *C. elegans*.

In humans about 300 genes are implicated in diseases. Of these about 42% are found in an equivalent form in *C. elegans*. These genes include the ones closely associated with Alzheimer's disease, colon cancer, spinal muscular atrophy and many other diseases and disorders. The effect of the absence of

the product normally coded for by one of these genes can be investigated by inactivating and **silencing** the equivalent gene in *C. elegans* and finding out what happens. By using *C. elegans* as a model organism in this way, it is hoped that a greater understanding of the biological functioning of these genes will be obtained and that it will in turn lead to the development of treatments.

Drosophila melanogaster, the fruit fly, has about 17 000 genes in its genome. Although fewer in number than *C. elegans*, they show a similar diversity of function. The fruit fly has many genes in common with vertebrates. It has been used by scientists to determine developmental and neurological pathways conserved through evolutionary time from invertebrates to humans.

The fruit fly also possesses equivalent versions of about 75% of the 300 genes in the human genome known to be involved in diseases and disorders. By disrupting these genes in fruit flies (and the proteins that they code for), it is possible to investigate some of the events that may also occur in humans. Therefore *Drosophila melanogaster* is also a valuable model organism in the study of diseases that affect humans and in the development of new treatments.

Comparison of human and chimp genomes

The genomes of humans and chimpanzees (our closest living relatives) are very similar. A chimpanzee has **24** chromosomes in a single copy of its genome; a human has **23** (see Figure 8.8). This difference is thought to be the result of the fusion of two ancestral ape chromosomes during evolution (see page 69).

Analysis of the difference in base sequence of the two genomes reveals that humans and apes have about **98.5%** of their DNA in common. Fossil evidence shows that they shared a common ancestor until about six million years ago when the two groups diverged.

Around 600 genes, common to both chimps and humans, have been identified that are thought to have been conserved by **positive selection**. Many of these genes are known to be involved in defence of the body by the immune system against pathogenic micro-organisms. For example one of them codes for granulysin, a membrane-disrupting protein that destroys microbes such as *Mycobacterium tuberculosis*.

Despite the very close similarities in genomes, some important differences exist between the two species. Several key genes that give resistance to the parasite that causes sleeping sickness are completely deleted from the chimpanzee genome. Humans, on the other hand, appear to have lost the function of a gene that produces an enzyme thought to give protection against Alzheimer's disease. Most of the differences in genome between humans and chimps take the form of gene duplications and single base-pair substitutions.

Of all the genetic differences that have arisen, one of the most striking involves a gene called HAR1. In the chimpanzee and the chicken, this gene is an exact match for 116 out of 118 bases, amounting to a total of two changes over a period of 310 million years. However, in the chimpanzee and the human genomes, this gene is a match in only 100 out of 118 bases, amounting to 18 changes over 6 million years.

The HAR1 gene encodes a form of RNA needed by a region of the brain for its proper development. The same cells with the active HAR1 gene also produce a protein that is essential to regulate proper **neural development** of the brain's cerebral cortex. It is thought that the genetic differences between the chimp and the human versions of the HAR1 gene account in part for the development of the more **advanced brain** present in humans. These differences in genome tend to support the idea that humans are 'naked apes with big brains'.

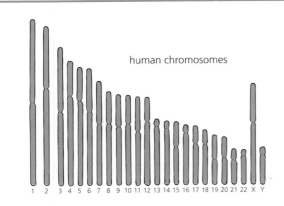
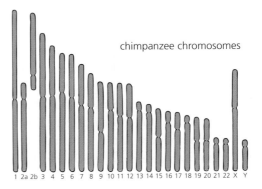

Figure 8.8 Chromosome complements of two primates

Testing Your Knowledge 1

1 a) What information is obtained by the process of genomic sequencing? (1)

   b) i) What is meant by the term *bioinformatics*?
     ii) What use do biologists make of bioinformatics? (2)

2 a) Name TWO examples of *model* organisms whose genomes have been sequenced. (2)

   b) Explain why model organisms are important for research. (2)

3 What is the purpose of comparing the genome of a harmless strain of *E. coli* with that of a pathogenic strain? (2)

4 a) 'Much of the genome is highly conserved across different organisms'. Explain what this statement means. (1)

   b) Suggest why a genetic sequence responsible for an enzyme used in photosynthesis is highly conserved among plant species. (1)

Phylogenetics

The study of evolutionary relatedness among different groups of organisms is called **phylogenetics**. It makes use of information obtained from comparisons of genome sequence data to deduce phylogenies (sequences of events involved in a group's evolution) and to construct phylogenetic trees (diagrams that show evolutionary relationships). Closely related species are found to have genomes that are very similar in the sequence of their nucleotide bases.

Divergence

Over time a group of closely related living things acquires its own set of **mutations** (such as nucleotide substitutions) which gradually alter its genome. If the group gives rise to two groups that become more and more different from one another and eventually **diverge**, then changes occur in each group's genome that are distinct from those occurring in the other group's genome. Therefore the more different the base sequences of two genomes are found to be, the more **distantly related** the two groups to which they belong and vice versa.

This use of molecular information to determine evolutionary relationships is called **molecular phylogenetics**. It has the advantage over the sole use of structural features for this purpose in that it can be used in a wider range of situations. These vary from the comparison of two groups that are not structurally alike (but may be related genetically) to those that are physically indistinguishable (including many species of bacteria).

When the base sequences for a selection of genes from two different groups are compared and found to differ by only a few bases, this suggests that the groups share a **common ancestor** and that they diverged fairly recently. The greater the number of differences, the longer the time since the point of divergence.

The number of differences per unit length of DNA sequence (in other words, quantity of genetic change) between the two genomes is regarded as a measure of **evolutionary distance** between the two groups. These distances can then be used to construct a **phylogenetic tree** which shows the probable evolution of related groups of organisms and their phylogenetic patterns of divergence.

An example of a phylogenetic tree is shown in Figure 8.9. It is based on differences between several genetic sequences possessed by five related species. In this tree the length of a branch represents the number of changes that have occurred in that species' genome

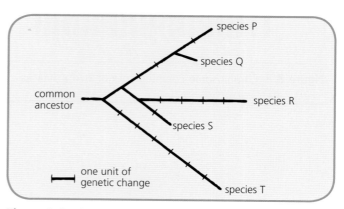

Figure 8.9 Phylogenetic tree

compared with the others. Species P and Q are the most closely related and species T is the most distantly related to the others.

Molecular clocks

Molecules of nucleic acid (and the proteins that they code for) gradually change over time as they are affected by mutations such as nucleotide substitutions. When equivalent genetic sequences for two related groups of organisms (that are known from fossil evidence to have diverged at a certain point in geological time) are compared, the **number of nucleotide substitutions** by which they differ is regarded as being proportional to the **length of time** that has elapsed since the groups diverged. In other words, the quantity of molecular difference that exists between the two groups is a measure of how long ago it is since they shared a common ancestor.

Therefore a molecule of nucleic acid (or a protein coded for by the nucleic acid) can be regarded as a **molecular clock**. It can be given an actual time scale by graphing the number of molecular differences it has evolved against a time scale based on fossil records. Molecular clocks are used as tools to try to date the **origins** of groups of living things and to determine the **sequence** in which they evolved.

Figure 8.10 shows the use of α-**globin** (a polypeptide present in haemoglobin) as a molecular clock. Each lettered point on the graph refers to a comparison of two groups of organisms. For example the groups compared at point A have nine molecular differences

between their versions of α-globin and diverged from one another about 450 million years ago. On the other hand, the groups compared at point E have only two differences and shared a common ancestor until about 100 million years ago when they diverged.

Molecular versus structural

Comparison of dolphins and bats using molecular clocks shows the two groups to be more closely related than sharks and tuna fish. This agrees with fossil evidence that suggests that sharks and tuna have been evolving along separate lineages for longer than dolphins and bats. In this case, changes in the molecules that have acted as molecular clocks give a more accurate indication of underlying evolutionary relationships than the changes that have occurred to the animals' body structure.

Shortcomings

Use of a molecular clock assumes that the mutation rate affecting that type of molecule has been relatively constant over time. Although this is often the case for closely related species, it may not be true for groups that diverged early in the evolution of life on Earth. Therefore molecular clocks are less reliable for use in dating the origins of distantly related groups.

Three domains of living things

RNA and DNA sequences have been used to trace the primary evolutionary lineages of all living things. This work was based largely on comparisons of nucleotide sequences of **ribosomal RNA (rRNA)** from many organisms. rRNA is used as a molecular clock for constructing phylogenies because the genes that code for rRNA are ancient, have suffered little or no horizontal gene transfer and are possessed by all living things. Molecular evidence obtained in this way has been used to construct a phylogenetic tree as shown in Figure 8.11. It supports the idea that living things are made up of three main **domains**:

- the **bacteria** (traditional prokaryotes)

- the **archaea** (mostly prokaryotes that inhabit extreme environments such as hot springs and salt lakes)

- the **eukaryotes** (fungi, plants and animals).

The three domains are compared in Table 8.4. Bacteria and archaea are found to be as different genetically as

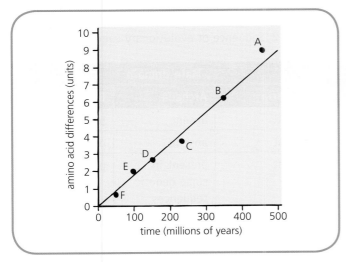

Figure 8.10 α-globin as a molecular clock

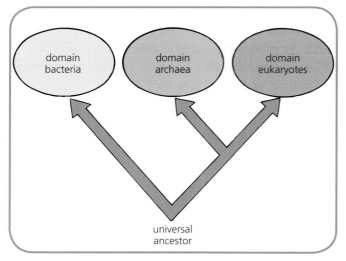

Figure 8.11 Three main domains

bacteria and eukaryotes. Sequencing of genomes has shown the archaean genes involved in DNA replication, transcription and translation to resemble much more closely those of eukaryotes than those of bacteria.

The deep evolutionary divisions that separate bacteria and archaea were not obvious from their phenotypes and only came to light following comparison of their rRNA. This work also revealed that the genetic material present in mitochondria and chloroplasts originated in prokaryotes (also see page 295).

Sequence of evolutionary events

Fossils

Fossilisation normally involves the conversion of hard parts of the body such as bone, teeth or shells into rock. The age of a fossil can be determined by estimating the age of the rock of which it is composed. The older the rock, the less radioactivity it emits.

Combined evidence

Scientists have used a combination of genome sequence data and fossil evidence to work out the **sequence** in which key events in evolution have taken place. The evidence strongly supports the theory that living things have undergone a series of **modifications** from the first emergence of life on Earth through to the present day, gradually becoming more and more **complex** as evolution has progressed. Some of the important events are shown in Figure 8.12.

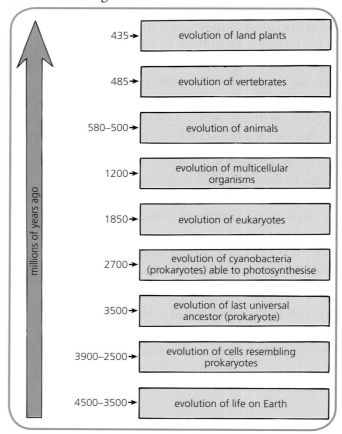

Figure 8.12 Sequence of evolutionary events

Characteristic	Main domain		
	Bacteria	**Archaea**	**Eukaryotes**
true nucleus bound by double membrane	absent	absent	present
membrane-enclosed organelles (such as mitochondria)	absent	absent	present
introns	absent	present in some genetic sequences	present
number of types of RNA polymerase	one	several	several
normal response to streptomycin (an antibiotic)	growth inhibited	growth not inhibited	growth not inhibited

Table 8.4 Comparison of three main domains

Personal genomics

The branch of genomics involved in sequencing an individual's genome and analysing it using bioinformatic tools is called **personal genomics**. As a result of advances in computer technology, the process of sequencing DNA is rapidly becoming **faster** and **cheaper**. Sequencing an individual's DNA for medical reasons will soon become a real possibility. In years to come, a person's entire genome may be sequenced early in life and stored as an electronic medical record available for future consultation by doctors when required.

Genetic variation

Many different types of **variation in genome** are found to occur among the members of a human population. These differences are largely the result of **mutations** and **rearrangements** of parts of the sequence of bases. They range from completely missing or extra chromosomes to single nucleotide changes (such as single nucleotide polymorphisms – see page 99) in a protein-coding gene or non-coding regulatory sequence.

Harmful and neutral mutations

Having located the mutant variants present in the genome, it is often difficult to distinguish between those altered genetic sequences that are genuinely **harmful** (for example those which fail to code for an essential protein) and those that are **neutral** (in other words have no negative effect).

Genetic disorders

A **genetic disorder** or **disease** is the result of a variation in genomic DNA sequence. The challenge for scientists is to establish a **causal link** between a particular mutant variant in a genomic sequence and a specific genetic

---

Related Topic

Comparison of individuals' genomes

The human genome consists of around 20 000 protein-coding genes, many non-coding regulatory sequences and vast stretches of DNA of little known function. The latter often take the form of repetitive sequences clustered together or distributed at regular intervals. In the past these were wrongly dismissed as 'junk' DNA but it is likely that many of these sequences function in ways that are not yet understood.

In all, a single human genome consists of around **three billion** base pairs, yet, on comparison, the genomes of two individuals normally vary by less than 1% from each other. This variation has arisen as a result of:

- **Point mutations** such as substitutions which result in single nucleotide polymorphisms (SNPs). Of the estimated total of ten million SNPs that exist in the human population, only about 1% are functional. The remainder are neutral.

- **Errors** in repetitive DNA sequences.

- **Copy number variation.** This means an alteration in the genome that causes an abnormal number of copies of one or more sections of DNA to arise. Fewer copies in the case of deletion where a relatively large section of DNA is lost; more in the case of a block of duplication where one or more copies of a section of DNA is gained. It is estimated that, on average, copy number variation accounts for about 0.4% of the variation between the genomes of unrelated people.

It is a combination of these differences that makes each person's genome unique and different from all others.

Personal genome sequence

A complete sequencing of a person's DNA bases is called a **personal genome sequence**. The first complete sequencing of the human genome (based on a combined genome of several donors) in 2003 was followed by the sequencing of several personal genomes. One of these was for Craig Ventor of USA in 2007. Comparison of his genome with the reference one revealed that SNPs made up the majority of his genetic variants and that non-SNPs, such as deletions, accounted for about 22% of the total number of his variants. The genomes of several thousand human individuals from all parts of the world are now being sequenced to investigate genetic variation among human beings.

disease or disorder. When this is achieved, the disease or disorder is said to be **molecularly characterised**.

The causal genetic sequence has been identified, at least in part, for around 2200 genetic disorders and diseases in humans. However, this does not mean that it is a simple matter to produce treatments for these disorders. The nature of disease is highly complex. Most medical disorders depend on both **genetic** and **environmental** factors for their expression, though the specific effects of these are not fully understood.

Personalised medicine (pharmacogenetics)

Already it is known that one in ten drugs (including the blood thinner warfarin) varies in effect depending on differences such as SNPs in the person's DNA profile. In the future it may be possible to customise medical treatment to suit an individual's exact metabolic requirements. The most **suitable drug** and the **correct dosage** would be prescribed as indicated by personal genomic sequencing (and *not* as shown in Figure 8.13!). Ideally this advance would increase drug efficacy while reducing side effects and the 'one-size-fits-all' approach would be consigned to history.

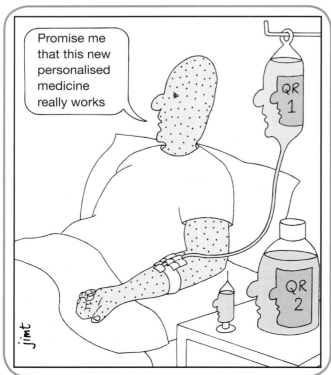

Figure 8.13 'Personalised' medicine

Risk prediction

Already variations in DNA have been linked to conditions such as diabetes, heart disease, schizophrenia and cancer. In the future, when the location in the human genome of many more markers for common diseases and disorders have been established, it should become possible to scan an individual's genome for **predisposition** to a disease and **predict risk** early enough to allow suitable action to be taken. Eventually reduction of risk may be achieved through appropriate drug treatment combined with a healthy lifestyle.

Ethical issues

If personal genomic sequencing becomes a routine predictive medical procedure then this raises many **ethical** issues. For example, if a person's genome contains genetic markers indicating a high risk of a debilitating or fatal disease later in life, who should have access to this information?

- The person's employer? Perhaps the company will refuse to employ anyone who is at risk of the disorder.

- The person's offspring? Maybe this would tell them more than they want to know about their own genome.

- The person's life insurer? Perhaps the insurance company will insist on charging a much higher premium or refuse to provide cover at all.

Many people believe that laws should be introduced to prevent **genetic discrimination** based on information obtained from an individual's genome. These issues need to be addressed by society before genomic sequencing becomes inexpensive and widely available.

Testing Your Knowledge 2

1 a) What is meant by the term *phylogenetics*? (1)

b) Identify the advantage of using molecular phylogenetics rather than structural features to determine the evolutionary relatedness of two groups of bacteria. (2)

2 Rewrite the following paragraph and complete the blanks using the answers given below it. (3)

Two related groups of organisms known from fossil records to have _____ at a certain point in _____ time are chosen. Many genetic _____ for the two groups are compared and the number of nucleotide _____ by which they differ is determined. The quantity of molecular change in their _____ that has occurred is a measure of how long ago the groups diverged from a common _____. The DNA can therefore be used as a molecular _____.

ancestor, clock, diverged, DNA, geological, sequences, substitutions

3 a) i) Name the THREE main domains of living things.
ii) Identify TWO features possessed by members of the most recently evolved domain that are absent in members of the other two domains. (3)

b) Draw a flow chart to show the evolution of plants using the following terms:

photosynthetic eukaryotes, last universal ancestor, photosynthetic land plants, photosynthetic prokaryotes, multicellular green plants. (2)

4 a) What is meant by the term *personal genomics*? (2)

b) Give TWO possible benefits of personalised medicine to patients in the future. (2)

What You Should Know

Chapters 7–8

(See Table 8.5 for word bank)

allopatric	environmental	non-random
archaea	evolution	non-representative
asexual	fertile	nucleotide
bioinformatics	founder	pharmacogenetics
change	frequency	phylogenetics
clocks	genomes	reproduction
closely	genomics	risk
conservation	geological	sampling
customised	horizontally	sequencing
decrease	hybrid	sexual
directional	interbreed	speciation
disruptive	life	stabilising
diverged	model	sympatric
domains	mutations	vertical
drift	natural	viruses

Table 8.5 Word bank for chapters 7–8

1 The gradual _____ in the characteristics of a population from generation to generation as a result of variations in its genome is called _____.

2 Genetic sequences of DNA are passed down from parent to offspring by _____ inheritance. This occurs as a result of both sexual and _____ reproduction.

3 In prokaryotes, genetic material may also be transferred _____ between one another and into the _____ of eukaryotes. DNA sequences can also be transferred horizontally into eukaryotes by _____.

4 Within a population, _____ selection brings about both the non-random increase in _____ of genetic sequences that increase the chance of survival and the _____ decrease in frequency of deleterious sequences that _____ the chance of survival.

5 _____ selection brings about the non-random increase in frequency of genetic sequences that increase the chance of successful _____ by the population.

6 _____ selection favours the intermediate versions of a trait and acts against the extreme variants. _____ selection favours a version of the trait that was less common and results in a progressive shift of the population's mean. _____ selection favours extreme versions of a trait at the expense of the intermediates.

7 The random increase or decrease in frequency of genetic sequences that occur due to _____ error, particularly in small populations, is called genetic _____. The _____ effect occurs when a splinter group containing a _____ sample of the gene pool breaks away from a large population. The small group develops into a new population with allele frequencies different from the original population.

8 A group of organisms that can _____ and produce _____ offspring belong to the same species.

9 The formation of new species by evolution is called _____. The barriers involved in _____ speciation are geographical whereas those involved in _____ speciation are normally behavioural or ecological.

10 _____ zones may exist in regions where the ranges of closely related species overlap.

11 Determining the sequence of _____ bases along an organism's genes or entire genome is called genomic _____. Use is made of _____, involving computing and statistics, to compare sequence data.

12 The study of genomes is called _____. Many genomes have been sequenced including those of _____ organisms important for research. In addition to many differences, comparative genomics shows that a high degree of _____ exists among different organisms.

13 _____ is the study of evolutionary relatedness found among different groups of organisms. The use of sequence data indicates that distantly related groups _____ at an earlier point in _____ time and that more _____ related groups diverged more recently.

14 Molecules such as DNA are affected by _____ and gradually change over time therefore they can be used as molecular _____.

15 Comparison of nucleic acid sequences provides evidence to support the idea that living things fall into three main _____: bacteria, _____ and eukaryotes. A combination of sequence data and fossil evidence has enabled scientists to determine the main sequence of events in the evolution of _____ on Earth.

16 In the future, routine sequencing of an individual's genome may lead to personalised medicine (_____). This could involve predicting _____ of disease through knowledge of the person's genome and administering _____ drugs in appropriate dosages. Diseases are complex and are often affected by both genetic and _____ factors.

Applying Your Knowledge and Skills

Chapters 1–8

1 Refer back to Figure 1.8 which shows Griffith's transformation experiment. Avery continued this line of investigation and isolated a chemically purified form of the 'principle' that transformed live R to live S cells. He then carried out the experiment shown in Figure 8.14.

   a) Find out and state the effect that
   i) the enzyme DNAase has on DNA, its substrate
   ii) the enzyme protease has on protein, its substrate. (2)

   b) Why did the transforming principle treated with DNAase have no effect on the mouse? (2)

   c) Why did the transforming principle treated with protease still work and affect the mouse? (2)

   d) Identify TWO factors from Figure 6.14 that must be kept constant throughout the experiment. (2)

   e) State the means by which the reliability of the experiment could be checked. (1)

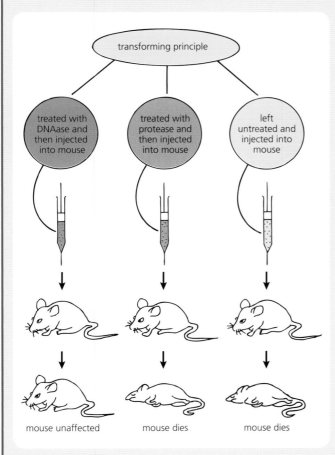

Figure 8.14

2 Refer back to Figure 2.4 and then draw a labelled diagram to show both the DNA strands and the test tube contents that would result after three DNA replications involving semi-conservative replication only. (4)

3 Figure 8.15 shows mRNA's codons and the amino acids that they code for.

   a) Which letters should have been inserted at positions **X** and **Y** in the wheel? (2)

   b) How many codons are able to trigger the process of translation? (1)

   c) Identify the codons that can bring translation to a halt. (3)

   d) Which amino acid is coded for by codon
   i) UUU
   ii) ACC
   iii) GGU? (3)

   e) Name all the codons that code for leucine. (2)

   f) Refer back to Figure 3.17 and then state which amino acid would become attached to this tRNA's site of attachment. (Remember that tRNA has an anticodon and that the wheel shows mRNA codons.) (1)

4 Figure 8.16 shows a possible use of stem cells in the future.

   a) Match blank boxes P, Q, R, S, T and U with the following possible answers. (6)
   i) stem cells induced to differentiate
   ii) nucleus removed and retained
   iii) stem cells removed and cultured in laboratory
   iv) egg lacking nucleus retained
   v) matching tissue transplanted to patient without fear of rejection
   vi) nucleus inserted into egg

   b) Which of the following is **not** represented in Figure 8.16? (1)

   A cytoplasmic hybrid cell

   B amniotic stem cell line

   C undifferentiated stem cells

   D nuclear transfer technique

   c) **i)** Name a source of the donor egg cells used at present in this line of research.
   ii) Why does this prevent the series of events shown in the diagram being put into practice? (2)

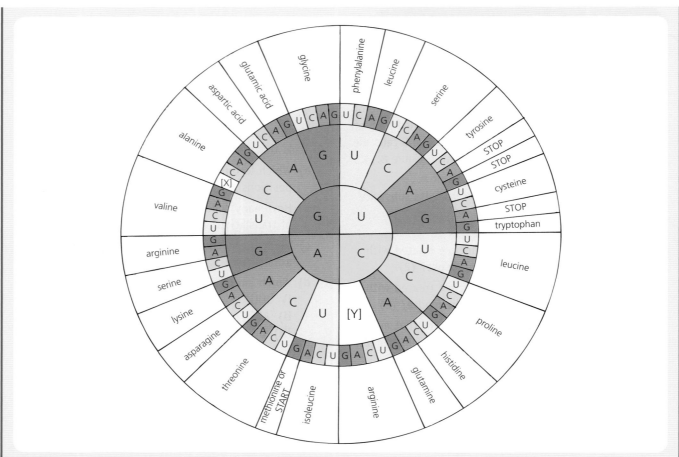

Figure 8.15

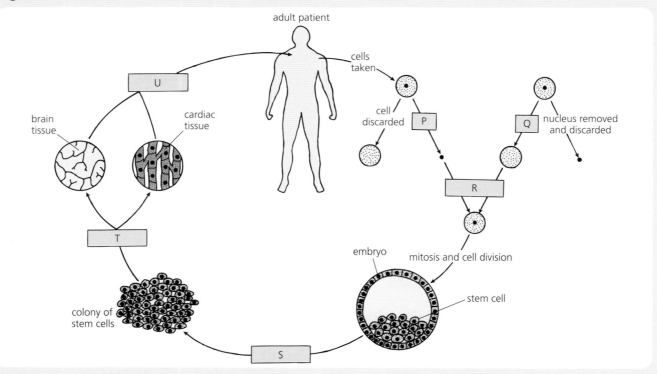

Figure 8.16

5 Figure 8.17 shows the base sequence on a region of DNA undergoing a type of point mutation.

  a) i) Identify the type of point mutation that occurred.
  ii) Describe the way in which the DNA has been altered. (2)

  b) Refer back to Table 3.6 (and Table 3.2) and work out the amino acid sequence for
  i) the original DNA
  ii) the mutant DNA. (2)

  c) i) State whether this mutation would be silent, neutral, missensical or nonsensical.
  ii) Explain your choice. (2)

  d) i) Refer back to Figure 6.4 and state whether the point mutation that results in the formation of haemoglobin S is silent, neutral, missensical or nonsensical.
  ii) Explain your choice. (2)

6 Figure 8.18 shows a map of the Galapagos Islands. Each figure in brackets refers to the number of different species of finch found on the island. Table 8.6 gives further information about six of the islands. Table 8.7 and Figure 8.19 refer to ground-living finches on two of the islands.

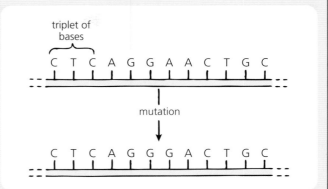

Figure 8.17

Name of island	Percentage number of finch species only found on this island
Culpepper	75.0
Pinta	33.3
Espanola	66.7
Isabella	22.2
Santa Cruz	0.0
Santa Fe	14.3

Table 8.6

  a) Calculate the actual number of finch species which are found on Culpepper and on no other island. (1)

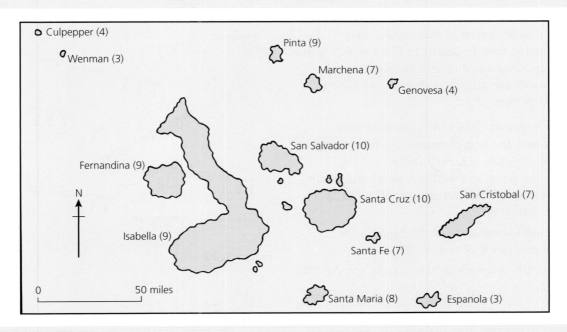

Figure 8.18

Species of ground finch		Island	
Body size	Food	Culpepper	Pinta
small	cactus	present (11.3 × 9.0)	present (9.7 × 8.5)
large	cactus	absent	present (14.6 × 9.7)
medium	seeds	present (15.0 × 16.5)	absent
large	seeds	absent	present (16.0 × 20.0)

Table 8.7 (numbers in brackets = length × depth of beak in mm)

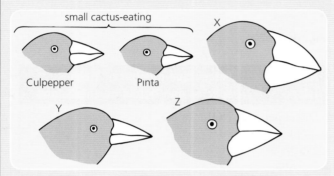

Figure 8.19

b) Two of the islands each have an actual number of two species which are found on that island and nowhere else. Identify the islands. (2)

c) Which island is populated by finch species which are all found on other islands? (1)

d) Identify birds X, Y and Z using the information in Table 8.7. (2)

e) i) If a large number of finch type Z were transported from Culpepper to Pinta, which native type on Pinta would face most competition?
ii) Predict the possible outcome over a long period of time. (2)

7 The DNA fragments shown in Figure 8.20 were formed during the type of sequencing technology illustrated in Figure 8.3. Each fluorescent tag indicates the point on the strand where replication of complementary DNA was brought to a halt by a modified nucleotide.

a) Work out the sequence of the bases in the complementary DNA strand. (1)

b) Deduce the sequence of bases in the original DNA strand. (1)

8 Give an account of personal genomics under the headings:

a) source of genomic information about a patient (4)

b) possible benefits to the patient (3)

c) possible disadvantages. (2)

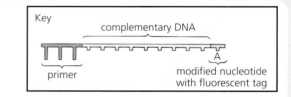

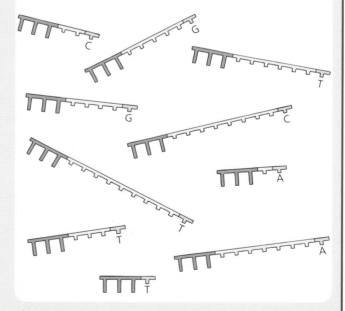

Figure 8.20

Since this group of questions does not include examples of every type of question found in SQA exams, it is recommended that students also make use of past exam papers to aid learning and revision.

Unit 2

Metabolism and Survival

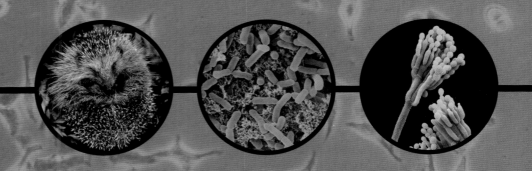

9 Metabolic pathways and their control

Cell metabolism

Cell metabolism is the collective term for the thousands of biochemical reactions that occur within a living cell. The vast majority of these are steps in a complex network of connected and integrated pathways that are catalysed by enzymes.

Metabolic pathways

The biochemical processes upon which life depends take the form of **metabolic pathways** which fall into two categories:

- **Catabolic** pathways which bring about the breakdown of complex molecules to simpler ones usually releasing energy and often providing building blocks.

- **Anabolic** pathways which bring about the biosynthesis of complex molecules from simpler building blocks and require energy to do so.

Such pathways are closely integrated and one often depends upon the other. For example aerobic respiration in living cells is an example of **catabolism** which releases the energy needed for the synthesis of protein from amino acids (an example of **anabolism**). This close relationship is shown in Figure 9.1. An important chemical called ATP (see chapter 10) plays a key role in the transfer of energy between catabolic and anabolic reactions.

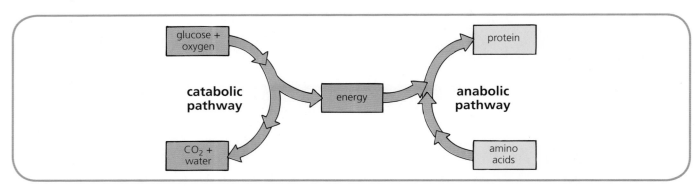

Figure 9.1 Two types of metabolic pathway

Case Study | **Toxic effects of poisons, toxins and venoms**

A **poison** (see Figure 9.2) is a substance that can impair function and damage the body, sometimes fatally. The damage often results from the disruption of metabolic pathways in cells following the absorption of the chemical through the skin, gut or lung lining.

Toxins

Strictly speaking a **toxin** is a poisonous (toxic) substance produced by a living organism.

Figure 9.2 Hazard symbol for poison

Venom

Venom is a poisonous fluid secreted by certain snakes and scorpions. It contains a mixture of substances including toxins and is transmitted by a sting or a bite (see Figure 9.3).

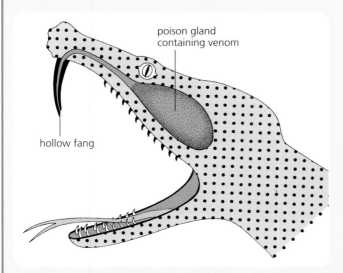

Figure 9.3 Source of snake venom

Under normal circumstances in the human body when a nerve impulse on the way to a muscle arrives at a synapse (a gap between two nerve cells), a chemical transmitter substance is released allowing the impulse to cross the gap. Then an enzyme breaks down the chemical transmitter before the next impulse arrives.

Some snake venoms contain toxin which destroys this enzyme. Therefore the transmitter substance is not broken down and the muscle remains stimulated causing uncontrollable muscle contractions (spasms). Other venoms contain toxin that mimics the molecular shape of the chemical transmitter, blocks the gap and causes paralysis of the victim's nerves and muscles.

Tetanus toxin

Tetanus (also known as lockjaw) is an acute disease caused by the bacterium *Clostridium tetani*. The bacteria release a toxin which acts in a similar way to the toxin in the venom of some snakes. It interferes with the nervous system and muscle contraction leading to sustained muscular spasms.

Curare

Curare is a black resin produced by certain trees in tropical regions of South America. It is a toxin that acts on an animal's motor nerves in a similar way to the toxin in the venom of some snakes and causes paralysis. Curare has long been used by the native inhabitants of the rainforest as an arrow poison.

Salmonella toxin

Some forms of food poisoning are caused by *Salmonella* bacteria. Following multiplication in the host's gut, the micro-organisms die and release toxins. These poisons cause inflammation of the cells lining the gut and disturb their metabolic pathways leading to the person suffering gastrointestinal disorders and diarrhoea which may contain blood.

Botulinum toxin

The bacterium *Clostridium botulinum* produces botulinum toxin which affects the functioning of the metabolites at neuromuscular junctions rendering them unable to transmit nerve impulses in the normal way. This results in paralysis of muscles including those responsible for breathing and therefore it is usually fatal.

Botulinum toxin is one of the most toxic substances known. As little as 90–270 nanograms is enough to kill a person of average size and 4 kg of the toxin would be sufficient to wipe out the entire population of the world. Very dilute concentrations of this neurotoxin (trade name – Botox) are used in some medical procedures (including treatment for rapid, involuntary blinking of eyelids) and in some cosmetic procedures (such as the suppression of frown lines between the eyebrows).

Other poisons

Some **poisonous chemicals** are not produced naturally by living things. A few examples are given below.

Paraquat

This chemical is widely used as a weedkiller because it inhibits photosynthesis by interfering with the electron transport chain in green plant cells (see page 235). It is also toxic to humans. When ingested or inhaled, it leads to acute respiratory distress syndrome which may be fatal. →

Cyanide

Cyanide, on being inhaled or ingested, very quickly starves the body of energy by inhibiting the enzymes located in mitochondria that are essential to produce ATP during aerobic respiration (see chapter 10). Hydrogen cyanide has been used in gas chambers as a method of execution.

Potassium chloride

A very high concentration of potassium chloride (given as an intravenous injection) quickly interferes with the metabolic processes that enable muscles to contract. As a result the heart soon stops beating and death follows. This poison has been used to execute prisoners in some parts of the USA.

Reversible and irreversible steps

Metabolic pathways are regulated by enzymes which catalyse specific reactions. A pathway often contains both **reversible** and **irreversible** steps which allow the process to be kept under precise control. **Glycolysis** (see page 142) is the metabolic pathway that converts **glucose** to an intermediate metabolite called **pyruvate** at the start of respiration. Figure 9.4 shows the first three enzyme-controlled steps in a long pathway.

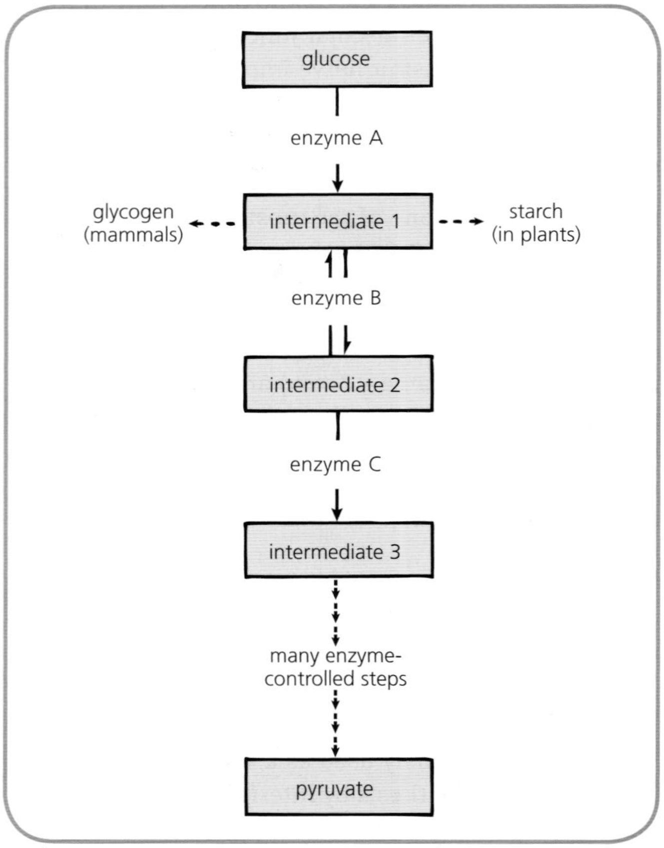

is of advantage to the cell because it maintains a low concentration of glucose inside the cell and therefore promotes continuous diffusion of glucose into the cell from the high concentration outside.

The conversion of intermediate 1 to intermediate 2 by enzyme B is **reversible**. If more intermediate 2 is formed than the cell requires for the next step then some can be converted back to intermediate 1 and used in an alternative pathway (for example to build glycogen in animal cells or starch in plant cells). The conversion of intermediate 2 to intermediate 3 by enzyme C is **irreversible** and is a key **regulatory point** in the pathway. There is no going back for the substrate

Figure 9.4 Metabolic pathway

Glucose diffusing into a cell from a high concentration outside to a low concentration inside is irreversibly converted to intermediate 1 by enzyme A. This process

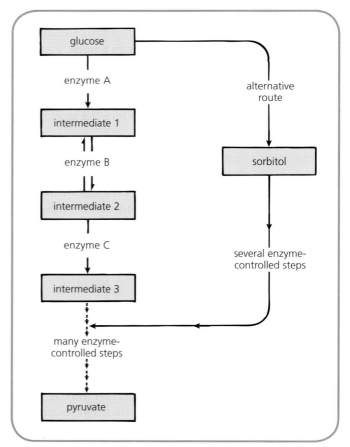

Figure 9.5 Alternative route

now. It is committed to following glycolysis through all the steps to pyruvate.

Alternative routes

Metabolic pathways may also contain **alternative routes** that allow steps in the pathway to be bypassed. Figure 9.5 shows a pathway from glucose via an intermediate (called sorbitol) that bypasses the steps controlled by enzymes A, B and C but returns to glycolysis later in the pathway. This bypass is used when the cell has a plentiful supply of sugar.

Membranes

The cell **membrane** is the boundary that separates the internal living contents of a cell from its external surroundings. The membrane regulates the flow of materials into and out of the cell by allowing selective communication between intracellular and extracellular environments.

Cell organelles are also bounded by membranes. In addition, some organelles such as mitochondria and chloroplasts have inner membranes which take the form of **folds** or **compartments**. This partitioning of the cell enables metabolic activity to be localised, with particular sites being exclusively responsible for specific biochemical reactions.

Compartmental function of membrane

Membranes may be employed to keep chemical metabolites close together or to keep them apart.

On many occasions certain metabolites need to be in close and continuous association in order to work in an efficient and integrated manner. For example the enzymes that control the citric acid cycle (a metabolic pathway in aerobic respiration – see page 143) are localised in a liquid-filled **compartment** called the central cavity (matrix) inside a mitochondrion (see Figures 9.6 and 9.7).

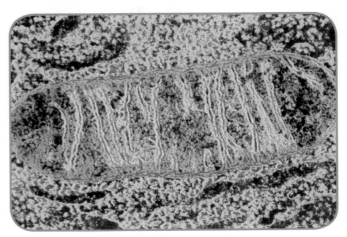

Figure 9.7 Electron micrograph of mitochondrion (This photo has had colour added to it but in reality the contents of a mitochondrion are never green.)

Similarly in a chloroplast (see Figures 9.8 and 9.9) the assemblies of proteins essential for ATP generation are attached to the membranes of flattened sacs containing chlorophyll. The fluid outside the sacs is in a **compartment** and contains the enzymes for the Calvin cycle, a metabolic pathway that makes up a major part of photosynthesis (see page 237).

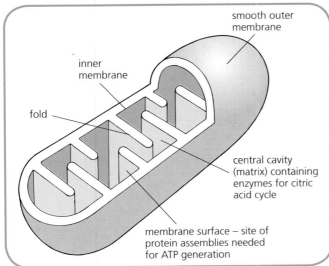

Figure 9.6 Compartments and membranes of mitochondrion

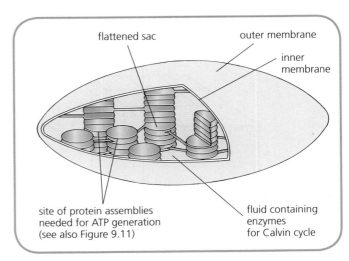

Figure 9.8 Compartments and membranes of chloroplast

cube has a **larger surface area relative to its volume**. Similarly tiny compartments in a cell (and folds in the membrane) present relatively large surfaces upon which metabolic reactions can take place. In addition, the high concentrations of reactants that are located in small compartments promote high rates of reaction between metabolites.

Structure of cell membrane

The cell membrane consists of **protein** and **phospholipid** molecules. Most evidence supports the **fluid mosaic model** of membrane structure (see Figure 9.11). This proposes that the cell membrane consists of a fluid bilayer of constantly moving phospholipid molecules that forms a stable boundary. It contains a patchy mosaic of protein molecules that vary in size and structure.

Molecular transport

Diffusion is the net movement of molecules or ions from a region of high concentration to a region of low concentration of that type of molecule or ion. During diffusion, molecules or ions always move down a **concentration gradient** from a high to a low concentration. The cell membrane is freely permeable to molecules such as oxygen and carbon dioxide that are small enough to diffuse through the phospholipid bilayer.

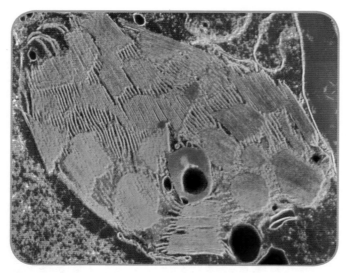

Figure 9.9 Electron micrograph of chloroplast

Lysosome

Some chemical metabolites must remain safely segregated from one another until certain circumstances arise. One group of digestive enzymes, for example, is so powerful that the enzymes would destroy the fabric of the cell if they were released into the cytoplasm. For this reason, they are compartmentalised inside membrane-bound organelles called lysosomes until required.

Surface area to volume ratio

Figure 9.10 compares the surface area to volume ratio of a small cube with that of a larger cube. The smaller

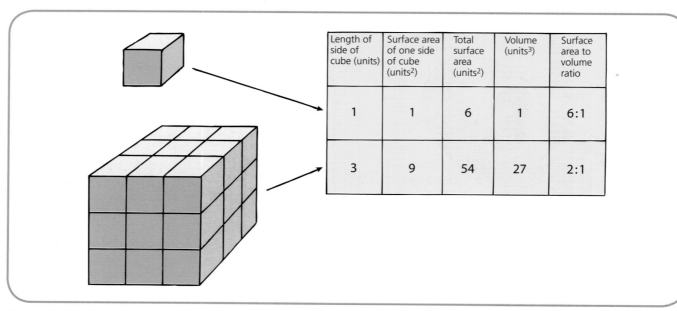

Length of side of cube (units)	Surface area of one side of cube (units^2)	Total surface area (units^2)	Volume (units^3)	Surface area to volume ratio
1	1	6	1	6:1
3	9	54	27	2:1

Figure 9.10 Effect of size on relative surface area

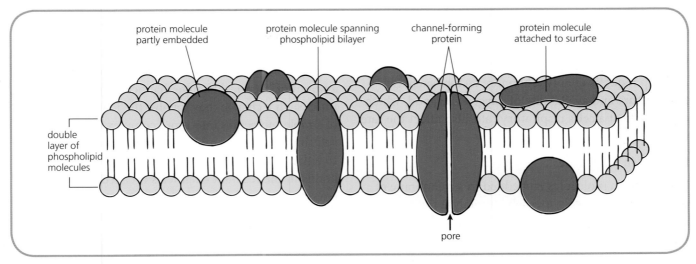

Figure 9.11 Fluid mosaic model of cell membrane structure

Role of protein pores

Larger molecules to be transported depend on certain protein molecules to let them move across the membrane into or out of the cell. These transport molecules contain **pores**. They are often described as channel-forming because they provide channels for specific substances to diffuse across the membrane.

Active transport

Active transport is the movement of molecules and ions across the cell membrane from a low to a high concentration, in other words **against** a concentration gradient. Active transport works in the opposite direction to diffusion and always requires energy.

Sodium/potassium pump

Certain protein molecules present in the cell membrane act as **carrier** molecules which recognise specific ions and transfer them across the cell membrane. These active transport carriers are often called **pumps**. Some of them play a dual role in that they exchange one type of ion for another. An example is the **sodium/ potassium pump** where the same carrier molecule actively pumps sodium ions out of the cell and potassium ions into the cell each against its own concentration gradient (as shown in Figure 9.12). Maintenance of the difference in ionic concentration by this pump is particularly important for the proper functioning of muscle and nerve cells. It accounts

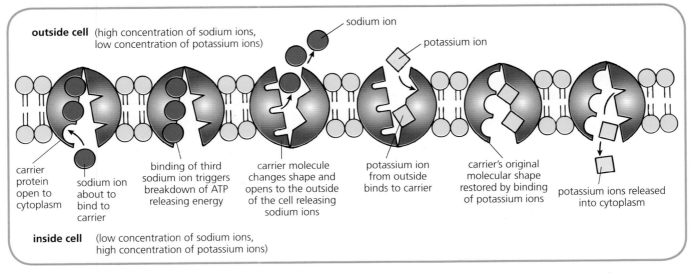

Figure 9.12 Active transport by the sodium/potassium pump

for around 30% of a typical animal cell's energy expenditure.

Conditions required by protein pumps

A pump requires energy. Therefore factors such as temperature and availability of oxygen and food, which directly affect a cell's respiratory rate, also affect the rate of active transport.

Enzymes in membrane

Some protein molecules embedded in a membrane of phospholipids are **enzymes** which catalyse the steps in a metabolic process essential to the cell. For example the enzyme ATP synthase (see page 142), which catalyses the synthesis of ATP, is a membrane protein present in mitochondria, chloroplasts and prokaryotes.

On some occasions, molecules of several different enzymes are arranged in a membrane as a multi-enzyme complex to promote a series of related steps in a metabolic pathway and ensure that they occur in a specific order.

Testing Your Knowledge 1

1 **a)** Define the term *metabolism*. (2)

   b) Describe TWO ways in which the two types of metabolic pathway differ from one another. (2)

2 **a)** Which cellular structure creates compartments within cells? (1)

   b) Why is it important that enzymes are compartmentalised in:
   i) mitochondria
   ii) lysosomes? (2)

3 Briefly describe the role played by **a)** protein pores and **b)** protein pumps present in the membrane that bounds a cell. (4)

Activation energy and enzyme action

The rate of a chemical reaction is indicated by the amount of chemical change that occurs per unit time. Such a change may involve the joining together of simple molecules into more complex ones or the splitting of complex molecules into simpler ones. In either case the energy needed to break chemical bonds in the reactant chemicals is called the **activation energy**.

The bonds break when the molecules of reactant have absorbed enough energy to make them unstable. They are now in the **transition state** and the reaction can occur. This energy input often takes the form of heat energy and the reaction only proceeds at a high rate if the chemicals are raised to a high temperature (see Figure 9.13).

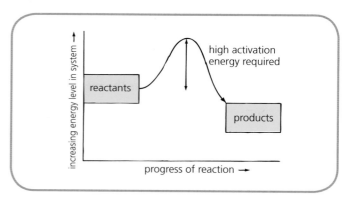

Figure 9.13 Uncatalysed reaction

Related Activity

Investigating the effect of heat on the breakdown of hydrogen peroxide

Hydrogen peroxide is a chemical that breaks down into water and oxygen as shown in the following equation:

hydrogen peroxide $\rightarrow$ water + oxygen
$(2H_2O_2)$ $(2H_2O)$ (O_2)

In the experiment shown in Figure 9.14, test tubes containing hydrogen peroxide and drops of

detergent are placed in five water baths at different temperatures. The detergent is used to sustain any oxygen bubbles that are released as a froth.

After 30 minutes the tubes are inspected for the presence of a froth of oxygen bubbles which indicates the breakdown of hydrogen peroxide. The diagram shows a typical set of results where the volume of froth is found to increase with an increase in temperature.

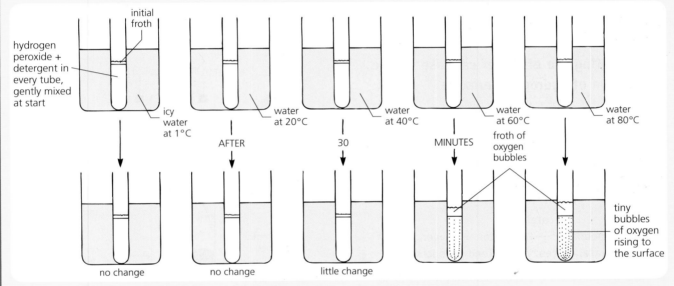

Figure 9.14 Investigating the effect of heat on the breakdown of hydrogen peroxide

Related Activity

Investigating the effect of manganese dioxide on the breakdown of hydrogen peroxide

In the experiment shown in Figure 9.15, the bubbles forming the froth in tube A are found to relight a glowing splint. This shows that oxygen is being released during the breakdown of hydrogen peroxide. In tube B, the control, the breakdown process is so slow that no oxygen can be detected.

It is concluded therefore that manganese dioxide (which remains chemically unaltered at the end of the reaction) has increased the rate of this chemical reaction which would otherwise have only proceeded very slowly. A substance that has this effect on a chemical reaction is called a **catalyst**.

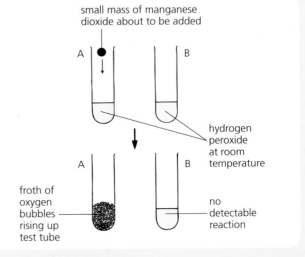

Figure 9.15 Effect of a catalyst

Properties and functions of a catalyst

A catalyst is a substance that:

- lowers the activation energy required for a chemical reaction to proceed (see Figure 9.16)

- speeds up the rate of a chemical reaction

- takes part in the reaction but remains unchanged at the end of it.

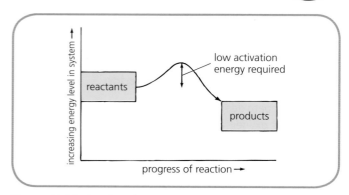

Figure 9.16 Catalysed reaction

Related Activity

Investigating the effect of catalase on the breakdown of hydrogen peroxide

Catalase is an enzyme made by living cells. It is especially abundant in fresh liver cells. In the experiment shown in Figure 9.17 the bubbles produced in tube C are found to relight a glowing splint. This shows that oxygen is being released during the breakdown of hydrogen peroxide as follows:

$$\underset{\text{(substrate)}}{\text{hydrogen peroxide}} \xrightarrow{\underset{\text{(enzyme)}}{\text{catalase}}} \underset{\text{(end products)}}{\text{water} + \text{oxygen}}$$

In tube D, the control, the breakdown process is so slow that no oxygen can be detected. It is concluded that the enzyme catalase has increased the rate of this chemical reaction which would otherwise have proceeded only very slowly.

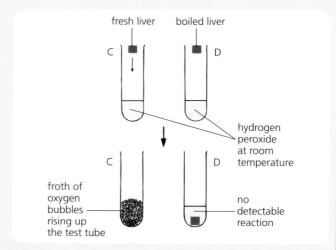

Figure 9.17 Effect of catalase

Importance of enzymes

Living cells cannot tolerate the high temperatures needed to make chemical reactions proceed at a rapid rate. Therefore they make use of **biological catalysts** called **enzymes**.

Enzymes speed up the rate of the reactions in a metabolic pathway by **lowering the activation energy** needed by the reactant(s) to form the transition state. It is from this unstable state that the end products of the reaction are produced.

By this means biochemical reactions are able to proceed rapidly at the relatively low temperatures (such as 5–40 °C) needed by living cells to function properly. In

the absence of enzymes, biochemical pathways such as respiration and photosynthesis would proceed so slowly that life as we know it would cease to exist.

Enzyme action

Enzyme molecules are made of **protein**. Somewhere on an enzyme's surface there is a groove or hollow where its **active site** is located. This site has a particular shape which is determined by the chemical structure of, and bonding between, the amino acids in the polypeptide chains that make up the enzyme molecule.

Specificity

An enzyme acts on one type of substance (its **substrate**) whose molecules exactly fit the enzyme's active site. The enzyme is **specific** to its substrate and the molecules of substrate are complementary to the enzyme's active site for which they show an **affinity** (chemical attraction).

Induced fit

The active site is not a rigid structure. It is **flexible** and **dynamic**. When a molecule of substrate enters the active site, the shape of the enzyme molecule and the active site change slightly making the active site fit very closely round the substrate molecule. This is called **induced fit** (see Figure 9.18). The process is like a rubber glove, slightly too small, exerting a very tight fit round a hand. Induced fit ensures that the active

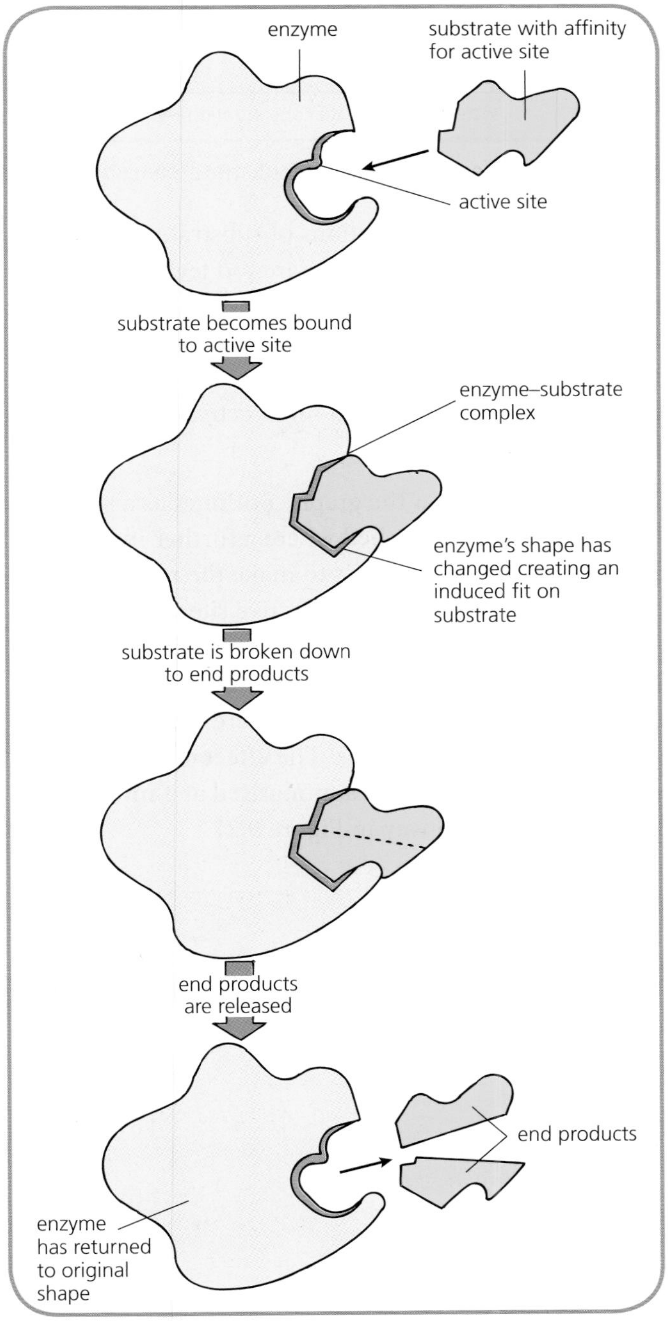

enzyme

substrate with affinity for active site

active site

substrate becomes bound to active site

enzyme–substrate complex

enzyme's shape has changed creating an induced fit on substrate

substrate is broken down to end products

end products are released

end products

enzyme has returned to original shape

Figure 9.18 Induced fit during an enzyme-catalysed reaction

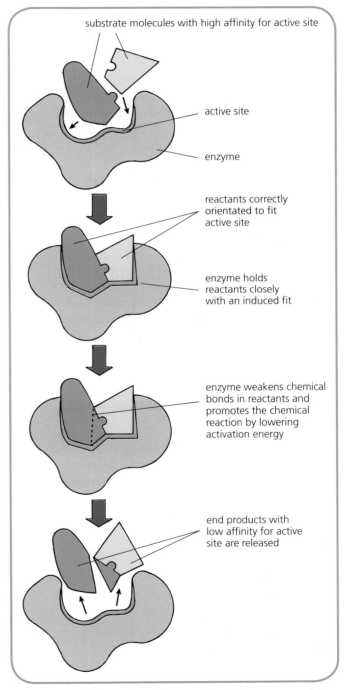

substrate molecules with high affinity for active site

active site

enzyme

reactants correctly orientated to fit active site

enzyme holds reactants closely with an induced fit

enzyme weakens chemical bonds in reactants and promotes the chemical reaction by lowering activation energy

end products with low affinity for active site are released

Figure 9.19 Orientation of reactants during an enzyme-catalysed reaction

site comes into very close contact with the molecules of substrate and increases the chance of the reaction taking place.

Orientation of reactants

When the reaction involves two (or more) substrates (see Figure 9.19), the shape of the active site determines the **orientation** of the reactants. This ensures that they are held together in such a way that the reaction between them can take place.

First the active site holds the two reactants closely together in an induced fit. Then it acts on them to weaken chemical bonds that must be broken during the reaction. This process **reduces the activation energy** needed by the reactants to reach the **transition state** that allows the reaction to take place.

Once the reaction has occurred, the products have a **low affinity** for the active site and are released. This leaves the enzyme free to repeat the process with new molecules of substrate.

Factors affecting enzyme action

To function efficiently, an enzyme requires a suitable temperature, an appropriate pH and an adequate supply of substrate. Inhibitors (see page 133) may slow down the rate of an enzyme-controlled reaction or bring it to a halt.

Effect of substrate concentration on enzyme activity

The graph in Figure 9.20 shows the effect of increasing substrate concentration on the rate of an enzyme-controlled reaction for a limited concentration of

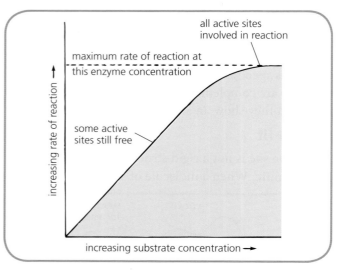

Figure 9.20 Effect of increasing substrate concentration

enzyme. At low concentrations of substrate, the reaction rate is low since there are too few substrate molecules present to make maximum use of all the active sites on the enzyme molecules. An increase in substrate concentration results in an increase in reaction rate since more and more active sites become involved.

This upward trend in the graph continues as a straight line until a point is reached where a further increase in substrate concentration fails to make the reaction go any faster. At this point all the active sites are occupied (the enzyme concentration has become the **limiting factor**). The graph levels off since there are now more substrate molecules present than there are free active sites with which to combine. The effect of increasing substrate concentration is summarised at a molecular level in a simplified way in Figure 9.21.

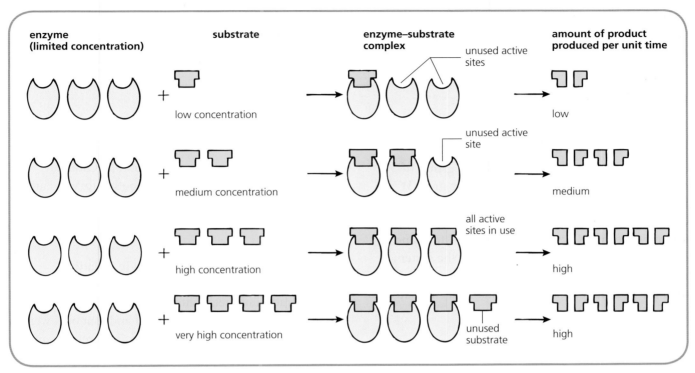

Figure 9.21 Effect of increasing substrate concentration at a molecular level

Related Activity

Investigating the effect of increasing substrate concentration

Liver cells contain the enzyme catalase which catalyses the breakdown of hydrogen peroxide to water and oxygen. In the experiment shown in Figure 9.22, the one variable factor is the concentration of the substrate (hydrogen peroxide). When an equal mass of fresh liver is added to each cylinder, the results shown in the diagram are produced. The height of the froth of oxygen bubbles indicates the activity of the enzyme at each concentration of substrate.

From the experiment it is concluded that an increase in substrate concentration results in increased enzyme activity until a point is reached (in cylinder G) where some factor other than substrate concentration has become the limiting factor.

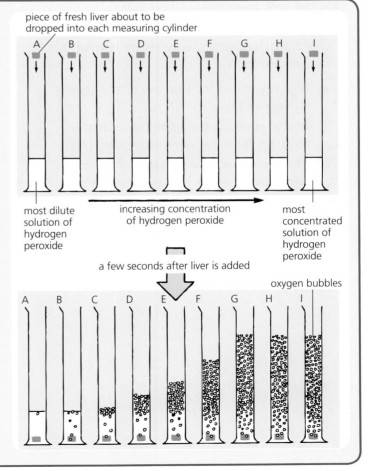

Figure 9.22 Effect of substrate concentration on enzyme activity

125

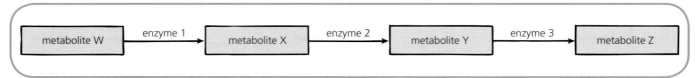

Figure 9.23 Action of a group of enzymes

Direction of enzyme action

A metabolic pathway usually involves a **group** of enzymes as shown in Figure 9.23. As substrate W becomes available, enzyme 1 becomes active and converts W to X. In the presence of metabolite X, enzyme 2 becomes active and converts X to Y and so on. A continuous supply of W entering the system drives the sequence of reactions in the direction W to Z with the product of one reaction acting as the substrate of the next.

Reversibility

Most metabolic reactions are **reversible**. Often an enzyme can catalyse a reaction in both a forward and a reverse direction. The actual direction taken depends on the relative concentrations of the reactant(s) and product(s).

A metabolic pathway rarely occurs in isolation. If, as a result of related biochemical pathways, the concentration of metabolite Y in Figure 9.23 were to increase to an unusually high level and that of X were to decrease, then enzyme 2 could go into reverse and convert some of Y back to X until a balanced state (equilibrium) was restored once more.

Testing Your Knowledge 2

1 Give THREE reasons why enzymes are referred to as *biological catalysts*. (3)

2 a) What determines the structure of an enzyme's active site? (1)

   b) What is meant by the *affinity* of substrate molecules for an enzyme's active site? (1)

   c) What term means 'the change in shape of an active site to enable it to bind more snugly to the substrate'? (1)

   d) Rewrite the following sentences choosing the correct answer from each underlined choice.

The shape of the active site ensures that the reactants are correctly orientated/denatured so that the reaction can take place. This is made possible by the fact that the enzyme increases/decreases the activation energy needed by the reactants to reach the transitory/transition state. (3)

3 a) What is meant by the term *rate of reaction*? (See page 120 for help.) (1)

   b) i) What effect does an increase in concentration of substrate have on the reaction rate when a limited amount of enzyme is present?
   ii) Explain why. (4)

Control of metabolic pathways

A **metabolic pathway** normally consists of several stages each of which involves the conversion of one metabolite to another. Each step in a metabolic pathway is driven by a specific enzyme (see Figure 9.24). Each enzyme is coded for by a gene (though complex enzymes composed of several polypeptides require several genes to be involved in their production). If the appropriate enzymes are present, the pathway proceeds. If one enzyme is absent, the pathway comes to a halt. Enzyme action can be regulated at the level of gene expression (see below) and at the level of enzyme action (see page 132).

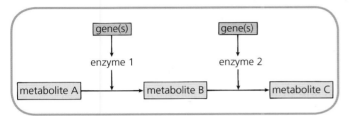

Figure 9.24 Control of two steps in a metabolic pathway

Control by switching genes on and off

Some metabolic pathways are only required to operate under certain circumstances. To prevent resources being wasted, the genes that code for the enzymes controlling each of their stages are 'switched on' or 'switched off' as required.

Lactose metabolism in *Escherichia coli* (*E. coli*)

Lactose is a sugar found in milk. Each molecule of lactose is composed of a molecule of glucose and a molecule of galactose (see Figure 9.25).

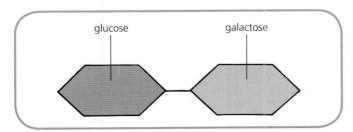

Figure 9.25 Molecule of lactose

Gene action in *Escherichia coli*

Background information

● Glucose is a simple sugar used in respiration by the bacterium *E. coli* for energy release.

● *E. coli* can only make use of the glucose in lactose if it is released from the galactose.

● Lactose is digested to glucose and galactose by the enzyme β-galactosidase.

● *E. coli*'s chromosome has a gene which codes for β-galactosidase.

● *E. coli* is found to produce β-galactosidase only when lactose is present in its nutrient medium and fails to do so when lactose is absent.

● Somehow the gene which codes for β-galactosidase is switched on in the presence of lactose and switched off in the absence of lactose.

● The process of switching on a gene, only when the enzyme that it codes for is needed, is called **enzyme induction**.

Lac operon of *E. coli*

An **operon** (see Figure 9.26) consists of one or more **structural genes** (containing the DNA code for the enzyme in question) and a neighbouring **operator** gene which controls the structural gene(s). The operator gene is, in turn, affected by a **repressor** molecule coded for by a **regulator** gene situated further along the DNA chain.

Absence of lactose

Environments inhabited by *E. coli* normally contain glucose but not lactose. The bacterium would waste some of its resources if it made the lactose-digesting enzyme when no lactose was present to digest. Figure 9.26 shows how the bacterium is prevented from doing so by the repressor molecule combining with the operator gene. The structural gene remains switched off and its DNA is not transcribed.

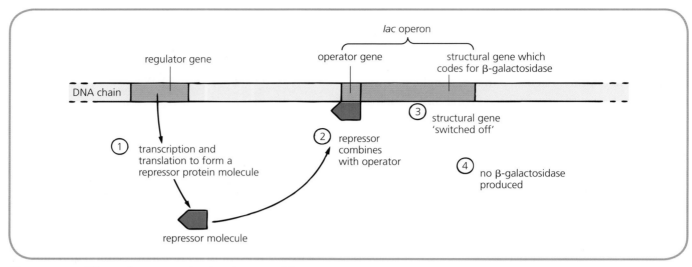

Figure 9.26 Effect of repressor in the absence of lactose

Presence of lactose

When the bacterium finds itself in an environment containing lactose, the events shown in Figure 9.27 take place and lead to the **induction** of β-galactosidase.

Lactose (the **inducer**) prevents the repressor molecule from binding to the operator gene. The system is no longer blocked, the structural gene becomes switched on and production of β-galactosidase proceeds.

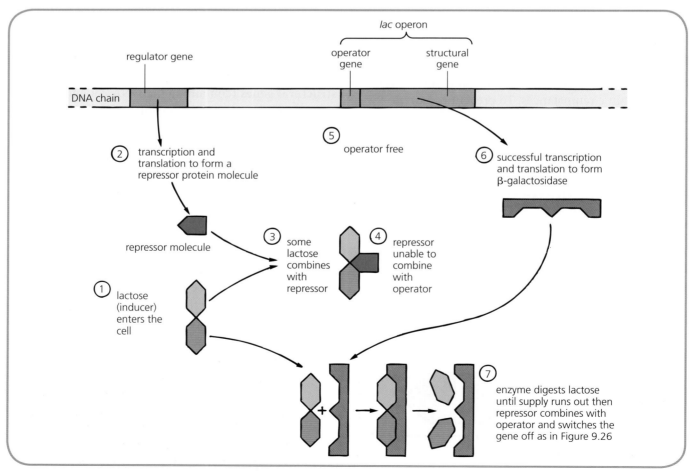

Figure 9.27 Effect of inducer (lactose)

When all the lactose has been digested, the repressor molecule becomes free again and combines with the operator as before. The structural gene becomes switched off and the waste of valuable resources (such as amino acids and energy) is prevented.

Hypothesis

This hypothesis of gene action was first put forward by two scientists called Jacob and Monod. It is now supported by extensive experimental evidence from work done using bacteria.

Related Activity

Investigating the *lac* operon of *E. coli*

ONPG is a colourless synthetic chemical which can be broken down by the enzyme β-galactosidase as follows:

$$\text{ONPG} \xrightarrow{\text{β-galactosidase}} \text{galactose + yellow compound}$$

The presence of the yellow colour indicates activity by β-galactosidase. The experiment is set up as shown in Figure 9.28.

From the results it is concluded that:

● In tube 1, lactose has acted as an inducer and switched on the gene in *E. coli* that codes for β-galactosidase. This enzyme has acted on the ONPG forming the yellow colour.

● In tubes 2 and 4, no yellow colour was produced because ONPG was absent.

● In tube 3, β-galactosidase has acted on ONPG forming the yellow compound.

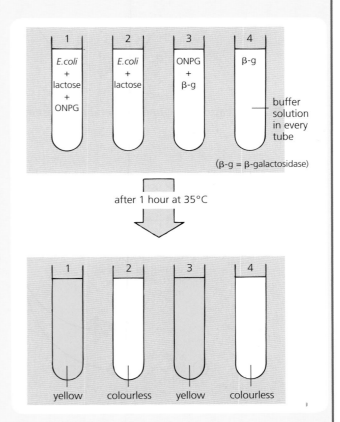

Figure 9.28 Investigating the *lac* operon

Related Topic

Ara operon of *E. coli*

Arabinose is a sugar that can be used by *E. coli* as its sole source of carbon and energy in the absence of glucose and lactose. To be of use to the bacterium, arabinose must be broken down by enzymes. The genes for these enzymes (the *ara* operon) are **switched off** in the absence of arabinose (see Figure 9.29) and **switched on** in its presence as a result of arabinose acting as an inducer (see Figure 9.30).

Transformation of the *ara* operon

E. coli cells can be genetically **transformed** (see chapter 13) using a modified plasmid called pGLO. This procedure brings about the replacement of the *ara* operon's structural genes with a gene (originally from a fluorescent jellyfish) which codes for **green fluorescent protein** (GFP) and a second gene that makes the transformed cells resistant to an antibiotic (called **ampicillin**). In the presence of arabinose, the inducer, these transformed bacteria produce GFP instead of arabinose-digesting enzymes as shown in Figure 9.31.

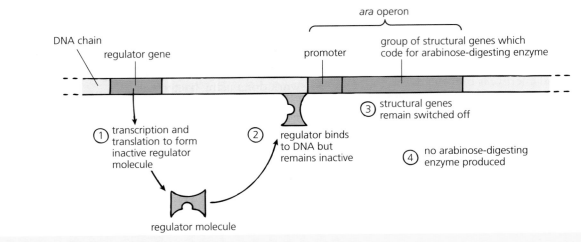

Figure 9.29 Situation in normal bacterium in absence of arabinose

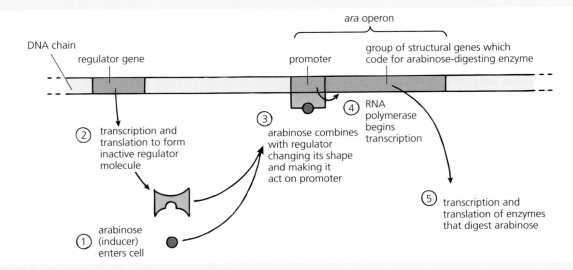

Figure 9.30 Situation in normal bacterium in presence of arabinose

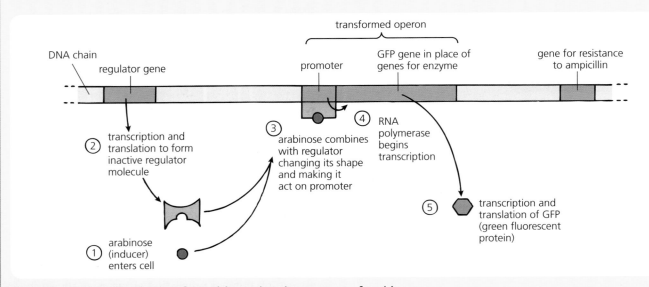

Figure 9.31 Situation in transformed bacterium in presence of arabinose

Related Activity

Investigating the transformed *ara* operon

This experiment is set up as shown in Figure 9.32. pGLO plasmids are added to tube 1 to transform the bacteria into cells containing the genes for GFP and ampicillin resistance. Tube 2 is the control.

After appropriate treatment to bring about the transformation, samples of bacteria are subcultured onto four nutrient agar plates as shown. Only transformed bacteria with the genes for GFP and ampicillin resistance grow on plates A and B. No bacteria grow on plate C because they are not

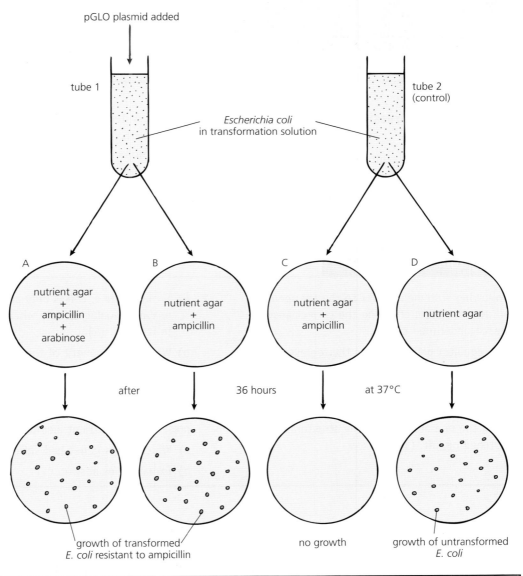

result in UV light	fluorescence	no fluorescence	no fluorescence	no fluorescence
reason	presence of arabinose (inducer) has switched GFP gene on	cells lack arabinose (inducer) needed to switch GFP gene on	cells have been killed by ampicillin	cells lack GFP gene and arabinose

Figure 9.32 Investigating the transformed *ara* operon

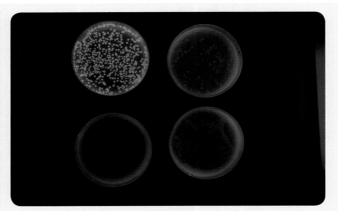

Figure 9.33 Expression of GFP gene

resistant to ampicillin antibiotic. Untransformed bacteria grow on plate D which lacks ampicillin.

When the plates are exposed to ultraviolet light, fluorescence occurs in plate A only (see Figure 9.33). It is concluded that the presence of arabinose, the inducer, has switched on the GFP gene in these cells resulting in the production of GFP.

Regulation of gene expression by signal molecules

In the *lac* operon system of control in *E. coli* (and in the *ara* operon – see Related Activity) a gene that was switched off becomes switched on in response to a **signal molecule** from the cell's environment. In the

lac operon system, the signal molecule is lactose. It combines with the product of the regulator gene (the repressor molecule) enabling the structural gene to be expressed and lead to the production of the required enzyme.

Testing Your Knowledge 3

1 The following statements refer to the *lac* operon of *E. coli*. Rewrite them choosing the correct answer from each underlined choice.

   a) The regulator gene produces the <u>repressor/inducer</u> molecule. (1)

   b) The inducer molecule combines with the <u>operator/repressor</u>. (1)

   c) When the operator is free, the structural gene is switched <u>on/off</u>. (1)

2 a) Explain why *E. coli* is only able to produce the enzyme β-galactosidase when lactose is present in its food. (1)

   b) What is the benefit of this on/off mechanism to the bacterium? (2)

3 A mutant strain of *E. coli* was found to produce β-galactosidase continuously whether lactose was present in its nutrient medium or not.

   a) Which of its genes had suffered a mutation? (1)

   b) Explain your answer. (1)

Control by regulation of enzyme action

Some metabolic pathways (for example glycolysis) are required to operate continuously. The genes that code for their enzymes are always switched on and the enzymes which they code for are always present in the cell. Control of these metabolic pathways is brought about by **regulating the action of their enzymes as** follows.

Effect of signal molecules

The activity of some enzymes is controlled by **signal molecules**. For example the hormone **adrenaline** (epinephrine), released into the bloodstream by the adrenal glands, binds to receptors in the membrane of liver cells where it acts as a signal molecule. It triggers a series of events in the liver cells which results in the activation of an enzyme that converts glycogen to glucose when the body needs energy urgently.

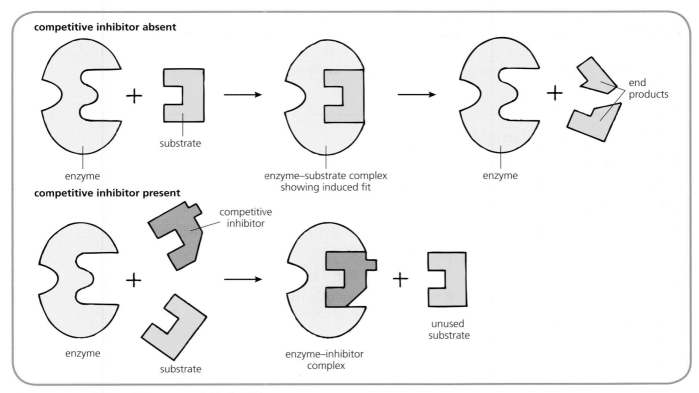

Figure 9.34 Effect of the competitive inhibitor

Some signal molecules that affect a cell's metabolism originate within the cell itself; others come from the environment (for example from other cells in the organism's body via the bloodstream).

Effect of inhibitors

An **inhibitor** is a substance which decreases the rate of an enzyme-controlled reaction.

Competitive inhibitors

Molecules of a **competitive inhibitor** compete with molecules of the substrate for the active sites on the enzyme. The inhibitor is able to do this because its molecular structure is **similar** to that of the substrate and it can attach itself to the enzyme's active site as shown in Figure 9.34. Since active sites **blocked** by competitive inhibitor molecules cannot become occupied by substrate molecules, the rate of the reaction is reduced.

Effect of increasing substrate concentration

The graph in Figure 9.35 compares the effect of increasing substrate concentration on rate of reaction for a limited amount of enzyme affected by a limited

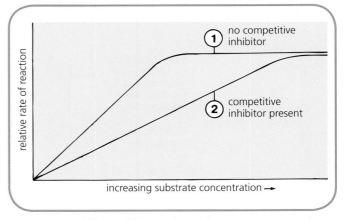

Figure 9.35 Effect of increasing substrate concentration on competitive inhibition

amount of inhibitor. In graph line 1 (the control), an increase in substrate concentration brings about an increase in reaction rate until a point is reached where all active sites on the enzyme molecules are occupied and then the graph levels off.

In graph line 2, an increase in substrate concentration brings about a gradual increase in the reaction rate. Although the competitive inhibitor is competing for and occupying some of the enzyme's active sites, the true substrate is also occupying some of the sites. As substrate molecules increase in concentration and outnumber those of the competitive inhibitor, more and more active sites become occupied by true substrate rather than inhibitor molecules. The reaction rate continues to increase until all the active sites are occupied (almost all of them by substrate).

Investigation

Inhibition of β-galactosidase by galactose

Normally the enzyme β-galactosidase catalyses the reaction:

$$\text{lactose} \xrightarrow{\text{β-galactosidase}} \text{glucose} + \text{galactose}$$

However, it is also able to break down a colourless, synthetic compound called ONPG as follows:

$$\text{ONPG} \xrightarrow{\text{β-galactosidase}} \text{galactose} + \text{yellow compound}$$

The experiment shown in Figure 9.36 is set up to investigate the inhibitory effect of galactose on the action of β-galactosidase as the concentration of the substrate, ONPG, is increased. The **independent variable** in this experiment is substrate concentration.

At the end of the experiment, an increasing intensity of yellow colour (indicating products of enzyme activity) is found to be present in the tubes, with tube 1 the least yellow and tube 4 the most yellow. The intensity of colour can be measured quantitatively using a **colorimeter**. This allows the results to be displayed as a graph.

A possible explanation for these results is that galactose acts as a **competitive inhibitor**, having the most effect at low concentrations of substrate. As the concentration of substrate increases, more and more active sites on the enzyme become occupied by substrate, not inhibitor, and the reaction rate increases.

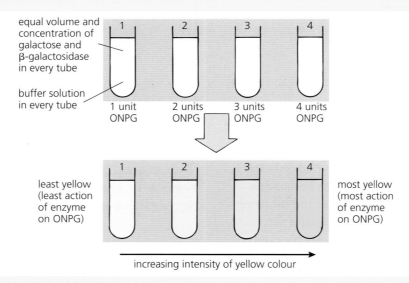

equal volume and concentration of galactose and β-galactosidase in every tube

buffer solution in every tube

1 unit ONPG   2 units ONPG   3 units ONPG   4 units ONPG

least yellow (least action of enzyme on ONPG)

most yellow (most action of enzyme on ONPG)

increasing intensity of yellow colour

Figure 9.36 Investigating the inhibitory effect of galactose

Regulation by changing the shape of the active site

Non-competitive inhibitors

A **non-competitive inhibitor** does not combine directly with an enzyme's active site. Instead it becomes attached to a non-active (**allosteric**) site and changes the shape of the enzyme molecule. This results in the active site becoming **altered indirectly** and being unable to combine with the substrate as shown in Figure 9.37. The larger the number of enzyme molecules affected in this way, the slower the enzyme-controlled reaction. Therefore the non-competitive inhibitor acts as a type of regulator.

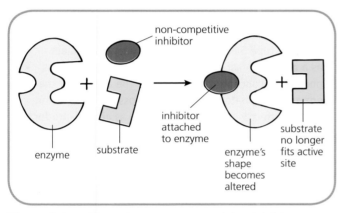

Figure 9.37 Effect of the non-competitive inhibitor

Some enzyme molecules are composed of several polypeptide subunits and each subunit has its own active site. The enzyme molecule also has several non-active (allosteric) sites. Depending on circumstances, the enzyme molecule may exist as an **active** form or an **inactive** form. These have different shapes as shown in Figure 9.38.

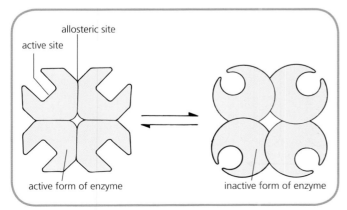

Figure 9.38 Active and inactive forms of enzyme molecule

The enzyme molecule changes shape if a **regulatory molecule** becomes bound to one of its allosteric sites (see Figure 9.39). If the regulatory molecule is an **activator**, the enzyme adopts its active form and enzyme activity is stimulated. If the regulatory molecule is a **non-competitive inhibitor**, the enzyme changes to its inactive state and enzyme action is inhibited. The more enzyme molecules affected by activators, the faster the reaction rate; the more enzyme molecules affected by inhibitors, the slower the reaction rate.

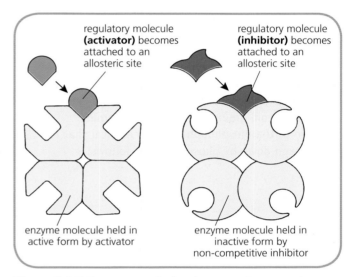

Figure 9.39 Enzyme regulation by an activator and an inhibitor

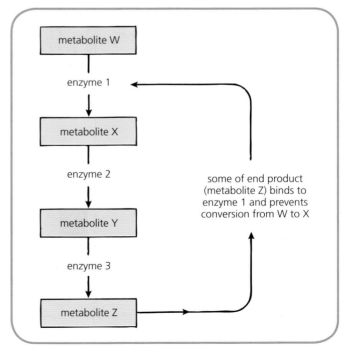

Figure 9.40 Regulation by feedback inhibition

135

Feedback inhibition by an end product

End-product inhibition (see Figure 9.40) is a further way in which a metabolic pathway can be regulated. As the concentration of end product (metabolite Z) builds up, some of it binds to molecules of enzyme 1 in the pathway. This slows down the conversion of metabolite W to X and in turn regulates the whole pathway.

As the concentration of Z drops, fewer molecules of enzyme 1 are affected and more of W is converted to X and so on. The pathway is kept under **finely-tuned control** by this means (called **negative feedback control**) and wasteful conversion and accumulation of intermediates and final products are avoided.

Related Activity

Investigating the effect of phosphate on phosphatase

Phosphatase is an enzyme that releases the phosphate group from its substrate for use in cell metabolism. Phosphatase is present in the extract obtained from ground-up mung bean sprouts. **Phenolphthalein phosphate** is a chemical that can be broken down by phosphatase as follows:

The experiment is set up as shown in Figure 9.41. At the end of the experiment a decreasing intensity of pink colour is found to be present in the tubes. Tube 1 is the most pink and tube 5 is the least pink. From these results it is concluded that tube 1 contains most free phenolphthalein as a result of most enzyme activity and that tube 5 contains least free phenolphthalein as a result of least enzyme activity. In other words as phosphate concentration increases, the activity of the enzyme phosphatase decreases. A possible explanation for this effect is that phosphate acts as an **end-product inhibitor** of the enzyme phosphatase.

$$\text{phenolphthalein phosphate} \xrightarrow{\text{phosphatase}} \text{phenolphthalein (pink in alkaline conditions)} + \text{phosphate}$$

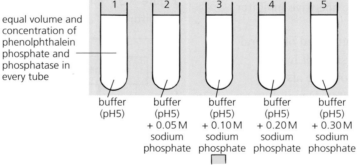

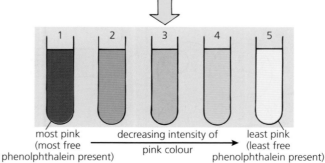

Figure 9.41 Investigating the effect of phosphate on phosphatase

Testing Your Knowledge 4

1 a) What property of a competitive inhibitor enables it to compete with the substrate? (1)

   b) i) What effect does an increase in concentration of a substrate have on the rate of a reaction when a limited amount of competitive inhibitor and enzyme are present?
      ii) Explain why. (3)

2 An enzyme molecule may possess several active sites and several allosteric sites and exist in an active or an inactive form. Explain how molecules of such an enzyme could be controlled so that they could bring about:

   a) an increase in the reaction rate

   b) a decrease in the reaction rate. (2)

3 Figure 9.42 shows a metabolic pathway where metabolites P, Q and R are present in equal quantities at the start.

   a) Name enzyme X's
      i) substrate
      ii) product. (2)

   b) Name enzyme Y's
      i) substrate
      ii) product. (2)

   c) In which direction will the pathway proceed if more of metabolite P is added to the system? (1)

   d) i) Metabolite R can act as an end-product inhibitor. Describe how this would work.
      ii) What is the benefit of end-product inhibition? (3)

metabolite P → enzyme X → metabolite Q → enzyme Y → metabolite R

Figure 9.42

10 Cellular respiration

Cellular respiration is a series of metabolic pathways which brings about the release of energy from a foodstuff and the regeneration of the high-energy compound **ATP**. It occurs in the cells of all members of the three domains of life.

Adenosine triphosphate

A molecule of **adenosine triphosphate** (**ATP**) is composed of adenosine and three inorganic phosphate (P_i) groups as shown in Figure 10.1. Energy held in an ATP molecule is released when the bond attaching the terminal phosphate is broken by enzyme action. This results in the formation of **adenosine diphosphate** (**ADP**) and inorganic **phosphate**. On the other hand, energy is required to regenerate ATP from ADP and inorganic phosphate. This relationship is summarised in Figure 10.2.

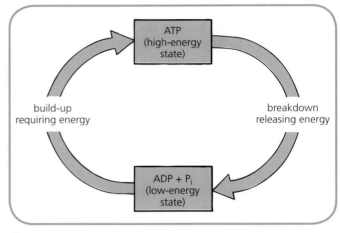

Figure 10.2 Relationship between ATP and ADP + P_i

Transfer of energy via ATP

ATP is important because it acts as the **link** between catabolic energy-releasing reactions (such as respiration) and anabolic energy-consuming reactions (such as the synthesis of proteins). It provides the means by which chemical energy is transferred from one type of reaction to the other in a living cell (see Figures 10.3 and 10.4).

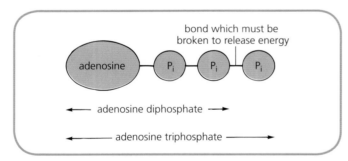

Figure 10.1 Structure of ATP

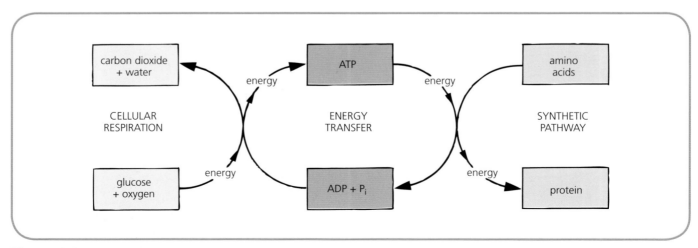

Figure 10.3 Transfer of chemical energy by ATP

Figure 10.4 'What do you mean, I need **ATP**? I thought you said **a tepee**.'

Turnover of ATP molecules

It has been estimated that an active cell (for example a bacterium undergoing cell division) requires approximately two million molecules of ATP per second to satisfy its energy requirements. This is made possible by the fact that a **rapid turnover of** ATP molecules occurs constantly in a cell. At any given moment some ATP molecules are undergoing breakdown and releasing the energy needed for cellular processes while others are being regenerated from ADP and P_i using energy released during cell respiration.

Fixed quantity of ATP

Since ATP is manufactured at the same time as it is used up, there is no need for a living organism to possess a vast store of ATP. The quantity of ATP present in the human body, for example, is found to remain fairly **constant** at around 50 g despite the fact that the body may be using up *and* regenerating ATP at a rate of about $400\,g\,h^{-1}$.

Related Activity

Measuring ATP using luciferase

Background

- **Luciferase** is an enzyme present in the cells of fireflies. It is involved in the process of bioluminescence (the production of light by a living organism).

- Luciferase catalyses the following reaction:

$$luciferin + ATP \xrightarrow{\text{luciferase}} end\ products + light\ energy$$

- The presence of **ATP** is essential for the production

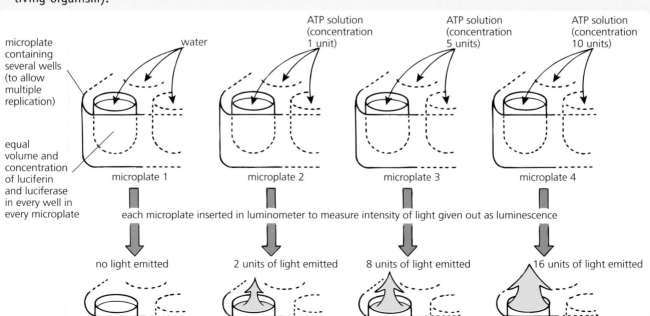

Figure 10.5 Measuring light emitted from known concentrations of ATP

of light energy and the reaction does not proceed in its absence.

● When luciferin and luciferase are plentiful and ATP is the limiting factor, the intensity of light emitted is proportional to the concentration of ATP present.

The experiment is carried out as shown in Figure 10.5 and the results used to draw a graph of known values of ATP concentration (see Figure 10.6). When the experiment is repeated using material of unknown ATP content, the ATP concentration can be determined from the graph. For example, the sample shown in Figure 10.7 would contain 7.5 units of ATP.

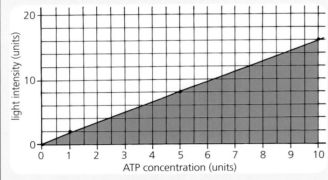

Figure 10.6 Graph of luciferase results

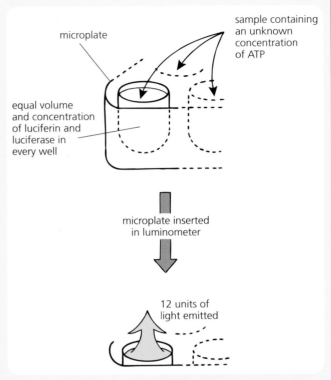

Figure 10.7 Measuring light emitted from an unknown concentration of ATP

Phosphorylation

Phosphorylation is an enzyme-controlled process by which a phosphate group is added to a molecule. Phosphorylation occurs, for example, when the reaction shown in Figure 10.2 goes from the bottom to the top and P_i combines with low-energy ADP to form high-energy ATP.

Phosphorylation of a reactant in a pathway

Phosphorylation also occurs when phosphate and energy are transferred from ATP to the molecules of a reactant in a metabolic pathway making them **more reactive**. Often a step in a pathway can proceed only

if a reactant becomes **phosphorylated** and energised. In the early stages of cellular respiration, for example, some reactants must undergo phosphorylation during what is called the energy investment phase. One of these steps is shown in Figure 10.8.

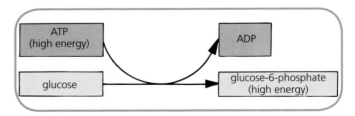

Figure 10.8 Phosphorylation of glucose

A phosphorylated substrate

Background

- **Glucose-1-phosphate** is a phosphorylated form of glucose.

- A molecule of starch is composed of many glucose molecules linked together in a long chain.

- Potato tuber cells contain **phosphorylase**, an enzyme that promotes the synthesis of starch.

- Potato extract containing phosphorylase is prepared by liquidising a mixture of potato tuber and water and then centrifuging the mixture until the potato extract (see Figure 10.9) is **starch free**.

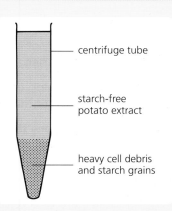

Figure 10.9 Preparation of potato extract

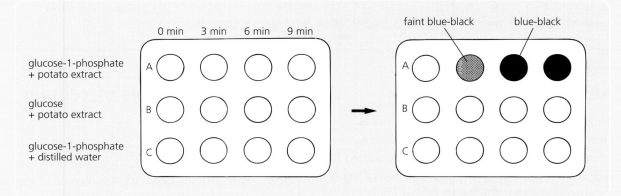

Figure 10.10 Investigating a phosphorylated substrate

The experiment is set up on a dimple tile as shown in Figure 10.10. One dimple from each row is tested at 3-minute intervals with iodine solution. Starch is found to be formed in row A only. It is concluded that in row A, phosphorylase has promoted the conversion of the phosphorylated (and more reactive) form of the substrate, glucose-1-phosphate, to starch as in the following equation:

$$
\underset{\substack{\text{glucose-1-phosphate}\\ \text{(phosphorylated substrate)}}}{} \xrightarrow{\text{phosphorylase}\\ \text{(enzyme)}} \underset{\substack{\text{starch}\\ \text{(end product)}}}{}
$$

In row B (a control), phosphorylase has failed to convert the more stable (and less reactive) form of the substrate, glucose, to starch.

In row C (a control), the molecules of glucose-1-phosphate have failed to become bonded together into starch without the aid of phosphorylase.

Positive and negative controls

A **positive control** is set up to assess the validity of a testing procedure or design and ensure that the equipment and materials being used are in working order and appropriate for use in the experiment being carried out. For example, a positive control for the above experiment could be set up as row D, which would contain starch in every dimple. If the addition of iodine solution at each 3-minute interval gave a blue-black colour, this would confirm that:

- the iodine solution being used was working properly as a testing reagent for starch

- the experiment was not adversely affected in some way, for example by the contamination of the spotting tile or by changes in room temperature.

If a positive control does not produce the expected result, then this indicates that there is something wrong with the design of the testing procedure or with the materials being used.

A **negative control** is one that should not work. It is a copy of the experiment in which all factors are kept exactly the same except the one being investigated. When the results are compared, any difference found between the experiment and a negative control must be due to the factor being investigated.

In the above investigation, starch is not synthesised in row B, showing that the glucose must be in a phosphorylated state to become converted to starch. If row B had not been set up, it would be valid to suggest that starch would have been formed whether or not the glucose was phosphorylated. Similarly, starch was not formed in row C showing that phosphorylase (in potato extract) must be present for phosphorylated glucose to be converted to starch. If row C had not been included, it would be valid to suggest that phosphorylated glucose would have become starch whether or not phosphorylase was present. Therefore rows B and C in this investigation are negative controls.

Synthesis of ATP

When an energy-rich substance such as glucose is broken down during cellular respiration in a living cell, it releases energy which is used to synthesise ATP from ADP and P_i. Cellular respiration consists of many enzyme-controlled steps which ensure that energy release occurs in an orderly fashion.

A flow of high-energy electrons from the respiratory pathway is used to pump hydrogen ions (H^+) across the inner mitochondrial membrane and maintain a region of higher concentration of hydrogen ions on one side of the membrane (see Figure 10.11).

Embedded in the membrane are molecules of the protein **ATP synthase** which is an enzyme. The return flow of hydrogen ions from the region of higher concentration to the region of lower concentration takes place via ATP synthase molecules. This makes part of the ATP synthase rotate and catalyse the synthesis of ATP from ADP and P_i. ATP synthase molecules operate in a similar way in the membranes of chloroplasts.

Metabolic pathways of cellular respiration

Glycolysis

The process of cellular respiration begins in the cytoplasm of a living cell with a molecule of **glucose** being broken down to form **pyruvate**. This process of 'glucose-splitting' is called **glycolysis**. It consists of a series of enzyme-controlled steps. Those in the first half of the chain make up the **energy investment phase** (where two ATP are used up per molecule of glucose); those in the second half of the chain make up the **energy payoff phase** (where four ATP are produced per molecule of glucose) as shown in Figure 10.12.

Phosphorylation of intermediates occurs twice during the first phase:

- at step 1 where an intermediate is formed that can connect with other metabolic pathways

- at step 3 which is an irreversible reaction leading only to the rest of the glycolytic pathway.

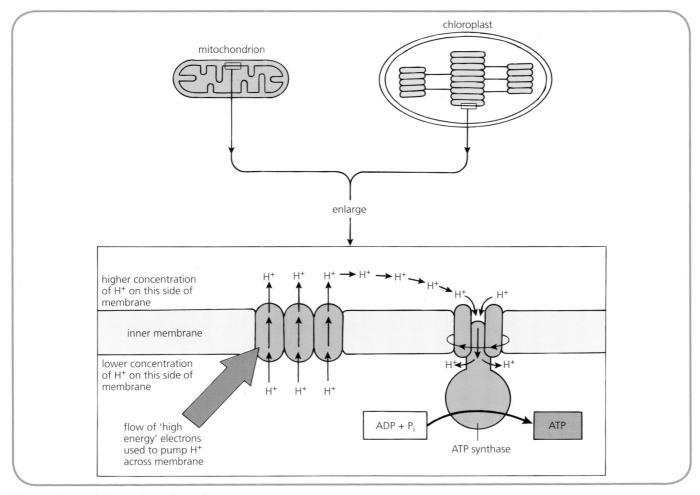

Figure 10.11 ATP synthase in action

The generation of four ATP that occurs during the second half of the pathway gives a **net gain of two ATP** per molecule of glucose during glycolysis. In addition, during the energy payoff phase, H ions are released from the substrate by a dehydrogenase enzyme. These H ions are passed to a coenzyme molecule called **NAD** (full name, nicotinamide adenine dinucleotide) forming **NADH**.

The process of glycolysis does not require oxygen. However, NADH only leads to the production of further molecules of ATP at a later stage in the respiratory process if oxygen is present. In the absence of oxygen, fermentation occurs (see page 154).

Citric acid cycle

If oxygen is present, aerobic respiration proceeds and pyruvate is broken down into carbon dioxide and an **acetyl group**. Each acetyl group combines with **coenzyme A** to form **acetyl coenzyme A**. During this process, further H ions are released and become bound to NAD forming NADH. A simplified version of the metabolic pathway is shown in Figure 10.13.

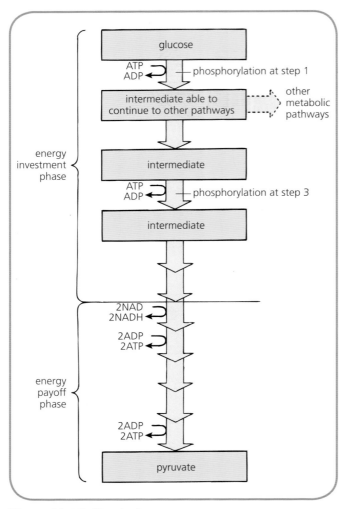

Figure 10.12 Glycolysis

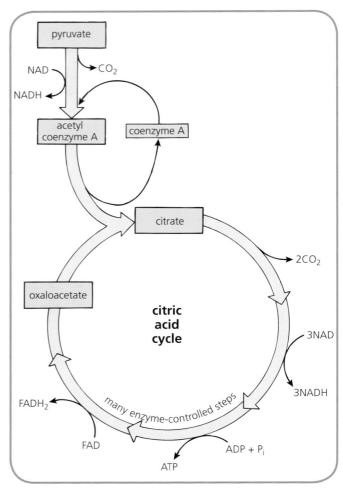

Figure 10.13 Citric acid cycle

The acetyl group of acetyl coenzyme A combines with **oxaloacetate** to form **citrate** and enter the **citric acid cycle**. This cycle consists of several enzyme-mediated stages which occur in the central matrix of mitochondria and result finally in the regeneration of oxaloacetate.

At three steps in the cycle, dehydrogenase enzymes remove **H ions** from the respiratory substrate along with associated **high-energy electrons**. These H ions and high-energy electrons are passed to the coenzyme NAD to form NADH. At one other step a similar reaction occurs but the coenzyme is **FAD** (full name, flavine adenine dinucleotide). On accepting H ions and electrons it becomes **FADH$_2$**. In addition, ATP is produced at one of the steps and carbon dioxide is released at two of the steps.

Many people refer to the citric acid cycle as the **Krebs cycle** in recognition of the contribution to its discovery made by **Hans Krebs**, a German biochemist. Prior to the work done by Krebs, scientists had established that a cell extract from respiring animal tissue in the presence of oxygen is able to rapidly break down chemicals such as citrate, fumarate, malate and succinate and release carbon dioxide. Then they found that the following sequence of reactions occurs:

succinate → fumarate → malate → oxaloacetate

And later they established that the following sequence also takes place:

citrate → isocitrate → α-ketoglutarate
→ succinyl-CoA → succinate

Therefore at the time of Krebs' discovery, this part of the biochemistry of respiration was thought to occur as the pathway shown in Figure 10.14.

However, Krebs, using extract from respiring muscle tissue, found that citrate could be formed if oxaloacetate and pyruvate were added to it. He therefore deduced that the process occurred as a **cycle** (see Figure 10.15) and *not* as a linear pathway. Further evidence to support this conclusion came from the fact that the addition of any of the intermediate reactants resulted in the generation of all the others. Experimental work involving **competitive inhibition** of the enzymes that convert one intermediate to another also lent support to what has now become accepted as fact.

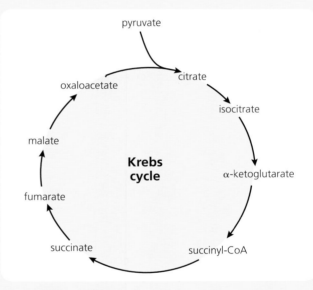

Figure 10.15 Krebs cycle

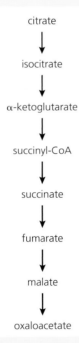

Figure 10.14 Possible pathway

Related Activity

Demonstrating the effect of malonic acid

Background

- Succinate and fumarate are two of the intermediates in the citric acid cycle.

- When succinate is converted to fumarate during respiration in a living cell, hydrogen is released and passed to the coenzyme FAD. The reaction is catalysed by the enzyme **succinic dehydrogenase** as follows:

$$\text{succinate} + \text{FAD} \xrightarrow{\text{succinic dehydrogenase}} \text{fumarate} + \text{FADH}_2$$

- **Malonic acid** is a chemical that inhibits the action of succinic dehydrogenase.

- In this investigation a chemical called DCPIP is used as the hydrogen acceptor. DCPIP changes colour upon gaining hydrogen as follows:

dark blue   →   colourless
(lacks hydrogen)   (has gained hydrogen)

The experiment is carried out as shown in Figure 10.16. From the results it is concluded that in tube A, succinic dehydrogenase in respiring mung bean cells has converted succinate to fumarate and that the hydrogen released has been accepted by DCPIP, turning it colourless. It is concluded that in tube B, the respiratory pathway has been blocked and no hydrogen has been released for DCPIP to accept because malonic acid has inhibited the action of succinic dehydrogenase.

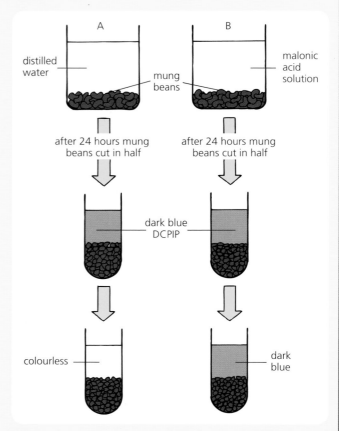

Figure 10.16 Effect of malonic acid

Electron transport chain

An **electron transport chain** consists of a group of protein molecules. There are many of these chains in a cell. They are found attached to the **inner membrane of mitochondria**. NADH and FADH$_2$ from the glycolytic and citric acid pathways release **high-energy electrons** and pass them to the electron transport chains (see Figure 10.17).

The electrons begin in a high-energy state. As they flow along a chain of electron acceptors, they release energy. This is used to pump **hydrogen ions** across the membrane from the inner cavity (matrix) side to the intermembrane space where a higher concentration of hydrogen ions is maintained. The return flow of hydrogen ions to the matrix (the region of lower H$^+$ concentration) via molecules of **ATP synthase** drives this enzyme to synthesise ATP from ADP and P$_i$. Most of the ATP generated by cellular respiration is produced in mitochondria in this way.

When the electrons come to the end of the electron

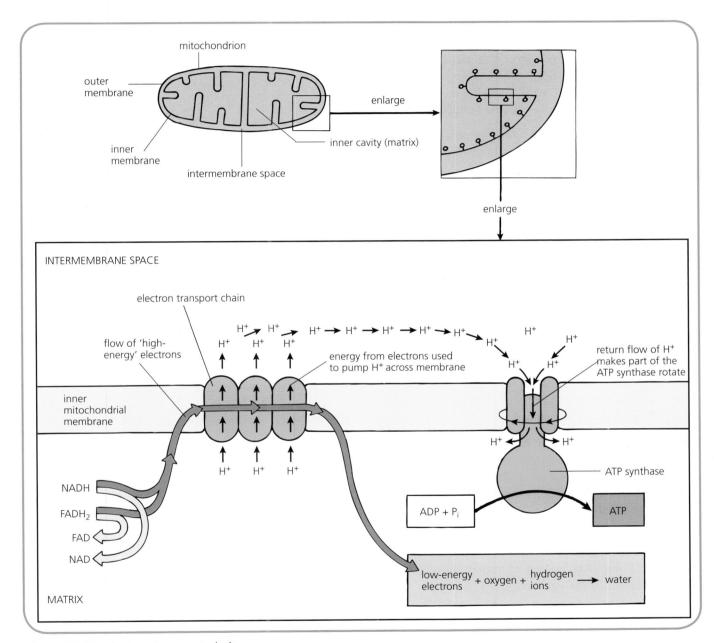

transport chain, they combine with **oxygen**, the final electron acceptor. At the same time, the oxygen combines with a pair of hydrogen ions to form **water**.

In the absence of oxygen, the electron transport chains do not operate and this major source of ATP becomes unavailable to the cell.

Figure 10.17 Electron transport chain

Investigating the activity of dehydrogenase enzyme in yeast

Background

- During respiration, glucose is gradually broken down and hydrogen released at various stages along the pathway. Each of these stages is controlled by an enzyme called a **dehydrogenase**.

- Yeast cells contain small quantities of stored food which can be used as a respiratory substrate.

- Resazurin dye is a chemical which changes colour upon gaining hydrogen as follows:

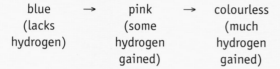

blue	→	pink	→	colourless
(lacks hydrogen)		(some hydrogen gained)		(much hydrogen gained)

- Before setting up the experiment shown in Figure 10.18, dried yeast is added to water and aerated for an hour at 35 °C to ensure that the yeast is in an active state.

Once the experiment has been set up, the contents of tube A are found to change from blue via pink to colourless much faster than those in tube B. Tube C, the control, remains unchanged.

It is concluded that in tube A, hydrogen has been released rapidly and has acted on, and changed the colour of, the resazurin dye. For this to be possible, dehydrogenase enzymes present in the yeast cells must have acted on glucose, the respiratory substrate.

In tube B, the reaction was slower because no glucose was added and the dehydrogenase enzymes could only act on any small amount of respiratory substrate already present in the yeast cells.

In tube C, boiling has killed the cells and denatured the dehydrogenase enzymes.

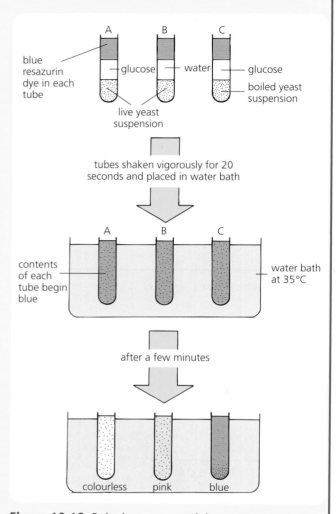

Figure 10.18 Dehydrogenase activity

Testing Your Knowledge 1

1 a) What compound is represented by the letters ATP? (1)

   b) What is the structural difference between ATP and ADP? (1)

   c) Give a word equation to indicate how ATP is regenerated in a cell. (2)

2 Explain each of the following:

   a) During the glycolysis of one molecule of glucose, the net gain is two and not four molecules of ATP. (1)

   b) Living organisms have only small quantities of oxaloacetate in their cells. (1)

   c) A human body can produce ATP at a rate of around $400\,g\,h^{-1}$, yet at any given moment there are only about $50\,g$ present in the body. (2)

3 Using the letters G, C and E, indicate whether each of the following statements refers to glycolysis (G), citric acid cycle (C) or electron transport chain (E). (Some statements may need more than one letter.) (8)

   a) It brings about the breakdown of glucose to pyruvate.

   b) It ends with the production of water.

   c) It begins with acetyl from acetyl coenzyme A combining with oxaloacetate.

   d) It involves a cascade of electrons which are finally accepted by oxygen.

   e) It has an energy investment phase and an energy payoff phase.

   f) It results in the production of NADH.

   g) It involves the release of carbon dioxide.

   h) It results in the production of ATP.

Substrates for respiration

Carbohydrates

Starch (a complex carbohydrate stored in plants) and **glycogen** (a complex carbohydrate stored by animals) are composed of chains of **glucose** molecules. They act as respiratory substrates since they can be broken down to release glucose as required (see Figure 10.19). Other sugar molecules such as maltose and sucrose can also be converted to glucose or intermediates in the glycolytic pathway and used as respiratory substrates.

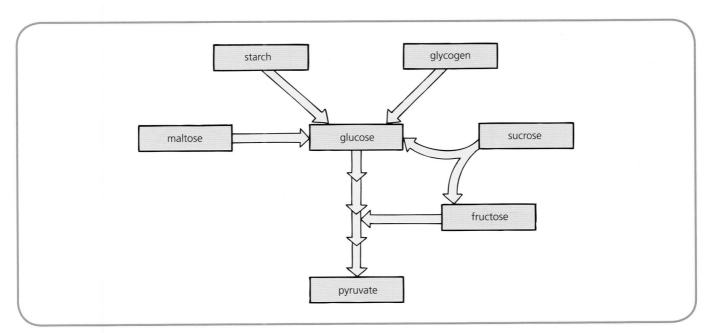

Figure 10.19 Carbohydrates as respiratory substrates

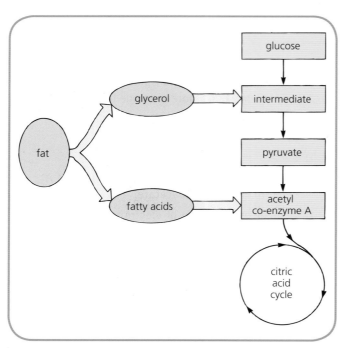

Figure 10.20 Fat as a respiratory substrate

Fats

When required for use as a respiratory substrate, a molecule of **fat** is broken down into **glycerol** and **fatty acids**. These products then become available for use in cellular respiration. Glycerol is converted to a glycolytic intermediate (see Figure 10.20) and fatty acids are metabolised into molecular fragments that enter the pathway as acetyl coenzyme A for use in the citric acid cycle.

Proteins

Proteins in the diet are broken down to their component **amino acids** by the action of digestive enzymes. Amino acids in excess of the body's requirements for protein synthesis undergo deamination forming urea and respiratory pathway intermediates as shown in Figure 10.21. These intermediates then enter the metabolic pathway and act as respiratory substrates regenerating ATP as before.

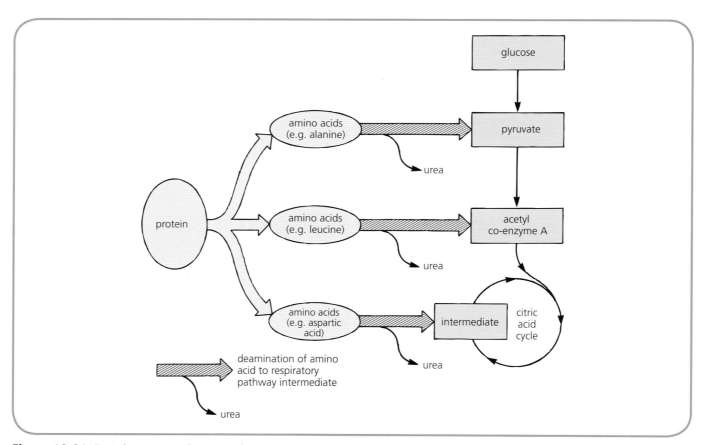

Figure 10.21 Protein as a respiratory substrate

Practical Activity and Report

Investigating the use of three different sugars as respiratory substrates by yeast

Information

- Figure 10.22 shows, in a simple way, the molecular structure of three types of sugar and the digestive enzymes needed to break down maltose and sucrose.

- Strictly speaking, this activity is really three investigations being carried out simultaneously.

- In each case the independent variable is time.

- The dependent variable that you are going to measure is the volume of carbon dioxide released as a result of yeast using a particular type of sugar as its respiratory substrate.

You need

three graduated tubes

three large beakers (such as 500 ml) of coloured tap water

three clamp stands

one container of glucose solution (10 g in 90 ml of water)

one container of maltose solution (10 g in 90 ml of water)

one container of sucrose solution (10 g in 90 ml of water)

three conical flasks (250 ml) each with a rubber stopper and delivery tube

three labels

three portions of dried yeast, each 1 g

a stopclock

What to do

1 Read all of the instructions in this section and prepare your results table before carrying out the experiment.

2 Fill each graduated tube with coloured tap water and clamp it in an inverted position in a beaker of coloured water as shown in Figure 10.23.

3 Label the conical flasks 'glucose', 'maltose' and 'sucrose', respectively, and add your initials.

4 Pour the appropriate sugar solution into each conical flask and add a portion of dried yeast.

5 Assemble the stoppers and delivery tubes as shown in Figure 10.23.

6 Start the clock and record, at 5-minute intervals, the total volume of carbon dioxide that has been released for each flask over a period of 2 hours.

7 If other students have carried out the same experiment, pool the results.

Reporting

Write up your report by doing the following:

1 Rewrite the title given at the start of this activity.

2 Put the subheading '**Aim**' and state the aim of your experiment.

3 a) Put the subheading '**Method**'.

   b) Draw a diagram of your apparatus set-up at the start of the experiment after the yeast has been added and bubbles of carbon dioxide are being released.

   c) Briefly describe the experimental procedure that you followed using the impersonal passive voice. (Note: The impersonal passive voice avoids the use of 'I' and 'we'. Instead it makes the apparatus the subject of the sentence. In this experiment,

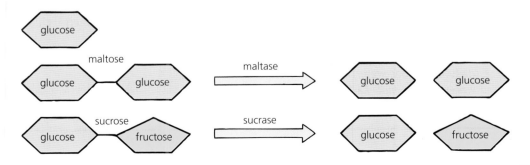

Figure 10.22 Relationship between three sugars

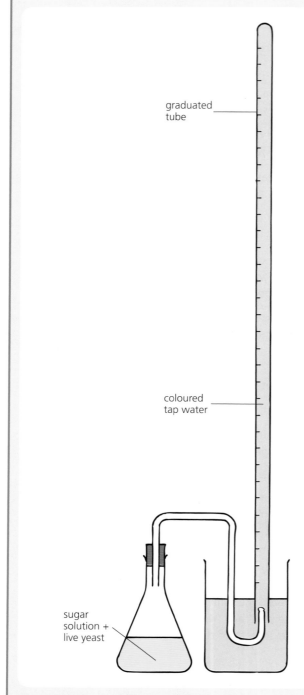

graduated
tube

coloured
tap water

sugar
solution +
live yeast

Figure 10.23 Yeast investigation set-up

for example, you could begin your report by
saying 'Three graduated tubes were filled
with coloured water ...' etc. *not* 'I filled three
graduated tubes with coloured water ...' etc.)

d) Continuing in the impersonal passive voice, state
how your results were obtained.

4 Put the subheading '**Results**' and draw a final version
of your table of results.

5 Put a subheading '**Analysis and Presentation of
Results**'. Present your results as three line graphs
with shared axes on the same sheet of graph paper.

6 Put the subheading '**Conclusion**' and write a short
paragraph to state what you have found out from a
study of your results. This should include answers to
the following questions:

a) Which respiratory substrate(s) was yeast able to
use effectively?

b) Which enzyme (see Figure 10.22) is probably
produced by yeast cells in adequate quantities
to digest its substrate before its use in cellular
respiration?

c) Which respiratory substrate(s) was yeast not able
to use effectively?

d) Which enzyme is probably not produced by
yeast in adequate quantities within the 2-hour
timescale to digest its substrate and make it
suitable for use in cellular respiration?

7 Put a final subheading '**Evaluation of Experimental
Procedure**'. Give an evaluation of your experiment
(keeping in mind that you may comment on any
stage of the experiment that you wish).

Try to incorporate answers to the following questions
in your evaluation. Make sure that at least one of
your answers includes a supporting statement.

a) Why is the same mass of yeast and the same
mass of sugar used in every flask?

b) Why is the same genetic strain of yeast used in
each flask?

c) Why must the rubber stoppers be tightly fitting?

d) Why should a control flask containing distilled
water and yeast have been included in this
investigation?

e) What is the purpose of pooling results with other
groups?

Research Topic | Use of respiratory substrates during exercise and starvation

Carbohydrate, fat and protein can all be used as **respiratory substrates**. Their individual contributions to the body's overall energy supply depend upon the body's circumstances.

Exercise

For several minutes, from the start of **aerobic exercise**, the body burns carbohydrates primarily. After 20–30 minutes of continuous exercise, respiratory substrate usage shifts to a balance of around 50% carbohydrate and 50% fat. During the first hour of exercise, protein makes up less than 2% of the respiratory substrate but its utilisation increases during prolonged exercise. It may reach 5–15% of fuel usage during the latter stages of prolonged exercise lasting 5 hours or more.

Marathon running

The respiratory substrates used in this lengthy athletic event (49.195 km) are glucose, glycogen and fat as shown in Figure 10.24. During the first few minutes of the race, readily available glucose from **muscle glycogen** is the main fuel used to generate energy. However, as the race continues and rate of blood flow increases, blood-borne fuels carried to the exercising muscles become the dominant sources of energy. **Blood glucose** (largely from liver glycogen) and slower-acting **fatty acids** provide most of the energy over the next 30 minutes or so. In the later stages of the race, fatty acids become increasingly important as supplies of glucose decrease.

A marathon runner therefore depends on a combination of carbohydrate and fat. The relative contribution made by each fuel depends on availability. The athlete may decide to 'load up' with carbohydrate during pre-race meals. He or she may consume an **approved refreshment** of glucose solution after 11 km and thereafter at intervals of 5 km. Under these circumstances the degree of

dependency on fat reserves is greatly reduced.

Starvation

Starvation results when the body continuously expends more energy than it takes in as food. During the early stages of starvation, the body uses up its store of **glycogen** and then mobilises its **fat** reserves. As starvation becomes prolonged, liver cells continue to use fatty acids from stored fats to form **acetyl coenzyme A**. Some acetyl coenzyme A enters the citric acid cycle (see Figure 10.13) and is used in the normal way; some becomes converted to water-soluble **ketones** which are transported in the bloodstream to the brain and provide it with a vital source of energy.

Tissue protein is used as a source of energy only during prolonged starvation when the reserves of glycogen and fat have become exhausted. Then skeletal muscle and other tissues rich in protein are used up to provide energy during the crisis. Eventually the person becomes emaciated and death soon follows.

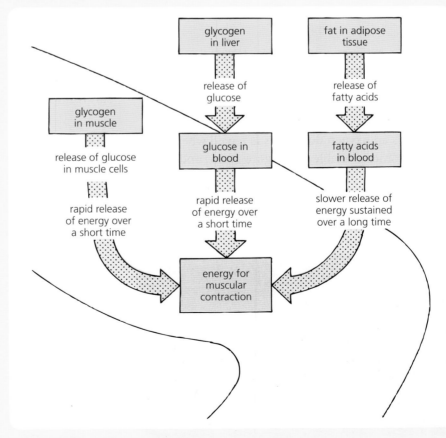

Figure 10.24 Fuelling a marathon

Fermentation

This is the process by which a little energy is derived from the **partial** breakdown of sugar in the absence of oxygen (anaerobic conditions). Since oxygen is unavailable to the cell, the citric acid cycle and electron transport chain cannot operate. Only glycolysis can occur. Each glucose molecule is converted to pyruvate and yields a net gain of two ATP. Then the pyruvate continues along an alternative metabolic pathway. The form that this takes depends on the type of organism involved.

Plants

The equation below summarises fermentation in plant cells such as yeast deprived of oxygen and cells of roots in water-logged soil:

glucose → pyruvate → alcohol (ethanol) + carbon dioxide

Animals (and some bacteria)

The equation below summarises fermentation in animal cells such as skeletal muscle tissue:

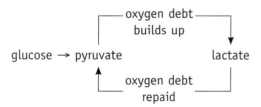

During the formation of lactate (lactic acid), the body accumulates an **oxygen debt**. This is repaid when oxygen becomes available (see Figure 10.25) and lactate is converted back to pyruvate which enters the aerobic pathway. Fortunately the biochemical conversion suggested in Figure 10.26 never really takes place.

Figure 10.26 Anaerobic nightmare

ATP totals

Fermentation is a less-efficient process since it produces only **two ATP** per molecule of glucose compared with **38 ATP** formed by cellular respiration in the presence of oxygen. The majority of living things thrive in oxygen and respire aerobically. They only resort to fermentation to obtain a little energy for survival while oxygen is absent.

Figure 10.25 Repayment of oxygen debt

Testing Your Knowledge 2

1 Name TWO complex carbohydrates composed of chains of glucose molecules. (2)

2 Figure 10.27 shows the relationship between carbohydrate and two other classes of food which can act as alternative sources of energy. Identify blanks 1–5. (5)

3 a) Give the word equation of fermentation in
   i) a plant cell
   ii) an animal cell. (2)

   b) Which of these forms of respiration is quickly reversed when oxygen becomes available? (1)

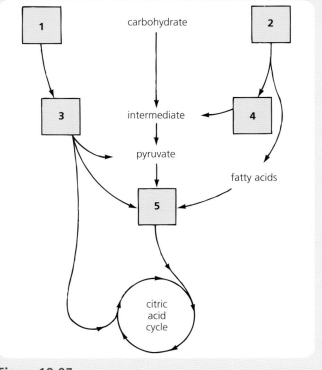

Figure 10.27

What You Should Know

Chapters 9–10

(See Table 10.1 for word bank)

acetyl	enzymes	on
activation	ethanol	orientation
ADP	FAD	oxygen
affinity	genetic	phosphorylation
anabolism	glycolysis	pores
ATP	hydrogen	product
ATP synthase	induced	proteins
break	inhibit	pumps
catabolism	inhibition	pyruvate
citrate	investment	regulated
compartments	irreversible	shape
competitive	lactate	structure
complex	lowering	substrate
concentration	metabolism	transferred
electron	NADH	transition
energy	negative	wasted
environment	off	water

Table 10.1 Word bank for chapters 9–10

1 Cell _____ encompasses all the enzyme-catalysed reactions that occur in a cell.

2 _____ consists of biosynthetic metabolic pathways that build up _____ molecules from simpler constituents and need a supply of energy; _____ consists of metabolic pathways that _____ down larger molecules into smaller ones and usually release _____.

3 A cell's metabolic activity is localised in _____ formed by membranes. Some protein molecules in the membrane have _____ that allow certain molecules to diffuse through the membrane; others act as _____ and actively transport ions across the membrane against a concentration gradient.

4 For a metabolic reaction to occur, _____ energy is needed to form a _____ state from which end products are produced. _____ catalyse biochemical reactions by _____ the activation energy needed by the reactants to form their transition state.

5 Substrate molecules have an _____ for the active site on an enzyme. The active site's shape determines the _____ of the reactants on it and it binds to them closely with an _____ fit.

6 The enzymes controlling a metabolic pathway usually work as a group. Although some steps are _____, most metabolic reactions are reversible. The direction in which the reaction occurs depends on factors such as concentration of the _____ and removal of a _____ as it becomes converted to another metabolite.

7 Each step in a metabolic pathway is _____ by an enzyme which catalyses a specific reaction. Each enzyme is under _____ control.

8 Some metabolic pathways are required continuously and the genes that code for their enzymes are always switched _____. Other pathways are only needed on certain occasions. To prevent resources being _____, the genes that code for their enzymes are switched on or _____ as required in response to signals from within the cell and from its _____.

9 Molecules of a _____ inhibitor resemble the substrate in _____. They become attached to the active site and slow down the reaction. Their effect is reversed by increasing the _____ of substrate.

10 Some regulatory molecules stimulate enzyme activity or _____ it non-competitively by changing the _____ of the enzyme molecule and its active site(s).

11 Some metabolic pathways are controlled by end-product _____, a form of _____ feedback control.

12 _____ is a high-energy compound able to release and transfer energy when it is required for cellular

processes. ATP is regenerated from _____ and P_i by phosphorylation using energy released during cellular respiration. _____ also occurs when P_i and energy are _____ from ATP to a reactant in a pathway.

13 Cellular respiration begins with _____, the breakdown of glucose to _____. This consists of an energy _____ phase and an energy payoff phase with a net gain of two molecules of ATP.

14 In the presence of oxygen, pyruvate is broken down into carbon dioxide and an _____ group. With the help of coenzyme A, the acetyl group enters the citric acid cycle by combining with oxaloacetate to become _____.

15 As one respiratory substrate is converted to another in the citric acid cycle, carbon dioxide is released, ATP is formed and pairs of _____ ions are removed and passed to coenzymes NAD and _____ forming NADH and $FADH_2$.

16 _____ and $FADH_2$ pass their high-energy electrons to _____ transport chains where the energy released is used to pump hydrogen ions across inner mitochondrial membranes. The return flow of these hydrogen ions makes part of each _____ molecule rotate and catalyse the synthesis of ATP. _____, the final electron acceptor, combines with hydrogen to form _____.

17 Complex carbohydrates, _____ and fats can all be used as respiratory substrates if they are first converted to suitable intermediates able to enter the pathway.

18 In the absence of oxygen, fermentation occurs. The final metabolic products are _____ and carbon dioxide in plant cells and _____ in animal cells and some bacteria.

11 Metabolic rate

Metabolic rate

The quantity of energy consumed by an organism per unit of time is called its **metabolic rate**. Normally this energy is generated by cells respiring aerobically as summarised in the following equation:

glucose + oxygen → carbon dioxide + water + energy

Therefore metabolic rate can be measured as:

- **oxygen** consumption per unit time

- **carbon dioxide** production per unit time

- **energy** production (as heat) per unit time.

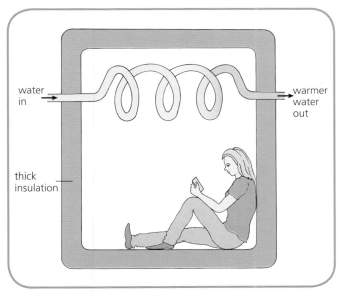

Figure 11.1 Calorimeter

Calorimeter

An organism's metabolic rate can be measured by placing it in a **calorimeter**. This is a well-insulated container containing a pipe through which water flows (see Figure 11.1). Heat generated by the organism causes a rise in temperature of the water in the pipe. By measuring the temperature of the water entering and leaving the calorimeter for a given period of time, the organism's metabolic rate can be calculated from the data collected.

Similarly an organism's metabolic rate can be measured by placing it in a **respirometer**. This is a chamber through which a continuous stream of air is pumped. Differences in oxygen concentration, carbon dioxide concentration and temperature between the air entering and the air leaving the respirometer are detected by **probes** (also see Related Activity). Table 11.1 compares metabolic rates (as oxygen consumption) of various animals at rest.

Animal	Volume of oxygen consumed $(mm^3 g^{-1}$ body mass $h^{-1})$
sea anemone	13
octopus	80
eel	128
frog	150
human	200
mouse	1 500
hummingbird	3 500

Table 11.1 Metabolic rates at rest

Measuring metabolic rate using probes (sensors)

The experiment is shown in Figure 11.2. Table 11.2 gives the purpose of each piece of equipment.

Equipment	Purpose
soda lime tube (containing sodium hydroxide)	to absorb all carbon dioxide from incoming air so that its initial concentration is not a variable factor
air pump	to pump a continuous flow of air through the system
flow meter	to maintain the flow of air at a steady rate that is low enough for the carbon dioxide sensor to work
animal chamber	to accommodate the animal whose metabolic rate is to be measured
temperature probe (sensor)	to measure changes of temperature in the animal chamber and send data to computer
condensing bath and drying column	to remove water vapour from passing air since the sensors need air to be dry
oxygen probe (sensor)	to measure percentage oxygen concentration and send data to computer
carbon dioxide probe (sensor) and analyser	to measure carbon dioxide in parts per million and send data to computer

Table 11.2 Purposes of respirometer equipment

The three probes (sensors) are calibrated in advance. The animal is inserted into the chamber and the experiment run for a set length of time (such as 30 minutes). The computer software monitors the data from the three sensors simultaneously and displays the information on the screen. From these data the animal's **metabolic rate** (as volume of oxygen consumed per unit time) can be determined.

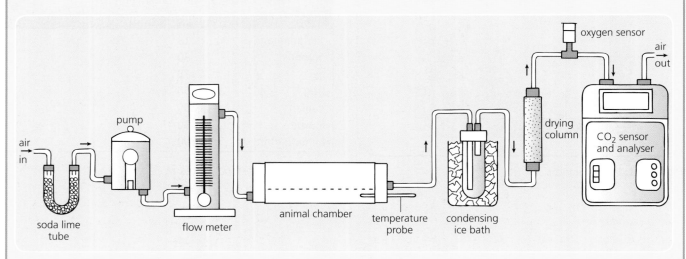

Figure 11.2 Investigating metabolic rate (connections to computer not shown)

Basal metabolic rate

The quantity of heat produced by the human body varies depending on level of activity and increases greatly during heavy exercise. Even when all voluntary muscular activity is brought to a halt and the person is at complete rest, some energy is still generated. This is the minimum rate of energy release needed by an endotherm (see page 167) to maintain essential body processes and it is called the **basal metabolic rate (BMR)**. It is normally expressed as kilojoules of heat released per square metre of body surface per hour. On average the BMR for a young adult male is about $165\,kJ\,m^{-2}\,h^{-1}$ and for a young adult female $150\,kJ\,m^{-2}\,h^{-1}$. Young children have higher BMRs and older adults have lower BMRs.

Oxygen delivery

As an organism's metabolic rate increases to meet an increasing demand for energy (for example for rapid movement or maintenance of body temperature), its rate of aerobic respiration and consumption of oxygen increase. Therefore aerobic organisms with high metabolic rates need **efficient transport systems** to deliver large supplies of oxygen to respiring cells.

Circulatory systems in vertebrates

All vertebrates have a **closed** circulatory system where the blood is contained in a continuous circuit of blood vessels and is kept moving by a muscular pump, the heart. In such a cardiovascular system, the heart pumps the blood into large vessels that branch into smaller and smaller vessels. The smallest of these vessels are thin-walled capillaries which allow **oxygen** to pass rapidly from the bloodstream to the fluid which bathes respiring cells and then on into the cells. Carbon dioxide moves in the opposite direction. The arrangement of the heart chambers and the circulatory system vary among the vertebrate groups.

Single circulatory system

The circulatory system in a fish is described as **single** because blood passes through the **two-chambered heart once only** for each complete circuit of the body (see Figure 11.3). In any closed circulatory system, a **drop in pressure** occurs when blood passes through a capillary

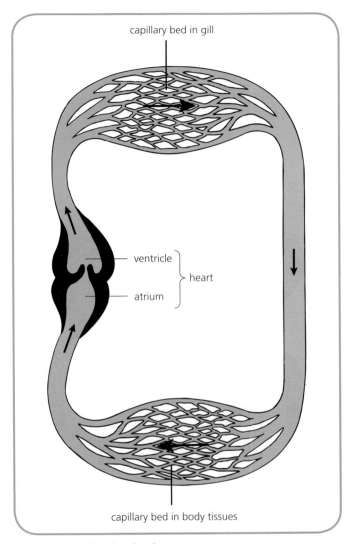

Figure 11.3 Single circulatory system

bed because it is a network of narrow tubes which offer resistance to flow of blood.

In a fish, blood flows to the gills at **high** pressure but is delivered next to the capillary beds of the body at **low** pressure. Therefore this is a primitive and relatively inefficient method of circulation compared to more advanced vertebrate groups.

Double circulatory system

The type of system present in the other vertebrate groups is described as **double** because blood passes through the heart twice for each complete circuit of the body. Blood is pumped to both the lungs and the body's capillary beds at **high** pressure ensuring a vigorous flow to all parts. Therefore a double circulation is more efficient than a single one.

Incomplete

In amphibians and reptiles, the system is described as **incomplete** because there is only **one ventricle** in the heart (see Figure 11.4) and some mixing of oxygenated blood from the lungs and deoxygenated blood from the body occurs.

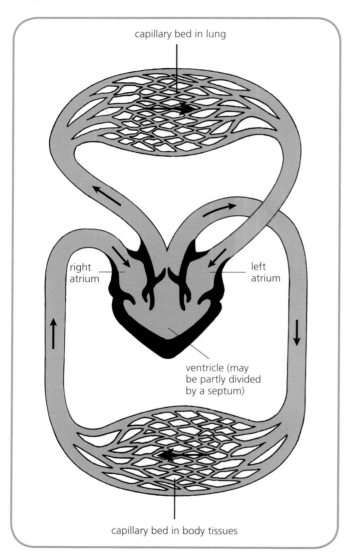

Figure 11.4 Incomplete double circulatory system

In amphibians, this mixing is not a major problem because blood returning from the body has been partly oxygenated by gas exchange through the animal's moist skin. In most reptiles, little mixing occurs because the single ventricle is partly divided by a septum.

Complete

In birds and mammals, the system is described as **complete** because the heart has **two ventricles**

completely separated by a septum (see Figure 11.5). Therefore no mixing of oxygenated and deoxygenated blood occurs. The complete double circulatory system is the most advanced and efficient circulatory system. It enables an endothermic ('warm-blooded') vertebrate to deliver large quantities of oxygen to respiring tissues which release heat during metabolism and keep its body warm.

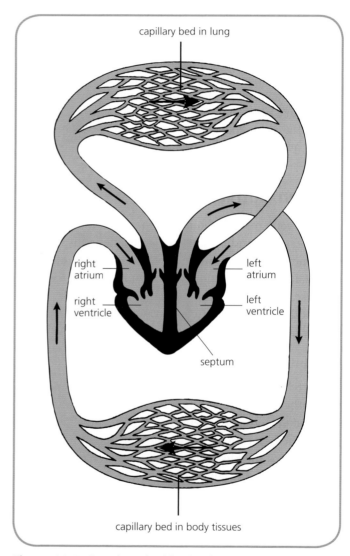

Figure 11.5 Complete double circulatory system

Complexity of lungs

Amphibians

Amphibians normally exchange gases through their skin and mouth cavity and only use their lungs during vigorous activity. Their lungs are small, thin-walled sacs that do contain some alveoli (tiny air sacs).

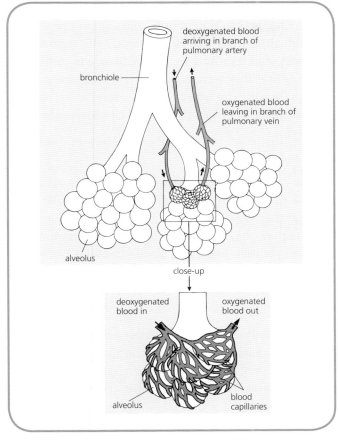

Figure 11.6 Alveoli and capillary network

However, the relative surface area that they present for gaseous exchange is small compared to that of more advanced vertebrates that depend entirely on lungs to exchange gases.

Reptiles and mammals

Reptiles and mammals possess a system of branching tubes that end in many alveoli as shown in Figure 11.6. Their inner lining is thin and moist and presents a relatively large surface area for gas exchange (about $100\,m^2$ in humans). This enables the large quantities of oxygen needed for aerobic respiration to pass into the bloodstream and be transported to metabolising tissues and organs.

Birds

Birds that fly are the most active of the vertebrate groups and need even more oxygen relative to their body size than the other vertebrates. In addition to lungs, birds possess several **large air sacs** that keep air flowing through the lungs by acting as bellows (see Figure 11.7).

When the bird inhales air, its posterior air sacs fill with fresh air while its anterior air sacs become filled with stale air from the lungs. When the bird exhales, the fresh air passes from the posterior sacs to the lungs

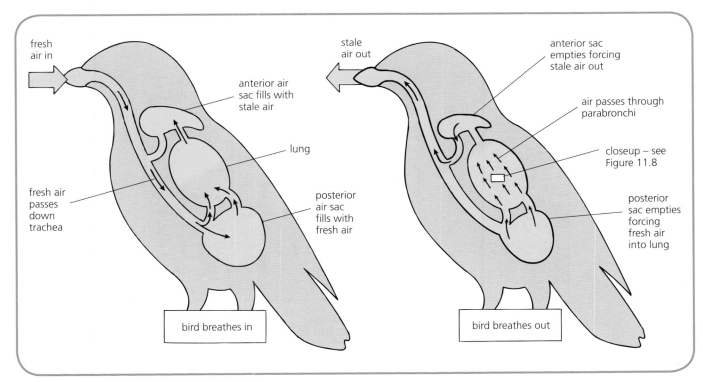

Figure 11.7 Bird's respiratory system

161

and the stale air passes from the anterior sacs to the external environment. By this means, air is forced in **one direction** through the lungs both times rather than into alveoli and back out again by the same route as in mammals.

Therefore the bird's lung does not possess 'dead-end' alveoli but instead has many tiny channels called **parabronchi** as shown in Figure 11.8. This highly efficient system of gas exchange allows birds to obtain the vast quantities of oxygen needed to maintain their very high metabolic rate.

Physiological adaptations for low-oxygen niches

High number of red blood cells

The human body functions best at sea level where the concentration of oxygen in the air is around 20%. At first, when a person moves to a high altitude, they gain less oxygen per breath than they did at sea level because at high altitudes the air is thinner and contains less oxygen per unit volume.

The body responds by secreting a higher concentration of the hormone which stimulates red blood cell production in the bone marrow. This results in the person's **red blood cell number** increasing from around $5 \times 10^{12} l^{-1}$ at sea level to around $6 \times 10^{12} l^{-1}$

at 4 kilometres above sea level. The latter red blood cell number is typical of people who live permanently at a high altitude. The extra red blood cells improve transport of oxygen and enable the people to perform activities as if they were at sea level. It takes about 46 days for a person who lives at sea level to become adapted in this way to an altitude 4 kilometres above sea level.

Deep-diving mammals

Marine mammals such as dolphins, seals and whales are able to make lengthy, deep-water dives despite the fact that they breathe air. This behaviour is possible because they possess certain **physiological adaptations**. For example their heart rate can be slowed down (125 to 10 beats per minute for seals on an extended dive). This conserves oxygen since less is used by cardiac muscle.

Their lungs are designed to **collapse** partially as hydrostatic pressure increases with increasing depth. Air is forced out of alveoli into the upper regions of the respiratory system. This air becomes compressed into a smaller and smaller volume but the animal's mass remains constant so it becomes **less buoyant** and sinks easily. Therefore during the dive, the animals are able to conserve energy and use it to hunt prey in deep waters. (Also see Case Study.)

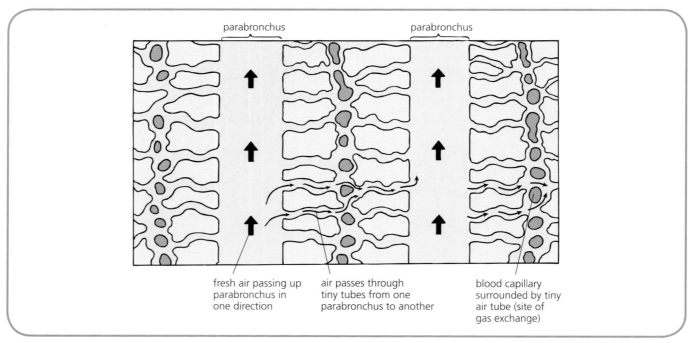

parabronchus   parabronchus

fresh air passing up parabronchus in one direction

air passes through tiny tubes from one parabronchus to another

blood capillary surrounded by tiny air tube (site of gas exchange)

Figure 11.8 Parabronchi (showing two of many)

Case Study   Weddell seal

The **Weddell seal** (see Figure 11.9) lives in the Antarctic Ocean. It is an excellent example of a mammal that possesses physiological adaptations required for deep diving. It begins a dive with a few powerful swimming strokes and then makes most of the rest of the descent as a relaxed glide while its lungs temporarily collapse and its buoyancy decreases. This enables the seal to reduce its oxygen consumption by 10–15%.

It is able to remain at depths of up to 500 metres for around 20 minutes as it hunts its prey of cod and other deep-sea fish. This type of behaviour is possible because it begins a deep-water dive with a large stockpile of oxygen. Figure 11.10 compares the percentage of total oxygen found at three locations in the body of a Weddell seal and of a human. The seal is able to hold much more oxygen in its blood because it has double the volume of blood per kilogram of body weight compared with a human. It is able to hold much more oxygen in its muscles because these contain an oxygen-storing protein called **myoglobin** in greater quantities than in other mammals.

In addition, during a dive, the seal's heart rate and rate of oxygen consumption decrease and blood is diverted to essential structures (such as the eyes, brain and nervous system). Muscles deprived of blood at this stage fall back on their reserves and may even respire by fermentation.

Figure 11.9 Weddell seal

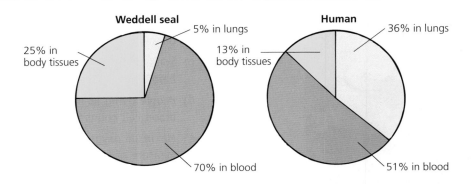

Figure 11.10 Distribution of oxygen in two animals

Fitness and maximum oxygen uptake

Maximum oxygen uptake (VO_2 **max**) is the maximum volume of oxygen that an individual's body can take up and use during intense exercise that is gradually increased incrementally (in other words, in a series of steps). VO_2 max is regarded as the best indicator of a person's **cardiovascular fitness**.

Measuring VO_2 max

Once the person has been fitted with an oxygen and carbon dioxide analyser, he/she performs the exercise on an **ergometer** such as a treadmill or exercise bicycle (see Figure 11.11). The workloads are gradually increased in increments from moderate to maximum. VO_2 max is reached when oxygen consumption stays steady despite the workload being increased. The VO_2 max value is calculated from measurements of ventilation rate and concentrations of oxygen and carbon dioxide in inhaled and exhaled air.

A young, untrained male has a VO_2 max of approximately $3.5 \, l \, min^{-1}$ and $45 \, ml \, kg^{-1} min^{-1}$ on average; a young, untrained female has a VO_2 max of approximately $2.0 \, l \, min^{-1}$ and $38 \, ml \, kg^{-1} min^{-1}$ on average. These scores improve with training and decrease with age.

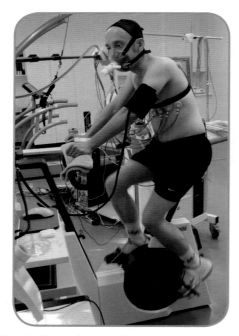

Figure 11.11 Measuring maximum oxygen uptake

Testing Your Knowledge

1 **a) i)** Define the term *metabolic rate*.
   ii) State TWO ways in which metabolic rate can be measured. (3)

   b) What is meant by the term *basal metabolic rate (BMR)*? (1)

2 Rewrite the following sentences, choosing the correct answer at each underlined choice. (3)

   The heart of a fish contains <u>two/three</u> chambers. Blood is pumped at <u>high/low</u> pressure to the gills and then on to the body's capillary beds at <u>high/low</u> pressure. The heart of a mammal contains <u>three/four</u> chambers. Blood is pumped to the mammal's lungs at <u>high/low</u> pressure and to the body's capillary beds at <u>high/low</u> pressure.

3 In what way are a bird's organs of gas exchange adapted to cope with the aerobic demands of flight? (3)

4 Decide whether each of the following statements is true or false and then indicate your choice using T or F. Where a statement is false, give the word that should have been used in place of the word in bold print. (6)

   a) Metabolic rate can be investigated using an oxygen **probe**.

   b) For each complete circuit of the body, blood passes through a fish's heart **twice**.

   c) Some mixing of oxygenated and deoxygenated blood occurs in the heart of a **bird**.

   d) People living at high altitudes have a **lower** red blood cell count than people living at sea level.

   e) Maximum oxygen uptake can be used as a measure of **fitness** in humans.

12 Metabolism in conformers and regulators

Conformers and regulators

Fluctuations in an external abiotic factor such as salinity or temperature may occur in an organism's environment. When this happens some organisms, called **regulators**, are able to alter their normal metabolic rate and maintain a steady state (see Figure 12.1) by employing physiological mechanisms.

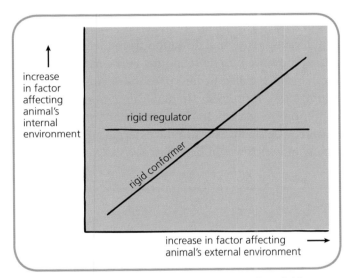

increase in factor affecting animal's internal environment

rigid regulator

rigid conformer

increase in factor affecting animal's external environment

Figure 12.2 Responses to an environmental variable

Other organisms, called **conformers**, are unable to alter their normal metabolic rate by these means.

Conformers

The state of a conformer's internal environment is **directly dependent** upon the abiotic factors that affect its external environment. However, this does not normally pose a problem because conformers live in environments that remain relatively stable (such as the ocean floor).

The advantage of this way of life is that the animal's metabolic costs are **low** since it does not employ energy-consuming physiological mechanisms to maintain its inner steady state. The disadvantage is that the animal is restricted to a **narrow range** of ecological niches and is **less adaptable** to environmental change.

Few organisms are complete conformers. Many employ **behavioural responses** to maintain their optimum metabolic rate. Lizards, for example, are unable to maintain their body temperature by employing physiological mechanisms such as shivering but they can manage it by behavioural means such as basking in sunshine.

Case Study | **Response of a conformer to a change in an environmental factor**

Thermal biology of *Anolis cristatellus*

Anolis cristatellus is the scientific name of a small lizard that lives in open lowlands and dense forests in Puerto Rico. Scientists have found that those members of the species living in open, sunny, lowland habitats are not complete conformers. They frequently raise their body temperature by basking in sunshine early and late in the day. For these animals the metabolic cost (energy expenditure) incurred by travelling a short distance to a sunny spot is low compared with the physiological benefits gained from this means of thermoregulation.

On the other hand, those members of the species that live in the shady, forest habitats tend to be almost complete conformers. They passively allow their body temperature to drop to that of their cool surroundings and very rarely bask in the sun. This behaviour is explained by the fact that the **metabolic cost** of travelling a relatively long distance in order to find a rare, sunny spot in the forest **outweighs any benefits** gained by raising their body temperature. It also increase the risk of capture by predators.

Regulators

The state of a regulator's internal environment is not directly dependent upon the abiotic factors that affect its external environment. Regulators employ physiological means to control their inner steady state. The Atlantic salmon, for example, spends part of its life in fresh water and part of its life in salt water. Yet it manages to maintain the solute concentration of its blood at a steady state by osmoregulation.

This is of advantage because the animal is able to exploit a wider range of ecological niches. For example, the Atlantic salmon is able to use the relatively safe, freshwater environment for breeding purposes but migrate to food-rich, marine waters during its growing years. The disadvantage is that the animal has to expend energy generated by its metabolism on the physiological mechanisms (such as osmoregulation) needed to maintain its inner steady state.

Physiological homeostasis

Physiological homeostasis is the maintenance of the body's internal environment within certain tolerable limits despite changes in the body's external environment. This regulation is brought about by **negative feedback control** and requires energy.

Principle of negative feedback control

When some factor affecting the body's internal environment deviates from its normal optimum level (called the **norm** or **set point**) this change in the factor is detected by **receptors**. These send out nerve or hormonal messages which are received by **effectors**.

The effectors then bring about certain responses which counteract the original deviation from the norm and return the system to its set point. This corrective mechanism is called **negative feedback control** (see Figure 12.3). It provides the stable environmental conditions needed by the body to function efficiently despite wide fluctuations in the external environment (many of which would be unfavourable).

Related Topic

Comparison of marine and estuarine invertebrates

The **spider crab** spends its life in sea water. The solute concentration of its blood is equal to that of the surrounding sea water. If it is placed in an environment with a higher or lower solute concentration than sea water, its body is unable to maintain a steady inner solute concentration by osmoregulation (see Figure 12.2). Instead it conforms to the environment by losing water or taking in water until its solute concentration is equal to that of the environment, even if this proves to be fatal.

The **shore crab**, on the other hand, can regulate the solute concentration of its body fluids to some extent. This enables the shore crab to operate in sea water and in river estuaries where the water contains far less salt than sea water. By being a regulator, the shore crab is able to exploit a wider range of environments than the spider crab, a conformer. However, the shore crab must find relatively more food to provide the energy expended during osmoregulation.

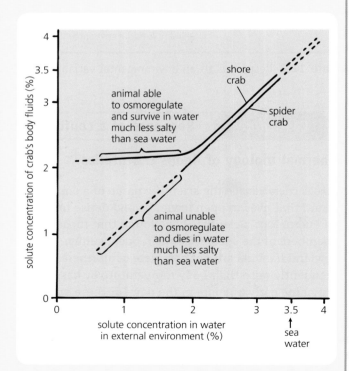

Figure 12.2 Comparison of conformer and regulator

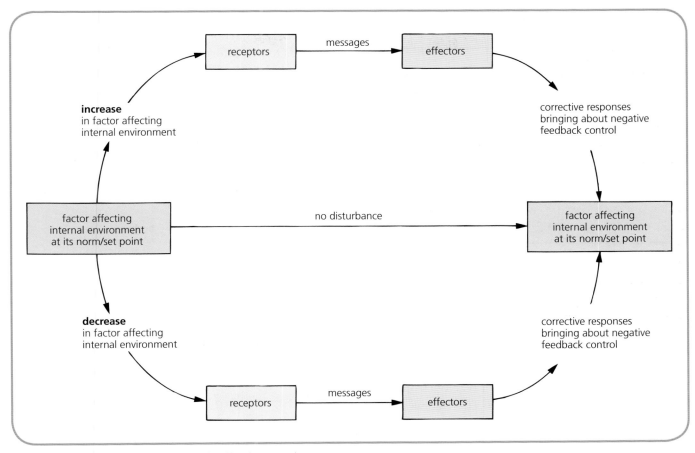

Figure 12.3 Principle of negative feedback control

Thermoregulation

Ectotherm

An **ectotherm** is an animal which is unable to regulate its body temperature by physiological means. Invertebrates, fish, amphibians and reptiles are, almost without exception, ectotherms and their body temperature normally varies directly with that of the external environment. They obtain most of their body heat by absorbing it from the surrounding environment.

Endotherm

An **endotherm** is an animal which is able to maintain its body temperature at a relatively constant level independent of the temperature of the external environment. All birds and mammals are endotherms. They have a **high metabolic rate** which generates most or all of their body's heat energy.

Most **enzymes** work best at 35–40 °C. Animals that can maintain their body temperature within this range possess an efficient and active metabolism. It consists of enzyme-controlled reactions and processes involving molecular diffusion that proceed at **optimal rates** regardless of the external temperature. Therefore terrestrial endotherms are capable of intense physical activity at all times of the day and night. They have an advantage over ectotherms whose metabolic rate slows down when the external temperature decreases.

The graph in Figure 12.4 summarises the effect of an increase in external temperature on body temperature of the two types of animal. Thermoregulation is brought about by **homeostatic control**.

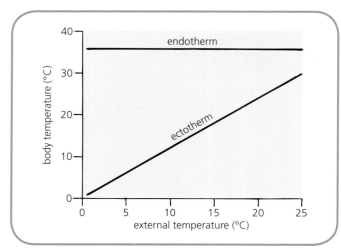

Figure 12.4 Effect of external temperature on body temperature

Role of hypothalamus

In addition to playing many other roles, the **hypothalamus** is the body's temperature-monitoring centre (see Figure 12.5). It acts as a **thermostat** and is sensitive to nerve impulses that it receives from heat and cold receptors in the skin. These convey information to it about the surface temperature of the body.

In addition, the hypothalamus itself possesses central **thermoreceptors**. These are sensitive to changes in temperature of blood which in turn reflect changes

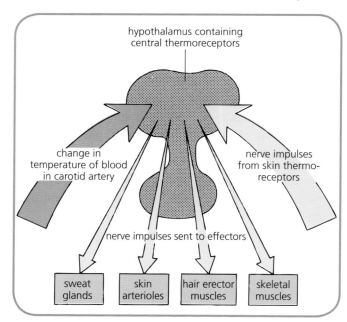

Figure 12.5 Hypothalamus as a temperature-monitoring centre

in the temperature of the **body core** (see Figure 12.6). The thermo-regulatory centre in the hypothalamus responds to this information by sending appropriate nerve impulses to effectors. These trigger corrective feedback mechanisms and return the body temperature to its normal level (set point).

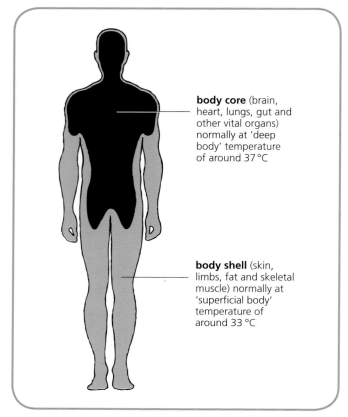

Figure 12.6 Body core and body shell

Role of skin

The **skin** plays a leading role in temperature regulation. In response to nerve impulses from the hypothalamus, the skin acts as an effector.

Correction of overheating

The skin helps to correct overheating of the body by employing the following mechanisms which promote heat loss.

Vasodilation

Arterioles leading to skin become **dilated** (see Figure 12.7). This allows a large volume of blood to flow through the capillaries near the skin surface. From here, the blood is able to lose heat by **radiation**.

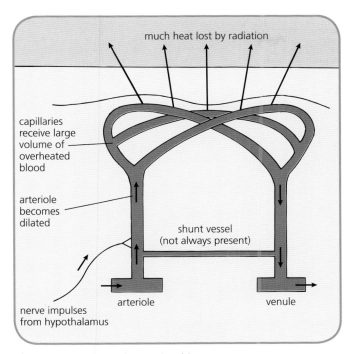

Figure 12.7 Vasodilation in skin

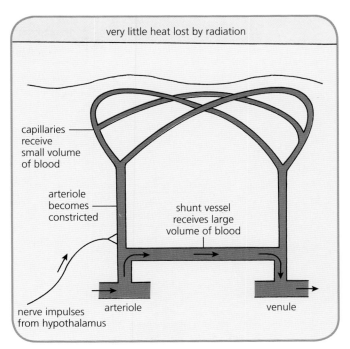

Figure 12.8 Vasoconstriction in skin

Increase in rate of sweating

Heat energy from the body is used to convert the water in sweat to **water vapour** and by this means brings about a lowering of body temperature.

Correction of overcooling

The skin helps to correct overcooling of the body by employing the following mechanisms which reduce heat loss.

Vasoconstriction

Arterioles leading to the skin become **constricted** (see Figure 12.8). This allows only a small volume of blood to flow to the surface capillaries. Little heat is therefore lost by radiation.

Decreased rate of sweating

Since sweating is reduced to a minimum, heat is conserved.

Contraction of erector muscles

This process (see Figure 12.9) is more effective in furry animals than in human beings. It results in hairs being raised from the skin surface. A wide layer of air, which is a poor conductor of heat, is trapped between the animal's body and the external environment. This layer of **insulation** reduces heat loss.

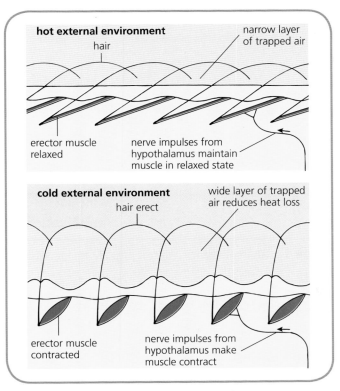

Figure 12.9 Action of hair erector muscles

The homeostatic control of body temperature is summarised in Figure 12.10. It includes further corrective mechanisms such as **shivering** and changes in **metabolic rate**.

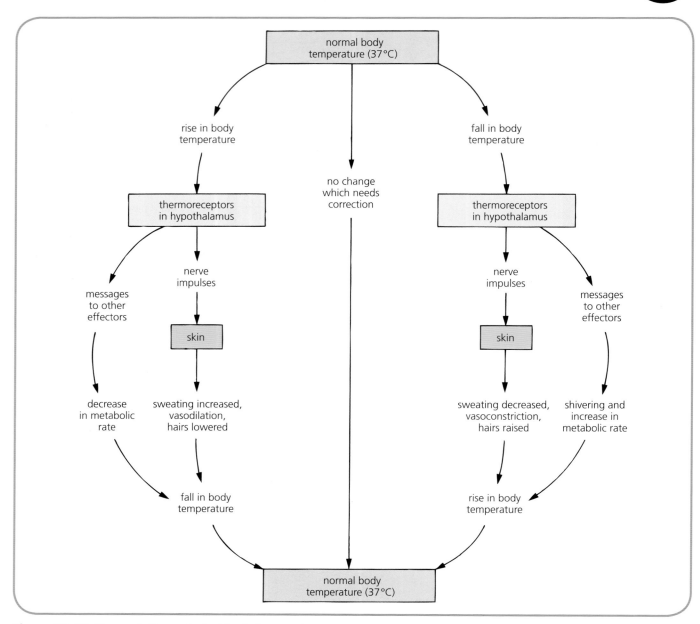

Figure 12.10 Homeostatic control of body temperature

Related Activity

Investigating response to sudden heat loss using a thermistor

A **thermistor** is a device which responds to tiny changes in temperature. In this investigation the thermistor is taped between two fingers of one hand, as shown in Figure 12.11, and the initial temperature of the skin is recorded from the digital meter. (Alternatively the thermistor can be connected up to an interface with a computer.)

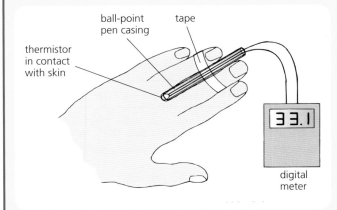

Figure 12.11 Use of a thermistor

The other hand is plunged into a container of icy water to cause a sudden heat loss. Temperature readings are taken every 30 seconds for 5 minutes. The skin temperature of the hand attached to the thermistor is found to drop by around 1 °C. A second thermistor positioned in the armpit during the experiment shows that the temperature of the body core remains constant.

It is therefore concluded that when heat is lost from one extremity (such as a hand in icy water), a **compensatory reduction in temperature** occurs in the other extremity but not in the temperature of the body core. This reduction in temperature is brought about by the following homeostatic mechanism: thermoreceptors in the skin in icy water send nerve impulses to the hypothalamus, which in turn sends impulses to the other hand causing **vasoconstriction** which reduces heat loss.

This response by the body's extremities helps to conserve heat when the body is exposed to extremes of temperature. The temperature of the body's extremities is therefore found to fluctuate more than that of the body core.

Testing Your Knowledge

1 Construct a table to compare conformers and regulators with respect to:

   a) ability to control the internal environment by physiological means (1)

   b) relative metabolic costs of lifestyle (1)

   c) extent of range of ecological niches that can be exploited. (1)

2 a) What is meant by the term *physiological homeostasis*? (2)

   b) i) Outline the principle of negative feedback control.

   ii) Why is such control of advantage to an organism? (5)

3 a) Is a human being an ectotherm or an endotherm? (1)

   b) Explain your answer. (1)

4 a) By what means does the hypothalamus in a mammal obtain information about the internal temperature of the body? (2)

   b) Name TWO effectors to which the hypothalamus sends nerve impulses when the body temperature decreases to below a normal level. (2)

13 Metabolism and adverse conditions

In some environments the extreme heat and drought of summer, and in others, the extreme cold and lack of food in winter, create conditions that are **beyond the tolerable limits** of an animal's normal metabolic rate. Homeostatic systems of control would break down when the animal's body could no longer generate enough energy to effect the corrective mechanisms needed to return it to its steady state. However, these cyclic seasonal fluctuations rarely prove to be fatal because animals are either adapted to **survive** them or are able to **avoid** them.

Surviving adverse conditions

A reduction in metabolic rate enables an organism to avoid expending excessive quantities of energy trying to stay warm in an extremely cold climate or to stay cool in an extremely hot one. This can be achieved by a period of **dormancy**.

Research Topic	Aspects of surviving adverse conditions

As a result of millions of years of evolution and natural selection, living organisms have become adapted to life in their particular ecosystem. If the ecosystem is affected by extreme fluctuations in climate or unpredictable environmental changes, then the organisms possess **adaptations** which enable them to survive the adverse conditions. These adaptations fall into three categories:

- **structural** (involving specialised structures possessed by the organism)

- **physiological** (depending on ways in which the organism's body and metabolism operate)

- **behavioural** (depending on the ways in which the organism responds to stimuli).

The discussion that follows considers these with reference to animals surviving adverse conditions in a cold climate.

Structural

Body size

The body size of birds and mammals tends to be larger in colder climates because a larger body size has a relatively smaller surface area from which heat energy can be lost (see Figure 13.1).

Appendages

Body appendages tend to be smaller in colder regions. For example, an Arctic fox (see Figure 13.2) possesses small ear flaps (pinnae) therefore exposing only a

breeding ground	average body length (mm)
Greenland	320
Norway	300
United Kingdom	290

Figure 13.1 Body size in puffins

Figure 13.2 Pinna size in Arctic and African foxes

small surface area to potential heat loss. On the other hand, an African bat-eared fox has large pinnae which promote heat loss in a hot climate. The legs and snouts of mammals are frequently shorter and stouter in colder regions to conserve heat energy.

Insulation

A layer of air (a poor conductor of heat) trapped by fur or feathers provides an animal with good insulation by cutting down loss of heat from its body core.

Colour of fur or plumage

Many mammals and birds undergo seasonal changes in their fur or feathers. For example, the hare and the ptarmigan (see Figure 13.3) change from brown to white in winter. Not only does the white colour serve as an effective camouflage against a background of snow, it also reduces heat loss from the animal's body since a

Figure 13.3 Ptarmigan in snow

lighter-coloured object radiates less heat than a darker one.

Physiological

Many organisms survive adverse cold conditions by spending part of their life cycle in a dormant state. During this time metabolic activity decreases to a minimum thereby conserving energy. In birds and mammals, specialised brown fat, produced and stored during the food-rich seasons of the year, is used as fuel. In addition to **hibernation** (see page 177), some additional forms of dormancy occur among animals as follows.

Diapause

This is commonly found in insects. It is a period during which growth and development are suspended and metabolism decreased. It is induced by certain stimuli (such as decreasing day lengths) and normally lasts from autumn until spring.

Brumation

This is a form of dormancy similar to hibernation found in 'cold-blooded' animals such as reptiles. Unlike hibernating mammals, brumating reptiles are not fully asleep and need to become active at times to drink water.

Behavioural

Collective den

Some mammals that are non-colonial during mild weather share a collective den in winter. This helps →

to reduce loss of heat from their body core by reducing the surface area exposed to the external environment.

Snow roost

Some types of grouse survive periods of extreme cold by resting in groups under the snow in a 'snow roost'.

Migration

Many animals avoid the adverse conditions of winter by migrating to warmer climes (see page 178).

Dormancy

Dormancy occurs as part of an organism's life cycle when its growth and development are temporarily arrested. The organism's **metabolic rate decreases** to the minimum needed to keep its cells alive. Therefore energy is conserved and the plant or animal is able to survive a period of adverse conditions such as winter cold, summer drought or scarcity of food.

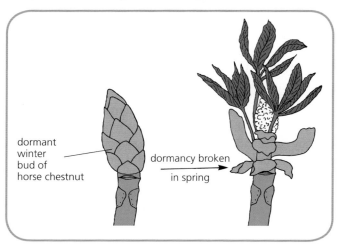

Figure 13.4 Dormant winter bud

Predictive dormancy

When an organism becomes dormant *before* the arrival of the adverse conditions, this is called **predictive dormancy**. For example, many trees respond to decreasing photoperiod (day length) and temperature in autumn by shedding their leaves and entering their dormant phase before the onset of winter. Their **winter buds** remain dormant until the spring (see Figure 13.4). Then the period of arrested growth and development is brought to a halt by the arrival of increasing day lengths and the action of plant growth substances.

Consequential dormancy

When an organism becomes dormant *after* the arrival of adverse conditions, this is called **consequential dormancy**. It is more common in regions where the climate is unpredictable. The advantage of consequential dormancy is that the organism can remain active for longer and continue to exploit available resources. However, a sudden, severe change in environmental conditions may kill off many organisms before they have had time to become dormant.

Related Activity

Seed dormancy

A dormant seed is one that fails to germinate when supplied with water, oxygen and a suitable temperature. Some forms of dormancy are caused by a **physical barrier** around the embryo. The seed coat, for example, may be thick and prevent the entry of water. This type of dormancy is only broken naturally after a long period in the soil during which micro-organisms decompose the seed coat. The dormancy can be broken artificially by cutting or weakening the seed coats. It is for this reason that machine-threshed legume seeds show a higher percentage of

germination than those that have been harvested by hand.

Inhibitors

Some forms of dormancy depend on **chemical inhibitors** to prevent the embryo from growing. Many desert plants survive drought for long periods as dormant seeds whose contents are in a highly desiccated, and almost completely inactive, state. When the short rainy season arrives the seeds germinate and grow into plants which quickly flower and produce seeds. These survive the next period of drought in a dormant state. The seeds do not germinate in response to a brief shower of rain but only to several centimetres of water which have passed down through the soil and dissolved the inhibitors in their seed coats. This is of survival value because if the seeds germinated in response to a light shower they would quickly die of dehydration.

The dormancy of some other types of seed is broken by a period of up to three months of cold conditions (for example below 4°C) which brings production of inhibitors in the seed to a halt allowing the embryo to grow and the seed to germinate. This type of dormancy is of survival value because it ensures that the seeds germinate in spring with a long period of mild weather ahead of them and not in autumn with the adverse conditions of winter about to arrive.

Related Activity

Seed dormancy experiments

Investigating the effect of scarification on dormant clover seeds

Scarification is the process by which the outer surface of a seed is scratched or worn down. In the experiment shown in Figure 13.5, the seeds have been rubbed with abrasive paper (such as emery paper) to break down their hard coats. From the results of the experiment it is concluded that scarification breaks the dormancy of clover seeds.

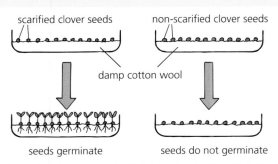

Figure 13.5 Effect of scarification on seed dormancy

Investigating the effect of low temperature on dormant apple seeds

The experiment is set up as shown in Figure 13.6. From the results it is concluded that a long period of cold conditions breaks the dormancy of apple seeds.

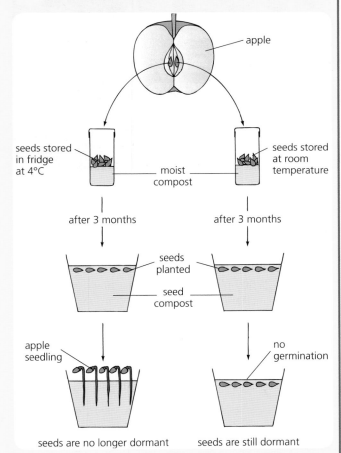

Figure 13.6 Investigating dormancy in apple seeds

Research Topic Seed banks

Storing seeds in a **seed bank** (see Figure 13.7) is a method of protecting potentially valuable species such as:

- food crops and their wild relatives
- plants with possible medicinal properties
- rare species threatened with extinction.

Figure 13.7 Seed bank

There are over 1300 seed banks worldwide which store around 6 million different seed types. One of these banks is the Millennium Seed Bank Project managed by the Royal Botanic Gardens at Kew, UK. Its aim is to safeguard 24 000 plant species from around the world against extinction. Another seed bank in Norway has been built 20 metres deep inside a mountain on an Arctic island. This site is permanently frozen and high enough to remain unaffected by any future rise in sea level. The bank's aim is to store seeds of **every food crop** from every country in the world.

The seeds in a seed bank are kept in conditions of **low temperature and humidity** to maintain their dormancy. Before seeds can be put into long-term storage, they must be assessed to **determine their response** to cold, dry conditions. Seeds that can tolerate these conditions and remain **viable** for many years are described as **orthodox** (desiccation-tolerant); those that are damaged by dry conditions and sub-zero temperatures are described as being **recalcitrant** (desiccation-intolerant). Seed banks are not suitable for storing species with recalcitrant seeds. Instead they can be conserved as a living collection but this requires space, maintenance work and protective measures against disease.

Practicalities of maintaining viable stocks

Orthodox seeds can be stored in a seed bank. Following collection and cleaning, a sample of the seeds is allowed to germinate to establish that at least 75% of the seeds are viable. The remaining seeds are dried to a moisture content of below 7%. Then they are sealed in moisture-proof containers (such as laminated foil bags, aluminium cans or glass jars) and stored at a low temperature ($-18\,^{\circ}$C) in sealed plastic boxes containing a drying agent. However, that is not the end of the matter.

The DNA in seeds degrades with time therefore the success of long-term conservation depends on **regular monitoring** of the seeds' viability. This involves periodic germination tests (normally on plain agar for evidence of root growth). When this drops below 75%, a new supply of seeds is required. New seeds may be obtained by planting the existing stock and growing them to flowering in a glasshouse or, better still, by collecting a new sample from the natural plant population, if it still exists. The batch of new seeds is then stored as before.

In addition to carrying out the above procedure, it is essential that the seed bank staff keep **accurate records** on a central database. This documentation normally includes information such as:

- identity of plant stored
- original location of sampling
- number of seeds stored
- viability level
- farming systems (such as rotation) in which the crop was grown.

If these data are unavailable, the seeds may not be requested for use in future plant improvement programmes.

The future

Experts forecast that global temperatures will rise by 3 °C in the next 50 years as a result of an increase in the 'Greenhouse Effect' (see page 329). If this occurs many of today's crops may fail in the warmer climate. However, it is not possible to store every variety of every species as a safeguard. Priority is being given to wild, **drought-resistant** relatives of **cereals** and **leguminous** plants which form **root nodules** containing nitrogen-fixing bacteria. It is hoped that it will be possible in the future to use the seeds stored in seed banks to develop new varieties able to survive global warming.

Dormancy in animals

Two examples of dormancy in animals are hibernation and aestivation.

Hibernation

Hibernation (or 'winter sleep') is a form of dormancy that enables some animals (usually mammals) to survive the adverse conditions of winter. It may last for weeks or even months. Before hibernating (often in a predictive way in response to shortening day length) the endothermic animal consumes extra food which becomes laid down as a **store of fat**.

During hibernation, the animal's **rate of metabolism drops** and this results in a **decrease in body temperature**. These changes are accompanied by a **slower heart rate**, a **slower breathing rate** and a state of general inactivity where the bare minimum of energy is expended to maintain the vital activities of cells. Together, these changes enable the animal (for example the hedgehog, as shown in Figure 13.8) to survive a prolonged period of low temperature in its surroundings. If, however, the external temperature drops too far, the hibernator will increase its metabolic rate slightly to prevent a fatal drop in body temperature.

Bears do not go into true, deep hibernation. The decrease in their metabolic rate is significant but less than that shown by smaller mammals such as the hedgehog. As a result, the bear's body temperature drops from 37 °C to around 31 °C and it can be aroused fairly easily. In contrast, the hedgehog's body temperature drops to around 6 °C and it cannot be wakened easily.

Aestivation

Aestivation (or 'summer sleep') is a form of dormancy employed by some animals to survive periods of excessive heat and drought in summer. For example, during a period of intense heat, a land snail seeks out a safe place (such as a spot high up in vegetation). It then retreats into its shell and the opening becomes sealed with dried mucus except for a tiny hole to allow gas exchange. The snail remains in this state with its **metabolic rate at a minimum level** until favourable conditions return.

Aestivation is also found to occur among vertebrates such as tortoises, crocodiles and lungfish. A lungfish (see Figure 13.9) buries itself in the mud of a dried-up lake and surrounds itself with a cocoon of dried mucus. It exchanges gases through a breathing tube and remains in a dormant state for many months until the arrival of the next rainy season.

Figure 13.9 Lungfish

Daily torpor

Daily torpor is the physiological state in which an animal's rate of metabolism and activity become greatly reduced for part of **every 24-hour cycle**. It is accompanied by a slowing down of heart rate and breathing rate and a decrease in body temperature. It is common among small birds and mammals.

Figure 13.8 Hibernating hedgehog

Hummingbirds (see Figure 13.10), for example, feed during the day and exhibit torpor at night; bats and shrews feed at night and become torpid during daylight hours. A small animal has a relatively **large surface area** from which heat is lost rapidly. Therefore when the animal is an active endotherm, it needs a very high rate of metabolism to maintain its body temperature. A daily period of torpor is of survival value to such an animal because it greatly **decreases the rate of energy consumption** during the time when searching for food would be unsuccessful or would leave the animal open to danger.

Figure 13.10 Hummingbird

Testing Your Knowledge 1

1 Give an example of a set of environmental conditions that would be beyond the tolerable limits for *normal* metabolic activity in a hedgehog. (1)

2 a) Identify
   i) a physiological
   ii) a structural
   characteristic typical of a deciduous tree during its period of dormancy. (2)

   b) Explain the difference between *predictive* and *consequential* dormancy. (2)

   c) **i)** Which type of dormancy is shown by deciduous trees?
   ii) Explain your answer. (2)

3 a) *Hibernation* and *aestivation* are forms of dormancy.
   i) Identify a characteristic they have in common.
   ii) Identify a characteristic by which they differ. (2)

   b) With reference to a named animal, explain the meaning of *daily torpor* and its importance to the animal. (2)

Migration

Migration is the regular movement by the members of a species from one place to another over a relatively long distance. By migrating to a favourable environment, an animal is able to avoid the conditions of metabolic **adversity** caused by shortage of food and low temperatures. Long-distance migration is carried out by many vertebrates and a few invertebrates. It normally involves an **annual round trip** between two regions, each of which offers conditions more favourable than the other for part of the year.

Birds

Some migratory birds such as the Arctic skua move all the way from one hemisphere of the world to the other. Figure 13.11 shows the migratory routes which it takes in autumn. It returns by the same route in spring. Other birds such as the yellow wagtail cover less distance by simply migrating from a temperate region to a tropical one within the same hemisphere.

Mammals

Many species of whale migrate. For example humpbacks spend the summer in polar regions where they gorge on plankton and build up a layer of blubber. At the start of winter they migrate up to 7 000 kilometres to subtropical waters where the females give birth and suckle their young. Although food for adults may be scarce in subtropical waters, the warm conditions suit the young whose small bodies would lose too much heat in polar regions.

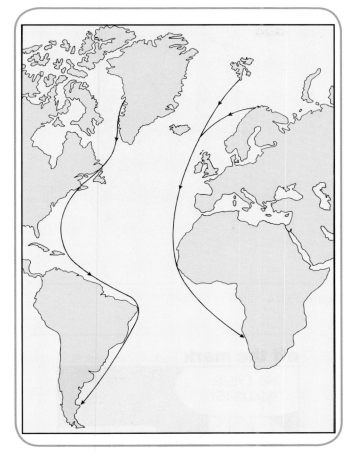

Figure 13.11 Migratory routes of Arctic skua in autumn

Invertebrates

Each spring, millions of Monarch butterflies migrate north from their winter territories in Mexico to their breeding areas in the USA and Canada. These areas contain abundant supplies of their exclusive food source – the milkweed plant. In autumn the butterflies migrate back to Mexico to avoid the cold winter conditions of northern regions. A Monarch butterfly only lives for a short time, so the butterflies that are found heading for Mexico are 3–5 generations removed from the ones that overwintered there the previous year. Somehow the information needed for successful migration has been passed on from generation to generation.

Specialised techniques

When studying long-distance migration, scientists want to find out information such as:

- when the animals migrated
- where they overwintered
- whether or not they **returned** to their original summer territory
- how long they lived for.

Many migratory animals travel thousands of miles which makes it very difficult to follow their route in detail. However, scientists have developed **specialised techniques** to overcome these difficulties.

Individual marking

Ringing with metal bands

This **ringing** technique (also known as **banding**) has been used ever since the beginning of scientific investigation into migration. A metal band (carrying the bird's unique number and the investigators' contact details) is attached to the bird's leg (see Figure 13.12). If the bird is recaptured and its information reported, then this record of its movements **contributes to an overall picture** of the migratory behaviour of the species. Details of the migratory flyways used by many species of birds have been built up over the years from information obtained in this way both inside and outside the country of the ring's origin.

Figure 13.12 Bird with leg band

Tagging

A small circular tag is attached to the underside of the hind wing of a Monarch butterfly (see Figure 13.13). This carries a code entered in a database. If the tag is recovered at a later date, the **route and distance** covered by the butterfly can be determined.

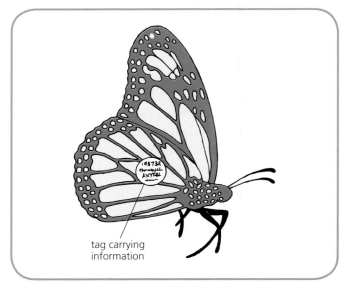

Figure 13.13 Tag on Monarch butterfly

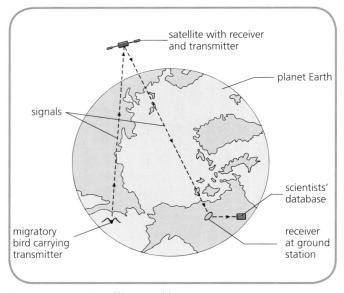

Figure 13.14 Satellite tracking

Colour marking

In recent years, the use of bright **coloured marks** (and **flags** on larger birds) has enabled scientists to observe the birds with binoculars without needing to recapture them. Individuals and their original locations can be identified using a combination of colours.

Tracking using transmitters

More recently lightweight **transmitters** have been developed that can be glued to the animal's body or implanted under its skin. The transmitter emits signals that are picked up by receivers on Earth-orbiting satellites as they pass overhead. The signals are beamed back to ground stations and the information relayed to scientists (see Figures 13.14 and 13.15). This technique of **tracking** an animal's route from space has yielded the most precise information so far on the exact location of flyways used by birds during their migratory cycle. It has also been used successfully to track several mammals including whales and seals.

Unlike a ringed animal, one bearing a 'high-tech' transmitter does not have to be recaptured to provide scientists with data. However, transmitters are much more expensive than 'low-tech' rings and may have a drag effect on some small birds.

Figure 13.15 Cat heaven

Migration triggers and adaptations

Photoperiod

Many experiments have been carried out on birds to investigate the effect of altering the length of the **photoperiod** (day length) on their migratory behaviour. One of these involved the indigo bunting, a bird that spends the summer in Eastern USA. It migrates nocturnally in autumn to overwinter in Central America and migrates back nocturnally in spring to Eastern USA for the summer. Under normal circumstances, prior to migration, the bird eats extra food, stores fat and becomes restless at night. Table 13.1 gives a summary of the experiment.

From this experiment it is concluded that in indigo bunting birds, the changes that occur prior to migration are triggered by changes in the photoperiod as summarised in Figure 13.16.

It is now known that **changing photoperiod** is the primary **trigger** for migration in many birds. It causes hormonal changes in the bird's body which result in the behavioural changes (such as night-time restlessness) and physiological changes (including storage of fat) that occur in preparation for migration. Decreasing environmental temperature may, in some cases, play a secondary role but length of photoperiod is a much more **reliable indicator** of time of year.

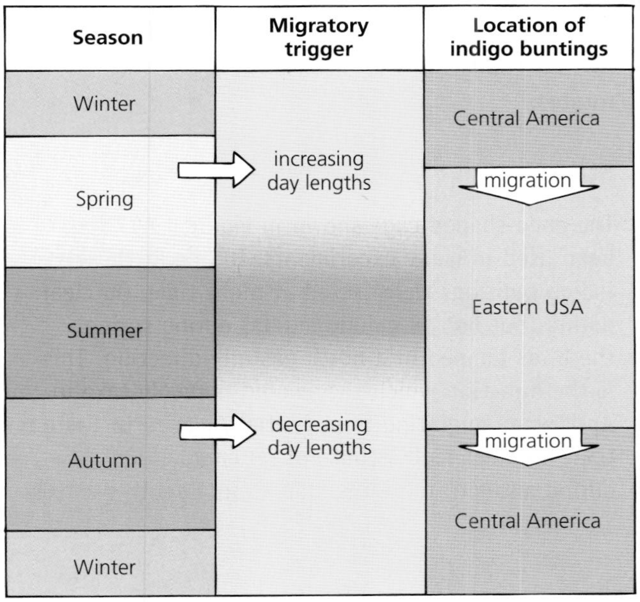

Sun

Many experiments have been carried out to investigate whether birds make use of the **Sun** as a **compass** to locate the **correct direction** in which to migrate. In one of these experiments, the importance of sunset as an indicator of direction for autumn migration was investigated using cone-shaped, funnel cages. These are lined with white blotting paper and each has an ink pad at its base as shown in Figure 13.17. If the bird tries to move in a particular direction, it leaves a tell-tale trail of inky footprints on the paper.

Season	Migratory trigger	Location of indigo buntings
Winter		Central America
Spring	increasing day lengths	migration
Summer		Eastern USA
Autumn	decreasing day lengths	migration
Winter		Central America

Figure 13.16 Triggers for migration

Group	Treatment in laboratory	Result
A	Birds exposed to normal day lengths from September to April.	When day length increased in spring, the birds binged on food and laid down a store of fat. In April they showed night-time restlessness.
B	Birds exposed to normal day lengths from September to December and then given artificially longer 'spring' day lengths in December.	The birds binged on food and laid down a store of fat. They then showed night-time restlessness.
C	Birds exposed to normal day lengths from September to March and then given artificially shorter 'autumn' day lengths in March.	The birds binged on food and laid down a store of fat. They then showed night-time restlessness.
D	Birds exposed to photoperiods of constant medium length.	The birds did not binge on food, store fat or become restless at night.

Table 13.1 Investigating effect of photoperiod on migratory behaviour

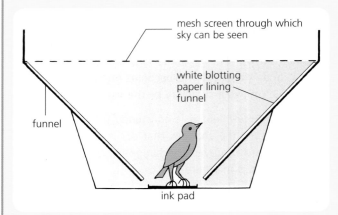

Figure 13.17 Funnel-cage experiment

Tests were conducted on sparrows during autumn under the following set of conditions:

- birds placed in cages at sunset under a clear sky (group A)

- birds placed in cages at sunset under a cloudy sky (group B)

- birds placed in cages after sunset under a clear sky (group C).

Figure 13.18 shows a typical footprint record for each condition and the resulting vector diagram. (A vector diagram gives a quantified version of the footprints.) The results for group A show a southerly trend in choice of direction. For B and C there is no

clear-cut directional choice. Therefore it is concluded that for sparrows, sunset is an important **visual cue** used in their autumnal migration to locate the direction to take. Other similar experiments show that if the perceived position of sunset is altered by using mirrors, then the direction chosen by the birds changes accordingly.

Internal clock

Many migratory animals make use of an **internal clock**. In an experiment where the only light source (acting as the Sun) was held in one position constantly, starlings were found to continue to change their angle of orientation by 15° per hour. This is their normal response in order to compensate for the change in the Sun's position as the Earth rotates.

Stars

The cone-shaped cage shown in Figure 13.17 has been used in many experiments. In one of these, indigo buntings were tested at night time. On clear nights (but not on cloudy nights) during spring, the birds jumped in a north-easterly direction. This is the direction which they would normally take in April when migrating from Central America to Eastern USA. On clear nights (but not on cloudy nights) during autumn, the birds jumped in a south-westerly

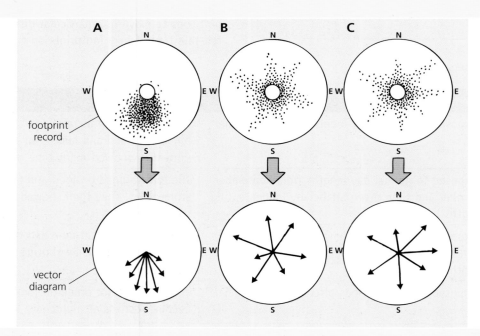

Figure 13.18 Results from an ink pad experiment

direction. This is the direction which they would normally take in September when migrating from Eastern USA to Central America.

The experiment was continued in a planetarium where results similar to those obtained for clear nights were obtained using an artificial, starry sky. In addition, it was possible to identify particular **patterns of stars** to which the birds were responding by shutting off various sections of the 'sky'. It was concluded that these birds possess a built-in **genetic mechanism** that makes them head in a particular direction in response to certain star patterns.

Magnetic field

Although many visual clues are used by birds for navigation, experiments with pigeons suggest that their navigational system also contains **non-visual components**. Out of a large group of pigeons released wearing frosted contact lenses, 60% were able to find their way home.

Experiments have also been carried out in which the birds have been subjected to **altered magnetic fields**. In one of these, bar magnets were attached to the backs of a group of pigeons and brass bars to those of the control group. During sunny conditions all the pigeons returned home quickly but on a cloudy day the 'magnet' birds, unlike the 'brass-bar' birds, became disorientated and many lost their way.

It is thought that homing pigeons and some long-distance migrants may use a **combination of navigational devices** including sun compasses and magnetic compasses. The latter are thought to enable the bird to sense changes in the Earth's **magnetic field**. Recent research indicates a connection between the eye and a part of the brain that is active during navigation, and suggests that some birds may actually 'see' the Earth's magnetic field. It is thought that this may appear as areas of light and shade superimposed on the normal images that the bird sees. Monarch butterflies are also thought to use some form of magnetic orientation to find their way during migration.

Innate and learned influences on migratory behaviour

Innate behaviour is inherited and inflexible. Innate influences are thought to play the primary role in migratory behaviour. This pattern of behaviour is performed in the same way by every member of the species. It occurs in response to an external stimulus such as a change in photoperiod.

Learned behaviour begins after birth and is gained by experience. It is flexible and occurs as a result of trial and error and the transmission of knowledge and skills among the members of a social group. Learned influences are thought to play a secondary role in migratory behaviour.

Displacement experiment

Starlings normally migrate from Eastern Europe to Northern France in autumn. An experiment was designed to investigate the effect of displacement on starlings. A large number of migratory birds were captured using fine netting in Holland and taken to Switzerland where they were released (see Figure 13.19).

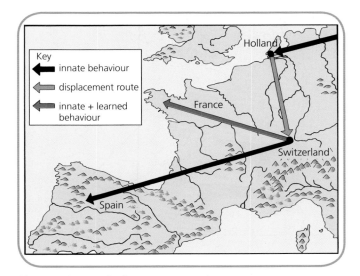

Figure 13.19 Displacement experiment

Adult birds that had migrated at least once before compensated for the displacement and arrived at the correct destination in France. Young, inexperienced birds failed to compensate and, on release, continued in the direction in which they had been travelling. As a result, they arrived in Spain instead of France.

It is concluded from this experiment that the migratory behaviour of the adult birds was based on a combination of both **innate and learned** influences. They made use of knowledge (gained from previous journeys) of familiar geographical features along the route to navigate their way to the correct location. On the other hand, the migratory behaviour of the young birds was **purely innate**. They possessed genetic information about the direction of the destination but had no previously learned information about its actual location that they could put to use.

Investigating directional tendencies

Figure 13.20 shows the **flight paths** taken by two distinct populations (A and B) of blackcap warbler birds during their autumn migration. Members of population A (in part of Germany) always head south-west; members of group B (in part of Austria) always head south-east and then south. An experiment was designed to investigate whether this behaviour is innate or learned.

Nestlings from both populations were hand-reared and then their orientation tested using funnel cages

(see Figure 13.17). Figure 13.21 shows the results. The directional choices made by the members of each test group (as indicated by the ink marks on the walls of the cages) corresponded to the actual direction of the flight path typical of their population of origin.

These results suggest that the young birds possess genetic information about the direction in which they are to migrate and that heading in this direction is a form of **innate** behaviour.

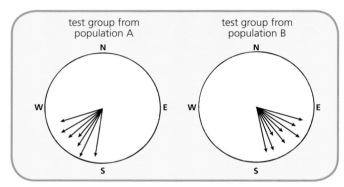

Figure 13.21 Vector diagrams of directional choice

Cross-fostering experiment

Herring gulls are non-migratory; lesser black-backed gulls are migratory. In an experiment, their eggs were switched round and the migratory behaviour of the 'fostered' offspring studied.

The black-backed gulls raised by the non-migratory herring gulls did migrate, supporting the idea of migration being **innate** behaviour. The herring gulls raised by the black-backed gulls did move with their migratory foster parents. They were thought to be simply following their foster parents and to be exhibiting learned behaviour.

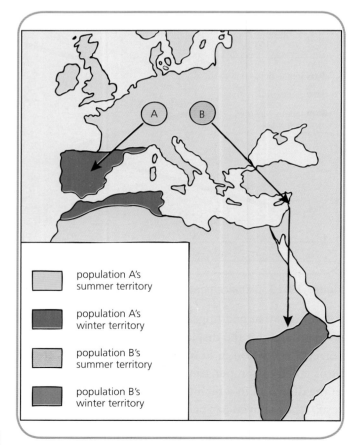

population A's summer territory

population A's winter territory

population B's summer territory

population B's winter territory

Figure 13.20 Two migratory flight paths

In an investigation, scientists chose six genes from the blackcap, a common European bird, as possible candidates for a 'migration gene'. These genes were known to influence behavioural traits linked to migration such as increased metabolism and level of night-time restlessness.

The scientists sampled the DNA of 14 populations of blackcap ranging from those in the Cape Verde Islands in the Atlantic Ocean that never migrate to those in Russia that travel over 3500 kilometres during migration. They found a link between one of the six genes (called ADCYAP1) and a certain form of behaviour. Different versions of this gene exist. They vary in the number of copies of a two-base repeat that they possess at one end of the genetic sequence. The greatest number of two-base repeats was found to match the highest level of night-time restlessness and the longest distance travelled during migration.

The ADCYAP1 gene codes for a peptide which influences daily rhythms and affects rate of metabolism and usage of fat – changes associated with preparations for migration. Scientists attribute about 3% of migratory behaviour to this gene. Clearly many other genes are also involved, in conjunction with the influence of environmental factors.

Extremophiles

Most **extremophiles** belong to the domain archaea. They are organisms which live in extreme conditions that would be lethal to most other living things. Extreme **thermophiles**, for example, thrive at high temperatures (such as 50–80 °C) and live in environments such as hot springs and hydrothermal vents in the seabed. They are able to survive in such extreme conditions because they possess **unusual enzymes** that function best at high temperatures.

Some of these enzymes have been put to use by scientists. For example, **heat-tolerant DNA polymerase** is used in the polymerase chain reaction (see page 22).

Many thermophiles that thrive in hot springs or deep-water vents have a unique form of energy metabolism. They are able to remove the high-energy electrons needed to generate ATP from **inorganic** molecules such as hydrogen sulphide (H_2S).

Table 13.2 gives some examples of extremophiles.

Extremophile	Extreme conditions in which organism thrives
acidophile	pH levels of 3 or less
alkaliphile	pH levels of 9 or more
cryophile	temperatures as low as -15 °C
halophile	salt solution of concentration of at least 0.2 M
hyperthermophile	temperatures between 80 °C and 120 °C
osmophile	presence of high concentration of sugar
piezophile	presence of high hydrostatic pressure
xerophile	extremely dry, desert-like conditions

Table 13.2 Extremophiles

Research Topic | Methanogens and sulphur bacteria

Methanogens

The **methanogens** make up a group of obligate anaerobic micro-organisms that belong to the domain archaea. They make use of carbon dioxide as their source of carbon and use hydrogen to change the CO_2 to **methane** (CH_4) thereby generating ATP. Methane gas is a by-product of their unusual metabolism which is summarised in the following equation:

$$CO_2 + 4H_2 \rightarrow CH_4 + 2H_2O$$

Methanogens are poisoned by the presence of oxygen and many thrive in environments such as swamps where other micro-organisms have depleted the oxygen supply. The methane released by the methanogens in these locations is called swamp gas. Other methanogens live in the guts of ruminants where they play a part in the digestion of cellulose (see page 293).

Sulphur bacteria

Purple and green **sulphur bacteria** (see Figure 13.22) are two groups of micro-organisms which contain bacteriochlorophyll. This enables them to trap light energy and carry out photosynthesis. Whereas green plants use water as an electron donor and produce oxygen, sulphur bacteria use **hydrogen sulphide** (H_2S) as their electron donor and produce tiny granules of sulphur. These are often deposited outside the cell.

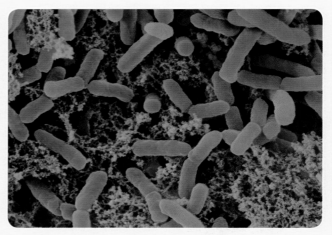

Figure 13.22 Sulphur bacteria

The chemical reaction is summarised in the following equation:

$$CO_2 + 2H_2S \rightarrow (CH_2O) + H_2O + 2S$$
$$\text{carbohydrate}$$

Purple sulphur bacteria thrive in illuminated aquatic environments lacking oxygen but rich in hydrogen sulphide such as sulphur springs. Green sulphur bacteria are found in sulphide-rich anaerobic conditions such as the mud in a lake.

Testing Your Knowledge 2

1 a) With reference to a named bird, explain what the term *migration* means. (2)

   b) In what way does the bird gain from migration considering that the process requires much energy to be expended? (1)

2 a) Identify TWO methods used to mark migratory animals. (2)

   b) Construct a flow chart of the events involved in the use of transmitters to track migratory animals. (3)

3 What is the difference between *innate* and *learned* behaviour? (2)

4 a) In general what is meant by the term *extremophile*? (1)

   b) Explain how a thermophile can survive at temperatures between 50 °C and 80 °C. (1)

What You Should Know

Chapters 11–13
(See Table 13.3 for word bank)

adaptations	external	migrating
aestivation	extremophiles	mixing
altitude	feedback	narrow
alveoli	fitness	niches
ATP	geological	optimum
avoid	heat-tolerant	oxygen
bellows	hibernation	parabronchi
body	high	physiological
carbon dioxide	homeostasis	predictive
collapse	hypothalamus	pressure
conformers	innate	probes
consequential	internal	regulators
deoxygenated	large-sized	temperature
dormancy	lungs	thermoregulation
drought	maximum	torpor
effectors	metabolic	tracking
electrons	metabolism	uptake

Table 13.3 Word bank for chapters 11–13

1 _____ rate is a measure of the quantity of energy consumed by an organism per unit of time. It can be measured as oxygen consumption, _____ production or heat production per unit time by using electronic _____.

2 Aerobic respiration consumes _____. Therefore aerobic organisms with high rates of _____ need systems that can deliver oxygen efficiently to cells.

3 Fish have a two-chambered heart which pumps blood at _____ pressure to the gills. Blood leaving the gills is transported to the _____ at low pressure. Amphibians and reptiles have a three-chambered heart which pumps blood at high pressure to both the _____ and the body but allows some mixing of oxygenated and _____ blood. Birds and mammals have a four-chambered heart which pumps blood at high _____ to both the lungs and the body with no _____ of blood.

4 Terrestrial vertebrates other than birds have lungs containing tiny air sacs called _____ where gas exchange occurs. Birds possess lungs containing channels called _____ which communicate with large air sacs outside the lungs. These sacs act

as _____ giving the very efficient gas exchange needed to obtain enough oxygen to generate energy for flight.

5 Some organisms possess _____ adaptations to survive in low-oxygen niches. People living at high _____ have a higher red blood cell count than those at sea level. Deep-diving mammals have lungs designed to _____ as hydrostatic pressure increases.

6 The _____ volume of oxygen that an individual's body can take up during intense incremental exercise is called maximum oxygen _____. It is used as a measure of _____.

7 When fluctuations in an external abiotic factor occur, some organisms called _____ are able to maintain their steady _____ state by using physiological mechanisms. This increases their range of possible ecological _____ but it requires energy. Other organisms, called _____, are unable to maintain their metabolic rate in this way and the state of their internal environment is influenced directly by changes in the _____ environment. Their range of ecological niches is _____ but their metabolic costs are low.

8 The maintenance of the body's internal environment within certain tolerable limits is called _____ and it requires energy. It is brought about by corrective mechanisms called negative _____ control.

9 Birds and mammals are able to maintain their body temperature at the _____ level for enzyme action. Such _____ keeps their metabolism at a high level regardless of low external _____.

10 The body's temperature-monitoring centre is in the _____. It sends nerve impulses to _____ which respond by bringing about changes that warm up or cool down the body as required. In extremely adverse conditions, these responses are inadequate and the organism needs to have further _____ which enable it to survive the conditions or to _____ them. One of these is reduction in metabolic rate during _____.

11 An organism that becomes dormant before the arrival of adverse conditions shows _____ dormancy; one that becomes dormant after their arrival shows _____ dormancy.

12 _____ is a form of dormancy that involves a decrease in metabolism and body temperature that enables an animal to survive a period of extreme cold; _____ is a form of dormancy that enables an animal to survive a period of intense heat or _____. Daily _____ is a period of decreased metabolism for part of each 24-hour cycle.

13 Some animals avoid adverse conditions by _____ to a more suitable environment for part of the year. Patterns of long-distance migration are studied using individual marking and _____ of animals.

Migration is basically a form of _____ behaviour but some aspects of it may be learned.

14 Organisms that live in extreme conditions that would be lethal to most other living things are called _____.

15 Thermophiles have unusual enzymes such as _____ DNA polymerase used in PCR. Some extremophiles are able to remove the high-energy _____ needed to generate _____ from inorganic molecules.

14 Environmental control of metabolism

An enormous variety of micro-organisms exist on Earth. Some are prokaryotes that take the form of **bacteria** (such as *Escherichia coli*) and **archaea** (such as thermophiles – see page 185). Others are species of **eukaryotes**. These may be unicellular algae that are able to photosynthesise or unicellular fungi such as yeast (see Figure 14.1) and multicellular filamentous fungi such as *Penicillium* (see Figure 14.2) that need a source of ready-made organic food.

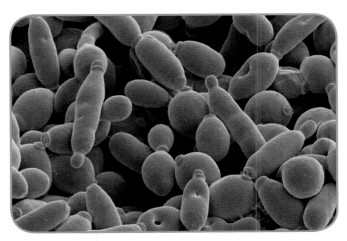

Figure 14.1 Yeast

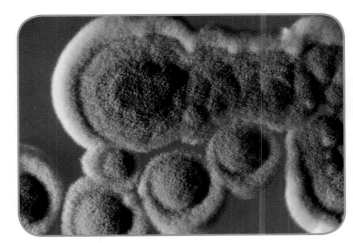

Figure 14.2 *Penicillium* colonies

Adaptability

In general, micro-organisms are **highly adaptable** and able to make use of a wide variety of substrates for their metabolism. Therefore they occur in every environment that supports life. Some can even make use of unusual ecological niches, such as hot sulphurous springs, that would be lethal to any other life form.

Useful products

In the course of their metabolic pathways, micro-organisms make a wide range of **metabolic products**, many of which are useful to humans. Employing micro-organisms to convert raw materials into useful substances dates back thousands of years to ancient times when people discovered gradually how to make products such as bread, beer and wine. In recent times, the use of microbes has escalated to an industrial level which provides humans with many products and services. Micro-organisms are ideal for a variety of **research and industrial uses** because:

- they are easy to cultivate (culture)
- they reproduce and grow quickly
- their food substrate is often a cheap substance (or even a waste product from another source)
- they produce many different useful products
- their metabolism can be manipulated relatively easily.

Environmental control of metabolism

Micro-organisms are of particular use in fermentation industries because their metabolism can be **controlled** much more easily than that of larger organisms. Scientists are able to control specific micro-organisms by manipulation of their environmental conditions during culture and, as a result, ensure optimum yield of a useful product.

Growing micro-organisms

Some micro-organisms, such as unicellular algae, are able to derive energy from light by photosynthesis. However, most micro-organisms used in industry are bacteria and fungi which derive their energy from a chemical substrate. It is to these microbes that the following text refers.

Types of growth media

Micro-organisms are normally grown under controlled conditions in a laboratory either in a liquid medium called broth or on a solid medium called agar jelly to which essential nutrients have been added. The **growth medium** is contained within Petri dishes, flasks or bottles (see Figure 14.3) for small-scale laboratory work

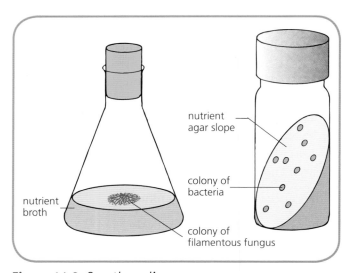

nutrient agar slope

colony of bacteria

nutrient broth

colony of filamentous fungus

Figure 14.3 Growth media

and within huge, stainless-steel fermenters in large, industrial processes.

Culture conditions

The growth of the micro-organism being cultured is affected directly by the chemical composition of its growth medium and by the environmental conditions to which it is exposed.

Chemical composition of growth medium

The microbe requires a supply of an organic compound such as carbohydrate as an **energy source**. It also needs a supply of raw materials to produce cellular building blocks such as amino acids and nucleotides needed in the **biosynthesis** of proteins and nucleic acids for new cells (see Table 14.1). Some micro-organisms can synthesise all of the complex molecules including a full range of amino acids from simple chemicals; others need specific complex compounds such as fatty acids or certain vitamins to be present in their growth medium. In some cases, a growth medium may include a complex non-specific substance such as beef extract.

Environmental conditions

Aseptic techniques are employed in the preparation and transfer of growth medium and the inoculation of the medium with the micro-organism. Every effort is made to keep conditions **sterile** to eliminate contaminants that would affect the growth of the microbe. Use of a fermenter allows a variety of environmental conditions to be monitored and controlled. This is done by computers when industrial-sized fermenters are being used (see page 192).

Chemical requirement	Typical source of chemical	Explanation
carbon	organic compound such as carbohydrate	organic compounds provide the microbe with energy and raw materials for biosynthesis
hydrogen	water and organic compounds	essential component of all organic materials
oxygen	water and air	oxygen is a component of many organic materials and the final electron acceptor in aerobic respiration
nitrogen	compound containing ammonium or nitrate group	nitrogen is needed for the synthesis of nucleic acids, amino acids and proteins
phosphorus	compound containing phosphate group	phosphorus is needed for the synthesis of ATP and nucleic acids
sulphur	compound containing sulphate group	sulphur is needed for the synthesis of some amino acids

Table 14.1 Nutritional requirements of micro-organisms

Effect of nutrients and temperature on growth of *E. coli*

The experiment is carried out as shown in Figure 14.4. From the results it is concluded that *E. coli* requires the presence of essential nutrients in its growth medium and that it grows better at 30 °C than at 20 °C.

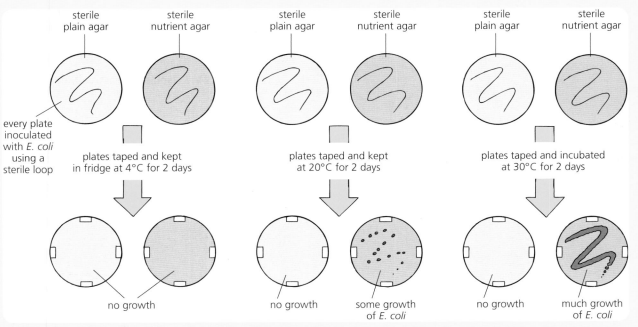

Figure 14.4 Investigating *E. coli*'s growth requirements

Related Activity

Isolation of yeast from grapes

A **selective medium** is designed to suit the growth requirements of a specific micro-organism. Therefore when the medium is inoculated with a mixed culture, it allows only the specific micro-organism to grow on it. Yeast extract peptone dextrose (YPD) agar is a selective medium designed to suit the growth of yeast cells.

Grape 'juice', known to contain a variety of micro-organisms, is prepared for this activity as shown in Figure 14.5. Using aseptic techniques, some of the juice is transferred to several plates of sterile YPD agar and then the juice is **streaked** as shown in Figure 14.6. The plates are then incubated at 30 °C for two days. Figure 14.7 shows the typical appearance of a streaked plate after incubation. Only yeast has grown and the streak method has isolated individual yeast colonies.

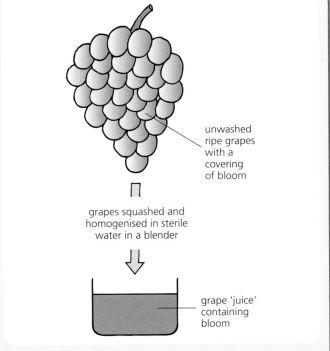

Figure 14.5 Preparation of grape 'juice'

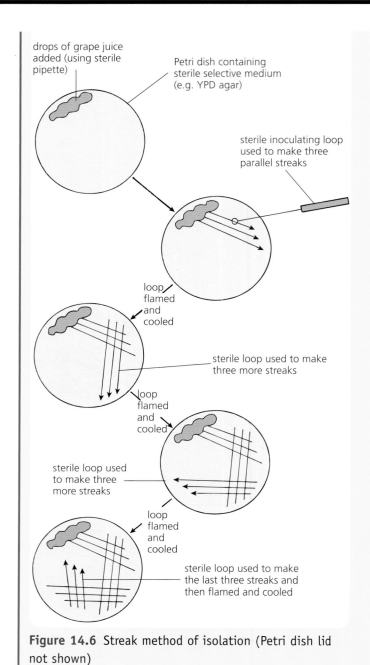

Figure 14.6 Streak method of isolation (Petri dish lid not shown)

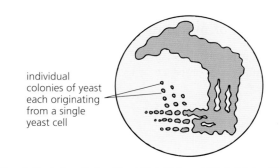

Figure 14.7 Isolated yeast colonies

Computer-controlled fermenter

In the context of industrial microbiology, the term **fermentation** refers to both aerobic and anaerobic processes (and not specifically to anaerobic reactions such as alcohol production). Fermentation industries grow micro-organisms on a vast scale in order to produce huge quantities of a useful product such as an antibiotic. Such commercial production of antibiotics (and other substances such as enzymes,

vaccines and cell metabolites) is made possible by the use of enormous **industrial fermenters** which are often able to hold thousands of litres of nutrient liquid.

Figure 14.8 shows a simplified version of an industrial fermenter being used to grow a fungus. The system is controlled automatically by **computers**. Sensors in contact with the nutrient solution monitor the various conditions that are needed for the best growth of the

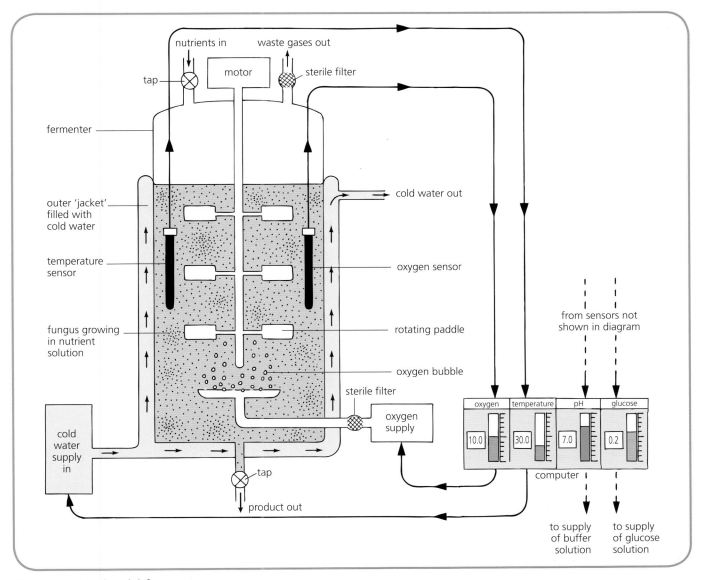

Figure 14.8 Industrial fermenter

micro-organism. Some examples of factors that affect its growth are:

- temperature
- oxygen concentration
- pH
- glucose concentration.

If any of these factors varies from the **optimum level**, the sensor picks up the change and sends information to the computer. The computer responds by communicating with the source of supply of the essential factor. The supply is adjusted accordingly until the required level is restored.

Imagine that the fungus being cultured in the fermenter in Figure 14.8 grows best under the following conditions:

- 30 °C
- 10% oxygen
- pH 7
- 0.2 molar glucose solution.

If the temperature rises above 30 °C then the **temperature sensor** picks up this information and sends it to the computer. The computer then sends out a message which causes an increase in the rate of flow of the cold water cooling system. This continues until the temperature drops back down to 30 °C.

If the growing fungus is using up oxygen so rapidly that the concentration has dropped below 10%, this information is picked up by the **oxygen sensor** and sent to the computer. It then sends out a message that brings

about an increase in supply of oxygen to the fermenter until the level returns to 10%.

Although not shown in Figure 14.8, further sensors for pH and nutrient levels would be monitoring these factors, allowing them to be adjusted as required.

Related Activity

Investigating the growth of yeast using a simple fermenter

The fermenter is set up as shown in Figure 14.9 and maintained at 25 °C. The magnetic stirrer is set at

maximum speed throughout the investigation. Growth is monitored over 4–5 days by sampling the culture medium and taking optical density readings in order to follow changes in **turbidity** (cloudiness) which gives an indication of cell mass.

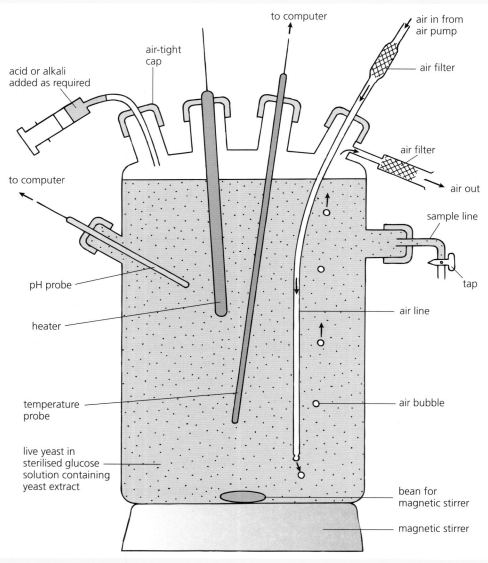

Figure 14.9 Simple fermenter

Monitoring the product

When given constant optimum conditions, the fungus grows rapidly and then produces the product which it normally releases into the surrounding medium. Computer-controlled technology also monitors this release and brings the process to a halt when the required level of antibiotic has been produced. This technology makes the system very efficient because it saves energy and prevents raw materials being wasted.

Testing Your Knowledge 1

1 Identify TWO properties of micro-organisms that make them highly useful for a variety of research and industrial purposes. (2)

2 Nutrient agar and nutrient broth are growth media.
  a) What is the basic difference between the two? (1)
  b) Which would be more likely to be used in an industrial fermenter? (1)

3 a) Explain why a micro-organism needs a supply of:
    i) nitrogen
    ii) phosphorus
    iii) organic compound. (3)
  b) Why must *aseptic conditions* be employed when setting up a culture of micro-organisms? (1)

4 Figure 14.10 shows a simplified version of an industrial fermenter.
  a) Identify THREE types of sensor missing from the diagram. (3)
  b) Match boxes 1–6 with the following answers:
  A products out
  B waste gases out
  C acid in
  D oxygen in
  E cold water in
  F cold water out (6)
  c) i) Identify part X.
    ii) State the function of part Y.
    iii) Of what material would part Z normally be composed? (3)

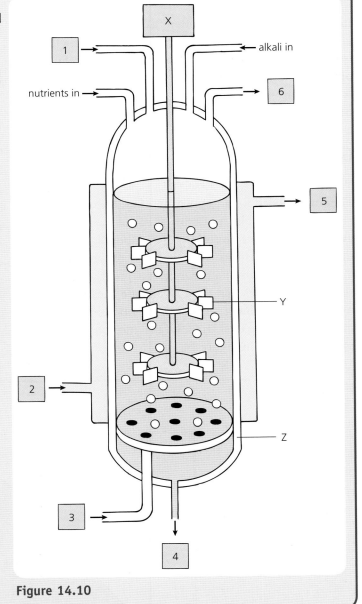

Figure 14.10

Patterns of growth

Dry biomass and fresh biomass

Growth occurs when the rate of synthesis of organic materials by an organism exceeds the rate of their breakdown. Growth involves an **irreversible increase in dry biomass**. Gain in dry biomass is a more reliable indicator of growth than gain in fresh biomass because an organism's fresh biomass varies depending on water availability.

Increase in dry biomass is often used to measure growth of a filamentous fungus. However, this method is less practicable for measuring growth of unicellular organisms. Therefore growth of bacteria and yeast cells is usually investigated by measuring **increase in cell number** over a period of time.

Growth of unicellular organisms

Generation time

The time needed for a population of unicellular organisms to double in number is called the mean **generation time** or **doubling time**. A population of unicellular organisms such as bacteria growing in a liquid medium use up the nutrients provided and secrete metabolites that they have made back into the medium. These changes result in the microbe's **pattern of growth** varying over time. It falls into **four distinct phases** as shown in Figure 14.11.

Lag phase

During the **lag phase** there is little or no increase in cell number. The cells adjust to the growth medium and show increased metabolic activity. They may need to **induce enzymes** for use in metabolising the new substrate(s). This phase is the flat part at the start of the graph.

Log or exponential phase of growth

During the **exponential phase** the cells grow and multiply at the maximum rate, provided that no factor is limiting. This phase is represented by the steep incline on the graph. The population doubles its number with each cell division. For example, the cell number of an organism that has a doubling time of 0.5 hours would increase as indicated in Table 14.2.

The cell number resulting from this phase of growth is so large after a few hours that it becomes difficult to plot accurately all the points (especially the lower values) on a sheet of normal graph paper (see Figure 14.12). One way of solving this problem is to create a scale that doubles in number at each interval on the vertical axis. Figure 14.13 shows how the full range of values in Table 14.2 can be plotted accurately on one sheet of graph paper by this means. In addition, this type of graph can depict an equal rate of growth as a line of equal slope.

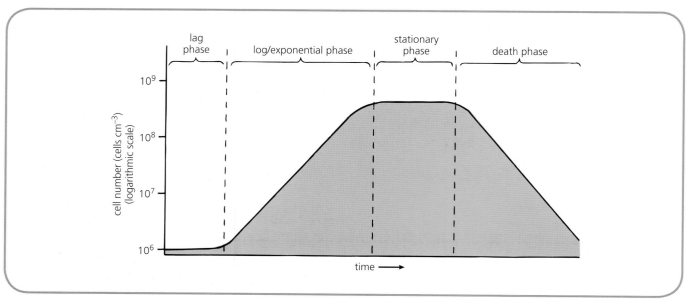

Figure 14.11 Growth pattern of an unicellular culture

Time (h)	Cell number
0.0	1
0.5	2
1.0	4
1.5	8
2.0	16
2.5	32
3.0	64
3.5	128
4.0	256
4.5	512
5.0	1 024
5.5	2 048
6.0	4 096

Table 14.2 Growth of bacteria

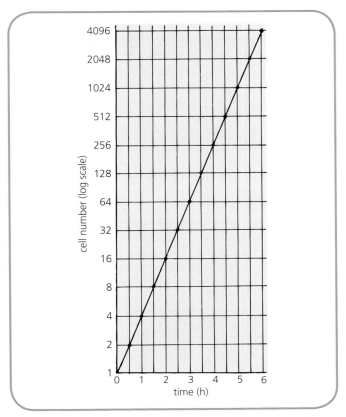

Figure 14.13 Graph with doubling of values on y axis

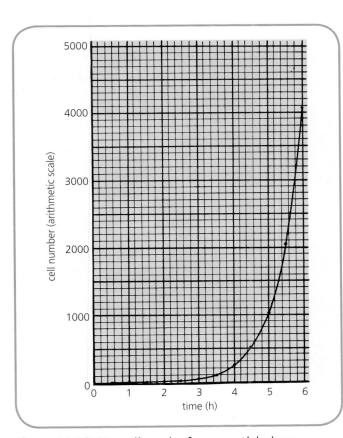

Figure 14.12 'Normal' graph of exponential phase

A similar graph (see Figure 14.14) can be produced by plotting the data on **semi-logarithmic** graph paper that shows all the subdivisions of the y-axis scale. This time the interval on the y axis from 1 to 10 is the same as that from 10 to 100 and so on. In each successive cycle, the values are **ten times** greater than the cycle below. This graph also depicts an equal rate of growth as a line of equal slope.

Stationary phase

The rapid phase of exponential growth does not continue indefinitely (see Figure 14.11). Nutrients begin to run out and/or **secondary metabolites** (see page 198) produced by the microbe may start to build up. In some cases these have a toxic effect on the micro-organism and cause its rate of cell division to decrease. At the point where the rate of production of new cells is equal to the death rate of the old ones, the population has reached the **stationary phase**. The graph's flat shape shows that the population number remains fairly steady during this phase.

of active growth (in other words, its lag and exponential phases) when it breaks down a substrate to obtain energy and produces **primary metabolites** such as amino acids essential for growth and increase in biomass. Some primary metabolites are of use to humans and industrial processes are carried out to collect them.

Secondary metabolism occurs at the very end of the exponential phase and during the stationary phase of the micro-organism's growth. It results in the production of **secondary metabolites**. Although these are not used by the micro-organism for growth and production of new cells (and may even be toxic), some may confer an ecological advantage on the filamentous fungus that makes them. Secondary metabolites such as **antibiotics**, for example, inhibit competing micro-organisms (such as bacteria) in the fungus' ecosystem (for example, soil). Other secondary metabolites promote spore formation (see Figure 14.15) which increases the microbe's reproductive potential and chance of surviving and expanding its range.

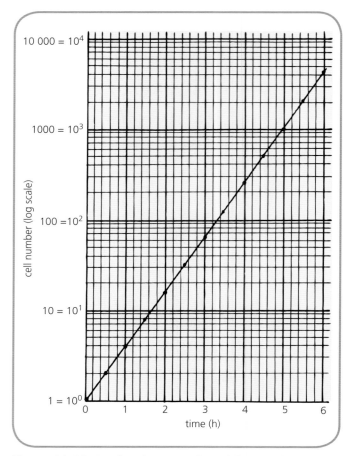

Figure 14.14 Graph using normal semi-log graph paper

Death phase

Finally the lack of nutrient substrate and/or the accumulation of a high concentration of **toxic metabolites** lead to the **death phase**. The number of cells dying now exceeds the number of new cells being produced. At this stage the cells are dying at a constant rate and they may undergo lysis (bursting). Figure 14.11 shows how the population enters a period of exponential decline. By the end of this phase, the population may be completely wiped out or it may survive in the form of a few resistant spores. A **viable cell count** gives the number of cells that are alive and capable of reproduction. A **total cell count** refers to all cells, dead or alive.

Controlling metabolism

Primary and secondary metabolism

Some micro-organisms such as filamentous fungi (and, less commonly, bacteria) exhibit two types of metabolism – primary and secondary. **Primary metabolism** occurs during the micro-organism's period

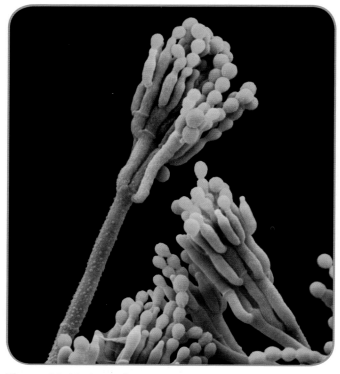

Figure 14.15 Spore formation in filamentous fungus

Many secondary metabolites have properties that are extremely useful to humans (see Table 14.3). Therefore the micro-organisms responsible are cultivated on an enormous scale in industrial fermenters in order to mass-produce certain metabolites.

Micro-organism	Secondary metabolite	Use
Blakeslea trispora	carotenoids	yellow pigment
Claviceps purpurea	ergot alkaloid	analgesic
Fusarium moniliforme	gibberellin	plant hormone
Penicillium chrysogenum	penicillin	antibiotic
Streptomyces testaceus	pepstatin (pepsin inhibitor)	ulcer treatment
Tolypocladium inflatum	cyclosporin	immunosuppressant

Table 14.3 Useful secondary metabolites

Manipulation of a micro-organism's metabolism

A micro-organism possesses a natural system of metabolic regulation. This involves several processes such as the **induction** or **inhibition** of enzymes, and regulation by **end-product inhibition** (see page 136).

When a micro-organism is being used in an industrial fermentation process, it is usually being employed to **overproduce one specific metabolite** that occurs at some point along a metabolic pathway. Often this metabolite is not the final product that would occur naturally. Therefore the micro-organism's metabolism may have to be **manipulated** to make it produce and accumulate large quantities of the desired product.

Imagine that the metabolic pathway shown in Figure 14.16 occurs naturally in the micro-organism being used but that metabolite C is the desired product. It may be possible to mass produce metabolite C by adding to the fermenter a continuous supply of one or more of the following:

- Metabolite A to act as a **precursor** (an earlier metabolite in the pathway) which will be acted upon by enzyme 1 and produce a continuous supply of metabolite B.

- Metabolite B to act as an **inducer** (and regulator) of enzyme 2. Provided that a supply of B is present, enzyme 2 will remain active and promote the conversion of B to C. (This would work in a similar way to lactose's effect on the *lac* operon as described on page 127.)

- An **inhibitor** that affects the activity of enzyme 3 (by acting competitively or non-competitively – see pages 133–136) or that inhibits production of enzyme 3 by binding to the operator region of the gene that codes for the enzyme 3, keeping the gene switched off.

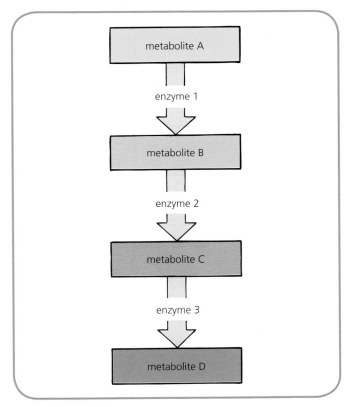

Figure 14.16 Pathway before manipulation to mass-produce metabolite C

It is for these reasons that certain fermentations are supplemented with various metabolites. For example phenylacetic acid is added as a precursor in the industrial production of penicillin.

Genetically modified micro-organisms (see chapter 15) often fail to function properly when attempts are made to switch on their imported, foreign genes. However, if the genetic sequence for a regulator is also included during the gene transfer process, then the foreign gene can be switched on as required by adding the specific chemical that acts as an inducer.

199

Some inhibitors are added to bring metabolic pathways to a halt at a certain point so that the desired product does not undergo further metabolism; others are used to redirect the metabolism towards the desired product and cut down the formation of other metabolites.

Glutamic acid production

Glutamic acid (glutamate) is an amino acid which is used to make **monosodium glutamate**, a flavour enhancer added to many foods such as soups, gravies and snacks. Glutamic acid is produced on an industrial scale in fermenters using special strains of micro-organisms such as *Microbacterium* and *Arthrobacter*. These have been developed to tolerate the high concentration of glutamic acid that builds up in their cytoplasm as a result of overproduction of the amino acid.

Figure 14.17 shows the normal relationship between glutamic acid and the citric acid cycle.

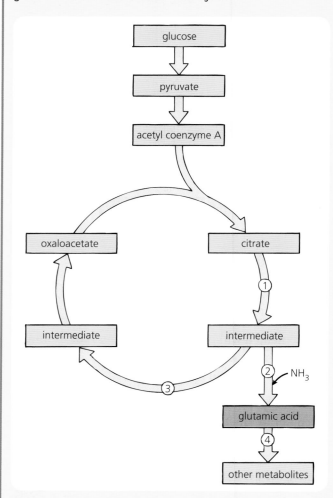

Figure 14.17 Citric acid cycle and glutamic acid

Overproduction of the amino acid by the microbe is achieved by employing **manipulative strategies** such as:

- promoting activity of enzymes that control steps in the pathway leading to the synthesis of glutamic acid (for example at arrows 1 and 2 in the diagram)

- inhibiting enzymes that promote pathways leading to formation of unwanted intermediates (for example at arrow 3 in the diagram) or using mutant strains of the micro-organism unable to make these enzymes

- inhibiting enzymes that promote the breakdown of glutamic acid to other metabolites (for example at arrow 4 in the diagram)

- removing feedback control mechanisms where an end product would act as an inhibitor (not shown in the diagram).

After 3–4 days in the industrial fermenter at 30–37 °C, the bacteria are treated to make them release the glutamic acid into the medium. The cells are then separated from the medium and the glutamic acid crystallised, filtered off, washed and made into monosodium glutamate.

Penicillin production

Penicillin is produced by growing the filamentous fungus *Penicillium chrysogenum* on an industrial scale. The process is begun by germinating spores of *Penicillium chrysogenum* in a small container of culture medium and then using the mycelium (mat of fungal threads) that develops to inoculate a much larger fermenter. The first part of the fermentation process is a 2–3 day **vegetative phase**. During this time the fungus receives optimum conditions of temperature and pH, and a high concentration of oxygen to allow continuous aerobic respiration to occur. It is also supplied with all the necessary nutrients in its liquid culture medium including a high concentration of a suitable carbohydrate to promote a rapid rate of growth (such as a doubling of biomass every 6 hours).

This phase is followed by the **antibiotic production phase** during the next 6–8 days when the balance of nutrients is deliberately altered and the supply of carbohydrate is reduced. The procedure causes a slowing down of growth and an increase in antibiotic production. During this time, as the fungus makes penicillin, it excretes it into the surrounding liquid medium. When the fermentation process is complete, the fungal mycelium is separated from the culture medium by a rotary vacuum filter and used as animal feed or fertiliser.

The penicillin is recovered from the medium by a series of chemical processes which eventually results in the formation of penicillin crystals that are **99.5% pure**. These are used in the manufacture of **pharmaceutical products** and **semi-synthetic penicillins**.

Therapeutic proteins

These are products made as a result of recombinant DNA technology (see page 213).

Testing Your Knowledge 2

1 Define the terms *growth* and *mean generation time*. (2)

2 a) Give ONE difference between the lag phase and the stationary phase of the pattern of growth shown by a population of bacteria. (1)

  b) Explain why the graph of the exponential phase of growth takes the form that it does. (1)

  c) Give TWO possible causes of death to bacterial cells during the death phase of growth. (2)

3 a) With reference to growth of micro-organisms, what is the difference between a primary and a secondary metabolite? (1)

  b) i) Give an example of a secondary metabolite.
     ii) Explain how it may confer an ecological advantage on the fungus that produces it. (2)

4 Identify TWO types of substance that may be added to a fermentation process to manipulate the metabolism of the micro-organism being cultured so that it will overproduce the required product. (2)

15 Genetic control of metabolism

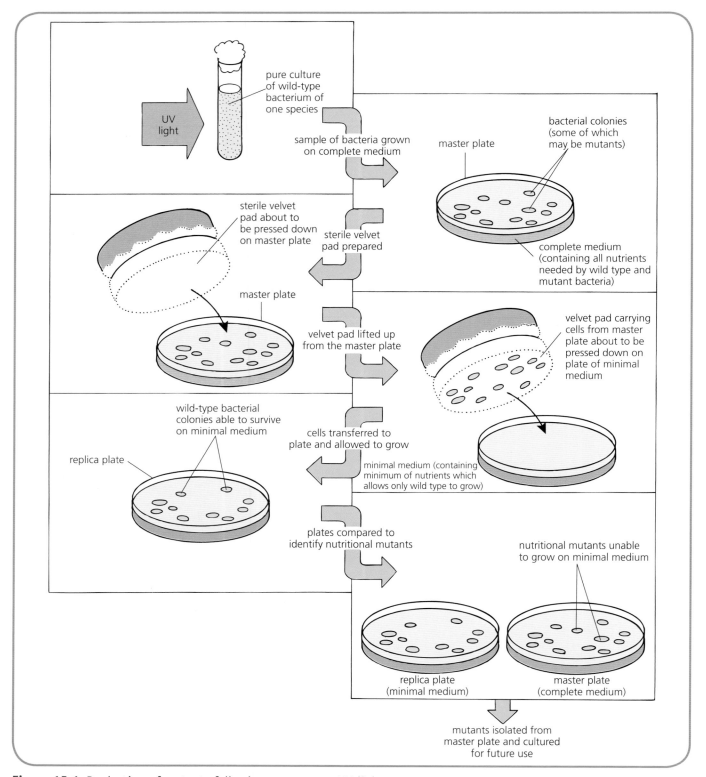

Figure 15.1 Production of mutants following exposure to UV light

Selection and isolation of micro-organisms

Wild strains of micro-organisms that may be of use in an industrial process are selected and cultured in enriched nutrient medium. They are given optimum growing conditions and then pure strains are isolated and screened for desired traits.

Strain improvement

Once a pure strain of wild micro-organism exhibiting a desired trait has been isolated, it may still lack many other important features such as:

- genetic stability

- ability to grow on low-cost nutrients

- ability to vastly overproduce the target compound for which it was selected

- ability to allow easy harvesting of the target product following the fermentation process.

Therefore strain improvement is employed to try to alter the wild microbe's genome and include the genetic material for these traits. This may be brought about by mutagenesis, breeding programmes or recombinant DNA technology.

Mutations and mutagenesis

A mutation is a heritable change in an organism's DNA that causes genetic diversity (see chapter 6). Usually the DNA sequence affected is no longer able to function, but on very rare occasions, there arises by mutation a mutant allele that confers an advantage on the organism or endows it with a new property that is useful to humans.

Mutagenesis is the creation of mutations. The rate of mutagenesis can be increased artificially by exposing organisms to mutagenic agents such as ultraviolet (UV) light, other forms of radiation or mutagenic chemicals, since all of these alter DNA and induce mutations. The experiment shown in Figure 15.1 shows the production of mutant strains of bacteria following exposure of the original strain to UV light.

Related Activity

Investigating the effect of UV radiation on UV-sensitive yeast cells

Normal yeast cells have genes which code for enzymes that repair damage done to their DNA by UV radiation. UV-sensitive yeast is a strain that has had these genes 'knocked out' by genetic engineering. Therefore it is unable to repair damaged DNA resulting from exposure to UV radiation.

The experiment is carried out as shown in Figure 15.2. After two days of incubation, plate X is found to lack yeast colonies whereas plate Y, the control, has many colonies. Therefore it is concluded that exposure to UV radiation has had a lethal effect on UV-sensitive yeast.

Investigating the effect of UV radiation on 'protected' UV-sensitive yeast

The previous experiment is repeated and extended to include two further Petri dishes V and W wrapped in cling film. Their top surfaces are smeared each with a different sun barrier cream (for example protection factors 6 and 20) and then exposed to the UV light source as before. If more yeast colonies grow on the plate with the higher protection factor then this result suggests that the higher factor has given them more protection from the harmful UV rays than the lower factor.

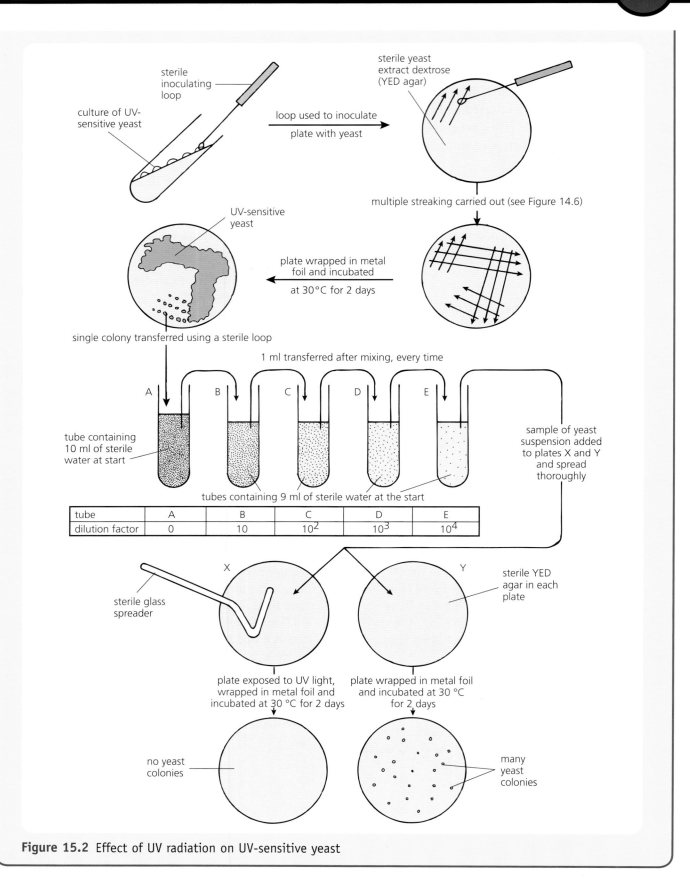

tube	A	B	C	D	E
dilution factor	0	10	10^2	10^3	10^4

Figure 15.2 Effect of UV radiation on UV-sensitive yeast

Improved strains

Occasionally a mutant strain induced by a mutagenic agent produces an **improved strain** of micro-organism. Many industrial micro-organisms have been improved by subjecting them to repeated sessions of mutagenesis followed by careful selection and screening of the survivors. Normally the improved strain that is selected **lacks an inhibitory control mechanism**. Therefore it no longer expresses some undesirable characteristic or it produces an increased yield of the desired product.

Genetic instability

Unfortunately mutant strains of micro-organisms are often **genetically unstable**. Therefore they sometimes undergo a reverse mutation (for example a deletion in DNA is repaired by an appropriate addition of DNA) and revert to the less-useful wild-type state. It is for this reason that an improved strain of industrial micro-organism must be monitored regularly to ensure that it is still in its mutated state before it is put to work in an industrial fermenter. A mistake would be very costly in terms of time and materials.

Site-specific mutagenesis

Spontaneous and induced mutations both occur randomly throughout a genome. However, geneticists normally want to study the effect of a mutation on one specific gene. In recent times this has become possible by producing many copies of a gene's DNA *in vitro* (see PCR page 21) and then making a change in the base pair sequence at a specific position in the DNA chain. This process is called **site-specific mutagenesis**. The mutated gene is then introduced back into the cell and the cell cultured to allow any changes in phenotype resulting from the mutation to be studied.

Breeding programmes

Most eukaryotic micro-organisms such as fungi are able to reproduce asexually and sexually. Asexual reproduction produces a clone of identical individuals. **Sexual reproduction** involves two parents and the fusion of a male and a female sex cell to form a zygote. It results in the production of offspring that show genetic (and phenotypic) **variation**.

By deliberately crossing different strains during **breeding programmes**, scientists are able to produce new strains. On some occasions a new strain combines two desirable characteristics, one from each parent, as shown in Figure 15.3.

Transfer of genetic material

Although bacteria do not reproduce sexually, **new strains of some species can arise as a result of**

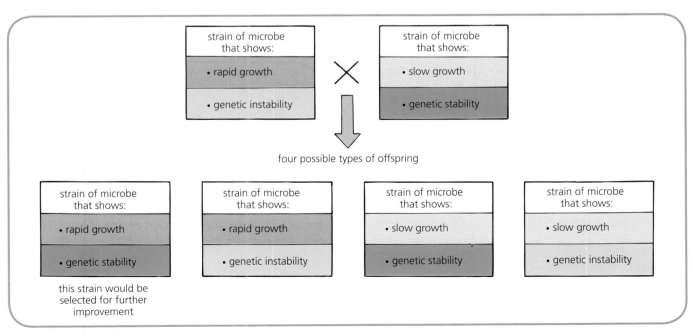

Figure 15.3 Breeding programme

horizontal transfer of genetic material. By this means plasmids or pieces of chromosomal DNA are transferred from one strain to another. New strains are also produced by bacteria taking up and incorporating DNA fragments from their environment (also see Related Activity below). Scientists attempt to produce new strains of useful bacteria by culturing existing strains together in conditions where horizontal transfer of DNA is most likely to occur.

Related Activity

Investigating transfer of DNA using bacteria

New strains of bacterial species can arise as a result of horizontal transfer of DNA occurring in one of the following ways.

Transformation

The bacterium's genome can be altered by **transformation** (see Figure 15.4 and Figure 1.8 on page 6). This occurs naturally when the cell takes up a piece of naked foreign DNA from the remains of a cell that has been destroyed and has undergone lysis (bursting). Some bacterial cells even have proteins on their surface specialised for the uptake of pieces of naked DNA from closely related species in their environment.

Transduction

When a bacteriophage (phage) virus multiplies inside a bacterial host cell, it produces many new copies of the virus (see Figure 1.10 on page 7). However, very occasionally, a fragment of *bacterial* DNA instead of viral DNA gets packaged inside a virus particle. If this unusual phage injects the bacterial DNA into another bacterial cell (see Figure 15.5), the bacterium may incorporate this DNA into its own chromosome. This process is called **transduction**.

Conjugation

A temporary bridge called a conjugation tube may form between two bacterial cells that differ in genome. The tube allows a copy of genetic material such as a plasmid to pass from the donor cell to the recipient cell (see Figures 15.6 and 15.7). This process is called **conjugation** and it results in the formation of a bacterial cell containing a new combination of

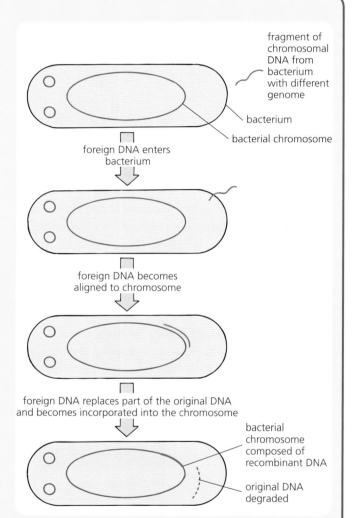

Figure 15.4 Transformation

genetic material. Conjugation is not regarded as a true form of sexual reproduction because it results in the production of an altered version of one of the original cells and not in a zygote.

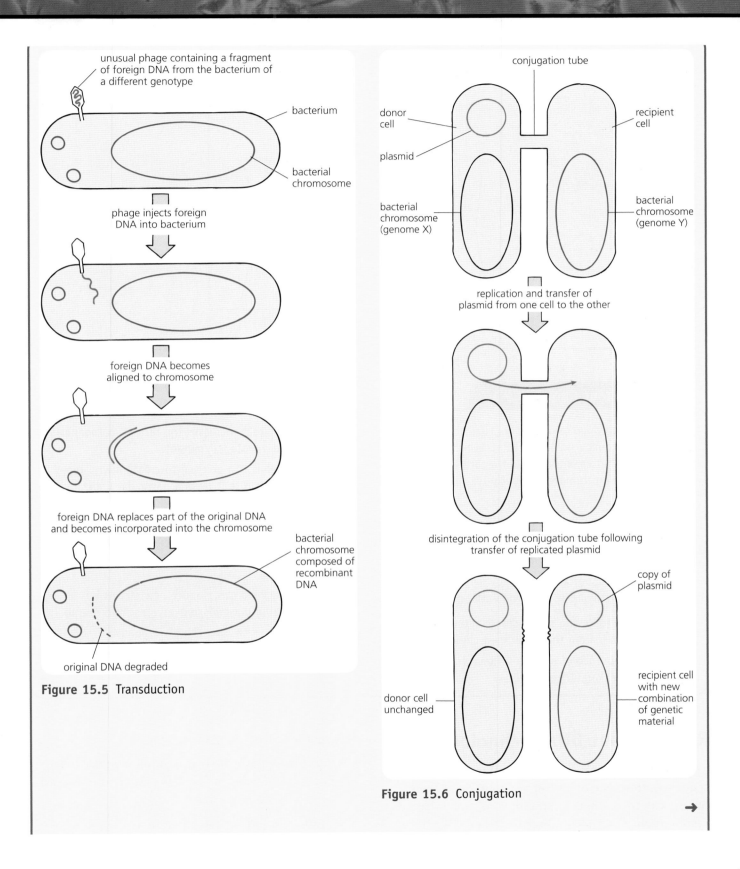

Figure 15.5 Transduction

Figure 15.6 Conjugation

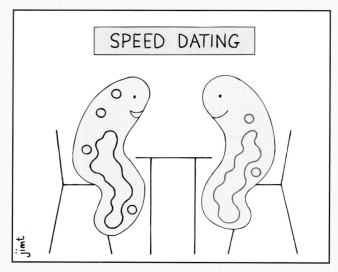

Figure 15.7 Fancy a plasmid?

Testing Your Knowledge 1

1 Imagine that a micro-organism (Y) is able to make a useful product (y). Name THREE other traits of microbe Y that scientists would regard as desirable when planning to make product y on an industrial scale. (3)

2 a) What is meant by the term *mutagenesis*? (1)

    b) Name TWO agents that could be used to increase an organism's rate of mutation. (2)

    c) Why is it important to monitor mutant strains of micro-organisms used in industrial processes? (1)

3 Rewrite the following sentences selecting only the correct answer from the underlined choice. (6)

    a) In the absence of outside influences, mutations arise very rarely/frequently.

    b) An agent that increases the rate of mutagenesis is called a mutagen/mutant.

    c) Mutagenesis can be used to create a wild-type/ mutant strain that lacks a particular undesirable characteristic.

    d) In prokaryotic/eukaryotic micro-organisms such as fungi, new genotypes can be produced by sexual/asexual reproduction between different strains.

    e) Some bacteria can produce new strains by transferring plasmids/prokaryotes from one to another.

Recombinant DNA technology

This technique enables scientists to transfer gene sequences from one organism to another and even one species to another. By crossing the species barrier, **recombinant DNA technology** makes possible the production of a plant or animal protein by a micro-organism that has been **artificially transformed**.

Improvement of existing strain

DNA technology can also be used to introduce to an existing micro-organism (such as a bacterium or yeast cell) one or more genes that:

- amplifies specific metabolic steps in a pathway or removes inhibitory controls affecting it, thereby **increasing yield** of the target product

- causes the cells to secrete their product into the

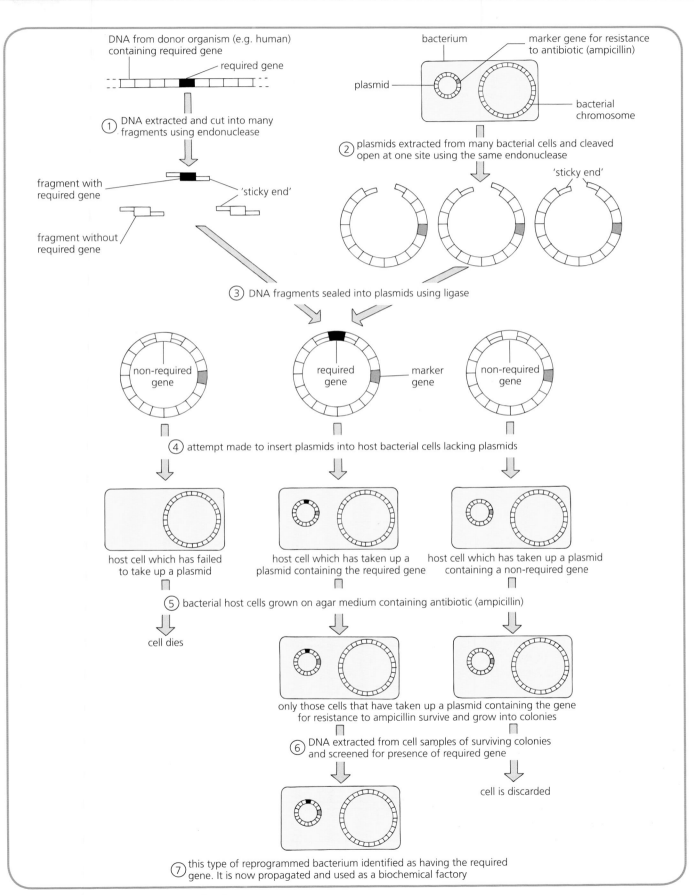

Figure 15.8 Recombinant DNA technology

surrounding medium allowing it to be **easily recovered**

- renders the micro-organism unable to survive in an external environment and therefore act as a **safety mechanism**.

Artificial transformation of a bacterium by recombinant DNA technology

Genetic engineers are able to select a particular gene for a desirable characteristic (such as the gene for human insulin), splice its DNA into the DNA of a vector (for example a plasmid from a bacterial cell) and insert the vector into a host cell (for example a bacterium such as *E. coli*).

The transformed host cell has its properties and functions altered and when it is cultured, it expresses the 'foreign' gene and produces the product (such as insulin). Since the host cell contains a **combination**

of its own DNA and that from another source joined together, it is said to contain **recombinant DNA**. Figure 15.8 illustrates the general principles of recombinant DNA technology involving several 'tools of the trade' as follows.

Restriction endonuclease

A restriction endonuclease is an enzyme extracted from bacteria which is used to cut up the DNA (containing the required gene from the donor organism) into fragments and to cleave open the bacterial plasmids that are to receive it.

Each restriction endonuclease recognises a specific short sequence of DNA bases called a **restriction site** (or recognition sequence). The sequence (four to eight nucleotides in length) is found on both DNA strands but running in opposite directions as shown in Figure 15.9. The enzyme cuts both DNA strands and may produce blunt ends or sticky ends. If the recognition sequence occurs many times (such as in a long DNA molecule) then the enzyme will make many cuts.

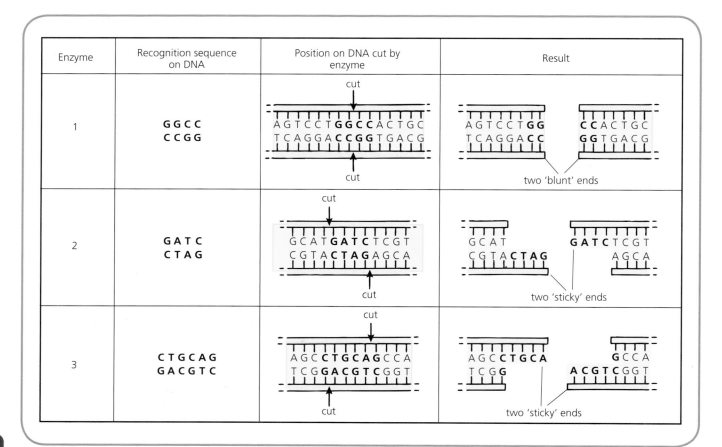

Figure 15.9 Action of restriction endonucleases

DNA ligase

DNA ligase is an enzyme which seals sticky ends (and blunt ends) together. It is used to seal a DNA fragment into a bacterial plasmid to form a **recombinant plasmid** containing recombinant DNA.

Vector (carrier)

Recombinant plasmids and artificial chromosomes (see below) are used as **vectors** to carry DNA from the genome of one organism (such as a human) into that of another (for example a bacterial host cell) and bring about **transformation** of the latter. To act as an effective vector, a plasmid must have the features shown in Figure 15.10.

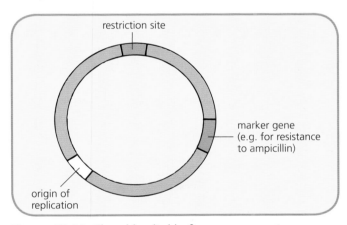

Figure 15.10 Plasmid suitable for use as a vector

Restriction site

This site must be able to be cut open by the same restriction endonuclease used to cut the DNA containing the gene to be transported so that the sticky ends will be complementary.

Marker gene

This is a gene that enables the scientist to determine whether a host cell has taken up the plasmid vector or not. For example if the plasmid contains the **marker** gene for **resistance to ampicillin** then this antibiotic can be used to select for the bacterial DNA. When cultured in a medium containing ampicillin, any host cells that have failed to take up a recombinant plasmid die since they lack the resistance gene (see Figure 15.8).

Origin of replication

This consists of genes that control **self-replication** of plasmid DNA and **regulatory sequences** that allow control of the existing genes and the expression of the

inserted gene. This site is essential for the generation of many copies of the plasmid (and the required gene) within the transformed bacterial host cell. When many copies of the gene are expressed, more product can be made by fewer cells.

Artificial chromosomes

Scientists have constructed **artificial chromosomes** that can also act as vectors in recombinant DNA technology. Each artificial chromosome possesses all the essential features of a vector described above but is able to carry much more foreign DNA than a plasmid. Therefore use of an artificial chromosome as a vector allows a **much longer sequence** of DNA to be carried from the donor organism to the recipient micro-organism.

Limitations of prokaryotes

Cloning and expressing a gene from a eukaryotic organism inserted into a prokaryotic organism may be problematic. The DNA of eukaryotes contains long stretches of non-coding DNA called **introns** interspersed among the protein-coding regions called **exons** (also see page 35). Primary transcripts of mRNA are modified by splicing. In addition, proteins, once synthesised, may be further modified after translation (see page 42).

The DNA of bacteria has exons but no introns. Therefore transcripts of mRNA in bacteria are not modified by splicing before translation. Furthermore, proteins synthesised by bacteria do not undergo post-translational modification.

As a result, a gene from a eukaryote expressed by a prokaryote may result in the formation of a polypeptide molecule which is **inactive** because it is not folded correctly or a molecule which **lacks certain post-translational modifications** essential for it to function. In addition, some bacterial cells do not secrete the desired protein into the surrounding medium. In fact they may even degrade it before it can be recovered.

Although many of these problems can be overcome by chemical means, there are situations where production of the desired protein by **genetically transformed** eukaryotic cells (such as yeast) is a preferable option despite their more demanding cultural conditions.

Case Study   Bacterial transformation

Insulin

This hormone is required to control blood sugar level. People whose bodies fail to produce adequate quantities of insulin develop **diabetes**. Traditionally diabetic patients were treated with **insulin** from animals but this often led to undesirable side effects. The problem has been overcome by recombinant DNA technology. Genetically modified micro-

organisms are used to make recombinant human insulin.

Under normal circumstances, human insulin following translation takes the form of a single polypeptide chain. This undergoes post-translational modification (see page 42) into two polypeptide chains A and B held together by sulphur bridges. The bacterium *E. coli* is a prokaryote and it is unable to

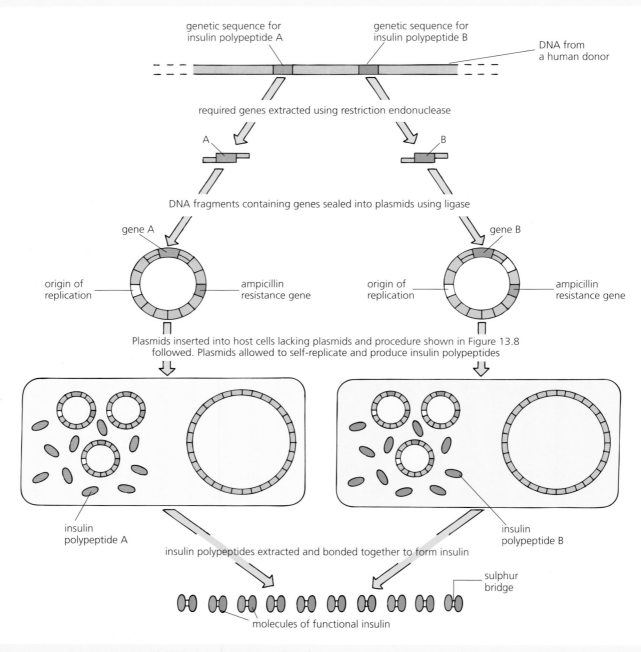

Figure 15.11 Using two strains of genetically modified *E. coli*

bring about this process typical of eukaryotes. However, the problem has been solved by using **two different strains of genetically modified** E. coli – one to produce polypeptide chain A and another to produce polypeptide chain B (see Figure 15.11). These are then combined to form a product identical to that made by cells in the human pancreas. Even more effective is **genetically modified yeast** which, being a eukaryote, is able to make and combine the two chains into an insulin molecule.

Related Topic

Therapeutic proteins

Therapeutic proteins are **low-volume, high-value** products made as a result of recombinant DNA technology involving the addition of genes to bacteria, yeast or mammalian cell cultures.

Human growth hormone

Human growth hormone (**HGH**) promotes growth by accelerating amino acid transport into the cells of both soft tissues and bones. This allows rapid synthesis of **tissue proteins** to occur. In particular it promotes an increase in length of **long bones** during growing years.

Preparations of HGH are used to treat children whose bodies fail to make sufficient quantities of this hormone. Figure 15.12 shows, in a simple way, the structure of **pre-HGH** and **active HGH** and the relationship between them.

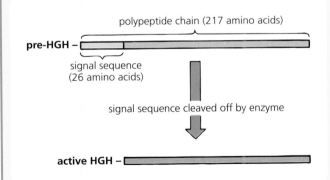

Figure 15.12 Structure of HGH

Figure 15.13 shows two methods involving recombinant DNA technology of producing active HGH for use with patients. In each case, cells of the bacterium E. coli are transformed into biochemical 'factories' to produce human growth hormone.

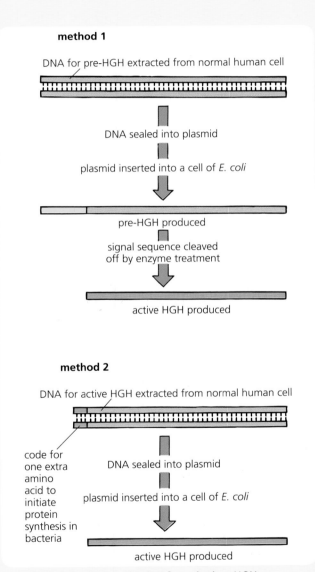

Figure 15.13 Two methods of producing HGH

Erythropoietin

Erythropoietin (**EPO**) is a hormone whose main site of production is the **kidneys**. It controls the production of red blood cells in the bone marrow. If the kidneys become diseased, the chain of events shown in

Figure 15.14 may occur and result in the person suffering **anaemia** (shortage of red blood cells).

EPO is a **glycoprotein** and it therefore requires post-translational modification to bring about the addition of a carbohydrate component to the protein molecule. Prokaryotic cells are unable to bring about this modification. Therefore **genetically modified animal cells** are used to produce EPO by recombinant DNA technology. The resulting product can then be used to treat a patient suffering from anaemia associated with kidney disease.

Use by cheats

Unnecessary use of EPO is made by some athletes in an attempt to dishonestly gain an advantage by boosting their red-blood-cell count and the oxygen-carrying capacity of their blood.

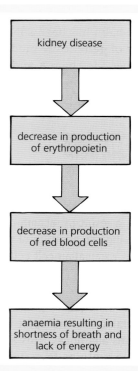

Figure 15.14 Anaemia associated with kidney disease

Testing Your Knowledge 2

1 a) With reference to TWO different species of living organism, describe a transfer of genetic material made possible by recombinant DNA technology. (2)

b) What benefit is gained by humans from the example that you have given? (1)

c) Which part of a bacterium's genetic material is often used as a vector? (1)

2 a) What is the difference between a *restriction endonuclease* and a *restriction site*? (2)

b) What is the function of the marker gene for resistance to the antibiotic ampicillin in the procedure shown in Figure 13.8? (1)

3 Which of the following is NOT a reason for introducing genes to an existing microbial strain by recombinant DNA technology? (1)

A To cause the cells to secrete their product into the surrounding medium.

B To amplify certain metabolic steps in the pathway and increase yield.

C To enable the micro-organism to survive in the wild outside the laboratory.

D To remove inhibitory controls affecting the pathway that leads to the product.

4 a) For which type of genetic transformation might a genetic engineer decide to use a eukaryotic rather than a prokaryotic micro-organism to make a recombinant protein? (1)

b) Give an example of a suitable eukaryotic microbe. (1)

5 So far, all applications by companies to patent segments of human DNA have been rejected. In your opinion, is this ethically correct? Justify your answer. (1)

16 Ethical considerations in the use of microorganisms

Ethics, risks and hazards

The development of microbiological products by biotechnology raises issues of **ethics**. It also requires that careful assessment of **risks** and possible **hazards** be carried out continuously and suitable safeguards be put in place.

Ethics

A pharmaceutical company must make a profit in order to survive. Therefore it is motivated to develop a new product that has the potential to offer treatment for a previously untreatable but common condition (such as dementia) since the product would be likely to be highly profitable and repay the time and money invested in its development. The same company would be less likely to finance the development of a drug for a rare disorder or a disease confined to a developing country. Therefore people with rare disorders or those living in poor countries are often in the unfair position of being less likely to benefit from the development of new microbiological products.

Research Topic | **Development of a microbiological product from discovery to market**

The discovery and development of a **new microbiological product** involves a combination of several contributory factors as shown in Figure 16.1. It then takes many years and vast sums of money to bring the new pharmaceutical product (such as a drug) to the market. The process is very long because the drug must pass a set of rigorous tests to ensure that:

- it is efficacious (in other words, it works)

- it is safe to use.

Figure 16.2 shows some of the stages involved in the development of a new antibiotic drug and some of the difficulties that may arise along the way.

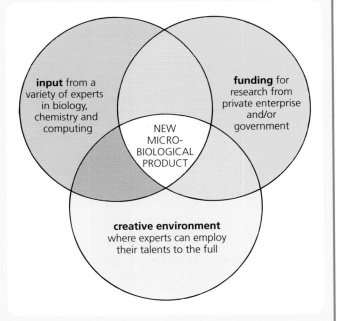

Figure 16.1 Factors affecting discovery and development of a new microbiological product

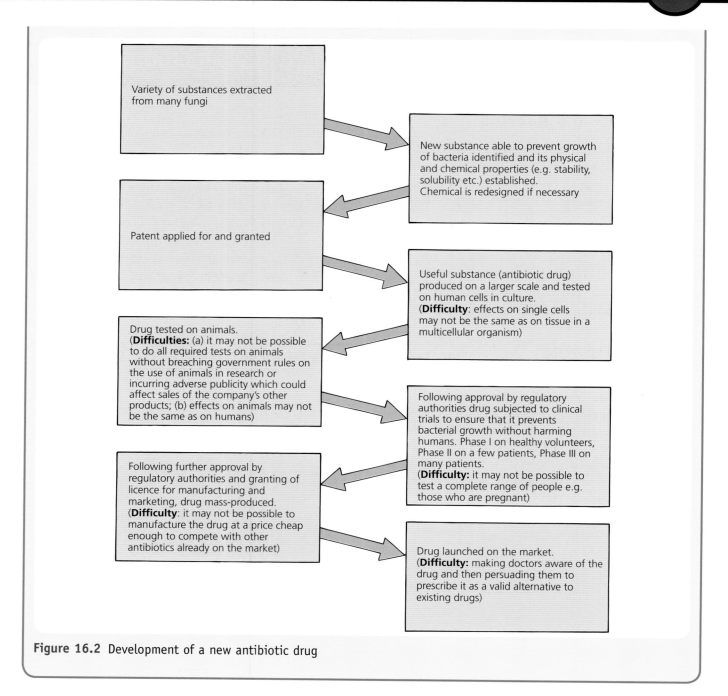

Figure 16.2 Development of a new antibiotic drug

The boxes in the figure contain the following text:

Variety of substances extracted from many fungi

New substance able to prevent growth of bacteria identified and its physical and chemical properties (e.g. stability, solubility etc.) established. Chemical is redesigned if necessary

Patent applied for and granted

Useful substance (antibiotic drug) produced on a larger scale and tested on human cells in culture. (**Difficulty**: effects on single cells may not be the same as on tissue in a multicellular organism)

Drug tested on animals. (**Difficulties:** (a) it may not be possible to do all required tests on animals without breaching government rules on the use of animals in research or incurring adverse publicity which could affect sales of the company's other products; (b) effects on animals may not be the same as on humans)

Following approval by regulatory authorities drug subjected to clinical trials to ensure that it prevents bacterial growth without harming humans. Phase I on healthy volunteers, Phase II on a few patients, Phase III on many patients. (**Difficulty:** it may not be possible to test a complete range of people e.g. those who are pregnant)

Following further approval by regulatory authorities and granting of licence for manufacturing and marketing, drug mass-produced. (**Difficulty:** it may not be possible to manufacture the drug at a price cheap enough to compete with other antibiotics already on the market)

Drug launched on the market. (**Difficulty:** making doctors aware of the drug and then persuading them to prescribe it as a valid alternative to existing drugs)

Patents

A **patent** is a certificate issued by a government's patent office that grants the inventor sole right to make, use and sell an invention for a limited period of time (see Figure 16.3).

Figure 16.3 'Been waiting long?'

Naturally occurring organisms and materials are *not* novel inventions or inventive steps in a manufacturing process and therefore cannot be patented. However, a **genetically modified** organism can be protected by a patent. In 1980, a scientist in the USA was the first to patent such an organism successfully. It was a species of *Pseudomonas*, a bacterium used to clean up oil spills. At the time it was decided that this new strain was 'the result of research and human ingenuity' and therefore eligible to be patented. Many people considered this landmark legal decision to be ethically wrong.

Controversy

In recent years a furious debate has raged about whether scientists should be allowed to **patent gene sequences** (or even whole organisms such as genetically modified crop plants and transgenic animals). This is a highly controversial and contentious area involving legal and ethical issues. Therefore, rather than apply for patents, many biotechnological companies choose instead to keep details of their discoveries, microbial strains, materials and processes secret. They make use of tight security arrangements and strict protocols to guard these trade secrets and keep them under lock and key. Some people argue that this lack of communication is unethical and a hindrance to true scientific progress.

Regulation of products and processes

Before a new microbiological product is granted a manufacturing and marketing licence, it must pass the following regulatory requirements.

- The product:
  - poses no threat or danger to the staff who manufacture it
  - is safe for use by consumers
  - is pure and uncontaminated by micro-organisms
  - is fit for purpose and accurately matches its product description.

- The **manufacturing process**:
  - maintains specified standards of purity of product
  - uses safe, well-designed facilities.

Risk assessment

The safety of the workforce in a manufacturing process is of paramount importance. Biotechnological industries make use of many types of micro-organism, some of which have the potential to act as allergens or irritants or even be pathogenic (disease causing). For this reason many of the regulatory requirements take the form of **risk assessment** (see Figure 16.4).

The risk assessments that need to be applied in a particular process depend on the micro-organism being used. The regulations are more complex and the quality criteria more stringent for products that are pharmaceuticals or foodstuffs or those whose production has involved genetically modified micro-organisms.

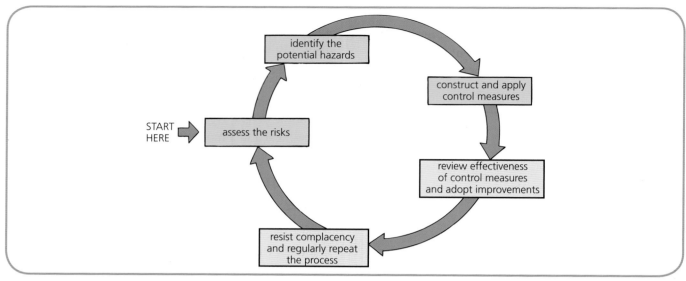

Figure 13.18 Risk assessment approach to safety

Testing Your Knowledge

1 Briefly explain why people suffering a rare disease confined to a developing country would be less likely to benefit from the development a new microbiological product than people suffering a common condition in a developed country. (2)

2 So far, all applications by companies to patent segments of human DNA have been rejected. In your opinion, is this ethically correct? Justify your answer. (1)

3 List THREE of the steps involved in a programme to assess and control risk in a place of work where microorganisms are used. (3)

What You Should Know

Chapters 14–16

(See Table 16.1 for word bank)

adaptable	exponential	polypeptides
amplify	generation	precursor
bacteria	genetic	recombinant
biosynthesis	growth	restriction
breeding	improved	risks
death	industry	safety
depleted	lag	secondary
DNA	ligase	self-replication
doubles	marker	sexual
endonucleases	metabolic	stationary
energy	mutagenesis	translation
environmental	mutations	unstable
equals	overproduce	useful
ethical	oxygen	vector
exceeds	plasmids	yeast

Table 16.1 Word bank for chapters 14–16

1 Micro-organisms such as _____, archaea and some eukaryotes are highly _____. They make use of many substrates, produce a wide range of _____ products and occur in any environment that can support life.

2 Much use is made of micro-organisms in research and _____ because they are easy to culture. They grow quickly if given nutrient medium containing a suitable _____ source and a supply of the raw materials needed for the _____ of complex molecules.

3 To grow rapidly, micro-organisms also require _____ conditions such as temperature, _____ concentration and pH to be maintained at optimum levels.

4 A microbe's pattern of _____ falls into four distinct phases. During the _____ phase, the cells adjust to the growth medium, metabolic rate increases and enzymes may become induced.

5 During the log or _____ phase, the cells multiply at maximum speed. The population _____ its number with each cell division. The time needed to do this is called _____ or doubling time.

6 During the _____ phase, the nutrient medium becomes _____, secondary metabolites are produced and the rate of production of new cells _____ the death rate of old ones.

7 During the _____ phase, the number of cells dying greatly _____ the number (if any) of new cells being produced.

8 Some _____ metabolites may be of advantage ecologically to the microbe that makes them; many are very _____ to humans.

9 An industrial fermentation process may need a metabolic _____, inducer or inhibitor to be added to it to make the micro-organism _____ the required product.

10 The processes of _____, selective _____ and recombinant DNA technology are used to try to improve wild strains of micro-organisms exhibiting useful traits.

11 _____ can be induced using ultraviolet light, other forms of radiation or mutagenic chemicals. On very rare occasions the result is an _____ strain but it may be genetically _____ and change back to the wild type.

12 Some bacteria are able to take up and incorporate pieces of _____ present in their environment.

Some bacteria can pass _____ or pieces of DNA on to other bacteria. These processes lead to the formation of new bacterial strains. In fungi, new strains can arise by _____ reproduction.

13 During _____ DNA technology, _____ sequences for useful products are transferred from a plant or animal to a micro-organism using plasmids. Genes that can _____ production of the required product or act as a _____ mechanism may also be introduced.

14 To act as an effective _____, a plasmid must contain a _____ site which will receive the genetic material to be transferred. It also contains a _____ gene to show whether the host cell has taken up the plasmid and an origin of replication consisting of genes for _____ and control of gene expression.

15 Enzymes called restriction _____ are used to cut out genetic sequences and cut open plasmids. An enzyme called _____ is used to seal the genetic sequence into a plasmid.

16 Genetically modified prokaryotes make _____ typical of eukaryotes but are unable to modify them following _____. In these situations, transformed _____ is more useful.

17 The use of micro-organisms to produce biotechnological products raises _____ issues and requires strict regulations to be applied so that potential hazards can be identified and _____ carefully assessed.

Applying Your Knowledge and Skills

Chapters 9–16

1 The graph shown in Figure 16.5 summarises the results from an experiment involving an enzyme-controlled reaction.

a) **i)** In this experiment, the enzyme concentration was kept constant. From the graph, identify the factor that was varied by the experimenter.
ii) Is this factor called the dependent or the independent variable?
iii) What effect did an increase in this factor have over region AB of the graph? (3)

b) Suggest which factor became limiting at point C on the graph. (1)

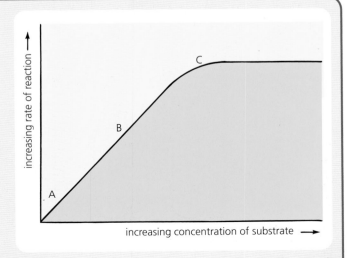

Figure 16.5

c) Which letter on the graph represents the situation where
  i) almost all of the active sites
  ii) none of the active sites
  iii) about half of the active sites on enzyme molecules are freely available for attachment to substrate molecules? (3)

d) Suggest what could be done to increase the rate of the reaction beyond the level it has reached at C. (1)

2 ONPG is a chemical which can be broken down as follows:

$$\text{ONPG} \xrightarrow{\text{β-galactosidase}} \text{galactose} + \text{yellow compound}$$

Figure 16.6 shows an experiment set up to investigate the *lac* operon in *E. coli* (where β-g = β-galactosidase).

a) Explain the yellow colour in:
  i) tube C
  ii) tube E. (2)

b) Explain the faint yellow colour in tube A. (1)

c) It could be argued that ONPG acts as an inducer. Draw a diagram of the control that should be set up to check out this possibility. (1)

d) How could the reliability of the results be improved? (1)

e) Return to page 131 and consider the experiment

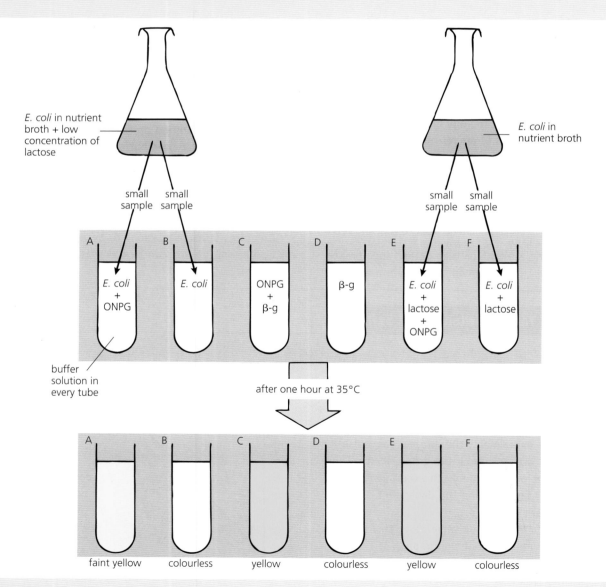

Figure 16.6

shown in Figure 9.32. Imagine that bacteria from plates B and D have been grown on plates E and F, respectively, which both contain nutrient agar and arabinose.

i) Predict the effect of exposing plates E and F to ultraviolet light.

ii) Explain your answer. (3)

3 Refer back to the investigation shown in Figure 10.16 on page 146. Based only on these results, it could be argued that malonic acid has simply killed the cells.

a) How could the experiment be adapted to investigate whether malonic acid really does act as a competitive inhibitor? (1) (Hint: see chapter 9, page 133.)

b) Explain how you would know from the results of your redesigned experiment whether or not malonic acid had acted as a competitive inhibitor. (2)

4 Give an account of the production of NADH and the role played by the electron transport chain during cellular respiration. (9)

5 The graph in Figure 16.7 shows the relationship between external temperature and the internal temperature of two animals.

a) What is the body temperature of the lizard when the external temperature is

i) 10 °C?

ii) 30 °C? (1)

b) What is the body temperature of the cat when the external temperature is

i) 10 °C?

ii) 30 °C? (1)

c) Which animal's body temperature is

i) independent of external temperature?

ii) dependent on external temperature? (1)

d) Which of these animals is

i) a conformer?

ii) a regulator? (1)

e) i) Based on the information in this graph, which of these animals will be better at hunting prey at night?

ii) Explain your answer. (3)

6 The initial direction that would be taken by a bird on a migratory flight can be investigated in the laboratory using the apparatus shown in Figure 16.8. It consists of a circular cage suspended inside an outer container with transparent windows. Mirrors can be inserted into the windows in such a way that to the birds in the cage the Sun seems to have rotated through 90°. The scientist observes the movements of the birds through the transparent floor. The details in Table 16.2 refer

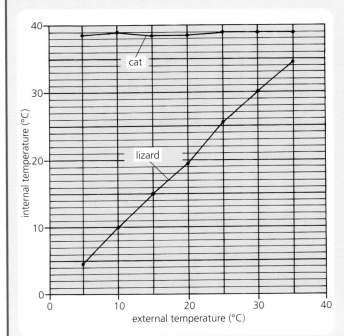

Figure 16.7

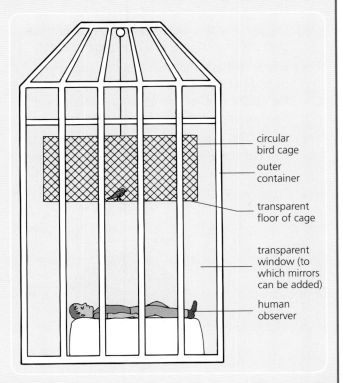

Figure 16.8

Experiment	State of outer container's windows	Actual time of year	State of sky	Direction taken by bird	Conclusion
A	transparent	spring	clear	north	normal migration direction chosen
B	transparent	autumn	clear	south	normal migration direction chosen
C	transparent	spring	overcast	random	clouds prevented bird getting a fix on Sun's position
D	mirrored	autumn	clear	west	Sun being at 90° from real position made bird alter direction by 90°
E	mirrored	spring	overcast	random	clouds prevented bird getting a fix on Sun's position
F	mirrored	autumn	overcast	random	clouds prevented bird getting a fix on Sun's position

Table 16.2

to a series of experiments carried out using a starling that had been hand reared from a nestling. Starlings normally migrate north in spring and south in autumn.

a) Which experiments produced results that are equivalent to the bird's natural migratory behaviour pattern? (1)

b) i) What is the main shortcoming of this investigation?
ii) How could it be overcome? (2)

c) Suggest why this equipment is less useful than that shown in Figure 13.17 on page 182. (1)

d) Which TWO experiments should be compared to find out the effect of the **time of year** on the choice of direction when the windows are transparent and the sky is clear? (1)

e) Which TWO experiments should be compared to find out the effect of the **state of the sky** on

choice of direction in autumn when the windows are mirrored? (1)

f) Which TWO experiments should be compared to find out the effect of the **state of the outer container's windows** in spring when the sky is overcast? (1)

g) What TWO further experiments should have been included to improve the design of the investigation? (2)

7 Read the passage and answer the questions that follow it.

Growth and sporulation of a fungus

Figure 16.9 shows the vegetative mycelium of *Trichoderma viride*. It produces antibiotics and therefore vast colonies of this fungus are surface-cultured on liquid media. Although fragments of mycelium can be used as the inoculum, spores

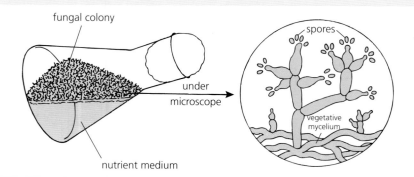

fungal colony

under microscope

spores

vegetative mycelium

nutrient medium

Figure 16.9

have been found to constitute a much more effective method of propagation. It is for this reason that many experiments have been carried out to examine the relationship between nutrition of the fungus and the production of its asexual spores. In such experiments the cultures are grown in triplicate, each flask being inoculated with 0.5×10^6 spores in 1 ml of water and incubated at 25 °C. Table 16.3 shows the effect of glucose concentration on growth and sporulation of *Trichoderma viride*.

a) Why is each culture in triplicate? (1)

b) Explain why culturing the fungus in flasks tilted to one side produces a greater yield of mycelium. (1)

c) Which type of nutrient medium in Table 16.3 brings about most overall growth of the fungus? (1)

d) i) Describe the effect of varying the glucose concentration on dry weight of mycelium.
   ii) Explain why this should be so.
   iii) What effect does increasing glucose concentration have on sporulation? (3)

e) i) Suggest why on some occasions scientists want to mass produce the vegetative mycelium of *Trichoderma viride*, while on other occasions they wish to obtain maximum sporulation.
   ii) From the information given, state the concentration of glucose that would be most suitable in each case.
   iii) Briefly describe how an even more accurate estimate of the optimum glucose concentration for sporulation could be obtained. (3)

Type of nutrient medium	% glucose	Flask	Dry mass of mycelium (mg)	Spore count ($\times 10^6$ ml^{-1})
A (rich in nitrate)	0.1	1	9	16
		2	11	15
		3	14	16
	1.0	1	111	137
		2	109	131
		3	108	128
	10.0	1	379	65
		2	382	67
		3	378	67
B (rich in sulphate)	0.1	1	8	11
		2	7	12
		3	5	9
	1.0	1	64	99
		2	65	103
		3	68	112
	10.0	1	301	54
		2	301	51
		3	284	47
C (rich in phosphate)	0.1	1	11	19
		2	14	18
		3	17	20
	1.0	1	79	151
		2	81	147
		3	89	143
	10.0	1	357	81
		2	343	76
		3	329	72

Table 16.3

8 Figure 16.10 shows a plasmid used as a cloning vector. It possesses several restriction sites each of which can be cut open by a specific restriction endonuclease enzyme. Table 16.4 gives information about four of these enzymes.

a) Which bacterium makes enzyme Bam HI? (1)

b) Which enzyme is made by *E. coli*? (1)

c) i) Which enzyme would cut the plasmid open to produce the result shown in Figure 16.11?
   ii) Are the structures shown in Figure 16.11 called blunt ends or sticky ends? (2)

d) Draw a simple diagram of the effect that the enzyme made by *Bacillus amyloliquefaciens* would have on the plasmid. (1)

e) As a result of an error in the laboratory, a plasmid was acted on simultaneously by Eco RI and Sal I. Draw a simple diagram of the result showing only the upper region of the plasmid affected. (2)

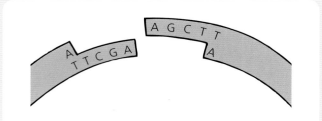

Figure 16.11

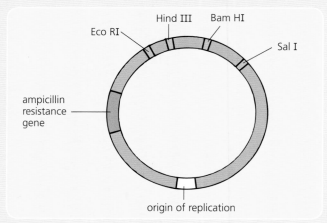

Figure 16.10

Organism which produces enzyme	Name of enzyme and of its restriction site on plasmid	Recognition sequence and positions of cut
Escherichia coli	Eco RI	↓ G A A T T C C T T A A G ↑
Haemophilus influenzae	Hind III	↓ A A G C T T T T C G A A ↑
Bacillus amyloliquefaciens	Bam HI	↓ G G A T C C C C T A G G ↑
Streptomyces albus	Sal I	↓ G T C G A C C A G C T G ↑

Table 16.4

Since this group of questions does not include examples of every type of question found in SQA exams, it is recommended that students also make use of past exam papers to aid learning and revision.

Unit 3

Sustainability and Interdependence

17 Food supply, plant growth and productivity

Food supply and food security

The human population depends on a sufficient and sustainable supply of food for its survival.

Food security may be defined as **access** (both physical and economic) to food of adequate **quantity** and **quality** by human beings (see Figure 17.1). Food security can refer to a small group such as a single household or to a large group such as the population of a country.

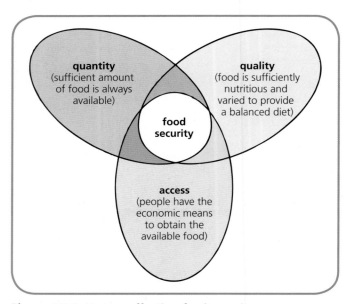

Figure 17.1 Factors affecting food security

Increasing demand for food

As the global human population continues to increase so also does the **demand for food**. The 'green revolution' in the 1960s transformed agricultural practices and raised crop yields but the effect is now levelling off. Current levels of food production will not meet the projected demand and already many people in the world lack food security. Therefore the demand for increased food production continues.

The 'green revolution' depended on the use of vast quantities of fertilisers and pesticides and intensive, multiple-crop farming methods which often led to environmental degradation. Attempts to reverse this unacceptable situation are now underway as society demands methods of increasing food production in a **sustainable way** that does not degrade natural resources such as the land and the water supply.

Increased plant productivity and **manipulation of genetic diversity** (see page 203) are two key factors that will continue to play important roles in the maintenance of sustainable food security.

Case Study | Food security

Challenge

Providing a secure supply of food for the global human population presents an enormous challenge for many reasons including the following:

- The global human population is increasing at a more rapid rate than food production.

- The world population in 2010 was 6 billion and it is projected to reach 9 billion by 2050.

- At present around 2 billion people lack food security.

- Malnourishment results in poor health. The individuals affected are unable to provide for their families. The resultant poverty is perpetuated from generation to generation.

- As the global human population increases, the demand for energy also increases.

- The drive to produce more biofuels (such as alcohol from sugar cane) leads to a reduction in arable land available for agricultural use.

- Farmers try to produce more food on less land, often with limited access to water.

- The price of storing and distributing food increases as the price of oil rises.

- Global warming alters environments and leads to change in what can be grown where. It may also increase the number and types of insects that are serious food pests and that may be resistant to traditional insecticides.

Contribution of biological science

Food security is a highly complex issue that involves many factors such as health, economic development, politics, trade and care of the environment. The problem of providing food for the global population cannot be solved by biological science alone. However, this branch of science, in close cooperation with other agencies as part of an interdisciplinary approach, can make a significant contribution to food security in several ways including the following:

- Development of high-yielding varieties of plants and animals by selective breeding or the incorporation of genetic variety from wild relatives into domestic strains and breeds.

- Use of genetic engineering to develop genetically modified varieties of crops that are resistant to pests or drought and in need of less fertiliser.

- Development and efficient use of biodegradable pesticides.

- Delivery of technology such as efficient irrigation schemes that enable farmers to increase agricultural productivity without exhausting irreplaceable ground water.

- Construction and delivery of programmes to educate people about birth control.

- Preparations made for the establishment of new agricultural zones in lands such as Canada and Siberia that will be warmed by climate change and will no longer be too cold for farming.

Agricultural production

Solar radiation drives the biological world. The first organism in every food chain, the green plant producer, obtains its energy from the Sun by photosynthesis. Some of this energy is passed on to animal consumers. Therefore all **food production** (plant or animal) depends on the process of photosynthesis.

Plant crops

Although the Earth possesses at least 75 000 species of **edible plants**, humans depend on only a small number of these to produce 95% of the world's food supply (see Figure 17.2).

These include cereals such as maize and rice, root crops such as cassava and leguminous (pod-bearing) plants such as soya bean.

Limited area

If the area suited to growing crops is **limited**, food production can only be increased by improving efficiency. This may be achieved by adopting one or more of the following practices:

- Identifying any factors that are **limiting** plant growth (for example shortage of mineral elements and water in the soil) and increasing the supply of these (such as by adding fertiliser and making use of a sprinkler system).

- Replacing the existing strain of crop plant with a **higher-yielding cultivar**.

- **Protecting** the crop from pests (such as insects), disease (for example those caused by fungi) and competition (from weeds) by using minimal doses of biodegradable pesticides, fungicides and herbicides.

- Developing **pest-resistant** crop plants. (Also see page 246)

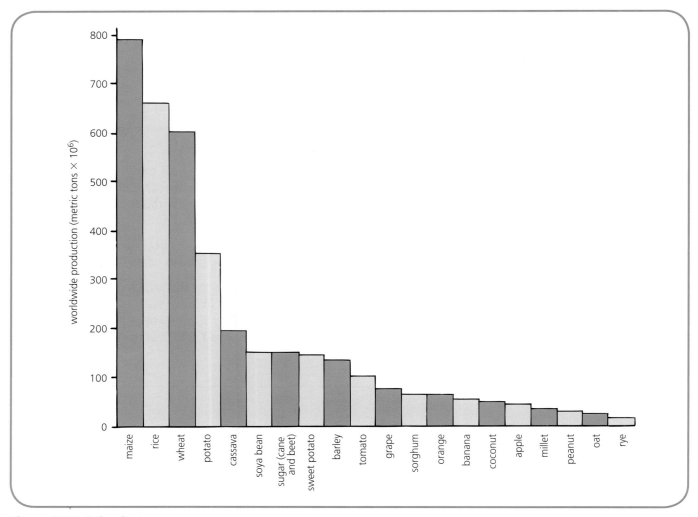

Figure 17.2 Main plant crops

Food chains and energy loss

Most of the energy gained by a consumer from its food is used for movement (and in endothermic animals, for maintaining body temperature). Therefore much of the energy taken in by an organism, and released as a result of cellular respiration, is lost and only about **10%**, on average, is incorporated into its body tissues and passed on along the food chain. Figure 17.3 shows a **pyramid of numbers** based on the food chain:

phytoplankton → zooplankton → herring → human

Each layer in the pyramid is called a **trophic level** and energy is lost between one trophic level and the next.

Length of food chain

More efficient use is made of food when humans consume plants rather than animals. In the food chain shown in Figure 17.4, 1000 kg of cereal plant could be used to feed many more people than can be fed by 100 kg of meat from farm animals. As a result of energy loss between trophic levels, livestock production generates far less food per unit area of land than plant production. In general, the **shorter** a food chain, the **greater** the quantity of energy held in the food.

Therefore arable farm land planted with crops produces far more food than the same land planted with grass to feed livestock. Some habitats (such as steep, grassy hillsides) are unsuitable for the cultivation of crop plants but efficient use can be made of them for livestock production (for example sheep farming).

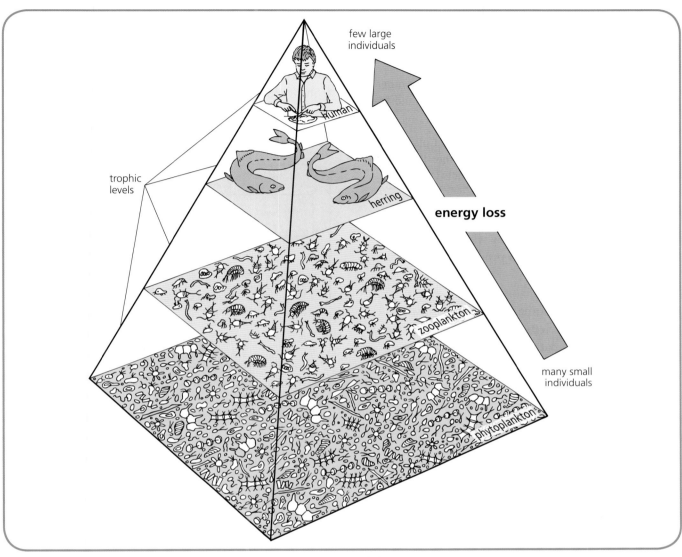

Figure 17.3 Energy loss in a food pyramid (organisms not to scale)

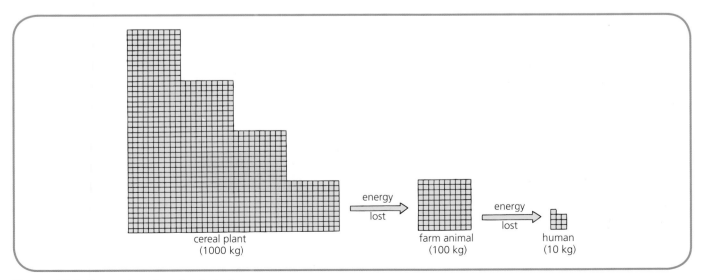

Figure 17.4 Energy loss in a food chain

1 What is meant by the term *food security*? (2)

2 State TWO practices that can be adopted in order to increase food production in an area of land that is limited in size. (2)

3 Why is more efficient use made of food plants by humans consuming them directly rather than first converting them into animal products? (1)

Photosynthesis

Photosynthesis is the process by which green plants trap light energy and use it to produce carbohydrates.

Light

Light is a form of electromagnetic radiation which travels in waves. **Wavelength** is the distance between two crests on a wave pattern as shown in Figure 17.5. Wavelengths of light are normally measured in nanometres (nm). ($1\,nm = 10^{-9}\,m$)

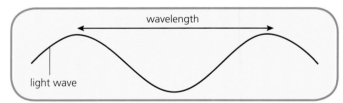

Figure 17.5 Wavelength

Spectrum of visible light

Out of the full range of radiation that falls on the Earth from the Sun and space, the most important, from a biological point of view, is the narrow band from wavelength 380 nm to 750 nm. This is called the **spectrum of visible light** (see Figure 17.6) because it can be seen by the human eye as a variety of colours.

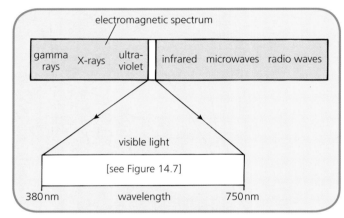

Figure 17.6 Electromagnetic radiation

Absorption, reflection and transmission

When light comes into contact with a substance, it may be **absorbed**, **reflected** or **transmitted**. A **pigment** is a substance that absorbs visible light. For example the wine in Figure 17.8 contains a red pigment which absorbs all the colours in the spectrum of visible light

Examining the spectrum of visible light

When a beam of white light is passed through a glass **prism** (or **spectroscope**) as shown in Figure 17.7, the **spectrum of visible light** is produced.

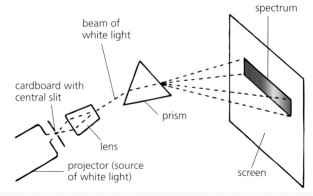

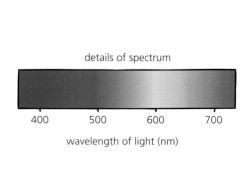

Figure 17.7 Spectrum of visible light

except red which it reflects and transmits. A pigment displays the colour of the light that it does *not* absorb.

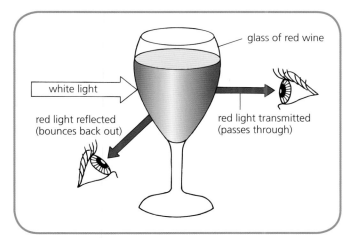

Figure 17.8 The reason why a red pigment is red

Thin-layer chromatography

During thin-layer chromatography the mixture to be separated is applied to a thin-layer strip (normally composed of a thin layer of silica gel attached to a backing material). As the solvent passes up through the thin-layer strip, it carries the components of the mixture to different levels depending on the degree of their solubility in the solvent (and the extent to which they are absorbed by the silica gel).

Related Activity

Extraction of leaf pigments

Fresh leaves are finely chopped up and then ground in a mortar containing propanone and a little fine sand as shown in Figure 17.9. The extract of soluble pigments is then separated from the cell debris by filtration.

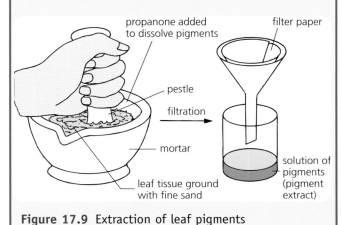

Figure 17.9 Extraction of leaf pigments

Related Activity

Separation of leaf pigments using thin-layer chromatography

A length of thin-layer strip is prepared as shown in Figure 17.10. This diagram illustrates the procedure followed during spotting of the extract and the use of the chromatography solvent.

Spotting and drying of the extract is repeated many times and then the end of the strip is dipped into the solvent. The chromatogram is allowed to run for

Design feature or precaution	Reason
plant tissue ground in fine sand	to rupture cells allowing release of contents
chromatography strip cut so that it does not touch sides of tube	to ensure that solvent rises uniformly through the strip rather than more rapidly up its edges
spotting and drying repeated many times	to obtain a concentrated spot of pigments
strip positioned in tube so that pigment spot is above solvent level at the start	to prevent extract dissolving in main bulk of solvent at bottom of tube
naked flames extinguished before starting experiment	to prevent fire risk since solvent chemicals are highly flammable

Table 17.1 Design techniques

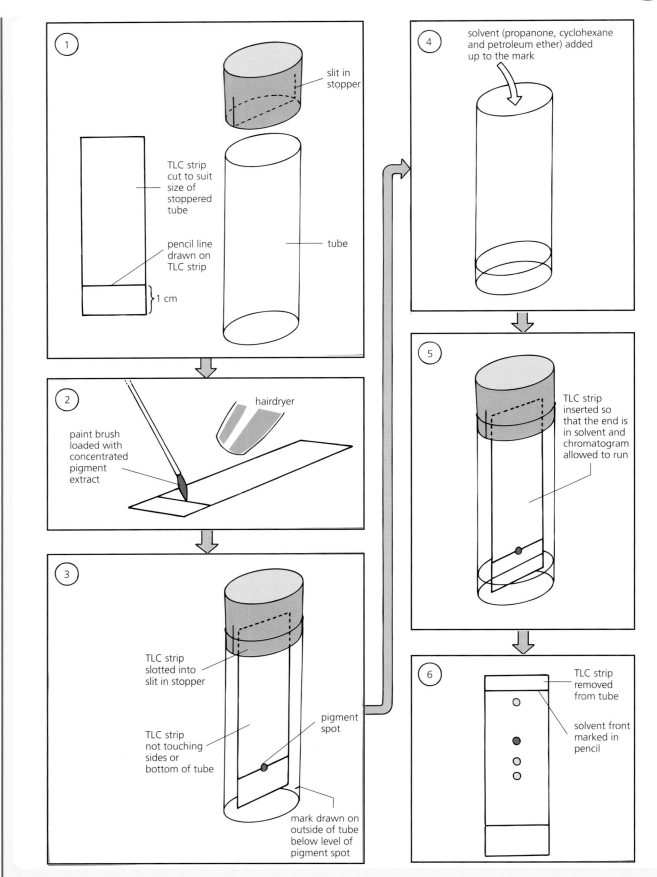

Figure 17.10 Separation of leaf pigments (TLC stands for thin-layer chromatography)

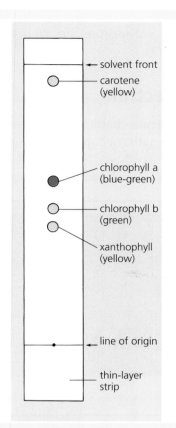

Figure 17.11 Thin-layer chromatogram of leaf pigments

a few minutes until the solvent has almost reached the top of the strip. The strip is then removed from the tube and a pencil used to mark the position of the solvent front. Table 17.1 gives the reasons for adopting certain techniques and precautions during this experiment.

Chromatogram

Figure 17.11 shows the **chromatogram** formed as a result of thin-layer chromatography with this particular solvent.

The solvent has carried the most soluble pigment (carotene) to the highest position and so on down the strip to xanthophyll, the least soluble. This has been carried the shortest distance.

Rf value

Each pigment separated by chromatography has an **Rf value** (also see chapter 3, page 28).

Absorption spectrum

When a beam of white light is first passed through a sample of extracted leaf pigments, placed at X in Figure 17.12, and then passed through a glass prism (or spectroscope), an **absorption spectrum** is produced.

Each **black** band is a region of the spectrum where light with a particular wavelength has been absorbed by the leaf pigments, and has therefore failed to pass through the prism and onto the screen. Most of the absorbed light is in the blue and red regions of the spectrum.

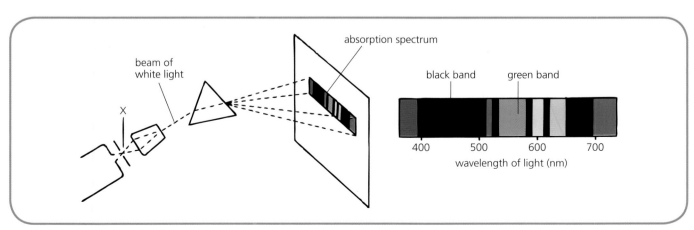

Figure 17.12 Absorption spectrum of leaf pigments

Each **coloured** band (such as green) is a region where light of a particular wavelength has *not* been absorbed by the pigment extract. Chlorophyll appears green to the eye because it does not absorb green light but instead reflects and transmits it.

Graph of absorption spectra of leaf pigments

The degree of absorption at each wavelength of visible light by each pigment (chlorophyll a, chlorophyll b and the carotenoids) can be measured using a spectrometer. The data obtained allow a detailed graph of each pigment's **absorption spectrum** to be plotted (see Figure 17.13).

Action spectrum

An **action spectrum** charts the effectiveness of different wavelengths of light at bringing about the process of photosynthesis. In the experiment shown in Figure 17.14, a set of coloured filters are used in

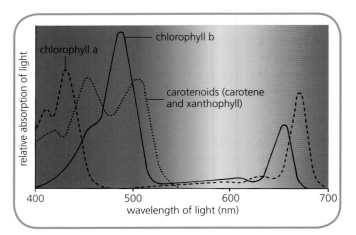

Figure 17.13 Graph of absorption spectra of leaf pigments

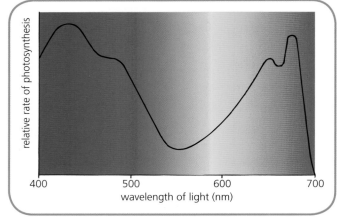

Figure 17.15 Action spectrum

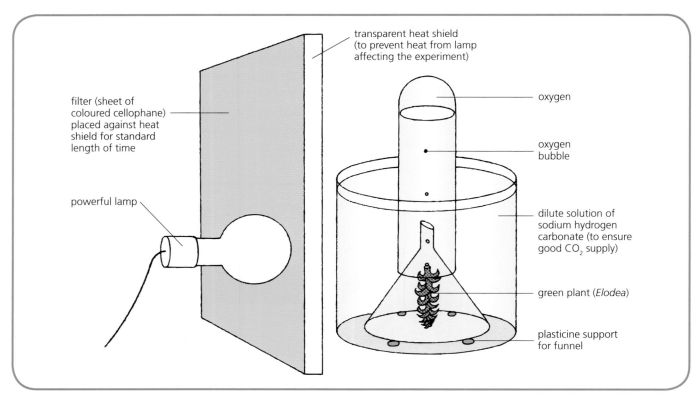

Figure 17.14 Investigating the action spectra of photosynthesis

turn to illuminate *Elodea*, an aquatic plant. Rate of photosynthesis is measured as number of bubbles or volume of oxygen released per minute. Figure 17.15 shows an action spectrum of photosynthesis when the results are graphed.

Comparison of absorption and action spectra

When Figures 17.13 and 17.15 are compared, a **close correlation** is found to exist between the overall absorption spectrum for the leaf pigments and the action spectrum for photosynthesis. It is therefore concluded that the absorption of certain wavelengths of light for use in photosynthesis is the crucial role played by the pigments.

Chlorophyll a and b absorb light energy mainly from the **blue** and **red** regions of the spectrum. The other pigments (such as carotenoids) absorb light energy from other regions (including the blue-green region of the spectrum) and pass the energy on to chlorophyll.

Advantage to plant

The fact that the different photosynthetic pigments absorb light of different wavelengths from one another is of advantage to the plant because it **extends the range** of wavelengths that the plant can use for photosynthesis.

Testing Your Knowledge 2

1 a) By what means can white light be split up into the spectrum? (1)

   b) Which colour in the spectrum has light with the
   i) shortest wavelength?
   ii) longest wavelength? (2)

2 a) Explain the difference between an *absorption* spectrum and an *action* spectrum. (2)

   b) Which TWO colours of light do chlorophylls a and b mainly absorb? (2)

   c) Why does chlorophyll b appear green in colour? (2)

3 Why is it of advantage to a green plant that the different pigments absorb different wavelengths of light? (1)

Capture and transfer of energy during photosynthesis

When light energy is absorbed by a molecule of chlorophyll a, its **electrons** become **excited** and raised to a higher energy state in the pigment molecule. Electrons excited in this way are captured by the primary electron acceptor associated with each chlorophyll a molecule in a chloroplast. This results

in the series of events shown in Figure 17.16 taking place.

The transfer of high-energy electrons through an electron transport chain releases energy that is used to generate **ATP** by the enzyme **ATP synthase**. Energy is also used for **photolysis** of water. During this process water is split into **oxygen** (which is released) and **hydrogen** which becomes bound to coenzyme **NADP** (acting as a hydrogen acceptor) to form **NADPH**.

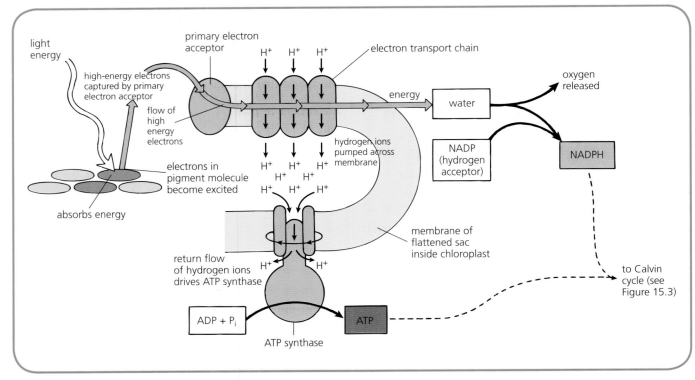

Figure 17.16 Transfer of energy during photosynthesis

Investigating photolysis (the Hill reaction)

DCPIP (dichlorophenol-indophenol) is a chemical that acts as a hydrogen acceptor by undergoing the following chemical reaction:

$$DCPIP + 2H^+ + 2e^- \rightarrow DCPIPH_2$$
(dark blue)   (colourless)

The experiment is set up as shown in Figure 17.17 with the three test tubes resting against the inner surface of the beaker of crushed ice.

From the results it is concluded that the contents of tube A have lost their dark blue colour because photolysis has occurred. Water in the presence of a hydrogen acceptor has been broken down by light energy into its components as in the equation:

$$2H_2O + 2DCPIP \xrightarrow[\text{chlorophyll}]{\text{light}} 2DCPIPH_2 + O_2$$

Tube B shows that light is necessary and tube C shows that chlorophyll is necessary for the reaction to take place.

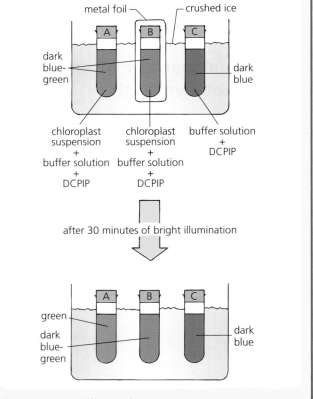

Figure 17.17 Hill reaction

The reaction is also known as the **Hill reaction**, named after the scientist who was the first to carry it out in the 1930s. In addition to showing that hydrogen was released from water, Hill demonstrated that oxygen was released also.

Calvin cycle

At the end of the first stage of photosynthesis (the light-dependent stage), the hydrogen held by NADPH and the energy held by ATP are essential for the second stage. This stage also takes place in the cell's chloroplasts but it is not light dependent. It consists of several enzyme-controlled reactions which take the form of a cycle – called the **Calvin cycle** after the scientist who discovered it. The cycle is summarised in Figure 17.18.

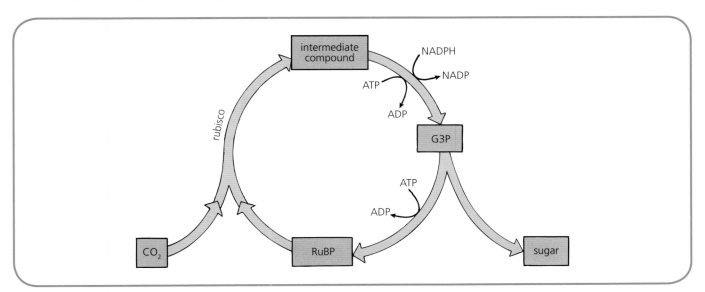

Figure 17.18 Calvin cycle

Carbon dioxide enters the cycle by becoming attached to **RuBP** (ribulose bisphosphate). This chemical reaction is controlled by the enzyme **rubisco** (sometimes written RuBisCO, full name – ribulose bisphosphate carboxylase/oxygenase). The intermediate (-3-phosphoglycerate) that is formed becomes combined with hydrogen from NADPH and becomes phosphorylated by receiving an inorganic phosphate (P_i) from ATP which supplies the energy to drive the process. This results in the formation of **G3P** (glyceraldehyde-3-phosphate), some of which is used to regenerate RuBP, the carbon dioxide acceptor. The remaining G3P is used for the synthesis of **sugars** such as **glucose**.

Research Topic	Inhibition of rubisco by oxygen

In most plants carbon dioxide combines with RuBP during photosynthesis. This 'carbon fixation' is controlled by the enzyme rubisco acting as a carboxylase. When a leaf's stomata are open, plenty of CO_2 enters the leaf's air spaces and becomes incorporated into the Calvin cycle. However, on hot, dry days, stomata close to conserve water. Now the concentration of CO_2 in the air spaces decreases and the concentration of oxygen produced by photosynthesis remains high. Under these circumstances, rubisco's normal activity as a carboxylase is inhibited. Instead it acts as an oxygenase and adds O_2 (*not* CO_2) to the Calvin cycle. This alters the process and decreases the photosynthetic output. At present, scientists are investigating this apparently inefficient system. If rubisco could be prevented from acting as an oxygenase, photosynthetic productivity and crop yield in plants such as rice and wheat would be significantly increased.

One solution would be to find a way of concentrating CO_2 in and around the leaf's green cells so that rubisco would take up CO_2 only and not oxygen. This already occurs naturally in some plants such as maize. Scientists are also trying to increase the specificity of rubisco for CO_2 relative to oxygen by genetic manipulation.

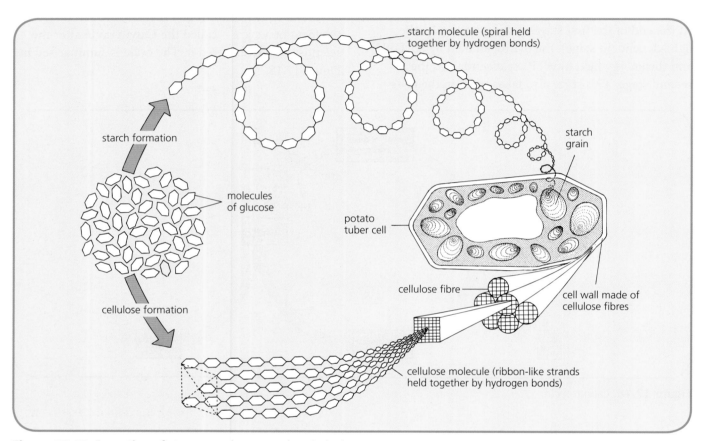

Figure 17.19 Formation of storage and structural carbohydrates

Use of sugar made by photosynthesis

Some of the carbohydrate (for example glucose) that is formed is used by the plant for cellular respiration to provide the plant with energy for **growth** and **reproduction**. Some of the remaining sugar molecules are synthesised into molecules of complex carbohydrate. For example they may become built into long chains of **cellulose** and used as a **structural** carbohydrate to build cell walls (see Figure 17.19). Alternatively they may become linked together into long chains and packed into spherical **starch** grains as a **storage** carbohydrate.

Other molecules of carbohydrate produced by photosynthesis may be passed to other **biosynthetic pathways**. These contribute to the production of a variety of further **metabolites** such as amino acids, proteins and nucleotides.

Related Activity

Investigating the effect of phosphorylase on glucose-1-phosphate

See page 141.

Testing Your Knowledge 3

1 a) When a molecule of chlorophyll a absorbs light energy, what happens initially to this energy? (1)

   b) High-energy electrons captured by a primary electron acceptor are transferred through an electron transport chain releasing energy. Give the equation for the enzyme-controlled process that is then driven by this energy. (2)

   c) Some of the energy is also used to split water. What happens to each component of water? (2)

2 a) i) Name the enzyme that attaches CO_2 to ribulose bisphosphate to form an intermediate in the Calvin cycle.

      ii) What TWO products from the light-dependent stage of photosynthesis are required to convert this intermediate to G3P? (3)

   b) G3P becomes converted into two substances. Name the substance that:
      i) remains in the cycle
      ii) leaves the cycle. (2)

3 a) Give an example of:
      i) a structural carbohydrate
      ii) a storage carbohydrate in plants. (2)

   b) Name TWO non-carbohydrate metabolites that result from biosynthetic pathways in green plants. (2)

Plant productivity

Biomass

The biomass of a population of plants is its total mass of organic material. Biomass is normally measured as dry mass of organic material because the water content of living organisms, especially land plants, can vary greatly over short periods of time.

Assimilation

Assimilation in plants is the process by which food produced by photosynthesis is converted into complex constituents of cell systems such as protoplasm and cell walls. This results in an increase in biomass of the growing plant.

Some of the carbohydrate made during photosynthesis is used up in respiration. Therefore net assimilation (the overall increase in biomass made by the plant) is the gain in mass made as a result of photosynthesis minus the loss in mass incurred by respiration.

Measurement of net assimilation rate

Net assimilation rate can be found by measuring the increase in dry mass per unit of leaf area per unit of time. The procedure outlined in Figure 17.20 shows how net assimilation rate for samples from leaves grown in a variety of conditions can be compared.

From the results it is concluded that:

- in group A, rate of respiration > rate of photosynthesis and the net rate of assimilation is negative

- in group B, rate of respiration = rate of photosynthesis and the net rate of assimilation is zero

- in group C, rate of respiration < rate of photosynthesis and the net assimilation rate is greater than zero. This rate can be expressed quantitatively by calculating the increase in dry mass per leaf disc per unit of time.

Productivity

In general, productivity refers to rate of production. In biology, productivity means the rate at which plants in an ecosystem generate new biomass. Productivity is measured as units of biomass per unit area per unit of time, for example grams per square metre per year $(g\,m^{-2}\,y^{-1})$.

Limiting factors

Rate of photosynthesis (and productivity) is affected by several environmental factors. These include temperature, light intensity and carbon dioxide concentration.

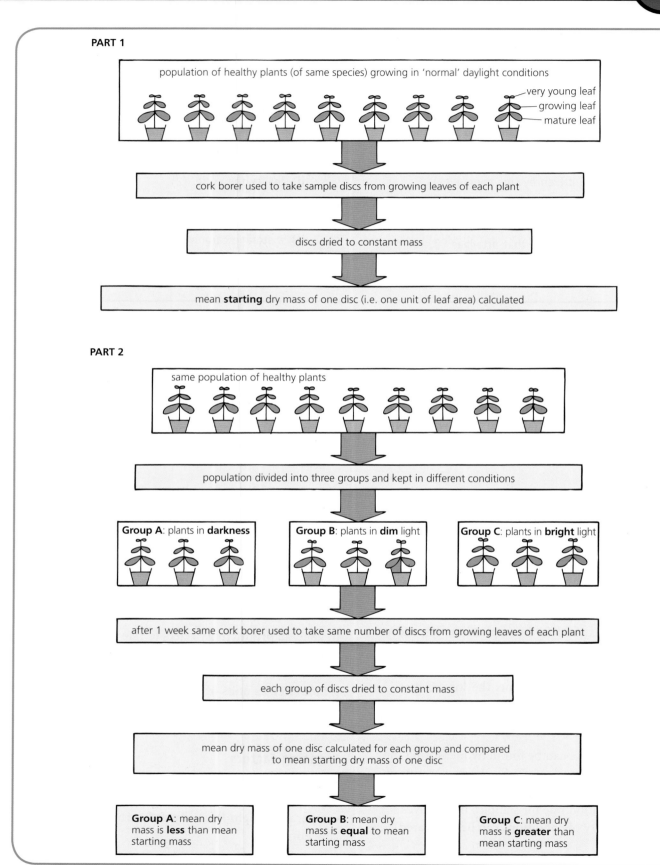

Figure 17.20 Measuring rate of net assimilation

The rate at which photosynthesis proceeds is limited by whichever one of these factors is in short supply. For example, light intensity would probably be the factor limiting photosynthesis on a dull, wet summer day.

The principle of **limiting factors** can be investigated using a water plant such as *Elodea* (see Figures 17.21 and 17.22). The carbon dioxide concentration can be varied by adding a chemical to the water. The light intensity can be varied by using a lamp with a dimmer switch. Photosynthetic rate is measured by counting the number of oxygen bubbles released per minute.

Graph ABC in Figure 17.23 refers to a water plant kept in conditions of constant low light intensity. When the plant is supplied with a CO_2 concentration of only one unit, photosynthetic rate is limited by this low concentration of CO_2 to three oxygen bubbles/min.

Figure 17.21 Release of oxygen bubbles from *Elodea*

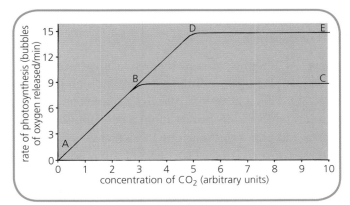

Figure 17.23 Limiting factors

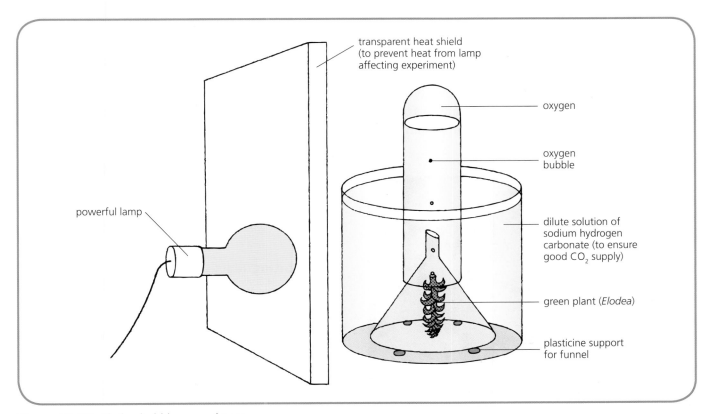

Figure 17.22 *Elodea* bubbler experiment

When CO_2 concentration is increased to two units, photosynthetic rate increases to six oxygen bubbles/min but no further since CO_2 concentration becomes limiting again.

A further increase in CO_2 concentration to three units brings about a further increase in photosynthetic rate. Beyond this point, the graph levels out and further increases in CO_2 concentration fail to affect photosynthetic rate. This is because light (which has been at constant low intensity throughout) has now become the factor limiting the process. Previously, CO_2 concentration had been the limiting factor (on the AB part of the graph).

Graph ADE represents a further experiment using the same plant kept in conditions of constant high light intensity. This time an increase in CO_2 concentration to four and five units brings about a corresponding increase in photosynthetic rate in each case because, at these concentrations, CO_2 concentration is still the limiting factor when light intensity is high. However, beyond five units of CO_2, the graph levels off again since light intensity (or some other factor) has become limiting.

Productivity and leaves

Photosynthesis is restricted to the plant's green parts – principally its leaves. Therefore productivity depends on the **arrangement, shape** and **number** of leaves. Leaves often grow in a **mosaic pattern** (see Figure 17.24) which presents the maximum surface area of leaf to the light with the minimum shading of the lower leaves.

Figure 17.24 Leaf mosaic pattern

Another effective arrangement is that of a plant shaped like a wide-based cone with its leaves arranged **spirally** around the stem. In theory the more leaves a plant possesses, the better. However, there is an optimum number for each plant because if too many leaves were present, many would become shaded and might use up more food during respiration than they gained by photosynthesis.

Leaf area index

The **leaf area index** (LAI) is the ratio of total leaf area to area of ground covered by the leaves. The LAI indicates the efficiency of light interception by the leaves. For example a cereal crop plant such as wheat has some leaves upright and some in part horizontal to the stem and in part drooping. Depending on density of planting, a crop of wheat may have a total leaf area three times that of the ground area covered by the leaves and therefore an LAI of 3.

The graph in Figure 17.25 shows that as LAI increases, net productivity increases initially and then levels off as a larger number of lower leaves become shaded by those above.

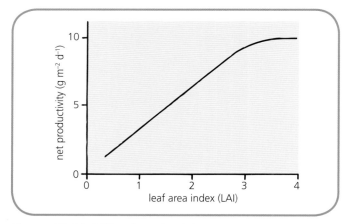

Figure 17.25 LAI and productivity

Crop planting density

When crop plants are too widely spaced, productivity will be relatively low because some light falls between the plants onto bare ground. In addition, space is available for weeds to grow and compete with the crop.

A more densely planted crop shows an increase in productivity because it makes maximum use of the available light with the minimum area of land left unused.

However, there comes a point when increased density of crop planting beyond a certain **optimum** level is *not* accompanied by an increase in productivity because many of the crop plants' leaves are shaded. In addition the plants may be competing with one another for water or minerals and be more prone to the spread of pests. Too dense a crop also wastes money on supplies of unnecessary seeds and fertiliser.

Maize

The data in Table 17.2 show the effect of increasing crop planting density on productivity of maize plants grown on two farms for the same length of time. Although farm 1's overall productivity is less than that of farm 2, the effect of crop planting density is the same on both farms. Increased density of crop planting is accompanied by increased productivity to an optimum level at 30 000 plants ha^{-1}. At the higher density of 40 000 plants ha^{-1}, productivity decreases.

Biological yield and economic yield

The **biological yield** of a crop (see Figure 17.26) is the total biomass of plant material produced (for example mature barley plants). The **economic yield** of a crop is the mass of the desired product (for example barley grains).

Harvest index

The **harvest index** is calculated using the formula:

$$\frac{\text{dry mass of economic yield}}{\text{dry mass of biological yield}}$$

This is often converted to a percentage.

Crop planting density (no. of plants × 10³ ha⁻¹)	Dry biomass at harvest (kg ha⁻¹)	
	Farm 1	Farm 2
10	6 413	6 691
20	10 526	14 547
30	14 307	18 662
40	11 802	16 935

[1 hectare (ha) = 10 000 m²]

Table 17.2 Effect of increasing crop planting density

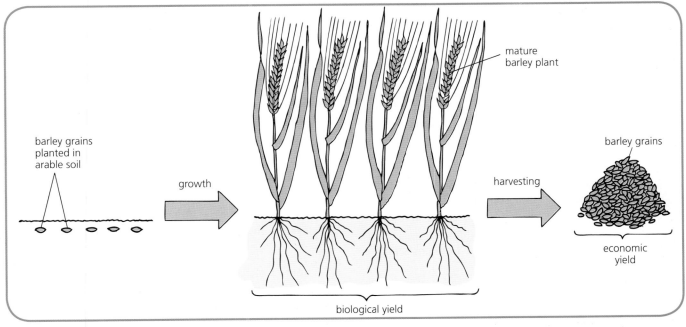

Figure 17.26 Biological and economic yield

Testing Your Knowledge 4

1 Decide whether each of the following statements is true or false and then use T or F to indicate your choice. Where a statement is false, give the word that should have been used in place of the word in bold print. (4)

a) Assimilation is the conversion of food into complex cell constituents such as **protoplasm**.

b) Net assimilation can be measured by the increase in **fresh** mass per unit of leaf area.

c) The biomass of a population of plants is its total mass of **inorganic** material.

d) The rate of generation of new biomass per unit area per unit of time is called **planting density**.

2 Name TWO environmental factors that can limit a plant's rate of photosynthesis. (2)

3 a) What is the difference between *biological* and *economic* yield of a crop? (2)

b) What value can be calculated by dividing the dry mass of economic yield by the dry mass of biological yield? (1)

What You Should Know

Chapter 17

(See Table 17.3 for word bank)

action	economic	pigment
assimilation	electrons	productivity
ATP	G3P	reflected
ATP synthase	harvest index	rubisco
biological	higher-yielding	RuBP
blue	less	security
carbohydrates	mass	spectrum
carbon dioxide	NADPH	sustainable
Calvin	phosphorylated	transport
carotenoids	photolysis	trophic
cellulose	photosynthesis	weeds

Table 17.3 Word bank for chapter 17

1 The ability to access food of sufficient quantity and quality by humans is called food _____. The continuous increase in the human population is accompanied by a demand for increased food production that is _____ but not damaging to the environment.

2 Food production depends on the process of _____. A small number of crops supply most human food. If agricultural land is limited, increased food production can be achieved by growing _____ cultivars and by protecting crops from pests and competitive _____.

3 As a result of energy loss between _____ levels in a food chain, production of livestock generates _____ food per unit area than crop plants.

4 The process by which light energy is trapped by green plants and used to produce _____ is called photosynthesis.

5 On coming into contact with a leaf, light may be absorbed, _____ or transmitted.

6 Chlorophyll absorbs light primarily in the _____ and red regions of the spectrum of white light. _____ absorb blue-green light and extend the range of wavelength absorbed for photosynthesis. A close correlation exists between the overall absorption _____ for leaf pigments and the _____ spectrum for photosynthesis.

7 Light energy absorbed by a leaf _____ molecule is transferred to _____ which become excited. These high-energy electrons are transferred through electron _____ chains where they release energy.

8 Some energy is used to generate ATP under the control of _____; some energy is needed to split water by _____. The oxygen produced is released by the cell; the hydrogen becomes attached to coenzyme NADP to form _____.

9 _____ and NADPH from the light-dependent first part of the process are needed to drive the _____ cycle – the second part of photosynthesis.

10 _____ becomes attached to RuBP under the control of the enzyme _____. The intermediate metabolite that results becomes _____ by ATP. Then it combines with hydrogen from NADPH to form _____.

11 Some G3P is used to regenerate _____. The rest becomes sugar. Some of these sugar molecules are built up into starch, _____ and other metabolites.

12 The increase in mass of a plant due to photosynthesis minus the loss due to respiration is called net _____; it is measured as increase in dry _____ per unit area of leaf.

13 The generation of new biomass per unit area of leaf per unit of time is called _____.

14 The total biomass of a crop plant is called its _____ yield. The biomass of the desired product of a crop is called its _____ yield. The economic yield divided by the biological yield gives the _____ of a crop.

18 Plant and animal breeding

Characteristics selected by breeders

Breeders of crop plants and livestock attempt to manipulate a chosen organism's heredity. This is done in order to produce a new and improved **cultivar** of plant or **breed** of animal that will provide a source of sustainable food for humans. Examples of the types of characteristics that breeders would select are shown in Table 18.1.

Heritable characteristic	Example
increase in yield	increase in mass of food produced by wheat crop
increase in nutritional value	increase in mass of protein produced by soya bean crop
resistance to pests	resistance of tomato to eelworm
resistance to disease	resistance of potato to late blight
possession of useful physical characteristic	growth of cereal crop to uniform height suited to mechanical harvesting
ability to thrive in a particular environment	ability of maize to grow in cold, damp climate

Table 18.1 Characteristics selected by breeders

Related Topic

Investigating resistance of potato varieties to *Phytophthora infestans*

In recent years agriculture has become overdependent on the use of chemical pesticides to protect crops from pests and diseases. Scientists are constantly seeking new ways of protecting food crops by breeding cultivars that are **resistant** to diseases.

Phytophthora infestans is a fungal pathogen that causes **late blight** in potato plants (see Figure 18.1). It was this devastating disease that led to the Irish potato famine in 1845–6. During the early twentieth century some resistance to *P. infestans* was achieved successfully by crossing existing (domestic) cultivars of potato with wild varieties possessing resistant genes. However, *P. infestans* soon evolved new aggressive races (strains) able to break down the potato plant's resistance.

Scientists in Scotland are investigating the resistance of potato varieties to *P. infestans* using a combination of approaches including the following:

- A variety of potato cultivars from many different parts of the world are being subjected to various

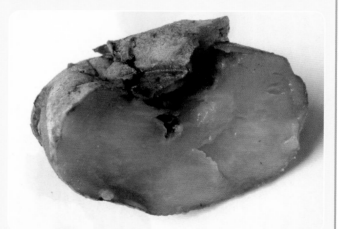

Figure 18.1 Potato infected with late blight

races of *P. infestans* to identify resistant strains of potato.

- Marker-assisted selection (MAS) is being used to locate markers (regions of a crop plant's DNA) that are associated with desirable traits, with the aim of transferring these from one variety to another. MAS is an advance on genetic modification involving single genes because it involves a set of interacting genes that contribute to a complex trait such as disease resistance.

● Multi-trait pre-breeding programmes are being carried out to combine disease resistance with other quality traits to create new varieties of potato.

● Field trials are being run where new and traditional varieties of potato are grown without fungicide and compared for incidence of late blight and for crop yield.

Discrete variation

The members of a species are not identical but **vary** from one another. An inherited characteristic shows **discrete variation** if it can be used to divide up the members of a species into two or more distinct groups. For example peas can be divided into two separate groups based on seed colour where each seed is either yellow or green (see Figure 18.2). Such information is often presented as a bar chart. Table 18.2 gives further examples of characteristics in pea plants that show discrete variation.

Figure 18.2 Discrete variation in pea seed colour

Characteristic	Dominant trait	Recessive trait
plant height	tall	dwarf
pod shape	inflated	constricted
pod colour	green	yellow
seed shape	round	wrinkled
flower colour	purple	white

Table 18.2 Discrete variation in pea plants

Single gene pattern of inheritance
Seed shape in pea plants

A characteristic that shows discrete variation is normally controlled by the alleles of a **single** gene. In pea plants the gene for seed shape has two alleles, round (R) which is **dominant** to wrinkled (r), the **recessive** form. Figure 18.3 shows three generations

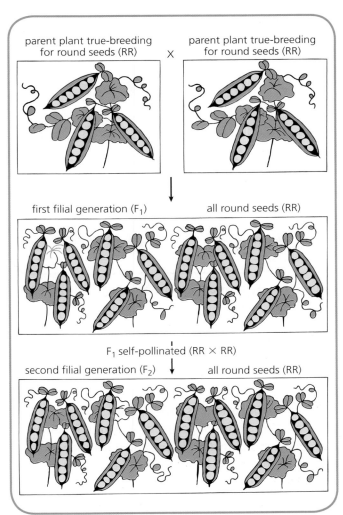

Figure 18.3 Cultivar of pea true-breeding for round seeds

of a strain of pea plant with round seeds. Figure 18.4 shows three generations of a strain of pea plant with wrinkled seeds. In each case the seed type is always identical to that of the parents which are **true-breeding** lines formed by self-fertilisation and inbreeding (see page 253).

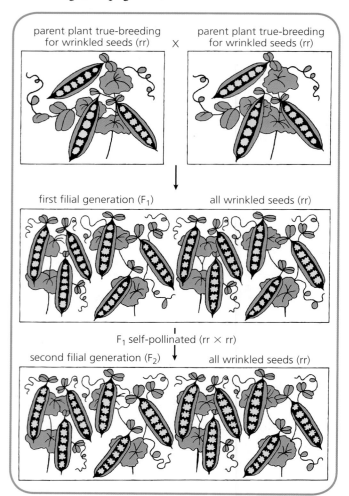

Figure 18.4 Cultivar of pea true-breeding for wrinkled seeds

Single gene cross

A single gene (**monohybrid**) cross is a cross that involves only **one difference** in an inherited characteristic between the original parents. Figure 18.5 shows a monohybrid cross between the two true-breeding strains of pea plant shown in Figures 18.3 and 18.4. Self-pollination is prevented between the parents so this cross is an example of cross-fertilisation and **outbreeding** (see page 253).

The phenotypes of the F₁ generation are uniform – they all have round seeds. The wrinkled characteristic

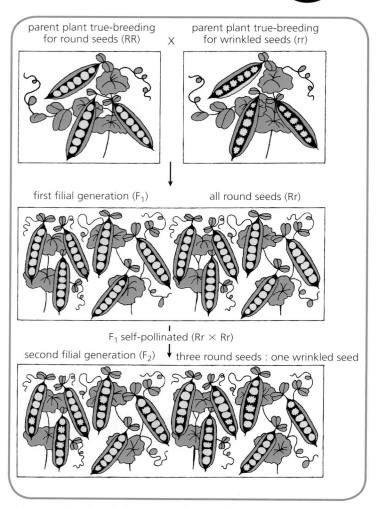

Figure 18.5 Monohybrid cross in pea plants

has disappeared in the F₁ because it is recessive and has been masked by the round characteristic which is dominant.

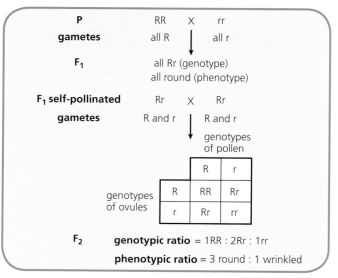

Figure 18.6 Monohybrid cross in symbols

When the members of the F_1 are self-pollinated, the members of the F_2 generation are found to occur in a **phenotypic ratio** of three round:one wrinkled as shown in Figure 18.6 which uses symbols to represent the cross. The F_2 generation does not contain any 'in-between' forms of seed shape. Both round and wrinkled appear in their original form unaffected by their union in the F_1 generation. This is typical of characteristics that exhibit discrete variation.

Presence or absence of horns in cattle

In European cattle, the presence or absence of horns is controlled by a single gene with two alleles. Polled (hornless) (N) is dominant to horned (n). Figure 18.7 shows a cross involving this trait. On average three out of four members of the F_2 generation would be polled but it would not be obvious whether each polled animal's genotype was homozygous (NN) or heterozygous (Nn) for this trait.

Test cross

A **test cross** is a cross between an organism whose genotype for a certain trait is unknown and an organism that is homozygous recessive for that trait.

If the farmer wanted to know the genotype of a polled member of the F_2 in Figure 18.7 (in other words, to identify NN animals for breeding purposes), then he/she could set up a test cross (see Figure 18.8). This would allow the unknown genotype to be deduced by considering the offspring produced.

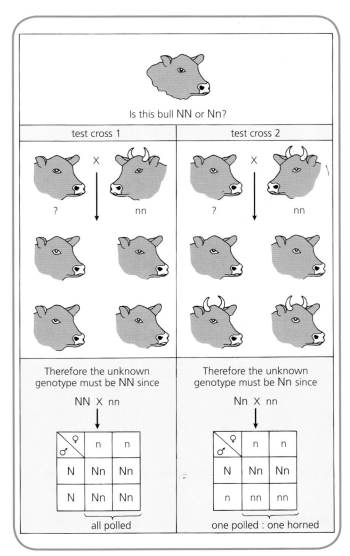

Figure 18.8 Test crosses

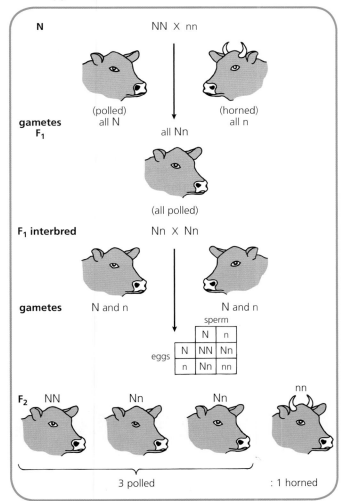

Figure 18.7 Monohybrid cross in cattle

Continuous variation

An inherited characteristic shows **continuous variation** when it varies among the members of the species in a smooth, continuous way from one extreme to another and does not fall naturally into distinct groups. For example seed mass varies from 'light' to 'heavy'. Such information is often presented as a **distribution curve** like the one shown in Figure 18.9 based on the mass of each of a group of castor oil seeds. The curve is found to be bell shaped because the majority of the seeds have a mass close to the centre of the range with fewer at the extremities.

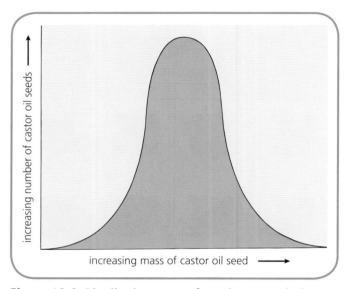

Figure 18.9 Distribution curve of continuous variation

Since the majority of the seeds have a mass close to the centre of the range, with fewer at the extremities, a curve drawn round the histogram gives a bell-shaped **normal distribution**.

Pattern of polygenic inheritance

A characteristic showing continuous variation is controlled by the interaction of alleles of more than one gene and is said to show **polygenic inheritance**. In cattle, for example, birth weight, weaning weight and marbling (streaks of fat in lean meat) are all examples of polygenic traits and each is controlled by alleles of several genes. The more genes that are involved, the greater the number of **intermediate phenotypes** that can be produced.

Environmental influences

Whereas characteristics that show discrete variation (such as seed shape) are largely unaffected by environmental factors, many traits that show continuous variation (including seed mass) are influenced by the environment. They are dependent on favourable environmental conditions (such as adequate sunshine and rainfall) for their full phenotypic expression.

Field trials

A plant **field trial** takes the form of an investigation. It could be set up, for example, to:

● compare the performance of two different plant cultivars under the same set of environmental conditions

● find out the effect of different environmental conditions on a new cultivar of a crop plant

● evaluate genetically modified (GM) crops.

Plots and treatments

The area of land to be used for a field trial is divided into equal-sized portions called **plots** (see Figure 18.10). A field trial involves **treatments**. A treatment refers to the way in which one plot is treated compared with other plots. For example one plot might be given a high concentration of fertiliser and another plot a low concentration. Therefore these plots would represent two different treatments of a variable factor under investigation.

Figure 18.10 Field trial

Designing a field trial

Once the plant breeder has established an objective (for example to investigate the effect of concentration of a nitrogenous fertiliser on a new cultivar of cereal plant), the next stage is to design the field trial. When doing so, the following factors must be taken into consideration.

Selection of treatments to be used

Each equal-sized plot might, for example, be given a high concentration or a low concentration or no application of fertiliser. If no other factor were varied, then a **fair comparison** could be made between treatments.

Number of replicates to be included

If only one treatment of each concentration of fertiliser were carried out, the results would be unreliable. This is because **uncontrolled variability** exists within the sample. Neither the three plots used nor the methods employed to apply the treatments to them would be exactly identical each time, however hard the scientist tried. Such variability is called **experimental error**.

Several **replicates** (normally a minimum of three) must be set up to take account of the variability and reduce the effect of this experimental error. It also allows valid statistical analysis of the results to be carried out. The more replicates that are set up, the more **reliable** the results.

Randomisation of treatments

If the plots in a field were treated in an orderly sequence then a **bias** could exist in the system. In the field shown in Figure 18.11, for example, soil moisture content decreases along the sequence of plots. Therefore within each replicate, each plot B treatment will have a built-in bias of less soil water compared with its corresponding plot A treatment and more soil water compared with its corresponding plot C treatment. **Randomising** the pattern of replicated treatments, as shown in Figure 18.12, eliminates this bias.

Repeats in other environments

If a plant field trial were restricted to one environment (such as sandy soil and temperate climate) then the conclusion that could be drawn from the results would be fairly limited. For example it might be the case that

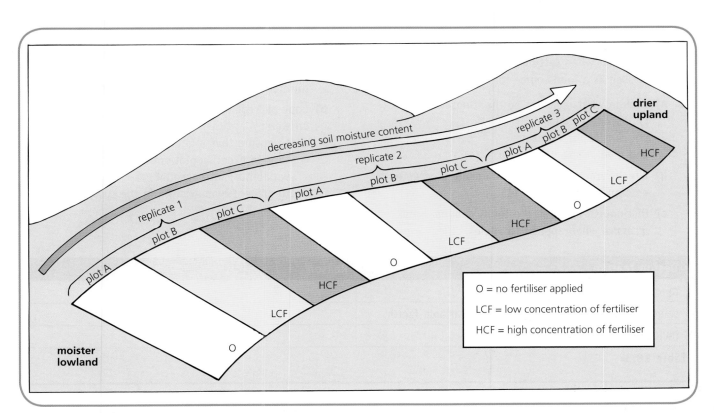

Figure 18.11 Poor design of field trial lacking randomisation

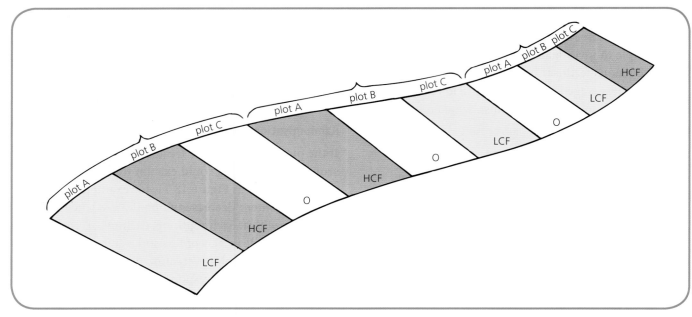

Figure 18.12 Design improved to include randomisation

the new cultivar being tested does not grow well in sandy soil regardless of how much fertiliser is added. Therefore a field trial is often repeated in several different environments to find out which soil type and climate conditions suit the plant best.

Testing Your Knowledge 1

1 Identify THREE heritable characteristics that breeders would select when setting out to improve a crop plant used as a food source for humans. (3)

2 a) Explain what is meant by the terms
   i) *discrete* variation
   ii) *continuous* variation
   and give an example of each. (4)

   b) Which form of variation is normally unaffected by environmental factors? (1)

   c) Distinguish between the terms *dominant* and *recessive* when applied to alleles. (2)

3 What is a *test cross* and why is it set up? (2)

4 a) With reference to field trials, what is the difference between a *plot* and a *treatment*? (2)

   b) Copy and complete Table 18.3 using the following answers:
   ● to ensure that a fair comparison can be made
   ● to take experimental error (uncontrolled variability) into account
   ● to prevent bias existing in the system. (2)

Design feature	Reason
randomisation of treatments	
selection of treatments involving one variable factor	
inclusion of several replicates	

Table 18.3

Selecting and breeding

A breeder selects those plants or animals with desired characteristics and uses them as the parents of the next generation. Normally the aim of a breeding programme is to combine the alleles of the genes for the desired traits present in one parent with those present in another parent thereby producing offspring superior to both parents.

Inbreeding and outbreeding

Inbreeding involves the fusion of two gametes from close relatives. The most intense form of inbreeding occurs among plants that are naturally self-fertile following self-pollination. Some crop plants such as peas, wheat and rice are natural **inbreeders**.

Outbreeding involves the fusion of two gametes from unrelated members of the same species. Animals and cross-pollinating plants are naturally outbreeding. Cross-pollinating plants often possess mechanisms that

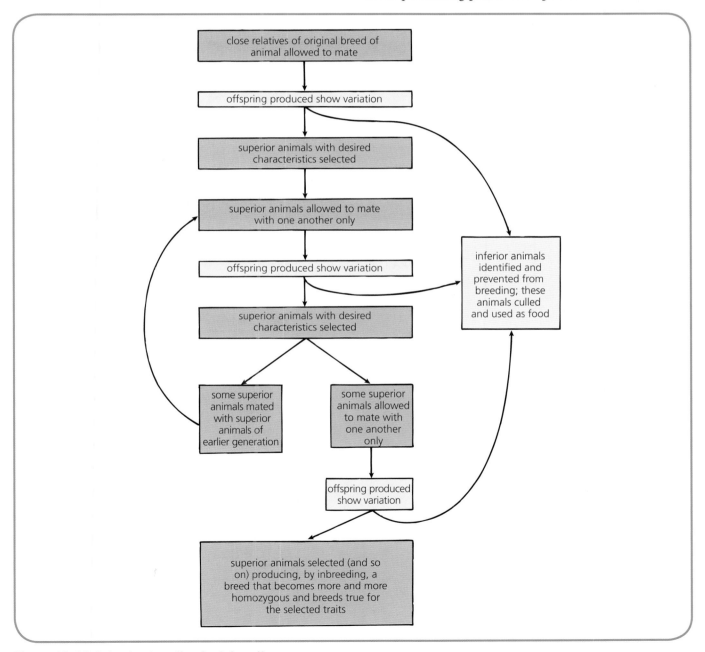

Figure 18.13 Selective breeding by inbreeding

prevent self-pollination such as the ripening at different times of the anthers and ovaries in the same flower. Some crop plants such as tomato, sugar beet and maize are natural outbreeders.

Effects of inbreeding

Inbreeding ensures that the members of each generation of a selectively bred strain of plant or animal receive the alleles for the desired characteristics. Inbreeding to produce a plant cultivar true-breeding for one or more desired traits is most effective if the plant is naturally self-pollinating.

Inbreeding to produce a breed of animal true-breeding for one or more desired characteristics is carried out by following a programme such as the one shown in Figure 18.13. This has the effect of concentrating the alleles for the selected traits into one line of the breed.

Comparison

Table 18.4 compares characteristics of inbreeders and outbreeders. When humans interfere with this natural state of affairs, problems may arise.

Inbreeders (self-pollinating plants)	Outbreeders (cross-pollinating plants and animals)
self-fertilisation employed	cross-fertilisation employed
homozygosity promoted	heterozygosity promoted
recessive, deleterious alleles normally eliminated over many generations by natural selection	recessive, deleterious alleles often present but masked by dominant alleles

Table 18.4 Characteristics of inbreeders and outbreeders

Generation	P_1	F_1	F_2	F_3
Genotypes resulting from inbreeding	Aa (selfed)	AA (selfed)	AA (selfed)	4AA
			AA (selfed)	4AA
			AA (selfed)	4AA
			AA (selfed)	4AA
		Aa (selfed)	AA (selfed)	4AA
			Aa (selfed)	AA:2Aa:aa
			Aa (selfed)	AA:2Aa:aa
			aa (selfed)	4aa
		Aa (selfed)	AA (selfed)	4AA
			Aa (selfed)	AA:2Aa:aa
			Aa (selfed)	AA:2Aa:aa
			aa (selfed)	4aa
		aa (selfed)	aa (selfed)	4aa
			aa (selfed)	4aa
			aa (selfed)	4aa
			aa (selfed)	4aa
Percentage heterozygosity remaining	100%	50%	25%	12.5%

Table 18.5 Effect of continuous inbreeding

Figure 18.14 Inbreeding depression in maize

Loss of heterozygosity

Continuous inbreeding leads to a **loss of heterozygosity** and development of **homozygosity** (see Table 18.5). This is not a problem for self-pollinating plants that are naturally inbreeding because harmful alleles have been weeded out of their genotypes by natural selection over millions of years.

Inbreeding depression

When a natural outbreeder is forcibly inbred, **inbreeding depression** occurs because genotypes emerge that are homozygous for an accumulation of recessive alleles of deleterious (harmful) genes. Expressed phenotypically, these result in a decline in vigour, size, fertility and yield of the plant or animal. This phenomenon is illustrated in Figure 18.14 for maize, a natural outbreeder. The plant on the left is the original parent forced to inbreed. The other plants represent the next three generations and show a decrease in growth.

Breeders often try to prevent natural outbreeders suffering inbreeding depression by choosing a population of parent plants that are homozygous for the desired characteristic(s) but are otherwise genetically diverse and heterozygous.

Case Study	Development of crop cultivars

Wheat

Red wheat has been bred over many generations for the excellent baking quality of its flour and its resistance to leaf rust (a fungal disease of cereal plants). In the past it was mainly grown in North America. However, in recent years cultivars of red wheat and other specially bred cultivars have been grown by thousands of British farmers. As a result, above 80% of the wheat used for bread making in the UK is now grown here and only 20% is imported from North America. This trend is expected to continue as a result of advances in wheat breeding and technology.

Swede

Swedes (Swedish turnips) (see Figure 18.15) have been grown in Scotland for more than 200 years.

Figure 18.15 Cultivar of swede

They are an important source of forage for sheep and cattle during the winter in addition to providing a wholesome source of food for people.

From the 1930s onwards swede plants were selected and inbred for high dry-matter content. This led to the development of a uniform, high-yielding cultivar. Then in the 1990s breeders turned their attention to other characteristics such as resistance to powdery mildew and clubroot.

After many breeding experiments involving both inbreeding of cultivars and crosses between different cultivars, scientists have developed varieties of swede that are high-yielding and resistant to both powdery mildew and the most prevalent strains of clubroot.

These cultivars outperform non-resistant varieties in environments where the diseases occur. However, the susceptible varieties do better than the resistant ones in regions where neither of the diseases is present. When either type of swede is grown under a fleece, it becomes attacked by root flies, so there is still plenty of work for the plant breeder to do to develop even better cultivars of swede.

Case Study | **Development of a livestock breed**

Ayrshire cattle

Development of the *Ayrshire* breed of cattle (see Figure 18.16) is thought to have begun about 300 years ago. Farmers are known to have crossed native local cattle, which were small and were poor milkers, with several other breeds. Of these, one breed that made a major contribution was the *Teeswater* which in turn contained genetic material from Dutch cattle (later used to develop the *Holstein* breed in Holland). The emerging *Ayrshire* breed was further improved over the years by crossing it with *Highland* cattle and with members of the *Shorthorn* breed.

The cow now known as 'the *Ayrshire*' is the result of breeders crossing and selecting various strains of cattle over many generations. Therefore *Ayrshire* cattle are well suited to the climate in Western Scotland and are efficient grazers. In addition, they are excellent milk producers. The milk itself is ideally

Figure 18.16 *Ayrshire* cow

suited to the production of butter and cheese. Top cows have been known to produce over 9000 litres of milk during their lactation period.

Testing Your Knowledge 2

1 Distinguish between the terms:

a) *inbreeding* and *outbreeding*. (2)

b) *homozygous* and *heterozygous*. (2)

2 Decide whether each of the following statements is true or false and then use T or F to indicate your choice. Where a statement is false, give the word that should have been used in place of the word in bold print. (5)

a) Self-pollinating plants are naturally **inbreeding**.

b) Continuous inbreeding results in loss of **homozygosity**.

c) Cross-pollinating plants and animals are natural **outbreeders**.

d) During **inbreeding** selected members of a species are bred for several generations until they breed true.

e) The accumulation of recessive deleterious alleles in a homozygous **phenotype** results in inbreeding depression.

3 **a)** Why are self-pollinating plants less susceptible to inbreeding depression? (1)

b) What can be done to try to avoid inbreeding depression when carrying out repeated inbreeding on species that are natural outbreeders? (2)

Crossbreeding

Although continuous inbreeding of a plant cultivar or animal breed may bring about an improvement in a desired trait, eventually the build-up of harmful recessive alleles in natural outbreeders tends to lead to inbreeding depression. It is for this reason that inbreeding is rarely carried out indefinitely. Instead new alleles are introduced to the plant or animal line by **crossbreeding** it with a strain possessing a different but desired genotype.

Breeding resistant tomato plants

Figure 18.17 shows a type of breeding experiment called a wide cross. A cultivar of tomato that produces high-quality fruit but is susceptible to eelworm is crossed with a wild strain of tomato which possesses the desirable trait for resistance to eelworm.

The members of the F_1 generation receive half of their genetic material from each parent. At this stage in the breeding programme, the breeder's job is to **dilute the genetic material** received by the F_1 plants from the wild parent while at the same time **retaining the allele for resistance** to eelworm. This is achieved by carrying out a series of back crosses. A **back cross** is a cross where an individual is crossed with one of its parents (or with an individual possessing exactly the same genotype as one of its parents).

In the tomato breeding programme, the offspring formed from each back cross are checked for resistance to eelworm. The resistant plants are then used as the parents of the next generation and back crossed again to the original cultivated strain. After two back crosses, the wild genetic material has been reduced to 12.5%. After six backcrosses, it would have been almost completely eliminated.

Similarly, new alleles can be introduced to animal breeds by crossing members of one breed with an individual from another breed that possesses a desired

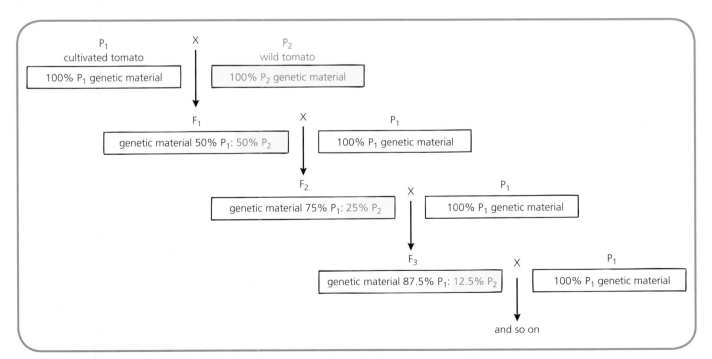

Figure 18.17 Backcrossing after a wide cross

trait. If the latter also contains undesirable genetic material, the cross would be followed up by a series of back crosses to eliminate it.

F_1 hybrids

An F_1 hybrid is an individual resulting from a cross between two genetically dissimilar parents of the same species. Breeders often deliberately cross members of one variety of a species which have certain desired features with those of another variety possessing different useful characteristics in an attempt to produce at least some F_1 hybrids which have both.

Hybrid vigour

Plants

Hybridisation between two different homozygous inbred cultivars of plant species produces an F_1 generation whose members are **uniformly heterozygous**. More importantly, they display **increased vigour, yield, fertility** or other characteristics that are improvements on those shown by either parent. This phenomenon is called **hybrid vigour**. Poorer recessive alleles are masked by superior dominant ones as shown in the example in Figure 18.18.

Figure 18.19 shows hybrid vigour in maize. Since the superior F_1 hybrids are not true-breeding, the hybridisation process using the original parental lines must be repeated every year. The number of F_1 crops produced in this way is limited because of the expense involved. If the F_1 hybrids, which are heterozygous, are allowed to self-pollinate, the F_2 generation produced is genotypically diverse and unsuitable as a crop. However, it is not completely worthless because it produces new varieties.

Figure 18.19 Hybrid vigour in maize

Animals

Similarly in animals, crossbreeding of members of two different breeds may result in the production of a new crossbreed with improved characteristics. The crosses

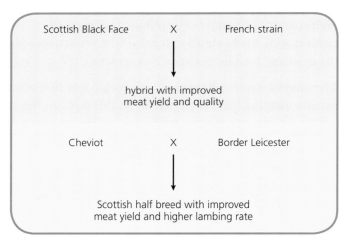

Figure 18.20 Hybrid vigour in sheep

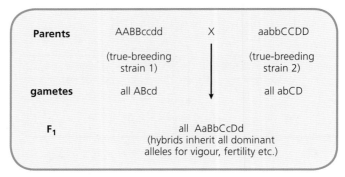

Figure 18.18 Hybridisation

Figure 18.21 'Now **that's** what I call hybrid vigour!'

Breed of cattle	Trait	Percentage improvement shown by hybrid
Dairy	birth weight	3–6
	live calves per calving	2
	feed conversion efficiency	3–8
	milk yield	2–10
Beef	birth weight	2–10
	calves weaned per cow mated	9–15
	feed conversion efficiency	1–6

Table 18.6 Hybrid vigour in cattle

in Figure 18.20 show the outcome of hybridisation between different breeds of sheep. Table 18.6 shows some examples of traits enhanced by hybrid vigour in cattle. (The cartoon in Figure 18.21 is wishful thinking!)

If F_1 hybrids are allowed to interbreed, the F_2 generation will contain a wide variety of genotypes with many animals lacking the enhanced characteristics. There are two possible solutions to this problem:

● The two original parental breeds can be maintained specifically for the purpose of crossing them with one another to produce crossbreed animals that express hybrid vigour.

● The F_1 hybrids can be prevented from breeding with one another and, instead, be back crossed repeatedly with a parental breed. This would be followed by selection to weed out the poorer animals for culling. By this means, a new improved crossbreed would be maintained.

Case History — Plant mutations in breeding programmes

The vast majority of mutations are deleterious. However, on very rare occasions a mutation arises spontaneously that is of benefit to an organism or that makes the organism useful to humans. A plant found to possess such a mutation for a desired trait (see rape seed example below) may be used in a breeding programme in an attempt to introduce the useful allele(s) into a cultivated strain of crop plant.

Increasing frequency of mutation

In 1928 an American scientist (L.J. Stadler) found that when barley seeds were exposed to X-rays, many more mutants were obtained than occurred naturally. This discovery led to the use of induced mutations in breeding programmes.

In the vast majority of cases, the mutants are inferior to the original wild type of the organism. For this reason deliberate use of radiation as a **mutagenic agent** is not a feasible method of improving breeds of farm animals. However, subjecting many thousands of a useful plant's seeds to radiation poses no such problem. By this means a **few** mutant plants with qualities beneficial to humans have been produced. These include tomatoes with increased yield and a strain of dwarf barley plant with erect ears that is more easily harvested than the original strain which tends to bend and lose its ears before the harvest.

Low euricic acid in rape seed

In the 1940s, Canadian scientists recognised that rape seed oil (at that time used as a lubricant in steam-powered engines) had potential for use as an edible oil. Rape seed oil differed in chemical composition from other edible oils in that it possessed a high level of euricic acid, a long-chain fatty acid (see Table 18.7).

It was known that Asian people had been consuming this type of rape seed oil for centuries with, apparently, no ill effects. However, research carried out on rats at the time indicated that a high intake of

259

Fatty acid	Percentage of fatty acid in vegetable oil		
	Sunflower seed	Soya bean	Rape seed before breeding programme
euricic	0.0	0.0	23.1
oleic	16.0	25.1	33.0
palmitic	7.2	12.0	4.9
stearic	4.1	3.9	1.6

Table 18.7 Fatty acid composition of vegetable oils

the oil rich in euricic acid caused unwelcome side effects such as enlarged adrenal glands.

Because of these nutritional concerns, scientists concentrated on developing a strain of rape plant whose seed oil would contain little or no euricic acid. First they located a low-yielding **mutant** variety of rape from Europe with a much reduced level of euricic acid in its oil. Then they carried out a series of breeding programmes involving careful selection over many generations in order to combine the allele(s) for low level of euricic acid of the mutant strain with the alleles (of the genes) for high yield and vigour found in the original strain. Eventually such a cultivar of rape was developed. Its edible oil, low in euricic acid, is found to be excellent as a cooking oil and as a salad dressing.

It is now known that consumption of a diet rich in **saturated** fatty acids leads to the build up of a fatty sludge on the insides of the artery walls. This restricts blood flow and may lead to circulatory problems and ill health. **Unsaturated** fatty acids have not been linked to this effect. In addition to being low in euricic acid, the developed strain of rape seed oil is rich in unsaturated fatty acids. It therefore enjoys worldwide success as a highly nutritious health food.

Genetic technology

Genome sequencing

Genome sequencing involves the construction of a 'library' of partially overlapping DNA fragments of an organism's genome and then assembling them into sequences of bases with the aid of computer technology (also see page 94). Genome sequencing can be used to identify organisms that possess a particular allele of a gene for a desired characteristic. This organism can then be used in a breeding programme to try to incorporate the useful gene into a new cultivar of crop plant or breed of domestic animal.

Genetic transformation

Genetic transformation is the process by which genetic information from one species is introduced into the cell of another species. This normally takes the form of DNA sealed into a bacterial plasmid acting as a vector (see also page 211). Genetic transformation can be used to insert a single gene from one species into the genome of a different species. The transformed genome can then be put to use in breeding programmes. The potential of this process to make significant improvements to crop plants is illustrated by the examples in the following three related topics.

Bt toxin gene for pest resistance

Bacillus thuringiensis (Bt for short) is a soil bacterium that makes a protein that is toxic to certain plant-eating insects. Once consumed, the Bt toxin becomes active and binds to receptors in the insect's gut, paralysing it and causing the insect to die of starvation. Many varieties of Bt toxin exist. For example one type is specific to butterflies whereas another type only works against beetles.

Genetic engineers have managed to extract the bacterial genes for Bt toxin and to insert them into certain crop plants. These genetically modified plants produce their own Bt toxin making them resistant to certain types of insect. (Consequently, they do not need to be sprayed with insecticide.)

Figure 18.22 shows a beetle feeding on a cob of maize. Some cultivars of Bt maize grown in the USA are resistant to this pest. The toxicity of each type

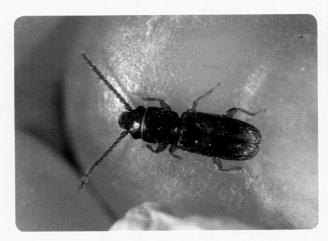

Figure 18.22 Beetle feeding on maize

of Bt toxin is limited to one or two insect groups. An insect that lacks the appropriate gut receptors remains unaffected. Bt toxins are non toxic to vertebrates and to most of the beneficial invertebrates.

Golden rice

Normal cultivated rice contains very little vitamin A in its grains. In regions of the world where this type of rice is the staple diet and people fail to obtain vitamin A from some other food source, vitamin A deficiency is common. Shortage of this vitamin leads to vision problems and even blindness and premature death.

Genetic engineers have now succeeded in transferring two genes into traditional rice to create a new cultivar called **golden rice** (see Figure 18.23). This new strain makes beta-carotene, the precursor to vitamin A, and deposits it in the rice grains turning them yellow. When the rice is consumed, the precursor is changed into vitamin A by the body.

When golden rice reaches the market, it is expected

Figure 18.23 Traditional and golden rice grains

to contain an improved content of iron and protein in addition to the vitamin A precursor.

Related Topic

Glyphosate-resistance gene for herbicide tolerance

Glyphosate is a weed killer (herbicide). It is absorbed through leaves and translocated throughout the plant. It inhibits an enzyme required for the synthesis of several amino acids, resulting in the death of the plant. Glyphosate is broken down into harmless products by micro-organisms within a few days.

Some plants are naturally resistant to glyphosate. Genetic engineers have successfully transferred the

gene responsible for this resistance from these plants to crop plants such as soya bean, maize and sorghum (see Figure 18.24).

When the genetically modified crop plants are sprayed with glyphosate, they remain unaffected but any weeds present among them are killed. Unfortunately some varieties of weeds resistant to glyphosate are beginning to emerge.

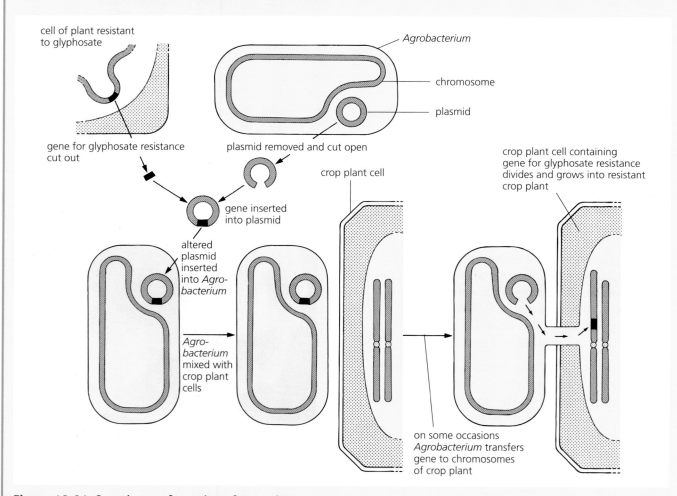

Figure 18.24 Genetic transformation of crop plant

Testing Your Knowledge 3

1 By what means (apart from genetic transformation) can new alleles be introduced to a plant cultivar that is beginning to show inbreeding depression? (1)

2 a) Why do F$_1$ hybrids from two homozygous inbred strains often display hybrid vigour? (1)

   b) i) Are such F$_1$ hybrids *homozygous* or *heterozygous* in genotype?
   ii) Are they *varied* or *uniform* in phenotype? (2)

   c) i) When this F$_1$ generation is selfed, is the F$_2$ generation varied or uniform?
   ii) What use can be made of the F$_2$ generation? (2)

   d) Why do some farmers continue to maintain the two homozygous parental strains? (1)

3 a) i) What is *genome sequencing*?
   ii) What use can be made of genome sequencing in a breeding programme? (2)

   b) i) In general what are scientists able to do by the process of genetic transformation?
   ii) In what way can the process of genetic transformation be of help in a crop plant breeding programme? (2)

What You Should Know

Chapter 18

(See Table 18.8 for word bank)

additive	environmental	sequencing
alleles	harmful	single
back-crossing	heterozygosity	sustainable
comparison	inbreeding	transformed
continuous	outbreeding	treatments
cross-pollinating	randomisation	trial
depression	replicates	uniform
desired	selection	variation
discrete	self-pollinating	vigour

Table 18.8 Word bank for chapter 18

1 During breeding programmes, breeders select organisms with _____ traits and use them as the parents of the next generation. The genetic material of crops and livestock is manipulated in this way to develop improved organisms that will provide sources of _____ food.

2 An inherited characteristic shows _____ variation if it can be used to divide the members of a species into two or more distinct groups. It is controlled by a _____ gene.

3 An inherited characteristic shows _____ variation if it varies among the members of the species in a smooth, continuous way from one extreme to the other. It is controlled by more than one gene and these are _____ in effect. It is also influenced by _____ factors.

4 A field _____ is set up to compare the performance of different plant cultivars or the effect of different _____ on one cultivar.

5 The design of a field trial must take into account: the treatments of the factor being investigated to allow for a fair _____, the inclusion of _____ to take uncontrolled variability into account and the _____ of treatments to eliminate bias.

6 _____ involves reproduction between close relatives. _____ involves reproduction between unrelated members of a species.

7 _____ plants and animals are naturally outbreeding. If they are forced to inbreed continuously, _____ is lost and _____ recessive alleles accumulate leading to inbreeding _____.

8 _____ plants are naturally inbreeding and do not tend to suffer inbreeding depression because the deleterious alleles have been weeded out of their genotypes by natural _____.

9 Crossbreeding a plant cultivar or animal breed with a member of a different strain that has a desired genotype allows new _____ to be introduced.

10 In plants, crossbreeding two different inbred homozygous strains results in the formation of

a _____ crop of F_1 hybrids that often exhibit increased vigour and yield. Although the F_2 is not uniform, it may provide a useful source of _____.

11 In animals, crossbreeding results in hybrid _____ among the members of the F_1 generation. The new breed can be maintained by rigorous selection and _____ or by maintaining the two parental breeds for the purpose of producing the crossbred offspring.

12 Breeding programmes can make use of those organisms that have been shown by genome _____ to possess desired genes and those organisms whose genomes have been genetically _____ by the insertion of a desired gene.

19 Crop protection

Balanced community

In a natural ecosystem, a balance exists between producers and consumers. A diverse variety of plant species compete with one another and co-exist with their insect pests and disease-causing micro-organisms. The members of plant, animal and microbial communities tend to live in small mixed populations. If the numbers of a certain species of green plant decrease then the numbers of animals and micro-organisms that depend on the plant fall accordingly. This allows the plant species to recover and soon the balance is restored.

Monoculture

In an agricultural ecosystem the variety of species that make up the community, the crop, is greatly reduced and may even take the form of a monoculture. A monoculture is a vast population of a single species of crop plant cultivated over a large area for economic efficiency. Often the members of the population are genetically identical and are members of a cultivar developed for its productivity.

However, a crop monoculture presents ideal growing conditions to weeds, pests and disease-causing micro-organisms whose activities, in turn, reduce the crop's yield. Insects and micro-organisms, for example, can feed on the plant and reproduce repeatedly without ever running out of food (see Figure 19.1). Therefore farmers employ a variety of control methods to protect their crops and avoid economic disaster.

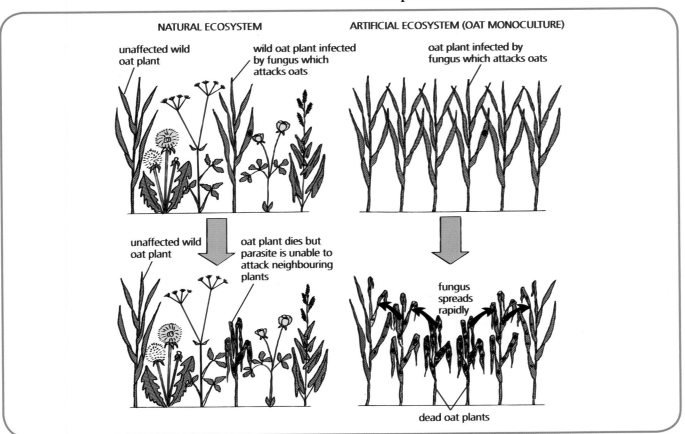

Figure 19.1 Effect of fungal parasite on two ecosystems

Weeds

Competition

Plants growing side by side in the same habitat compete for light, water, soil nutrients and space. Competition among the members of a monoculture is reduced by spacing out the seeds during sowing. However, these spaces tend to become occupied by weeds. A **weed** is any kind of plant that grows where it is not wanted. When weeds overrun a cultivated field, they pose a serious economic problem for the following reasons. They may:

- cause a **significant reduction** in the productivity of the crop due to competition

- release **chemical inhibitors** into the soil which further reduces crop growth

- **contaminate grain crops** with their seeds and reduce the crop's value

- act as **hosts for crop pests and diseases**, for example clubroot (a fungal disease that affects cabbage) is harboured by the weed Shepherd's purse.

Properties of common weeds

Weeds (see Figure 19.2) are perfectly adapted to their life as opportunists.

Annual weeds are able to colonise vacant land or an 'empty' field where the monoculture has yet to establish itself because they:

- grow very **quickly**

- rapidly produce flowers since their **life cycle is short**

- produce **vast numbers** of seeds which are often dispersed effectively by wind

- produce seeds that remain dormant but **viable for long periods** (even years) in the soil.

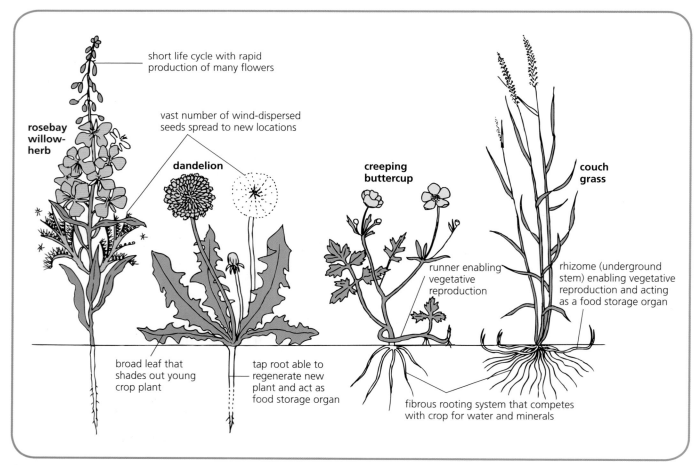

Figure 19.2 Adaptations of weeds (not drawn to scale)

Perennial weeds are able to compete successfully with the crop plant from the very start of the growing season because the weeds:

- are already **established** in the habitat

- have **storage organs** from the previous year that provide food even if environmental conditions do not favour rapid photosynthesis

- are able to **reproduce vegetatively** using specialised structures such as runners.

Invertebrate pests

A monoculture of a crop plant presents ideal conditions to herbivorous pests to feed and reproduce extensively. Pests that attack crop plants mainly fall into three groups of **invertebrates**:

- nematode worms

- molluscs

- insects.

Nematodes

Nematode worms (see Figure 19.3) occur in almost all environments and are particularly numerous in soil. Many of these tiny worms attack crops and establish themselves as **parasites** within the host plant's roots. A common example is potato cyst nematode (see page 271) which causes millions of pounds worth of damage annually to the UK potato crop.

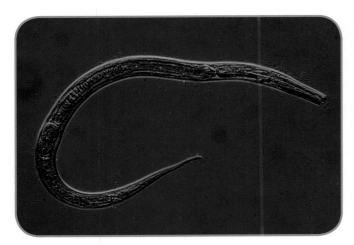

Figure 19.3 Nematode worm

Molluscs

Molluscs such as snails and slugs (see Figure 19.4) can do extensive damage to crops. They are most active at night and possess rasping mouth parts that are ideally suited to dealing with tough green plant parts such as cabbage leaves.

Figure 19.4 Molluscs

Insects

Herbivorous insects pose the greatest threat to food crops and cause many millions of pounds of damage annually by feeding on leaves, stems, roots and underground storage organs.

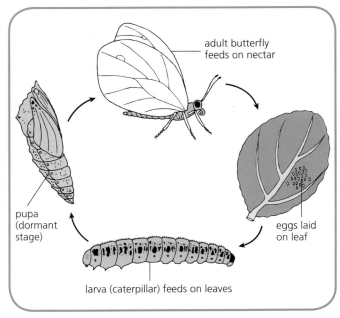

adult butterfly feeds on nectar

eggs laid on leaf

larva (caterpillar) feeds on leaves

pupa (dormant stage)

Figure 19.5 Life cycle of cabbage white butterfly

An insect often has several distinct stages in its life cycle. In the case of the cabbage white butterfly (see Figure 19.5) it is the larval stage that does the damage to the crop's leaves.

Aphids (greenfly and blackfly) are tiny insect pests that exist as winged and wingless forms (see Figure 19.6). They use their needle-like mouth part to pierce plant tissue in search of the sugary solution present in the phloem tissue.

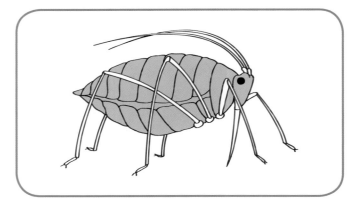

Figure 19.6 Wingless aphid

Decreased yield

Damage to leaves reduces photosynthesis; loss of transported sugar denies growing plant tissues their energy supply. As a result the crop plant's vigour and yield are adversely affected by insect pests. Some invertebrate pests also act as vectors of disease. Aphids, for example, transmit viruses that cause diseases such as potato leaf roll.

Plant diseases

Plant diseases are caused by pathogens such as fungi, bacteria and viruses. A few examples are given in Table 19.1. The pathogens may be soil borne, airborne or spread by insect vectors.

Poorer yield

Plant diseases also result in a poorer yield of the crop. In addition, a product that is blemished or infected by a pathogen such as a fungus (see Figure 19.7) is less marketable than a healthy, unblemished product. The storage life of a crop infected by a pathogen is also reduced because the stored crop is less healthy and more susceptible to attack by a storage disease.

Figure 19.7 Apple scab (fungal disease)

Type of pathogen	Examples of pathogen	Host plant	Disease caused
fungus	*Phytophthora infestans*	potato	late blight
	Puccinia graminis	wheat	black rust
bacterium	*Pseudomonas solanacearum*	tomato	wilt
	Pectobacterium corotovorum	parsley	soft root
virus	tomato bushy stunt virus	tomato	bushy stunt
	potato leaf roll virus	potato	leaf roll

Table 19.1 Plant pathogens

1 a) Which is normally more complex: the community structure of an *agricultural* ecosystem or that of a *natural* ecosystem? (1)

   b) **i)** Which of these two types of ecosystem offers ideal conditions for the growth of disease-causing micro-organisms?
      ii) Briefly explain why. (2)

2 Give TWO examples of adverse effects caused by weeds to a farmer's crop. (2)

3 a) Identify TWO properties of annual weeds that contribute largely to their success. (2)

   b) Give TWO reasons why perennial weeds are able to compete successfully with a crop. (2)

4 a) Explain how insects such as aphids cause a decreased yield of a crop plant. (2)

   b) Identify TWO other invertebrate groups that damage crops. (2)

   c) State TWO means by which pathogenic micro-organisms may be spread from one host plant to another. (2)

Control of weeds, pests and diseases

Cultural means

The process of agriculture involves preparing the soil to provide a good seed bed and then planting, tending and harvesting the crop. **Cultural** means of controlling weeds, pests and diseases have evolved from traditional, non-chemical methods of cultivation by trial and error over time. They tend to be **preventative** rather than **curative** and often require long-term planning. They do not offer the 'quick-fix' solution to the problem associated with chemical sprays. Some examples are given below.

Ploughing

The top 20 cm of soil is turned over by this process (see Figure 19.8) and many of the perennial weeds are buried to a depth at which they die and decompose. The crop seed can then be planted and become established before the weeds return.

Time of sowing

It is critical to know the **best time** to plant the seeds. Winter wheat, for example, is sown between late September and early November. At this time of year, annual weeds are in the form of dormant seeds and perennial weeds have been ploughed underground. In addition the soil is still relatively warm. Under these conditions, winter wheat grains will germinate, become established and survive the winter as young plants. Growth of the crop resumes in the spring well before the weeds can re-establish themselves.

Critical time for removal of weeds

Some competitive weeds that bring about a decrease in crop yield are known to cause most damage to young crop plants. If these weeds are removed **early** in the life of the crop, often the crop plants become sufficiently sturdy to tolerate competition by weeds when they return at a later stage. Therefore the yield of the crop is largely unaffected.

Removal of alternative hosts

In the absence of their favoured host plant (the crop), many insect pests are able to survive and breed on **alternative hosts** such as weeds bordering the field. Bramble plants, for example, harbour aphids and other insect pests that harm raspberry crops. The removal of these alternative hosts is a cultural means of controlling both pests and the viral diseases that they carry.

Figure 19.8 Ploughing (weeds)

269

However, this practice may have an adverse effect on the local wildlife.

Destruction of crop residue

Some fungal pathogens can survive as spores on **straw or stubble** left on the ground after a cereal crop (such as wheat) has been harvested and then infect the next crop. This type of plant disease can be controlled by removing the infected crop residue before sowing the next crop.

Cover crop

Some crops such as red clover (see Figure 19.9) may be grown as a **cover crop** on a fallow area as part of a crop rotation. During its growth period, the cover crop competes so well with the weeds that most of them fail to grow properly or to produce seeds. When its growth is completed, the cover crop is often left as a mat on the soil surface. This smothers any germinating weed seeds beneath it. Decomposing clover also enriches the nitrogen content of the soil.

Figure 19.9 Red clover

Crop rotation

Crop rotation is the practice by which each of a series of very different types of crop plant is grown in turn on the same piece of ground. Once the first crop has been harvested it is followed, the next season, by a dissimilar type of plant that does not act as host to the pest being controlled.

In the plan shown in Figure 19.10, for example, the cabbages follow the pea plants and are followed by the potatoes in the rotation. A pest that can only attack a certain type of host plant (such as brassicas) may be controlled effectively because it is unlikely to survive for four years until its host returns. It is for this reason that crop rotation works best against soil-inhabiting pests that are only able to attack a **narrow range** of host plants. For example, long crop rotations help to control potato cyst nematodes that are specific to one type of crop.

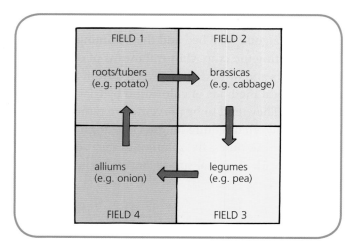

Figure 19.10 Crop rotation

Incidence and viability of potato cyst nematode cysts in two soil types

Potato cyst nematode is a common soil-borne parasite of potato plants. It attacks the roots (but not tubers) of the plant from which it obtains all of its food. This results in a reduced yield of potato tubers. Its life cycle is shown in Figure 19.11.

The investigation is carried out by following the procedure shown (in a simplified way) in Figure 19.12 using soil from an area continuously cropped with potatoes and soil from an area cropped with potatoes as part of a rotation.

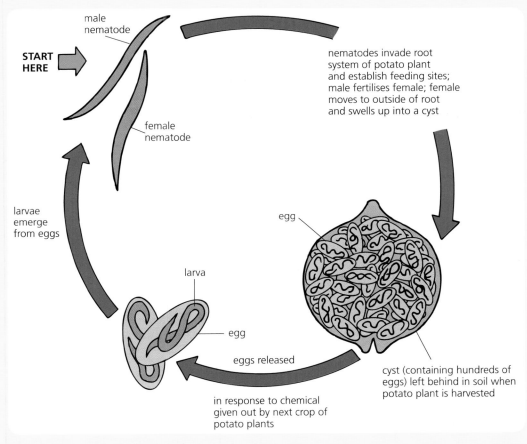

Figure 19.11 Life cycle of potato cyst nematode

Table 19.2 shows a specimen set of results which are presented as a bar chart in Figure 19.13.

	Soil type	
	Continuously cropped with potatoes	**Cropped with potatoes as part of a rotation**
total number of cysts per 100 g of soil	24	10
number of viable cysts out of the random sample of eight cysts	6	2
percentage of viable cysts in the random sample	75	25

Table 19.2

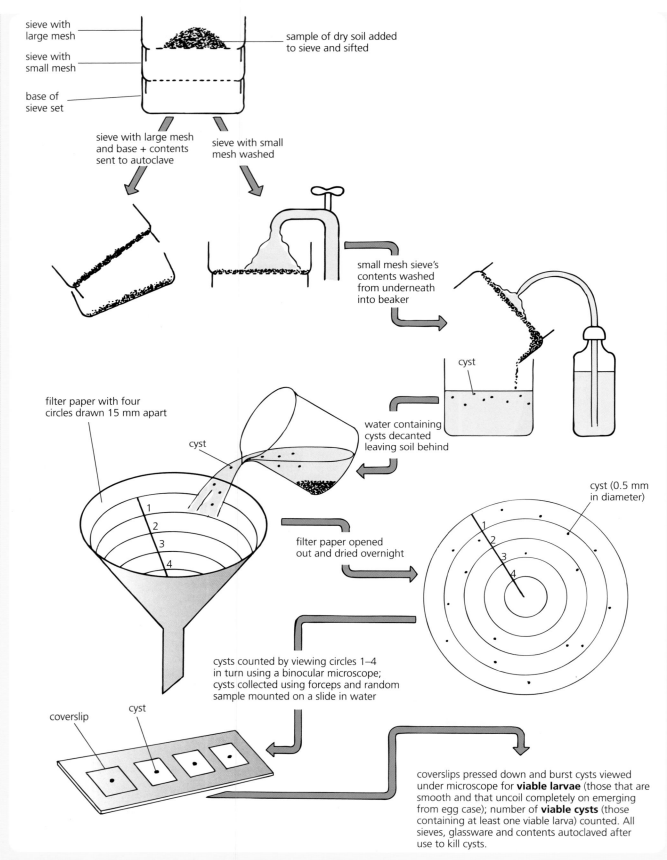

sieve with large mesh

sieve with small mesh

base of sieve set

sample of dry soil added to sieve and sifted

sieve with large mesh and base + contents sent to autoclave

sieve with small mesh washed

small mesh sieve's contents washed from underneath into beaker

cyst

water containing cysts decanted leaving soil behind

filter paper with four circles drawn 15 mm apart

cyst

cyst (0.5 mm in diameter)

filter paper opened out and dried overnight

cysts counted by viewing circles 1–4 in turn using a binocular microscope; cysts collected using forceps and random sample mounted on a slide in water

coverslip

cyst

coverslips pressed down and burst cysts viewed under microscope for **viable larvae** (those that are smooth and that uncoil completely on emerging from egg case); number of **viable cysts** (those containing at least one viable larva) counted. All sieves, glassware and contents autoclaved after use to kill cysts.

Figure 19.12 Procedure for potato cyst nematode cyst investigation

From the results it is concluded that there is a higher incidence and viability of cysts of the potato cyst nematode in soil that has been continuously cropped with potatoes than soil that has been cropped with potatoes as part of a rotation.

If even **one viable cyst** is found when a field is tested, that land cannot be used to grow seed potatoes. This strict rule is in place because seed potatoes pose a great risk of potato cyst nematode cross-contamination from one location to another.

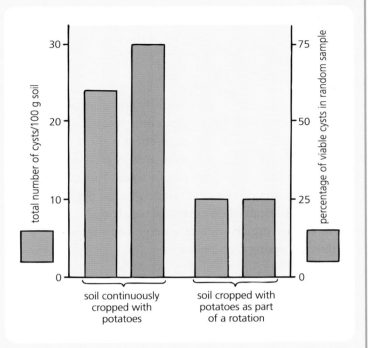

Figure 19.13 Bar chart of nematode cyst investigation results

Control of weeds, pests and diseases by chemical means

Unfortunately, traditional cultural control methods alone are often not sufficient to control vast populations of unwanted weeds, pests and pathogenic micro-organisms. Therefore, in addition, the farmer may have to make use of chemical agents to ensure high crop yields.

Herbicides

Chemicals used to kill weeds are called herbicides (weed killers).

Selective

Some herbicides act selectively by mimicking the action of naturally-occurring plant hormones (growth substances). They stimulate the rate of growth and metabolism of broad-leaved plants (in other words, the weeds) to such an extent that the plants exhaust their food reserves and die (see Figure 19.14). The narrow vertical leaves of the cereal plants absorb little of the chemical and are hardly affected.

Selective herbicides are similar in chemical structure to plant hormones. Therefore they are normally

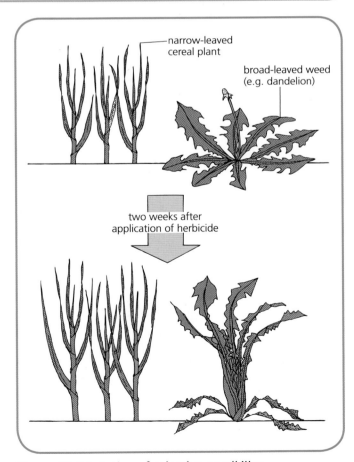

Figure 19.14 Action of selective weedkiller

273

biodegradable and broken down by soil bacteria. They do not cause harm to the soil community. However, some may leave residues which enter the food chain (see page 278).

Contact

Contact herbicides act non-selectively and destroy all green plant tissue with which they come in contact. Since they are biodegradable, their effect is short-lived and they can be used to prepare an area by clearing the ground completely before the crop is sown. However, contact herbicides do not affect underground organs. Therefore well-established perennial weeds with tap roots or storage organs soon re-emerge and compete with the new young crop plants.

Systemic

Molecules of systemic herbicide are absorbed by an annual or perennial weed and enter its circulatory system. The chemical is transported internally to all parts of the plant where it has a lethal effect. Although slower to act than contact herbicides, systemic herbicides are more effective because they are able to reach underground storage organs and intricate rooting systems and kill them (see Figure 19.15).

Pesticides

Chemicals used to control pests are called pesticides. The examples given in Table 19.3 refer to those used to kill three groups of common invertebrate pests. However, the term 'pesticide' is sometimes used more widely to include herbicides and fungicides (see below). Over 60% of crop-growing farms in Scotland apply pesticides to their crops. It is estimated that almost 30% of crops would be lost in the absence of pesticides.

Contact

A contact pesticide acts by:

- killing the invertebrate when it comes into contact with the pest (for example a spray acting directly on aphids)

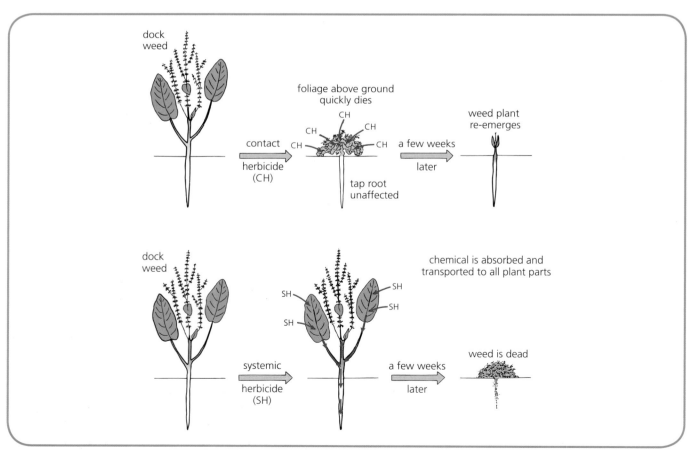

Figure 19.15 Action of contact and systemic herbicides

Pesticide	Pest targeted	Common method of application
insecticide	insects (such as greenfly)	applied as a spray to leaves
molluscicide	molluscs (such as slugs)	mixed with food bait
nematocide	nematodes (such as potato cyst nematodes)	applied as a vapour to fumigate soil

Table 19.3 Pesticides

- remaining as a protective layer of poisonous residue on the plant and taking effect when the pest comes into contact with it.

Systemic

Like a systemic herbicide, a **systemic** pesticide is absorbed by the plant and transported to all of its parts. If a sap-sucking insect such as an aphid pierces the plant's phloem, it will ingest poison along with the plant's sugary sap and die.

Fungicides

Fungicides are chemicals used to kill fungal parasites that cause diseases of crop plants.

Contact

Contact fungicide is sprayed on to crop plants prior to fungal attack (see Figure 19.16). When the fungal spores land and begin to germinate they absorb poison and die. However, rain tends to wash the chemical off and new leaves, on emerging, are unprotected and left vulnerable. Therefore repeated applications are required.

Systemic

Systemic fungicides are absorbed by the crop plant and transported throughout its body (in its vascular system). Therefore they tend to give better protection against fungal attack than contact fungicide.

Using weather data to predict disease outbreak

Potato blight is a disease caused by the fungus *Phytophthora infestans* whose spores are airborne. Infection of potato plants by the pathogen depends on the occurrence of a specific set of environmental conditions. This is called a **Smith Period** and it occurs when a minimum air temperature of 10 °C is accompanied by a relative humidity greater than 90% for at least 11 hours on two consecutive days.

It is for this reason that air temperature and humidity in all parts of the UK are monitored every hour

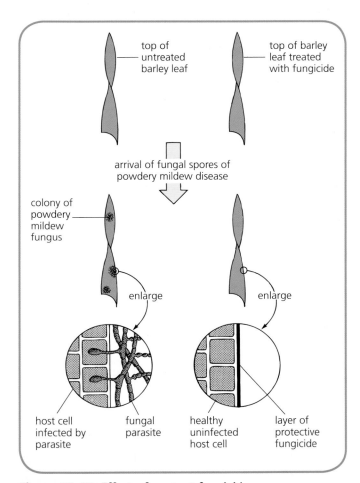

Figure 19.16 Effect of contact fungicide

by a blight watch service supported by the Potato Council. By this means, Smith Periods can be forecast and a warning system made available to growers. Armed with this information, farmers can spray their potato crops with fungicide in advance of infection. Such protective application acting as a **preventative** measure is normally much more effective than waiting until the crop is diseased and then trying to treat it. In addition, it prevents needless applications of fungicide at times when the crop is not under threat.

275

Case Study   Control of weeds, pests and diseases of wheat crops

Wheat is widely grown in Britain and needs to be protected from the activities of weeds, invertebrate pests and fungal pathogens.

Weeds

Competition with the crop by perennial weeds is reduced by **ploughing**. **Autumn sowing** of grains gives winter wheat plants an opportunity to establish themselves in a 'weed-free' environment. **Crop rotation** disrupts germination and growth of some weeds.

Invertebrates

If slugs have survived on plant debris left from the previous harvest, they often feed on newly-germinated wheat seedlings. These invertebrate pests can be controlled by cultural means such as **removing the debris** or by chemical means such as the **application of a molluscicide**. Soil-borne pests such as wheat bulb fly are, in part, controlled by crop rotation.

Fungal pathogens

Wheat crops in the UK can become infected by several fungal diseases such as mildew, stem rust (see Figure 19.17), eyespot and leaf blotch via airborne spores. Although fungal diseases rarely kill the host plant, they greatly reduce the yield of wheat grains.

Figure 19.17 Stem rust

Knowledge of the pathogen's life cycle

Some fungal pathogens (such as rust) spend part of their life cycle on a second host plant (for example barberry). **Removal of this secondary host** from agricultural areas helps to control the pathogen by making it difficult for the fungus to complete its life cycle.

Farm hygiene

Some fungal pathogens (such as eye spot and leaf blotch) survive as spores in wheat stubble and debris left on the soil surface after the harvest. They produce airborne spores capable of infecting the next crop of wheat plants especially if the weather is wet. Cultural practices that clean up the field and **reduce wheat residue**, by ploughing it back into the land or by removing it for use as animal feed, help to control the fungal diseases. In the absence of stubble, the fungus is a poor competitor in the soil. A crop rotation giving the field a 2-year break from the growth of cereals normally reduces the risk of eyespot, for example, to a very low level.

Timing of nitrogenous fertiliser

A small dose of fertiliser is given in March followed by the main dose in May when growth rate increases. This pattern of application of **nitrogenous fertiliser** has been found to promote the growth of healthy wheat plants and help them to resist infection by fungi.

Cultural versus chemical

On some farms wheat is grown as part of a rotation over several years alternating with crops such as oilseed rape and beans. This wheat is often used to supplement the diet of farm animals. On other farms crop rotation has been abandoned and farmers have chosen to specialise in the **intensive cultivation** of higher-quality wheat for human consumption. However, repeated use of the same field for wheat tends to encourage fungal pathogens. Despite the use of cultivars of wheat resistant to some pathogenic strains, the farmer becomes increasingly reliant on chemical means of control.

Many farmers attempt to make judicious use of fungicide sprays by applying them only when certain risk factors prevail, such as the advance of an epidemic. However, forecasts of epidemics are imprecise and it is tempting to play safe and resort to routine chemical control. Excessive use of chemical sprays leads to short-term gain but long-term problems such as **environmental degradation** and the evolution of **fungicide-resistant** strains of fungal pathogens.

Problems with plant protection chemicals

Ideal characteristics of a pesticide

A plant pesticide (using the term in its broader sense to mean a chemical designed to protect plants from the activities of weeds, invertebrates and pathogenic micro-organisms) should be specific to the pest, short-lived in its action and safe. It should not persist when released into the environment but instead break down into simple chemicals that are harmless to the host plant, the environment and the human consumer. However, in reality, some pesticides have proved to be toxic, to some extent, to humans and other animals.

Persistence of pesticide

Some protective chemicals may be persistent and, although harmless at very dilute concentrations, accumulate along food chains.

DDT

This chemical, which is now known to be both persistent and very toxic, was widely used as an insecticide on crops in the past. However, it was found to pass easily through food chains and webs and become more and more concentrated at each level. Consider the example shown in Figure 19.18. The producers (green leaves of various plant species) become contaminated with a very low concentration of

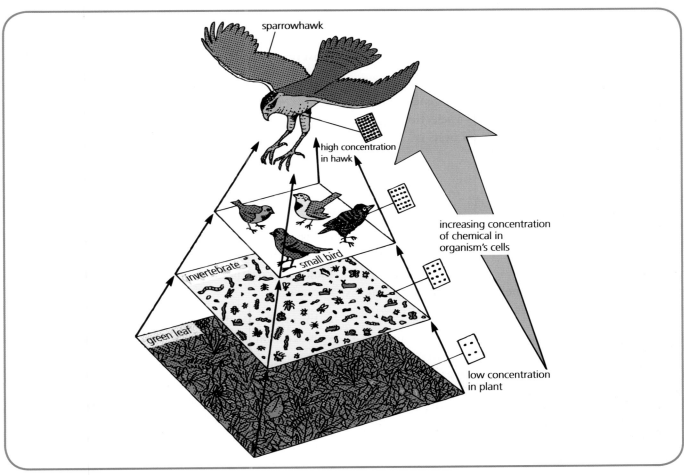

Figure 19.18 Accumulation of chemical in a food pyramid

277

chemical pesticide blown off neighbouring farmland during spraying of crops.

The concentration increases, however, as much plant material is eaten by primary consumers and the chemical **persists** in their cells. Progression on up the pyramid of numbers and biomass leads to an ever-increasing concentration of the chemical accumulating in living cells. Finally the few large tertiary consumers (such as the sparrowhawk) at the very top suffer severe poisoning. Once this effect became apparent, use of DDT was banned by developed countries though its use continues in many developing countries.

Resistance to pesticide

When a pesticide is applied to a crop, a few individuals among the pest population may already be **resistant** to the chemical. This is because they just happen to have some unusual feature which is now of advantage to them. This could be, for example, the possession of a thick coat or the ability to produce an enzyme that breaks down the toxin.

These individuals are **naturally selected** and survive to breed the next generation which may also be resistant. As a result, the number of resistant individuals in the population increases generation after generation. Continued use of the pesticide exerts a **selection pressure** and a population of resistant pests is produced.

Biological control

Biological control is the reduction of a pest population by the deliberate introduction of one of its natural enemies. This could be:

- a **predator** (for example the ladybird, an insect that feeds on greenfly – see Figure 19.19)

- a **parasite** (such as *Encarsia*, a wasp that lays its eggs inside a whitefly; the developing wasp larvae feed on the insect host and destroy it – see Case Study on page 279)

- a **pathogen** (such as *Bacillus thuringiensis*, a bacterium that infects butterfly caterpillars and kills them with a poison called Bt toxin – see Case Study on page 279).

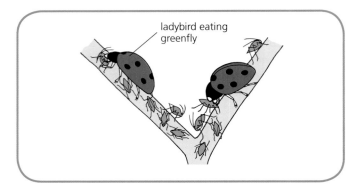

ladybird eating greenfly

Figure 19.19 Biological control of greenfly by ladybirds

The natural enemy acts as the **control agent** in place of a pesticide. Therefore biological control does not introduce persistent and potentially harmful chemicals to the food chain. In addition, this type of control does not exert a selection pressure that could produce a population of resistant pests.

Timing

In biological control the **timing** of the introduction of the agent of biological control is critical. The predator must be able to find its 'prey' or it will be ineffective. Therefore the agent is normally introduced when:

- infestation of the crop has begun

- environmental conditions are present that favour the establishment of the useful predator, parasite or pathogen.

Glasshouse

A heated **glasshouse** ('greenhouse') provides an environment that can be controlled carefully during the growth of a crop (such as tomatoes or cucumbers). Biological control is very effective in a glasshouse because:

- the system is enclosed so the predator is unable to move away to an alternative environment

- the temperature can be controlled to suit the control agent (for example, control of red spider mites using predatory mite *Phytoseiulus* [see pages 280–281] normally works well when the minimum temperature of 20 °C needed by the predator to reproduce rapidly is maintained).

Case Study **Control of glasshouse whitefly with the parasite wasp *Encarsia***

Glasshouse whiteflies are tiny insects about 2 mm in length and closely related to greenfly. They establish themselves in greenhouses where tomato or cucumber plants are being cultivated. Whiteflies weaken the crop plant by sucking its sap in the same way as aphids do. They also cover the plant surface with excreted 'honeydew' which may promote the growth of moulds. They take in sap greatly in excess of their need for carbohydrate because they also need to obtain amino acids which are much less concentrated in the sap. Each female whitefly lays up to 200 eggs in a circle on the underside of a leaf. The larvae that develop are scale-like and are often referred to as 'scales'.

Control

Glasshouse whitefly can be **controlled biologically** by a minute parasitic wasp called *Encarsia*. The female wasp lays her eggs inside the larvae of the whitefly (see Figure 19.20). Those larvae that are successfully parasitised by the wasp turn black, usefully indicating the effectiveness of the treatment.

To introduce the wasp, special cards bearing whitefly scales already parasitised by wasp pupae are

Figure 19.20 Whitefly and *Encarsia* wasp

purchased from a supplier and hung up in shady positions among the foliage in the greenhouse. Adult *Encarsia* wasps emerge from the pupae and lay their eggs in any whitefly scales present in the crop plant's leaves. Since whitefly and *Encarsia* are native to tropical regions, the biological control is only effective if the glasshouse temperature is maintained at a minimum of 18 °C during the day and 14 °C at night.

Case Study **Control of butterfly caterpillars with bacterium *Bacillus thuringiensis***

Bacillus thuringiensis is a naturally occurring soil bacterium. Some strains can infest and kill plant-eating insects (see page 261). When *Bacillus thuringiensis* (Bt for short) produces spores, it makes a protein that is toxic to certain insects. The toxin works by paralysing the insect's digestive system. As a result the animal stops feeding and dies of starvation several days later.

Different strains of Bt make different forms of the toxin, each specific to a particular group of insects. For example Bt *kurstaki* only works against leaf- and needle-feeding caterpillars. This strain of Bt is used as an insecticide spray containing a mixture of bacterial spores and crystalline toxin (see Figure 19.21) to protect crops against butterfly caterpillars (see Figure 19.22).

Advantage

This form of Bt insecticide is environmentally friendly in that it is specific to caterpillars and has very little or no effect on beneficial insects and other living organisms.

Disadvantages

Most versions of Bt insecticide are degraded by sunlight and only remain effective for a few days. Constant exposure of a crop to the same toxin creates a selective pressure which favours any pests that are resistant to the toxin.

→

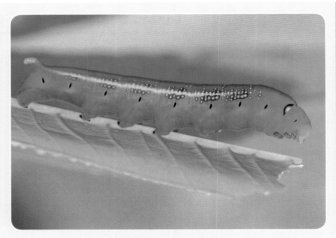

Figure 19.21 Bt spores and crystals of toxin

Figure 19.22 Leaf-eating caterpillar

Biological and chemical control of red spider mites

Background

- Glasshouse red spider mites (see Figure 19.23) are tiny invertebrates that feed on many different species of plant including some that are grown for food.

- Red spider mites pierce cells on the underside of the leaf with their mouthparts to obtain food.

- A female adult lives for several weeks and lays hundreds of eggs.

- A second type of mite, called *Phytoseiulus*, is longer than the red spider mite and has a shiny, orange-red body.

- It is a predator and its long legs enable it to move around the leaves quickly, in search of prey.

- A miticide is a type of pesticide developed specifically for use against mites.

The investigation is carried out by following the procedure outlined in Figure 19.24.

From the results it is concluded that biological control has been effective. *Phytoseiulus* has predated on the red spider mites in tray A and reduced their number significantly. The results from tray B are not found to differ significantly from those in tray C (the control). Therefore it is concluded that in this case, chemical control has not been effective, probably because the population of red spider mites was resistant to this type of miticide.

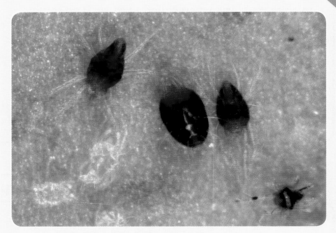

Figure 19.23 Red spider mite

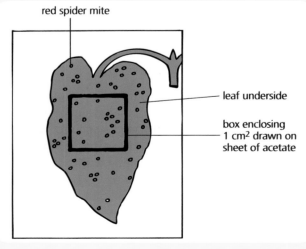

red spider mite

leaf underside

box enclosing 1 cm² drawn on sheet of acetate

Figure 19.25 Sampling technique

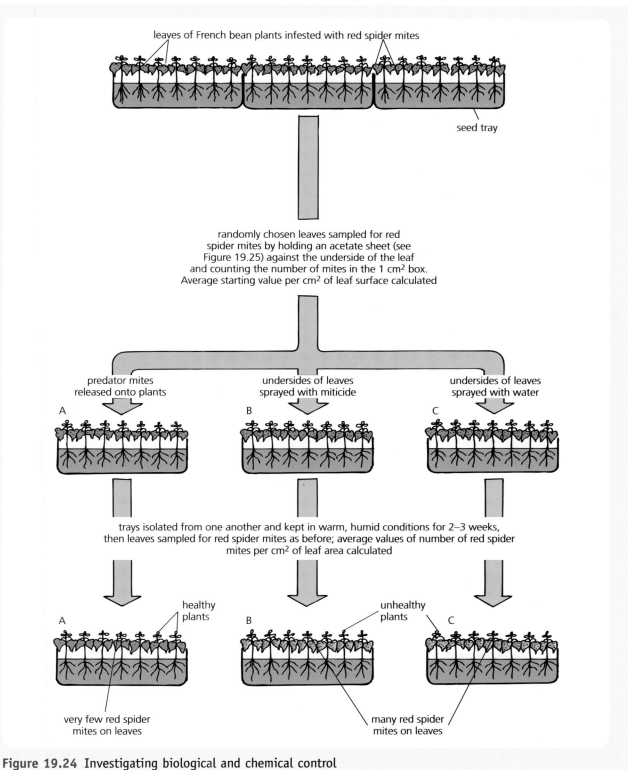

Figure 19.24 Investigating biological and chemical control

Integrated pest management

Integrated pest management (IPM) is a combination of techniques including chemical control, biological control, cultural means and host plant resistance. It sets out to reduce the use of pesticides while bringing pest populations down to a level at which they no longer cause economic damage. The emphasis is on control rather than eradication of the pest.

Cautious use of chemicals

Where chemicals need to be used, they are chosen because:

- they are effective even when only used infrequently at specific points in the host's or pest's life cycle

- they show low persistence

- they reduce pest numbers to a level at which methods of biological control can take over

- they do not disrupt biological control since they are selective and kill pests while leaving the useful predators unharmed.

Future

Ideally a situation would be reached where the target species would neither die out nor increase in number to become a pest. It would simply remain under control while at the same time the crop species and the surrounding wildlife would be unaffected.

Testing Your Knowledge 2

1 **a)** Agricultural pests can be controlled to some extent by *cultural means*. What does this term mean? (1)

   b) Crop rotation is a cultural means of control. Briefly explain how it works. (3)

   c) Name TWO other cultural means of controlling pests. (2)

2 **a)** What is the advantage of using a selective weedkiller on a cereal crop? (1)

   b) Explain why a *systemic* fungicide may be more effective than a *contact* one on a crop. (2)

3 **a)** Redraw Figure 19.26 which shows a pyramid of biomass for a food chain and add the following

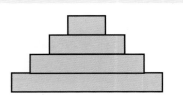

Figure 19.26

   labels: *primary consumer, secondary consumer, tertiary consumer, producer*. (1)

   b) i) Using dots to represent molecules of persistent pesticide, complete your pyramid.
   ii) Explain the distribution of dots you have chosen for your diagram. (3)

4 Copy the following sentences, choosing the correct answer at each underlined choice. (8)

   a) Continued use of pesticide exerts a <u>reduction/ selection</u> pressure on a population producing a <u>resistant/susceptible</u> population of pests.

   b) The reduction of a <u>crop/pest</u> population by the deliberate introduction of one of its natural enemies is called <u>biological/chemical</u> control.

   c) The use of a combination of techniques such as chemical and biological control and host plant <u>persistence/resistance</u> is called <u>cultural/ integrated</u> pest management.

   d) The form of management referred to in c) aims to make <u>maximum/minimum</u> use of chemicals on the farm and to <u>control/eradicate</u> pests.

Animal welfare

Wellbeing of domesticated animals

Traditionally the wellbeing of domesticated animals was judged solely on their physical health as indicated by their ability:

- to grow
- to reproduce and raise offspring successfully
- to resist disease.

However, this narrow view of animal wellbeing has been overtaken in recent times by the work of the Farm Animal Welfare Council (see Research Topic – The five freedoms for animal welfare). It is now agreed that an important part of an animal's welfare is the provision of opportunities for the animal to express its normal, natural behaviour patterns.

Hens, for example, given adequate space to stretch their wings and wag their tails, take far less time to settle and begin egg-laying than those that are crowded and short of space. An animal's state of wellbeing is therefore regarded as acceptable only if the animal is able to behave in a natural way, live free from disease and grow vigorously.

Costs and benefits

Providing domesticated animals with improved environmental conditions requires an initial financial outlay by the farmer. However, the increased costs of an improved level of welfare result in long-term benefits. Contented, unstressed animals (see Figure 20.1) grow better, breed more successfully and generate products (meat, milk, eggs etc.) of higher quality.

The opposite is true of animals that are stressed. Research in pigs, for example, shows that pregnant sows exposed to stress, such as competition for food, produce piglets with a slower rate of growth after being weaned. In addition, these young pigs in turn show poor maternal behaviour towards their own offspring.

The standards of animal welfare maintained in the UK are among the highest in the world but they add to the cost of the produce. It is for this reason that animal

Figure 20.1 High level of welfare

products from farms in Britain are normally more expensive than those imported from countries with lower standards of animal welfare.

Ethics

Ethics refer to the moral values and rules that ought to govern human conduct. Clearly it is unethical to subject domesticated animals to a regime of negative experiences such as pain and distress simply to provide humans with supplies of cheap food.

It is hard to believe that chickens raised in the overcrowded conditions of a battery farm (see Figure 20.2), and often with their beaks trimmed using infrared radiation to prevent them from injuring one

Figure 20.2 Battery chicken farming

Farm Animal Welfare Council (FAWC)

The **FAWC** is an independent advisory body set up by the government to review the welfare of farm animals (on farmland, in transit, at the market and at the slaughterhouse). The FAWC advises the government on changes to the law that it considers to be necessary. The Animal Welfare Act 2006 requires that an animal's needs are met. These needs are based on the five freedoms for animal welfare (see Table 20.1) identified by the FAWC. These freedoms place great emphasis on the **avoidance of negative experiences**.

The work of the FAWC continues to press for ever more **humane treatment** of farm animals. It advises farmers to move beyond the minimum standard to the provision of one where the animals have a life worth living during their relatively short life time. This could be achieved by including positive experiences such as opportunities for exercise and play within the overall programme of animal welfare.

Freedom:	Means by which this freedom should be delivered
from hunger and thirst	provision of access to water and to a diet that maintains full health and vigour
from discomfort	provision of an appropriate environment that includes shelter and an area for resting comfortably
from pain, injury and disease	application of preventative measures and, where necessary, rapid diagnosis and treatment of the problem
to express normal behaviour	provision of adequate space, proper facilities and company of other members of the animal's own kind
from fear and distress	provision of conditions and treatment that avoid causing the animal mental suffering

Table 20.1 The five freedoms for animal welfare

---

another, are enjoying anything other than a very low quality of life. Surely supplies of cheap eggs and meat do not justify this treatment of a domesticated animal.

Behavioural indicators of poor welfare

When animals are kept confined in unnatural or substandard conditions, they often exhibit behaviour patterns that differ from those shown in a natural environment. These unusual forms of behaviour act as indicators of poor animal welfare and involve factors such as ill health, stress and a general lack of wellbeing.

Stereotypy

A stereotypy is a behaviour pattern that takes the form of repetitive movement often lacking variation. At first sight it may appear to the onlooker to lack purpose. A stereotypy is often displayed by an animal

housed in bare and/or confined quarters. Pigs in small pens, for example, often make continuous chewing movements without having food in their mouths, many cattle tethered in stalls are found to roll their tongues continuously (see Figure 20.3) and some animals in small enclosures pace the same monotonous path endlessly.

Figure 20.3 Stereotypy

It could be argued that such behaviour does have a purpose in that it enables the animal to express frustration and unconsciously communicate its need for sensory stimulation. In addition, pacing back and forth in a confined space exercises muscles, generates heat energy and releases endorphin hormones that block pain. Some experts claim that rather than being abnormal, this form of behaviour indicates a natural response to confinement in an unnatural environment.

The incidence of stereotypies is greatly reduced when the animal's environment is **enriched** by including features present in its natural habitat and by increasing the size, to supply space for normal, natural exercise.

Misdirected behaviour

When a normal pattern of behaviour is directed inappropriately towards the animal itself, another animal or its surroundings, this is described as **misdirected behaviour**. It is a common occurrence among animals that are confined or kept in isolation. Such an animal may **mutilate** itself by excessively licking, plucking or chewing its own feathers, hair or even limbs. Many birds in confinement overgroom themselves to a damaging level; some performing monkeys have even been known to chew off their own tail.

Misdirected behaviour of one animal towards another may occur in response to boredom or stress. Chicks raised in cages without access to suitable flooring material for foraging will peck one another's feathers and skin (see Figure 20.4). Since fowl are attracted

Figure 20.4 Chicken's skin exposed by inappropriate pecking

Figure 20.5 Misdirected behaviour

to damaged feathers, this can lead to a rapid spread of injurious pecking throughout a flock of chickens. This activity is thought to be misdirected foraging behaviour.

Behaviour may be misdirected towards the animal's surroundings. This may take the form of excessive sucking of inanimate objects (especially among mammals separated very early from their mother), chewing cage bars (see Figure 20.5) and gnawing any solid object available.

Misdirected behaviour can be reduced by enriching the animal's environment. One way of doing this is to provide the animal with companions of its own type in a large, stimulating enclosure that includes objects, sounds and scents found in the animal's natural environment.

Failure in sexual or parental behaviour

Poor welfare and prolonged isolation can be responsible for the failure of animals to reproduce successfully. On the other hand they may produce young but then **reject** them and fail to act as effective parents. This affects the farmer whose livelihood depends on the production of generation after generation of livestock.

During their early development young mammals and birds need **social contact** with members of their own kind in a spacious environment in order to develop into normal healthy adults capable of successful reproduction. When they are given these conditions, reproductive failure is normally overcome.

Level of activity

If an animal displays a very high level of activity such as **hyper-aggression** (see Figure 20.6) or a very low level of activity such as **excessive sleeping** this indicates that it may be suffering as a result of poor welfare.

Observing behaviour (ethology)

Ethology is the study of animal behaviour. Scientists are able to establish the normal behaviour patterns of domesticated animals by observing them in their natural or semi-natural surroundings and then making an ethogram.

Ethogram

An **ethogram** is a list of all the different observed behaviours shown by an animal. It provides evidence

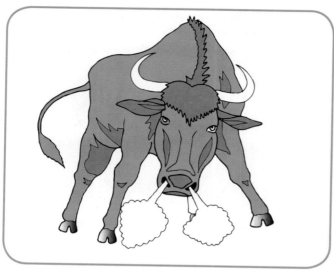

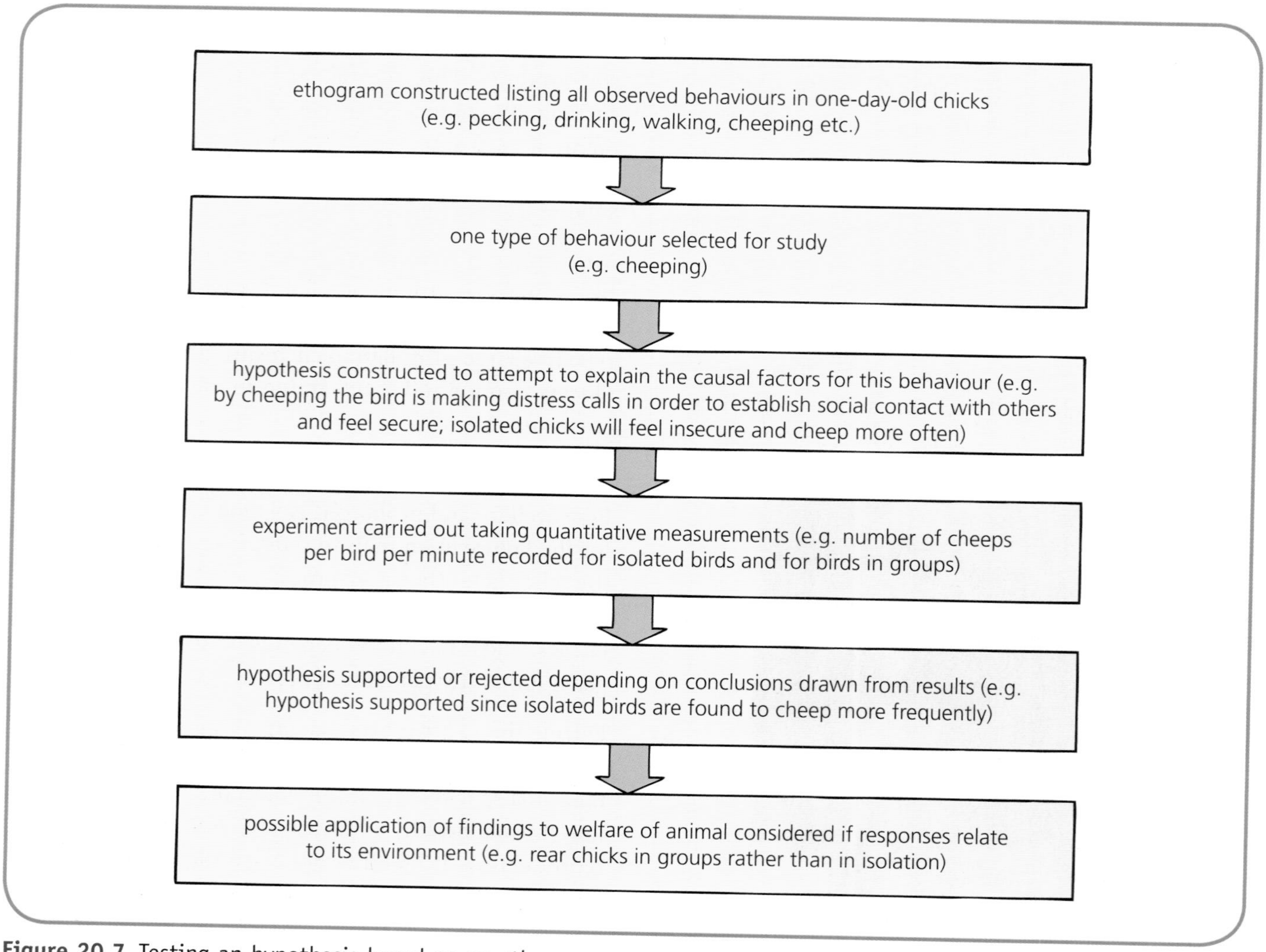

Figure 20.6 Hyper-aggression

ethogram constructed listing all observed behaviours in one-day-old chicks (e.g. pecking, drinking, walking, cheeping etc.)

↓

one type of behaviour selected for study (e.g. cheeping)

↓

hypothesis constructed to attempt to explain the causal factors for this behaviour (e.g. by cheeping the bird is making distress calls in order to establish social contact with others and feel secure; isolated chicks will feel insecure and cheep more often)

↓

experiment carried out taking quantitative measurements (e.g. number of cheeps per bird per minute recorded for isolated birds and for birds in groups)

↓

hypothesis supported or rejected depending on conclusions drawn from results (e.g. hypothesis supported since isolated birds are found to cheep more frequently)

↓

possible application of findings to welfare of animal considered if responses relate to its environment (e.g. rear chicks in groups rather than in isolation)

Figure 20.7 Testing an hypothesis based on an ethogram

of an animal's responses to its environment. Evaluation of the data in an ethogram may allow an **hypothesis** to be constructed. When this is tested by an appropriate **investigation**, it may be possible to draw **conclusions** from the results about the animal's welfare needs. The example in Figure 20.7 refers to 1-day-old chicks.

Related Topic

Anthropomorphism

Animals in the wild have undergone structural, physiological and behavioural adaptations which make them suited to their environment. Since human animals have adapted differently, we can only try to imagine what it feels like to be a non-human animal.

Therefore care must be taken not to give the behaviour of the animal a human interpretation. Attributing human behaviour to an animal is called **anthropomorphism** (see Figure 20.8). The meeting of the welfare needs of a domestic animal and the creation of a suitable environment for it should be based on scientific data (for example from an ethogram study) and not on what human beings would like in their own environment.

Figure 20.8 Anthropomorphism

Preference test

A **preference test** is a test that is set up to give an animal a choice between two conditions and therefore determine which one it prefers. The results from this type of research can be used to enhance the living conditions and wellbeing of farm animals such as hens and pigs.

Choice of two conditions

Figure 20.9 shows the apparatus used in a preference test on hens which were offered a choice between two conditions that relate to the same foraging behaviour. Each cage was dressed with two flooring materials and the hens were allowed to move freely between the two areas.

In order to identify the preferred type of flooring, scientists recorded the length of time spent by each bird on each side of the cage. In order to reduce experimental error and increase the reliability of the results, four replicates of each pair of flooring materials were set up and the behaviour of a large number

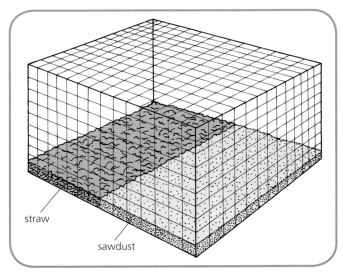

Figure 20.9 Cage for preference test between two flooring materials

of hens was recorded. They were found to prefer the materials in the order straw > sawdust > sand. Similarly when hens, as groups of five, were given the choice between a $1\,m^3$ space and a $9\,m^3$ space, they chose the larger space.

Motivation

Basic needs

Like all other creatures, a domesticated animal has a **basic set of needs** that must be satisfied if it is to thrive. These include adequate food, water, sleep and freedom from discomfort and pain.

Motivation is the process that arouses and directs the behaviour of an animal to satisfy one of these basic needs. Motivation **drives** the animal to act in the way that it does. An animal deprived of food, for example, has a high feeding drive and is strongly motivated to find and consume food. On the other hand, an animal whose basic needs are satisfied lacks motivation (see Figure 20.10).

Strength of motivation

When the dog in the preference test shown in Figure 20.11 is hungry, it is motivated to make an effort, extend the leash and reach the food. The strength of this motivation can be measured using a spring balance attached to the leash. If the dog is not

Figure 20.10 Lack of motivation

hungry, it is not motivated and does not extend the leash.

Pigs choose to be in the company of other pigs rather than to be alone. However, if the pigs have to make an effort and expend energy to reach and associate with other pigs, they lack sufficient motivation to do so.

Figure 20.11 Investigating strength of motivation

Motivation for different behaviours

A preference test can be used to compare the motivation for two different behaviours by offering the animal a choice between two desirable factors such as:

- comfortable bedding *or* the company of others of its own kind

- access to food *or* access to an area suitable for dust-bathing

- access to drinking water *or* access to a sexually receptive mate.

In each case, the motivation for the two different behaviours can be compared to find out which is the greater.

Testing Your Knowledge

1 a) Why does it pay in the long run to invest money in facilities and accommodation that will improve the welfare of farm animals? (1)

b) Some people claim that it is unethical to eat meat and eggs from chickens raised in battery farms. Explain this point of view. (1)

2 a) Which of the forms of behaviour listed below is an example of:
   i) stereotypy
   ii) misdirected behaviour
   iii) failure in parental behaviour
   iv) altered level of activity? (4)

   A a sow in a small enclosure smothering her newborn litter

   B a mare repeatedly biting the door-frame of her small stall

   C a bull alone in a small field charging aggressively at a fence post

   D caged game birds pecking one another's feathers and causing injury

   b) In general what could be done in an attempt to eliminate these forms of undesirable behaviour from future generations of domesticated animals? (2)

3 a) i) What is an *ethogram*?
   ii) To what use can the data contained in an ethogram of a domesticated animal be put? (3)

   b) What is the purpose of a *preference test*? (2)

   c) Give TWO examples of situations where an animal would be highly motivated to behave in a certain way. (2)

What You Should Know

Chapters 19 and 20

(See Table 20.2 for word bank)

agricultural	forecast	pressure
annual	fungi	resist
behaviour	hypothesis	resistant
biological	indicators	rotation
crop	integrated	selective
cultural	motivation	stereotypies
cycle	natural	systemic
diseased	nematodes	toxic
domesticated	parental	vegetatively
ethically	perennial	viable
ethogram	persist	weeds
experiment	preference	welfare

Table 20.2 Word bank for chapters 19 and 20

1 Compared to a natural ecosystem, the variety of species that make up the community in an _____ ecosystem is greatly reduced. Such conditions present ideal growing conditions to _____, pests and disease-causing micro-organisms. Their activities reduce the productivity of the _____.

2 _____ weeds are successful because they grow rapidly, have a short life _____ and produce a huge number of seeds which remain _____ for a long time. _____ weeds owe their success to the possession of storage organs, the ability to reproduce _____ and the fact that they are already established and therefore at a competitive advantage.

3 Animal pests that attack crops are mainly invertebrates such as _____, molluscs and insects. Diseases that affect crops are caused by bacteria, _____ and viruses.

4 Weeds, pests and diseases of crops can be controlled to some extent by _____ means such as crop _____ and by the use of protective chemicals. Use of a _____ herbicide is advantageous because it kills broad-leaved weeds but not the narrow-leaved crop. Use of _____ fungicide is advantageous because it protects all parts of the crop from within.

5 Applying a fungicide in response to a disease _____ is more effective than treating the crop once it has become _____.

6 Some protective chemicals are _____ to other living organisms in addition to the pest. They may _____ and accumulate in food chains. They may exert a selection _____ on the pest population and produce a _____ population.

7 The use of a natural enemy of the pest or parasite as the agent of control is called _____ control. A combination of several control techniques is called _____ pest management.

8 In the past, the ability of a _____ animal to grow, to reproduce and to _____ disease successfully were regarded as adequate indications of its wellbeing. However, in recent times, the animal being able to behave in a _____ way has been added to the list.

9 The provision of a high standard of animal _____ is costly but worth the financial outlay both economically and _____.

10 Animals kept in conditions of low level welfare express their discomfort as behavioural _____. These take the form of _____, misdirected _____, altered levels of activity and failure in sexual or _____ behaviour.

11 A list of all the observed behaviours of an animal is called an _____. This can be used to form an _____ about the animal's welfare needs which can then be tested by _____.

12 A _____ test is one that presents an animal with a choice between two conditions. The process that drives an animal to act in a way that satisfies one of its basic needs is called _____. It can be measured using preference tests.

21 Symbiosis

Symbiosis

Symbiosis is an ecological relationship between organisms of two different species that live in direct contact with one another. Symbiotic relationships are intimate relationships that have evolved over millions of years. In some cases the two species involved have become adapted in such a way that their metabolisms are complementary to some extent. This coevolution of adaptations is essential because a change in one partner is likely to affect the survival of the other.

Two categories of symbiosis are:

● **parasitism** – one organism, the **parasite**, benefits at the expense of the other organism, the **host**, which is often damaged

● **mutualism** – both organisms benefit from the relationship.

Parasitism provides illustrations of **dependence** since the parasite is always dependent on the host whereas mutualism illustrates **interdependence** since the two partners are mutually dependent upon one another.

Parasitism

In parasitism one organism, the parasite, derives its nutrition from another organism, the host, which it exploits. The host is harmed or at least loses some energy and/or materials to the parasite.

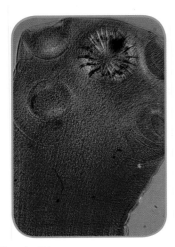

Figure 21.1 Head of tapeworm

In many cases of parasitism, a relatively stable relationship has evolved and a **balance** exists between defence mechanisms used by the host and damage inflicted by the parasite. Parasites often possess a **limited metabolism**. For example a tapeworm (see Figure 21.1) lacks a digestive system since its host has already digested the food. However, this means that many parasites such as an adult tapeworm cannot survive if they lose contact with their host. It is for this reason that the most effective parasite is one that does not cause its host to die (or at least not until completion of the parasite's life cycle is ensured).

Some parasites such as malarial *Plasmodium*, liver fluke and tapeworm live and feed *inside* their host. Some parasites such as aphid, flea and mosquito (see Figure 21.2) live and feed *outside* their host.

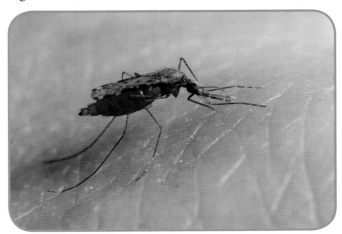

Figure 21.2 Mosquito

Transmission

The transmission of parasites to new hosts involves a variety of mechanisms such as:

● **direct contact** (for example head and body lice are passed from person to person during physical contact)

● **release of resistant stages** able to survive adverse environmental conditions for long periods until they come into contact with a new host (for example the resistant larvae and pupae of the cat flea shown in Figure 21.3 transmit the parasite to new hosts)

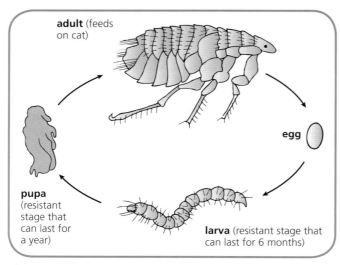

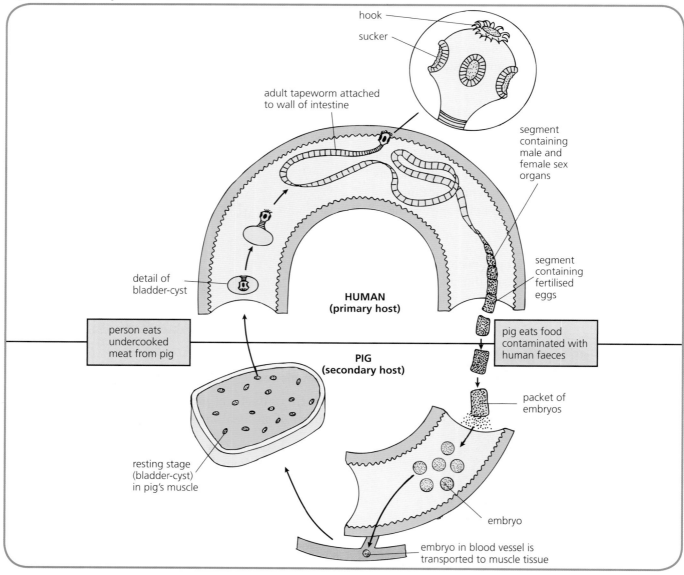

Figure 21.3 Life cycle of cat flea

- **use of a vector** (for example mosquitoes carry *Plasmodium*, the unicellular organism that causes malaria, from human to human).

Evolution of parasitic life cycles involving a secondary host

There are two types of parasitic life cycle. In a **direct** life cycle, eggs are shed and pass to a new member of the host species. This cycle involves one species of host only, and is common among parasites such as flea and louse that live and feed outside of their host.

More highly evolved is the **indirect** life cycle. In addition to using a **primary** host species as the site of the sexual stage of its reproduction, the parasite has

Figure 21.4 Life cycle of tapeworm

become adapted by evolution to employ a **secondary** (intermediate) host species in its life cycle.

A new primary host becomes infected when it is invaded by or consumes the infected **secondary** host (or the parasite that has been released from it). This type of life cycle is commonly found among parasites such as tapeworm (see Figure 21.4) that live and feed inside their host. The involvement of a second (or even third) host in the cycle would seem to complicate matters needlessly for the parasite yet this type of life cycle has evolved by natural selection over millions of years. Therefore the parasite must be gaining some advantage.

Advantage

It is often a difficult, risky business for a parasite that lives inside its host to move from one primary host to another. An adult tapeworm, for example, has no means of locomotion and its eggs are unlikely to be consumed by potential human hosts unless their food or drink is contaminated with raw sewage.

However, the parasite can complete its life cycle with ease once it is established in the secondary host which can be eaten by humans, the primary hosts. Completion of the cycle depends only on the infected meat being **inadequately cooked** and eaten by humans.

In addition to reproducing sexually within its primary host, the parasite may further exploit its secondary host by using it as a site of **asexual reproduction**. By this means it increases enormously its reproductive capacity and chance of survival.

Mutualism

Cellulose digestion

Many herbivorous mammals lack the genes required for the synthesis of cellulose-digesting enzymes despite the fact that cellulose, in the cell walls of plants, is a major constituent of their diet. These herbivores are found to possess special gut chambers containing **cellulose-digesting micro-organisms** (bacteria, archaea and protozoa) that form a **mutualistic** relationship with the herbivore. They are found, for example, in the first two chambers of a cow's complex, four-chambered 'stomach' (see Figure 21.5).

The micro-organisms produce enzymes which digest cellulose to simple sugars used by the herbivore as its

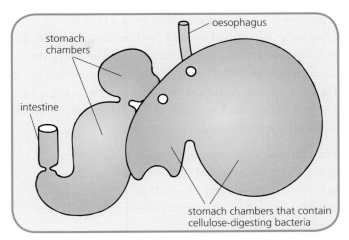

Figure 21.5 'Stomach' of cow

energy source. The microbes also convert some of the sugar to other metabolites essential to the animal (and make by-products such as methane). In exchange the microbes receive protection, warmth and a constant supply of food.

Humans depend on **ruminants** such as cattle and sheep for supplies of food and other products. Therefore the symbiosis between these animals and cellulose-digesting micro-organisms is of great economic importance.

Coral polyps

A **coral polyp** (see Figure 21.6) is an animal that resembles a sea anemone. However, it is unable to move from place to place. It secretes a hard skeleton which attaches it to the skeletons of earlier polyps forming a **coral reef**. It feeds on microscopic organisms and tiny bits of organic debris in the sea water.

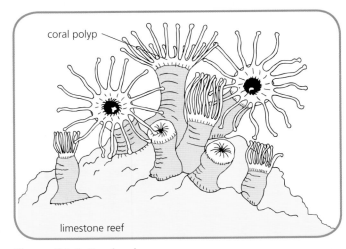

Figure 21.6 Coral polyps

It has a **mutualistic** relationship with a type of unicellular alga called **zooxanthella** which lives within and between its cells (see Figure 21.7). The polyp may use as much as 80% of the carbohydrate made by the algae for energy. In return the algae are provided with a secure habitat and a supply of the polyp's nitrogenous waste which they convert to protein.

The fact that coral reefs are known to have been in existence for over 200 million years and that they occupy more than 280 000 km^2 of tropical and sub-tropical waters demonstrates the success of this symbiotic relationship.

Figure 21.7 Coral polyps containing zooxanthella

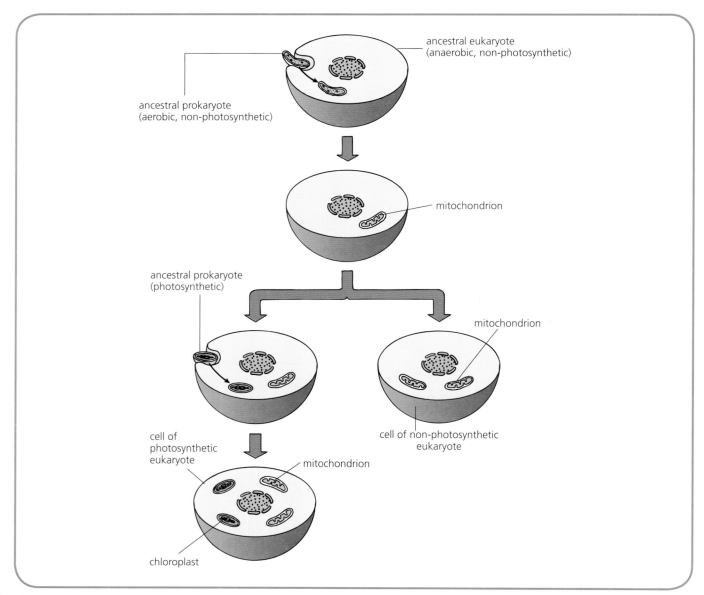

Figure 21.8 Origin of mitochondria and chloroplasts in eukaryotes

Symbiotic origin of mitochondria and chloroplasts

It is thought that **mitochondria and chloroplasts** evolved from two different types of small **prokaryotic** cells that had initially become residents inside larger anaerobic cells (see Figure 21.8). The ancestors of mitochondria are thought to have been aerobic, non-photosynthetic prokaryotes and those of chloroplasts to have been photosynthetic prokaryotes.

It is easy to imagine a form of **mutualism** developing between the larger cell (probably a eukaryote) and its smaller residents. The latter would gain security and the former a greatly improved energy output and a supply of food made by photosynthesis. These benefits would enable the larger cell to expand its environmental range. Mitochondria are thought to have evolved before chloroplasts. Chloroplasts only evolved in those cell lines that eventually became green plants and not in those lines that evolved into animals and fungi.

Evidence

The hypothesis of the endosymbiotic origin of mitochondria and chloroplasts is supported by the following evidence:

- Mitochondria and chloroplasts have their **own DNA** (see page 10) and it is circular like that of prokaryotes.

- The two types of organelle contain **ribosomes** more similar to those found in prokaryotes than those in their own eukaryotic cell.

- A strong similarity in **structure and size** exists between bacteria (prokaryotes) and mitochondria and chloroplasts (organelles) present in eukaryotes.

- The inner membrane of the two types of organelle bears **enzymes and transport systems** reminiscent of those found in the membrane of bacteria.

- The method by which mitochondria and chloroplasts **replicate** is similar to cell division in bacteria.

- Molecular studies of the **ribosomal RNA** of chloroplasts and mitochondria indicate that it originated in bacteria.

Research Topic — Symbiosis and anthropogenic climate change

Coral

When the zooxanthellae (yellow algae) inside coral polyps die, the coral is said to become 'bleached'. Many cases of bleaching have been reported in recent years and attributed to **thermal stress**. Warmer temperatures also seem to weaken a coral's immune system and leave it open to attack by pathogens. The situation is expected to become even worse in the future as coral reefs are further challenged by **anthropogenic climate change** (i.e. man-made global warming).

A glimmer of hope is provided by research that some types of zooxanthellae are able to tolerate an increase in temperature of about 1–1.5 °C. Therefore a coral polyp that associates with a variety of types of zooxanthellae may contain the tolerant type and may be able to effect some degree of thermal acclimatisation. However, on its own this is unlikely to be sufficient to enable the coral to survive the changes in sea surface temperature of tropical waters which are forecast to increase by up to 3 °C over the next 100 years.

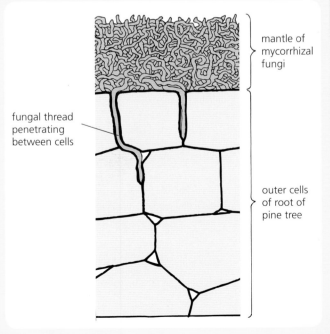

mantle of mycorrhizal fungi

fungal thread penetrating between cells

outer cells of root of pine tree

Figure 21.9 Mycorrhiza

295

Mycorrhiza

A **mycorrhiza** is an intimate **mutualistic** association between the roots of a plant and a fungus. The fungal threads (hyphae) greatly increase the absorptive surface in contact with the soil solution and help the plant to gain an adequate supply of water and soil nutrients. The fungus receives photosynthetic products in exchange.

The vast majority of vascular plants are in a mycorrhizal relationship with a fungus. Many types of tree such as oak, beech and pine (see Figure 21.9) are heavily dependent on this form of symbiosis because the presence of a mantle of fungal threads enables older regions of their roots lacking root hairs to absorb water and nutrients.

Anthropogenic climate change in the future is expected to alter regional rainfall and result in some forest ecosystems becoming warmer and drier. In extreme cases this may cause desiccation and death of the mycorrhizal fungi followed by death of the trees, their mutualistic partners.

Testing Your Knowledge

1 a) What is meant by the term *symbiosis*? (2)

   b) Copy and complete Table 21.1 using the symbols:
      + = benefit and − = harm. (2)

Type of symbiosis	Species 1	Species 2
		+
parasitism		

   Table 21.1

2 Briefly describe THREE methods by which parasites may be transmitted from one host to another. Include named examples in your answer. (6)

3 Explain why:

   a) a parasite such as an adult tapeworm is unable to survive out of contact with its host (1)

   b) coral polyps are restricted to waters less than 100 metres deep (1)

   c) it is of advantage to a parasite to involve a secondary host in its life cycle. (1)

22 Social behaviour

Many animals live in **social groups**. A social group may consist of as few as two members or as many as several thousand. The members of a group react to **social signals** given by other members of the same species. The successful cohesion of the group requires its members to exhibit certain **behavioural adaptations** as in the following examples of social behaviour.

Social hierarchy

This is a system where the members of a social group are organised into a graded order of **rank** resulting from aggressive behaviour between members of the group. An individual of higher rank **dominates** and exerts control over other subordinate individuals of a lower rank.

Birds

If newly-hatched birds such as pigeons are kept together, one will soon emerge as the **dominant** member of the group. This bird is able to peck and intimidate all other members of the group without being attacked in return. It therefore gets first choice of any available food. Below this dominant bird there

is a second one which can peck all others except the first and so on down the line. This linear form of social organisation is called a **pecking order**.

Table 22.1 summarises the results from observing a group of hens over a period of time. Bird A dominates all of the others, bird B dominates all others except A and so on down the line to bird J which is dominated by all the other birds. A pecking order is an example of a **social hierarchy**.

Mammals

Although not so clear cut, a similar system of social organisation exists among some mammals such as wolves. Because of his rank, the dominant male has certain rights such as first choice of food, preferred sleeping places and available mates. This dominant individual asserts his rank by employing social signals as shown in Figure 22.1.

The dominant wolf's visual display of **ritualised threat gestures** is normally impressive enough to assert his authority over other members of the social group. These in turn demonstrate their acceptance of his status by making **submissive responses**.

		Hen receiving pecks									
		A	B	C	D	E	F	G	H	I	J
Hen giving pecks	A		✓	✓	✓	✓	✓	✓	✓	✓	✓
	B			✓	✓	✓	✓	✓	✓	✓	✓
	C				✓	✓	✓	✓	✓	✓	✓
	D					✓	✓	✓	✓	✓	✓
	E						✓	✓	✓	✓	✓
	F							✓	✓	✓	✓
	G								✓	✓	✓
	H									✓	✓
	I										✓
	J										

Table 22.1 Pecking order for a group of ten hens

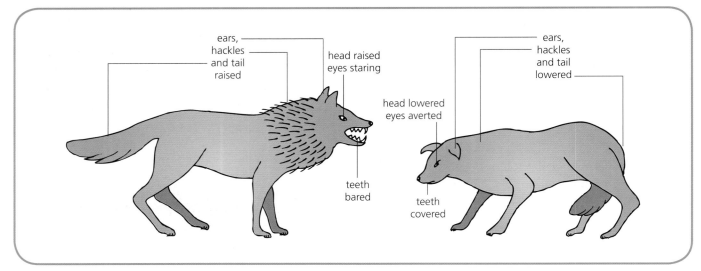

Figure 22.1 Dominant and submissive responses

Advantages of social hierarchy

A system of social hierarchy increases a species' chance of survival because:

- aggression between its members becomes ritualised

- real fighting is kept to a minimum

- serious injury is normally avoided

- energy is conserved

- experienced leadership is guaranteed

- the most powerful animals are most likely to pass their genes on to the next generation.

Cooperative hunting

Some predatory mammals such as killer whales, lions, wolves and wild dogs rely on **cooperation** between members of the social group to hunt their prey. Killer whales hunt in packs called pods (see Figure 22.2) and employ various strategies. In a river mouth, a pod will sweep along in a line to catch migrating salmon. In coastal waters the same pod will encircle a shoal of herring and concentrate them into a seething mass. The whales then thrash the herring with their tails to stun them and gorge themselves on a catch of food that would be unavailable to a solitary predator.

The **ambush strategy** employed by lions involves some predators driving prey towards others that are hidden in cover and ready to pounce. Dogs and wolves, on the

Figure 22.2 Pod of killer whales

other hand, take turns at **running down** a solitary prey animal to the point of exhaustion and then attacking it (see Figure 22.3). In the case of lions, wolves and dogs, the group of predators tends to concentrate its efforts on a prey animal that has become separated from the rest of the herd. This is often a young and inexperienced or old and infirm animal, making it an easy target.

Figure 22.3 Cooperative hunting

Advantages of cooperative hunting

When a kill is achieved, all members of the predator group obtain food (some of which may be disgorged later by females to feed the young). Thus **cooperative hunting** benefits the subordinate animals as well as the dominant leader of the group. By working together, the animals are able to tackle large prey animals and, as a result, all gain more food than they would by hunting alone. Provided that the food reward gained by cooperative hunting exceeds that from hunting individually, the social group will continue to share food regardless of the fact that the dominant member(s) receives a much larger share than the subordinate ones.

Social mechanisms for defence

By staying together as a large group (such as a school of fish or herd of mammals), many types of animals rely on the principle of 'safety in numbers' as a means of defence. Among a flock of birds, for example, there are many eyes constantly on the lookout for enemies. Following an **alarm** call, the bunching and swirling tactics adopted by the flock confuse the predator who finds it much more difficult to capture a member of a large, unpredictable, milling crowd than a solitary individual.

Defence is strengthened further by the members of a social group adopting a **specialised formation** as in the following examples.

Musk ox

Musk oxen (Figure 22.4) are native to Arctic regions of Canada and Greenland. Their natural environment is completely open and offers no scrub or woodland to use for concealment. Their natural enemy (apart

from human beings) is the wolf. When threatened, a herd of musk oxen form a **protective group** with cows and calves in the centre and mature males at the outside with their huge horns directed outwards. Individual wolves are gored and packs are driven off by a combined charge. This form of social defence is called **mobbing**.

Figure 22.4 Social defence (musk oxen)

Quail

Bobwhite quails roost in **circles** with their heads to the outside as shown in Figure 22.5. If disturbed, the circle acts as a defensive formation by 'exploding' in the predator's face. By the time their enemy has recovered from the confusion, the birds have flown away to safety.

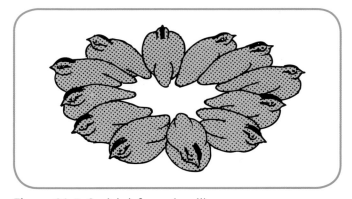

Figure 22.5 Social defence (quail)

Baboon

A strict social hierarchy is observed by the members of a troop of baboons. When the baboons are on the march (see Figure 22.6), the dominant males stay in the centre close to the females with infants. Lower-ranking adult males and juveniles keep to the edge of the troop and raise the alarm if the group is threatened (for example by a leopard).

Figure 22.6 Social defence (baboons)

Altruism

Members of the same species compete with one another because they need the same resources. However, variation exists among the members of a species. Those that are able to compete most successfully would be expected to selfishly exploit to excess the available resources and produce the maximum number of offspring at the expense of the poorer competitors who would lose out. As a result of this process, the fittest members would pass many copies of their genes on to the next generation.

However, on some occasions, an animal is found to behave in a way that is disadvantageous (harmful) to itself, the **donor**, and beneficial (helpful) to another animal, the **recipient**. This unselfish behaviour is called **altruism** (see Figure 22.7) and at first glance it would seem to contradict the idea of the survival of the fittest. However, on closer inspection, this is not found to be the case.

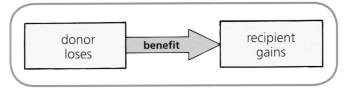

Figure 22.7 Altruism

Reciprocal altruism

Reciprocal altruism involves one individual, at some cost to itself, giving help to another provided that there is a very real prospect of the **favour being returned** at a later date when the roles of donor and recipient become reversed. It requires members of the social group to

be sufficiently intelligent to be able to remember who is indebted to whom and how to recognise and expel cheats.

Vampire bats

After a night of hunting, vampire bats that have been successful may return to the roost bloated with blood while other unsuccessful members of the same social group may return hungry. The hungry individuals then beg blood from the bloated ones by licking their face (see Figure 22.8 part a). The latter are often willing to regurgitate some blood (see Figure 22.8 part b) but tend to give it only to those who had been altruistic to them in the past.

In reciprocal altruism, the benefit gained by the recipient **exceeds the cost** to the donor. This is illustrated by vampire bats because a hungry bat (the potential recipient) is likely to die if it fails to find a blood meal on two consecutive nights.

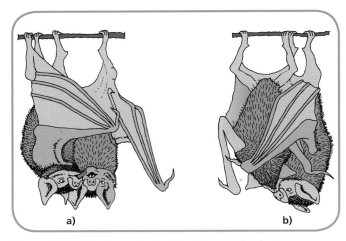

Figure 22.8 Reciprocal altruism in vampire bats

The prisoner's dilemma

Imagine two suspects (X and Y) jointly charged with a crime which they *did commit*. The police do not have sufficient evidence to be sure of a conviction for the crime but they do have enough to be sure of a conviction for a minor offence. The police interview the prisoners separately and offer each the following deal:

- If you testify for the prosecution against your accomplice and your accomplice remains silent, you will go free and your accomplice will receive the full 8-year jail sentence.

	X remains silent	X betrays Y
Y remains silent	X and Y each serve 1 year	X goes free; Y serves 8 years
Y betrays X	Y goes free; X serves 8 years	X and Y each serve 4 years

Table 22.2 Four outcomes of the prisoner's dilemma

- If you testify for the prosecution against your accomplice and your accomplice testifies against you, you will each receive a 4-year jail sentence.

- If you both remain silent, you will each be sentenced to 1 year in jail for the minor offence.

Each prisoner must choose whether to betray their accomplice or remain silent. The situation is summarised in Table 22.2.

If the two members of the group both make a self-interested decision and betray the other in an attempt to gain their own **best personal outcome** (complete freedom regardless of the 8-year jail sentence for their accomplice) then this results in the **worst possible mutual outcome** for both (a 4-year jail sentence each).

On the other hand if they trust one another, they can choose to cooperate and remain silent. This course of action results in the **best possible mutual outcome** (a 1-year jail sentence each) though not the best possible personal outcome.

Investigation

Reciprocal altruism using the prisoner's dilemma

The **prisoner's dilemma** can be investigated by playing it as a game. The jail sentences in Table 22.2 are converted into a scoring system of points as shown in Table 22.3.

	X remains silent	X betrays Y
Y remains silent	X and Y each receive 3 points	X receives 5 points; Y receives 0 points
Y betrays X	Y receives 5 points; X receives 0 points	X and Y each receive 1 point

Table 22.3 Points for prisoner's dilemma game

Within each group there are two players and a banker. Each player holds two cards, one bearing the words 'remain silent', the other bearing the words 'betray accomplice'. Each player puts one card face down in front of the banker who then turns them over and awards points accordingly. The game is played repeatedly to represent a series of interrogations. The score from each round is recorded and running totals kept. The object is to gain the maximum number of points before reaching game over. Game over is determined by the banker choosing a random number between 20 and 30 before the game begins which remains unknown to the players. The banker brings the game to a halt at the round indicated by the random number.

Since many rounds are played, each player has several opportunities to punish the other player for previous non-cooperative play. Eventually the incentive to make purely self-interested decisions may be overcome by the threat of punishment.

The final scores are compared with the scores that would have been obtained if X and Y had cooperated with one another and remained silent throughout. Table 22.4 shows a typical set of results. From the results it is concluded that the prisoner's dilemma is a simple model of **reciprocal altruism**. By cooperating from the start, X and Y would have both been better off at the end than they were by operating independently. Table 22.5 shows precautions that are 'adopted' during this investigation and the reasons for doing so.

Round	X				Y			
	Actual score	Running total	Score if silent and cooperating throughout	Running total	Actual score	Running total	Score if silent and cooperating throughout	Running total
1	1	1	3	3	1	1	3	3
2	5	6	3	6	0	1	3	6
3	3	9	3	9	3	4	3	9
4	5	14	3	12	0	4	3	12
5	3	17	3	15	3	7	3	15
6	0	17	3	18	5	12	3	18
7	1	18	3	21	1	13	3	21
8	1	19	3	24	1	14	3	24
9	5	24	3	27	0	14	3	27
10	5	29	3	30	0	14	3	30
11	0	29	3	33	5	19	3	33
12	0	29	3	36	5	24	3	36
13	1	30	3	39	1	25	3	39
14	1	31	3	42	1	26	3	42
15	1	32	3	45	1	27	3	45
16	3	35	3	48	3	30	3	48
17	3	38	3	51	3	33	3	51
18	5	43	3	54	0	33	3	54
19	0	43	3	57	5	38	3	57
20	1	44	3	60	1	39	3	60
21	0	44	3	63	5	44	3	63
22	5	49	3	66	0	44	3	66
23	1	50	3	69	1	45	3	69
24	3	53	3	72	3	48	3	72
25	3	56	3	75	3	51	3	75

Table 22.4 Results of prisoner's dilemma game

Precaution adopted	Reason
the decision of one player remains unknown to the other player until they have both made their decision	to prevent the second player's decision being influenced by that made by the first player
the exact number of rounds is not known in advance to the players	to prevent the players choosing to betray one another repeatedly in a last ditch attempt to enhance their score

Table 22.5 Precautions adopted during investigation

Kin selection

When one member of a flock of birds nesting in long grass in a marsh gives a warning call on spotting the approach of a predator, the other birds respond by remaining motionless, which keeps them safe. However, the bird that made the call has put itself in harm's way and may be caught by the predator. Therefore if an 'altruistic' gene for making the warning call exists, it would be reasonable to expect that the animals possessing it (and the gene itself) would become **eliminated** from the population. However, if the useful gene is also possessed by the bird's offspring and close relatives, the loss of one individual is easily offset by the survival of many.

Apparent altruism

When a parent sacrifices itself to ensure the survival of its offspring, this **apparent altruism** is not a sacrifice in terms of evolution because the parent's genes are successfully passed on to the next generation. But what about an individual that is harmed as a result of being helpful to other close relatives? A useful gene would only spread through the population if the cost to the individual that sacrifices its chance to reproduce and pass on the gene were more than made up for by the additional number of close relatives also possessing the gene and passing it on to future generations.

Coefficient of relatedness

The **coefficient of relatedness** (see Table 22.6) refers to the proportion of genes on average that are identical in two individuals because of shared ancestors. For example, for siblings it is 0.5 because they have, on average, 50% of their genes in common.

Natural selection favours an altruistic individual helping its siblings or helping its parents (or close relatives) who have the potential to produce more offspring. The donor benefits indirectly provided that many copies of the shared genes reach the next generation, ensuring their 'immortality'. This process, which favours acts of apparent altruism carried out to help close relatives, is called **kin selection** (see Figure 22.9).

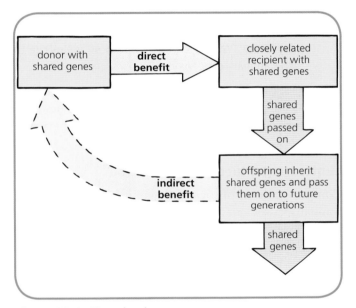

Figure 22.9 Kin selection

Relationship	Coefficient of relatedness
parent – son/daughter	0.5
brother/sister – brother/sister	0.5
half brother/half sister – half brother/half sister	0.25
uncle/aunt – nephew/niece	0.25
grandparent – grandchild	0.25
cousin – cousin	0.125

Table 22.6 Coefficients of relatedness

Testing Your Knowledge 1

1 Instead of fighting, wolves perform a ritual.

a) Describe FOUR features of a dominant wolf's visual display that are on show when it is asserting its authority. (2)

b) Describe the corresponding responses displayed by a subordinate animal. (2)

c) i) What name is given to the type of social organisation that results from this behaviour pattern?
ii) State TWO ways in which it is of advantage to the animals concerned. (3)

2 A pack of African wild dogs catches a large prey animal such as a wildebeest by running it down to the point of exhaustion. Give TWO advantages gained by the dogs from this form of *co-operative* hunting. (2)

3 Musk oxen live in a completely open environment. How do they defend themselves against wolves? (2)

4 a) Using the terms *harmful, recipient, behaviour, helpful* and *donor*, explain the meaning of altruism. (3)

b) What is *reciprocal* altruism? (1)

c) What is the survival value of behaviour that may require an individual to die in order to save its close relatives? (2)

Social insects

Limited reproductive contribution

Complex patterns of social behaviour have evolved in some insect societies such as termites, ants, wasps and bees. Close cooperation occurs between the individuals in caring for the young. A **division of labour** exists as follows.

- Food gathering and defence are carried out by numerous sterile members of the society.

- Reproduction is the responsibility of a few fertile individuals.

The evolution of this type of society is thought to have gone through several stages as shown in Figure 22.10.

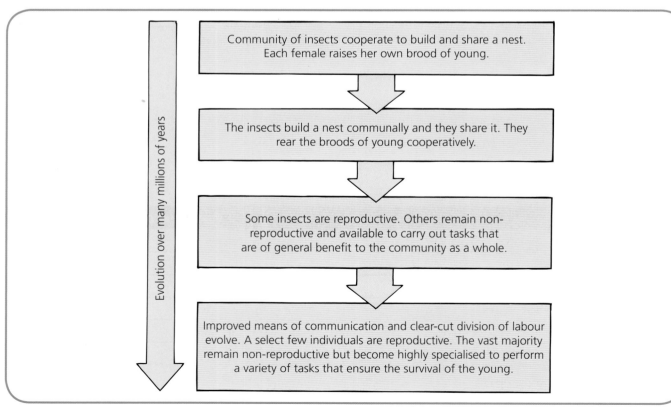

Figure 22.10 Possible steps in evolution of insect colony

Honey bee

Among honey bees, three castes exist – **queens, workers** and **drones**. Within a colony the single queen and the many thousands of workers are females and the few hundred drones present are males. Only the queen produces eggs. When these are fertilised by drones they develop into workers.

All sister workers share the same mother (the queen) and therefore have very many of their genes in common. The most efficient method of ensuring that these genes are passed on to future generations is by the workers **maintaining and defending the hive** rather than each attempting to produce and look after her own brood.

The drones play a purely reproductive role but the workers display a complex series of behavioural acts within their short adult life (4–6 weeks). These acts are all aimed directly or indirectly at **ensuring the survival of the offspring**. They include:

- cleaning out cells in the brood area
- feeding and grooming larvae (see Figure 22.11)
- building new cells
- storing pollen
- guarding the hive from enemies
- foraging for food.

Similarly among colonies of ants, termites and wasps, only a few individuals contribute reproductively to the society. Most members are workers who cooperate with one another to raise the young – not their own offspring but those of their close relatives. This is a further example of **kin selection**.

Keystone species

Removal of the keystone from the arch in Figure 22.12 makes the structure collapse.

Similarly a **keystone species** is one that plays a critical role in the structure and working of an ecosystem. Often the keystone species' impact on the ecosystem is disproportionately large relative to its numbers.

Social insects are often considered to be keystone species within their ecosystems because loss of their ecological contributions to the ecosystem could lead to its collapse. Fertility of soil in semi-desert and savannah ecosystems depends on the activity of subterranean termites (and their symbiotic cellulose-digesting micro-organisms) to break down dead wood and other plant debris. Such **decomposition** releases chemicals and enables nutrient cycles to turn. Bees (see Figure 22.13) play a vital role in the **pollination** of plants in an ecosystem. Insect pollination is especially important to plant species that are natural outbreeders and unable to pollinate and fertilise themselves.

Figure 22.11 Worker bees feeding larvae

Figure 22.12 Keystone in an arch

Figure 22.13 Pollination by bee

Figure 22.14 Parental care

Ecosystem services

The benefit that humans gain from the many resources supplied and processes carried out by natural ecosystems are called **ecosystem services**. Therefore species of insect that provide supportive processes such as decomposition by termites, pollination of crop plants by insects or pest control by parasitic wasps (see page 279) are of economic importance to humans.

Primate behaviour

The **primates** are animals that belong to an order of placental mammals. They normally possess dextrous hands and feet with opposable first digits, stereoscopic vision and, in the higher apes, a highly developed brain. Examples include lemurs, monkeys, apes and humans.

Parental care

Unlike less highly evolved animals that produce an enormous number of young on the basis that a few will survive, primates produce a small number of young and then take great care of them. Primate offspring are almost helpless initially although they do possess the strong hand grip needed to grasp on tightly to their mother. During the long period of **parental care** (see Figure 22.14), the parents feed their young, keep them clean, protect them from extremes of temperature, transport them from place to place and defend them against enemies.

During this time many opportunities arise for the young primates to **learn** complex social behaviours essential for their survival. At quiet times, very young,

playful, tree-living primates, for example, are allowed to explore under the watchful eye of their mother and crawl short distances along the branches by themselves. As the young primates grow older, they watch and learn while the adults perform important behaviour patterns such as **foraging**, **hunting** and **recognising danger**.

Language

As the young primates experiment and imitate others, they learn how to communicate with the members of their social group using **language**. Language is a system used to express thoughts and feelings and normally consists of a mixture of sounds and gestures.

Play

Eventually there comes a time when the young primates are well enough developed to leave their mother for long periods each day and **play** with other juveniles (see Figure 22.15).

Figure 22.15 Young primates at play

During social play, the youngsters **practise** the rudiments of adult social behaviour. They chase or flee from companions, play-fight with one another and test the physical limits of their own bodies. The behaviour is exaggerated so that it is recognised by other members of the social group as harmless and 'not-for-real'. By practising the rudiments of adult social behaviour during play, the youngsters learn skills such as **communication**, **cooperation** and **sharing** that they will need to survive as adults.

Reducing conflict

If rival animals engage in a real fight, the loser may be killed but, at the same time, the winner may be seriously injured. This means that the winner may be unable to find food or escape from enemies and therefore, like the loser, fail to survive. It is for this reason that many higher animals have evolved behaviours that make them go to great lengths to **reduce conflict** and avoid engaging in serious fighting.

Ritualistic display

When two social primates find themselves competing for a resource such as a mate, they are likely to exhibit a **threat display** to one another. Such a display normally makes them look larger and fiercer and involves the adoption of certain postures (see Table 22.7). Eventually one of the rivals succeeds in making itself more intimidating and the other responds by conceding defeat, abandoning its threat display and adopting **appeasement behaviour**.

Primate	Features of threat display between rival males of near-equal rank
chimpanzee	bipedal swaggering, shoulders hunched, arms held out, hair bristling, mouth open, teeth covered by lips
gorilla	chest-beating, roaring, strutting walk, hair bristling, eyes staring
marmoset monkey	back arched, tail raised, fur erect, eyes staring
vervet monkey	head bobbing, mouth open, eyes staring, tail arched over body

Table 22.7 Threat display features

Appeasement

Appeasement behaviour consists of a **submissive** display that is the reverse of a threat ritual. The animal's body is made to look smaller, flatter, motionless and as **unthreatening** as possible. A vulnerable part of the body may even be exposed to further defuse the hostile situation.

Once a male has established himself at the top of the **social hierarchy** within a social group of primates, females and subordinate males display their acceptance of the dominant male by employing appeasement behaviours (see Figure 22.16).

Figure 22.16 'He's still to learn that appeasement means grovelling not growling.'

Grooming

Chimpanzees and other primates employ **grooming** (see Figure 22.17) as an effective way of reducing tension within the group. One animal picks plant material, fleas and scabs from the fur of another. This often takes the form of reciprocal altruism. In addition to maintaining hygiene, it cements friendships between grooming partners who are more likely to assist one another in a crisis than non-grooming partners. Social grooming may even be used to bring about reconciliation after a fight.

Figure 22.17 Grooming

Facial expression

If a primate closes its eyes during an encounter with a rival, it is indicating that it accepts that it has been dominated and is giving up the struggle. It wants to be regarded as subordinate and submissive. Within a social group of monkeys, if an individual opens and closes its lips rapidly making a gentle smacking noise, this is recognised by others as a friendly, submissive greeting. It is derived from the act of grooming and acts as a form of appeasement helping to keep hostilities at bay. A grinning, open mouth exposing the teeth is employed by a chimp to appease a more dominant individual that it fears.

Body posture

Among chimpanzees, subordinate males greet a dominant male in a **servile** manner. They emit soft, grunting noises, make a series of quick bows and prostrate themselves low enough to be able to look up respectfully at the dominant male.

Sexual presentation

Female chimpanzees, on the other hand, employ a **sexual** approach to appease a dominant male by offering their rumps for sniffing and possible mounting. By doing this they are arousing a response that is an **alternative** to aggression.

Survival value

Ritualistic displays and appeasement behaviours are of survival value because they **reduce conflict** to a minimum within a closely-knit social group. They make it possible for weaker members to live in close proximity to stronger members without threats of needless hostility constantly erupting.

Social status and alliances

Within a primate society, a social hierarchy exists and each member accepts its place (in other words, its rank or status) on the social ladder. The individual tends to refrain from challenging those members of the group that are of higher rank. However, in reality such a hierarchy is both **complex** and in a state of **flux**. An

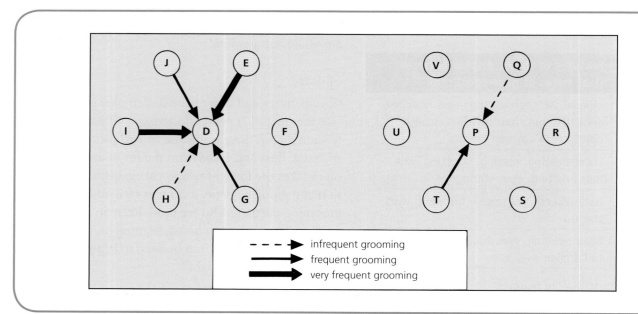

Figure 22.18 Grooming received by two vervet monkeys of different rank

individual's status does not necessarily remain fixed at a certain level.

Change of status

In a society of vervet monkeys, the males are forced to leave the group on reaching puberty. The females remain in the group and form a social hierarchy where a daughter inherits her mother's rank. Individuals of high status enjoy priority access to resources such as food. Female vervets of all ranks form long, close relationships with their offspring. These relationships are maintained by frequent grooming and may be extended to include non-relatives which results in the formation of **alliances**.

Females of high status attract more non-kin grooming partners into their alliances than do females of low status. In Figure 22.18, for example, vervet monkey D is a high-ranking female who attracts grooming from five other females, whereas P is a low-ranking female who attracts grooming from only two other females.

However, early in the breeding season when there are very few babies present in the group, a newborn baby, regardless of the mother's rank, acts as a magnet to all ranks of females. Therefore a mother of low rank who gives birth at this time can **increase her status** because many other females are keen to become her grooming partners (see Figure 22.19). If a low-ranking female continues to give birth, season after season, to more daughters than her rivals, she may continue to improve her status within the hierarchy and retain it.

Complexity of social structure

Primate societies are extremely complex and variable. The social structure of such a society is closely related to its **ecological niche**, the distribution of its **resources** and the **taxonomic group** to which it belongs.

Ecological niche

The ecological niches occupied by societies of primates vary, for example, from the insectivorous, tree-dwelling bushbaby to the omnivorous, bipedal, semi-terrestrial gorilla. A few examples are given in Figure 22.20. Underlying the success of these primates is the fact that they all belong to social groups.

Group size

The size of a group and the degree of social organisation that exists within the group vary from species to species and even within the same species. They are affected by factors such as predator pressures and the availability and distribution of resources – principally food. Group size tends to increase in times of plenty and decrease when food is scarce.

A large group containing many rival males in a hierarchy (such as chimpanzees) has a more complex social structure than a group consisting of a single mature male, three females and a few youngsters (for example gorillas).

Versatile use of resources

Almost all primates are **omnivorous** and although they may have a preferred food type, they are able to exploit a variety of foods, widely distributed throughout the forest ecosystem.

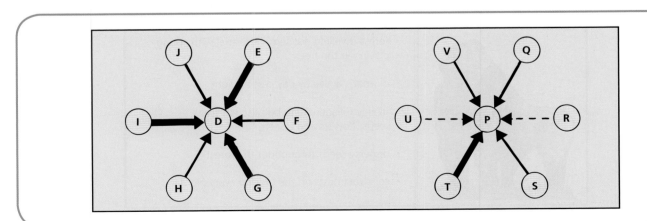

Figure 22.19 Grooming received by two vervet monkeys after giving birth

Primate	Ecological niche (way of life including the animal's use of all the resources in its environment)
Bushbaby 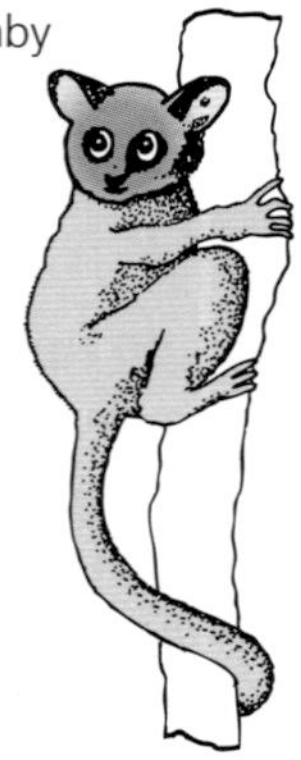	• forest-dwelling in upper branches of trees • nocturnal – active by night, rest in groups in dense foliage during the day • mainly insectivorous but also eat fruit, seeds and birds' eggs • disperse seeds throughout the forest • may pollinate some flowers that open at night
Spider monkey 	• forest-dwelling in upper parts of trees • diurnal – active by day, rest in groups at night • mainly fruit-eating but also eat leaves, seeds and insects • disperse seeds throughout the forest • are predated upon by large cats and snakes
Chimpanzee 	• forest-dwelling but semi-terrestrial • diurnal – active by day, rest at night • mainly fruit-eating but also eat seeds, insects, eggs and other vertebrates • disperse seeds throughout the forest • construct nests close together up the trees every night
Gorilla 	• forest-dwelling but semi-terrestrial with young playing in the trees • diurnal – active by day, rest at night • mainly foliage-eating but also eat fruits, seeds, flowers and insects • disperse seeds throughout the forest • construct nests on the ground every night

Figure 22.20 Ecological niches of primates

If fruit is in short supply, for example, chimpanzees will try to obtain some other source of food. Young adult males, who have become integrated into the group's hierarchy, have **bonded** with one another during grooming. Occasionally, these males form bands and go hunting for monkeys, pigs or antelopes (see Figure 22.21). If the hunt is successful, the food is shared and all members of the group benefit. The success of this strategy depends on **cooperation** between members of the social group. It would not work if chimpanzees were solitary animals.

Figure 22.21 Successful hunt

Chimpanzees also 'fish' for termites and ants by probing the insects' nests with sticks (see Figure 22.22). Infants learn this method of obtaining a valuable food resource by watching and imitating their mother.

Figure 22.22 Using a tool to obtain insect food

Collective defence against predators

Spider monkeys and baboons live in **fission–fusion** societies. The members of such a society split up during the day to forage (with the males protectively roaming around) and then reunite at night to sleep as a group. This gives the group maximum opportunity to find food by day and minimum chance of attack by predators at night.

Distribution of resources

Each group of primates has a **home range**. This is a geographical area within which it spends much of its time moving around, searching for food and places to rest or sleep. The size of the range depends on the distribution of the main resource – the animal's preferred food.

Leaf-eating primates can survive on a relatively small home range because they eat a huge variety of leaf types that are widely distributed and available all the year round. Fruit-eaters need a larger home range because many trees do not produce edible fruit and those that do may only produce it for a brief period each year.

Taxonomic group

All the members of a **taxonomic group** of primates tend to occupy similar ecological niches and possess a similar social structure. For example, bushbabies are small, nocturnal, tree-dwelling insectivores that live in large social groups whereas gorillas are large, diurnal, semi-terrestrial leaf-eaters that live in small social groups. Normally the more distantly related two taxonomic groups are, the more different their ecological niches.

Case Study | Primate behaviour

Tool-using by chimpanzees

As a result of many hours of observation by field workers, chimpanzees in the wild are now known to employ various objects as **tools** to carry out specific functions.

If approached by a predator they will launch an attack using wooden branches as **clubs** or **missiles**. If their fur becomes soiled, they may wipe it clean by using a leaf as a **cloth**. When thirsty they use a mass of leaves as a **sponge** to collect water that has gathered in a tree fork. Then they raise the sponge to their lips and suck out the water. If pestered by flies they may use a small, leafy twig as a **fly-whisk**.

When feeding they frequently crack open nuts. This is achieved by the animal placing the nut on a flat stone, the **anvil**, and pounding on it using a second stone, the **hammer** (see Figure 22.23). Chimpanzees are also fond of eating live insects. An ant nest or termite hill contains a rich supply and access presents no difficulty if a **probe** is used.

A chimpanzee selects a twig, removes all the side branches and breaks it into a suitable length. It then

Figure 22.23 Tool-user

inserts this tool into the nest or hill to 'fish' for insects. When the probe is withdrawn it is bristling with insects. The chimpanzee wipes the stick across its mouth and quickly swallows them before being bitten. Since chimpanzees both make *and* use the insect probe, they can be described as tool-*makers* as well as tool-users.

Testing Your Knowledge 2

1 The housefly lives a solitary life during which it finds food and searches for mates. In what TWO main ways does the behaviour of the members of a society of social insects differ from that of a housefly? (2)

2 Identify TWO examples of ecosystem services provided by insects that are of economic importance to humans. (2)

3 a) Give TWO examples of complex social behaviours learned by young primates during the period of parental care. (2)

   b) What is the survival value of appeasement behaviour among the members of a group of primates? (1)

4 Decide whether each of the following statements is true or false and then use T or F to indicate your choice. Where a statement is false, give the word that should have been used in place of the word in bold print. (7)

a) When mounting a threat display, a primate makes its body look as **small** as possible.

b) Grooming reinforces **rivalry** between social primates.

c) Social primates use appeasement behaviour to reduce **conflict** to a minimum.

d) A primate that closes its eyes during an encounter with a rival is indicating **aggression**.

e) Some female primates use a sexual approach to **appease** a dominant male.

f) Female vervet monkeys use **subservience** to improve their rank within their social group.

g) The complexity of a primate group's social structure may be related to the **distribution** of its resources.

What You Should Know

Chapters 21 and 22
(See Table 22.8 for word bank)

alliance	kin	ritualistic
altruism	metabolism	secondary
chloroplasts	mutualism	shared
cooperative	niche	services
donor	parasite	status
genes	parental	subordinate
grooming	prokaryotic	symbiosis
hierarchy	related	taxonomic
host	reproduction	vectors
keystone	resistant	workers

Table 22.8 Word bank for chapters 21 and 22

1 An intimate, co-evolved relationship between members of two different species is called _____.

2 In parasitism, one organism, the _____, depends on another organism, the _____, for its food and harms the host. Parasites often have a limited _____. They are transmitted from host to host by direct contact, by _____ and by _____ stages in the parasite's life cycle which often involves a _____ host.

3 In _____ the two organisms help and depend on one another and they both benefit.

4 Mitochondria and _____ are thought to have evolved from tiny _____ cells that became resident inside larger cells with which they developed a symbiotic relationship.

5 Many animals are adapted to life in social groups by exhibiting behaviours such as social _____ and _____ hunting. This form of hunting allows food to be _____ and benefits both dominant and _____ animals.

6 A form of behaviour that benefits the recipient but harms the donor is called _____. Behaviour that seems to be altruistic may be of benefit to both the _____ and the recipient if they are closely _____. Since they have many genes in common, the behaviour increases the chance of the donor's _____ surviving in the recipient's offspring. This phenomenon is called _____ selection.

7 Within societies of certain social insects, only a few members of a colony contribute to the _____ of the group. Most members are sterile _____.

8 Many social insects make an impact on their ecosystem that is disproportionately large relative to their numbers and therefore they are described as _____ species. Some social insects benefit humans by providing ecosystem _____ such as pollination of crop plants.

9 Young primates learn complex social behaviours during the extensive period of _____ care that they receive. Unnecessary conflict among social primates is reduced by _____ displays and appeasement behaviours which may involve _____, facial expressions and sexual presentation.

10 An ape or monkey's social _____ within a group may increase by it forming an _____ with other non-related members of the group. The complexity of social structure of a primate society is closely related to its ecological _____, the distribution of its resources and the _____ group to which it belongs.

23 Mass extinction and biodiversity

Extinction

Extinction, the complete demise of a group of organisms, is a natural process that has always occurred. Ever since life evolved on Earth, new species better suited to the environment have appeared and older, less-successful forms that have failed to adapt to a changing environment have become extinct.

Mass extinction events

Fossil evidence shows that life on Earth has been punctuated by several **mass extinction events**. The graph in Figure 23.1 shows the pattern of mass extinction that is thought to have occurred over a period of 300 million years. The peak at point 1 on the graph indicates the Permian extinctions (named after their period on the geological timescale). It was at this point that, for example, a major group of animals called the trilobites vanished completely, the corals came close to extinction and the fish were severely affected. The peak at point 2 on the graph indicates the Cretaceous extinctions. At this point many groups, including most of the dinosaurs, became extinct.

Such waves of mass extinction are closely related to changes in global climate. During an ice age, for example, sea levels drop and vast areas of frozen land appear. As a result, many animals native to warm, sheltered, marine waters and estuaries perish.

Winners and losers

When the environment becomes disrupted, species that were previously successful may suddenly find themselves at a major disadvantage and become extinct. However, species belonging to different taxonomic groups that had been enjoying minimum success in a hostile environment may now find themselves well suited to the new environment and evolve rapidly.

Mammals, for example, existed for many millions of years as a relatively insignificant group during the age of the dinosaurs. They only became the Earth's dominant life form when some major change in the environment, such as global cooling, caused the dinosaurs to die out.

Unlike 'cold-blooded' (ectothermic) dinosaurs, 'warm-blooded' (endothermic) mammals were able to withstand extremes of temperature in their environment. Their success was further promoted by the development of **milk** for their young and the improved level of **parental care** that is associated with suckling. From the original mammals, many different groups evolved over time as they became adapted to the variety of ecological niches that had become available (see Figure 23.2). This process is called **adaptive radiation** and it often follows a wave of mass extinction. It is the means by which biodiversity is slowly regained.

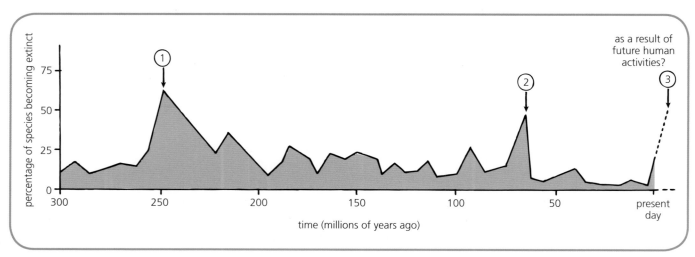

Figure 23.1 Mass extinction events

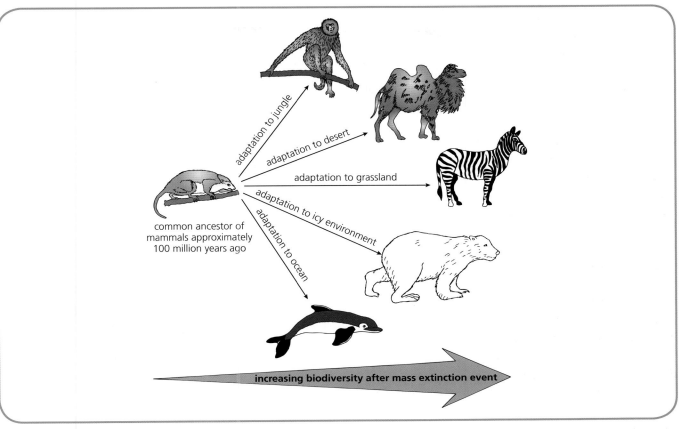

adaptation to jungle

adaptation to desert

adaptation to grassland

adaptation to icy environment

adaptation to ocean

common ancestor of mammals approximately 100 million years ago

increasing biodiversity after mass extinction event

Figure 23.2 Adaptive radiation in mammals

Research Topic   Mass extinction events

A mass extinction event is caused by a change in the global environment that is so rapid and disruptive that many species are unable to adapt in time and therefore perish.

The Permian mass extinction event of about 250 million years ago (point 1 in Figure 23.1) wiped out about 95% of all marine species and about 70% of life on land. It is thought that volcanic eruptions lasting tens of thousands of years helped to trigger the sudden climate changes. These volcanoes sent masses of lava and ash into the atmosphere and probably released enough carbon dioxide to bring about global warming. The temperature of the sea may have risen. This would have reduced the quantity of dissolved oxygen available to marine life and it would explain the drastic effect of the Permian mass extinction event on marine species.

The Cretaceous mass extinction event of about 65 million years ago (point 2 in Figure 23.1) wiped out about 50% of marine species and many land-living organisms including the dinosaurs. At that time the climate became cooler. This may have been in part caused by volcanic eruptions that released materials that blocked out sunlight.

However, many scientists favour the theory that an asteroid collided with Earth sending an enormous cloud of debris into the atmosphere and wiping out half of the world's species in a geological instant. The cloud could have darkened the Earth for months or even years, reducing photosynthesis and disturbing food chains. Other scientists attribute the change in climate to volcanism and continental drift. Perhaps a combination of all of these factors contributed to the Cretaceous mass extinction event.

The Holocene extinction event (point 3 in Figure 23.1) is happening now and is largely the result of **human activities** rather than natural phenomena. It remains to be seen whether humans will be the first, single, biological cause of a mass extinction event on the scale of the earlier ones.

Extinction rate

Extinction rate measures the number or percentage of species that become extinct in a given area per unit time. The most accurate extinction rates are based on well-known higher animals such as birds and mammals. Birds are also considered to be good indicators of the presence or absence of other less-well-known taxonomic groups such as insects. However, estimating the rate of extinction for species both past and present is extremely difficult and at best very approximate.

Extinction of megafauna

Humans have been causing the extinction of other life forms for tens of thousands of years. Fossil records show that the arrival of *Homo sapiens* in a new territory was quickly followed by the disappearance of the largest land animals (the **megafauna**).

When humans reached North America about 12 000 years ago, for example, four-horned antelopes, sloths and woolly mammoths (see Figure 23.3) were soon hunted to extinction. When humans arrived in South America about 11 000 years ago, they soon wiped out several llama-like megafauna and glyptodon (a giant armadillo-like animal). To date, North America has lost about 73% of its large mammals, South America 79% and Australia 86%.

Effect of ecosystem degradation

In an attempt to satisfy the demands of the ever-increasing population, humans chop down, plough up, dam and pollute natural habitats. As the rate of this ecosystem degradation escalates (see Figure 23.4), it causes the current wave of species extinction to run at a level many times greater than the natural (background) rate.

Since the early seventeenth century hundreds of species of birds and mammals have been wiped out by **over-hunting** and **habitat destruction**. Figure 23.5 shows a few 'high-profile' examples of the many species now threatened with extinction.

"Hello! We can't be far from civilisation."

Figure 23.4 'Hello! We can't be far from civilisation.'

blue whale

tiger

Californian condor

brown bear

black rhinoceros

snow leopard

mountain gorilla

panda

Figure 23.5 Endangered species

Figure 23.3 Hunting a woolly mammoth

Biodiversity

Biodiversity (a contraction of **biological diversity**) can be defined as the **total variation** that exists among all living things on Earth. It refers to the total number, the complexity of structure and the underlying genetic variation that exists among all living organisms. It also takes into account the variability of the ecosystems to which they belong. It has taken about 3 billion years for the vast variety of life forms that exist on Earth to evolve.

Measuring biodiversity

Measurements of biodiversity are important because they provide information which helps conservationists to decide which areas and species to support in order to sustain biodiversity for the future. The information is also useful for monitoring ecosystem change and pollution.

The conservation of biodiversity is critical, not only to preserve the wonders of the planet but also to ensure that as many species as possible are able to avoid extinction and adapt to changing environmental conditions. This will maintain a rich variety of resources which humans may be able to find uses for in the future.

Although some biologists have tried to create a 'single currency' approach, no single measure of biodiversity has proved to be satisfactory so far. Most biologists agree that the measurable components of biodiversity are threefold:

- genetic diversity
- species diversity
- ecosystem diversity.

Genetic diversity

The **genetic diversity** of a population results from the genetic variation shown by the **number** and **frequency** of all the alleles of the genes possessed by its members.

Figure 23.6 represents four populations of a species. Each symbol represents a diploid individual which possesses two alleles of one gene. Six alleles of this gene exist among the members of the population in different frequencies. The red allele, for example, occurs most frequently in population 1 and least frequently in population 4. The green, orange and purple alleles are rare and each is only present in one population.

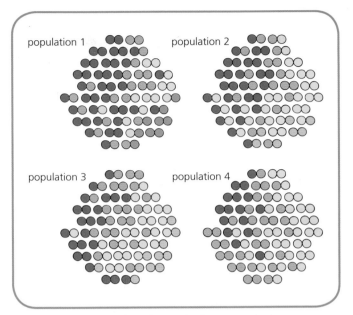

Figure 23.6 Genetic variation in four populations

If any one of populations 1, 2 or 3 dies out then an allele vanishes. If the lost allele is no longer present in any other population, then the species has lost some of its genetic diversity as illustrated by population 4. Loss of a useful allele from a population may limit the species' ability to adapt to changing environmental conditions in the future. This problem is particularly serious when a species is reduced in number to a few scattered populations.

Species diversity

When quantifying the **species diversity** of an ecosystem, the two factors that are taken into account are:

- the **richness** of species – the number of different species present in the ecosystem
- the relative **abundance** of each species – the proportion of each species in the ecosystem.

Table 23.1 compares two communities from two different ecosystems. They share the same species richness in that each possesses species A, B, C, D, E and F. However, they differ in relative abundance. Community P is dominated by species A and has a lower species diversity than community Q which is not dominated by one particular species.

Ecosystem divertsity

Ecosystem diversity refers to the number of distinct ecosystems present in a defined area.

Species	Relative abundance (%)	
	Community P	Community Q
A	50	20
B	10	15
C	10	15
D	10	20
E	10	15
F	10	15

Table 23.1 Differing relative abundances

Related Activity

Simpson's diversity index

The **Simpson index** is a measure of biodiversity. It uses number of individuals of each species as a measure of abundance. It is obtained by using the following formula:

$$D = \frac{N\,(N-1)}{\Sigma n\,(n-1)}$$

where D = biodiversity index

N = total number of individuals of all species

n = number of individuals per species

Σ = sum of

This formula can be applied to the data in Table 23.2 for community X as follows:

$$D = \frac{90+3+4+3(90+3+4+3-1)}{90(89)+3(2)+4(3)+3(2)} = \frac{9900}{8034}$$

$$= 1.23$$

Species	Number of individuals	
	Community X	Community Y
J	90	24
K	3	25
L	4	28
M	3	23

Table 23.2 Data for Simpson's index

And it can be applied to the data for community Y as follows:

$$D = \frac{24+25+28+23(24+25+28+23-1)}{24(23)+25(24)+28(27)+23(22)} = \frac{9900}{2414}$$

$$= 4.10$$

These calculations show that community X with dominant species J has a lower biodiversity index than community Y with the same species richness but no dominant species.

Case Study   Comparison of biodiversity indices

A monoculture of a cereal crop is intended by the farmer to grow as a community consisting of one plant species, the cereal. However, some weed species often manage to grow among the crop. Set-aside is land that is temporarily taken out of crop production to reduce surpluses. This land is often left uncultivated and allowed to revert to nature for a few years.

Table 23.3 shows the results from a survey of two equal-sized plots, one carried out in a wheat field, the other on neighbouring set-aside land.

Species	Number of individuals	
	Wheat field	Set-aside land
wheat	99	2
poppy	7	0
dandelion	2	20
creeping fescue	0	43
rye-grass	1	38

Table 23.3 Data for two ecosystems

The Simpson diversity index formula can be applied to the data in Table 21.3 as follows:

$$D \text{ (wheat field)} = \frac{109(109-1)}{99(98)+7(6)+2(1)+1(0)} = \frac{11\,772}{9746}$$

$$= 1.21$$

$$D \text{ (set-aside)} = \frac{103(102)}{2(1)+20(19)+43(42)+38(37)}$$

$$= \frac{10\,506}{3594}$$

$$= 2.92$$

From these results it is concluded that the monoculture community has a lower species diversity than a community of plants on set-aside land. (However, many more plots would need to be surveyed to give results that were reliable.)

Research Topic	Need for central database

The total number of different species on Earth is unknown. Most large organisms have been studied, classified and named. However, only a rough guess can be made about the number of the many types of smaller organism (such as protozoa and bacteria) and about the number of organisms of all sizes that live in ecosystems yet to be fully explored by humans (including the deep ocean bed and remote tropical rainforest).

It is estimated that there are about 2 million **known** species on Earth. Of the 50% that are animals, most are species of insect. Among the vertebrates, the most numerous are fish. The remaining 50% of known species is made up of bacteria, fungi and green plants. Of these about 250 000 are species of flowering plant.

However, there remains an enormous lack of accurate information particularly about groups of smaller organisms. Therefore estimates of the total number of species on Earth vary. Many experts believe that the true figure lies somewhere between 5 and 20 million.

Storehouse

The world's biodiversity comprises a **natural storehouse** of genetic variation. So far, humans have barely scratched the surface of this vital resource. The vast majority of living species have not been tested for their potential use (for example as producers of food, medicine, useful chemicals etc.) yet many of them are in danger of becoming extinct and the potential riches stored in their genes being lost.

There is no way of knowing in advance which species are most likely to be of value to us. Unexpected ones can turn out to be of great use. For example, scientists

Figure 23.7 Fluorescent jellyfish

have developed a fluorescent chemical made by a species of jellyfish (see Figure 23.7) which acts as a marker for tracing cancer cells.

Database

Clearly a detailed profile of every known species held in a **central database** is needed. Many databases of species already exist. The United Nations World Conservation Monitoring Centre's database contains details of over 75 000 animal species and about 90 000 plant species of conservation interest. The European Environment Agency runs a database containing details of European species. The European Register of Marine Species records all the species known to be present in European seas. The International Species Information System is a database of wild species held in captivity.

However, the ideal database would be one that is centralised and that holds comprehensive information on **every known species** on Earth. To construct →

such a database would require vast international cooperation and funding. In addition it would be difficult to ensure that every item of information entered was completely accurate because an observer may fail to identify a species correctly. Previously

undiscovered species might be wrongly classified due to inadequate identification guides. Therefore the information from all contributors would need to be checked thoroughly by experts to ensure that the database maintained high standards of quality control.

Island biogeography

Island biogeography is the study of the factors that affect the distribution and diversity of species on islands. In a biogeographical context an island can refer to:

- a **true island** – a land mass permanently surrounded by water (such as an oceanic island)

- a **habitat island** – an area surrounded by an unlike

ecosystem that cannot be colonised by the enclosed area's species (such as an oasis surrounded by desert).

The more **isolated** a habitat island, the lower the extent of the diversity found among its species. Similarly the **smaller** a habitat island's surface area, the lower the level of its species diversity.

Case Study   Colonisation of new islands

Figure 23.8 shows a new uninhabited volcanic island formed at some distance from the mainland that is populated by a diverse community. It is likely that many of these mainland species will migrate to the island and try to colonise it. However, once on the island, many of them will fail and become extinct. At the point where the rate of **immigration** is equal to the rate of **extinction**, the **equilibrium species number** that the island can support is reached (see Figure 23.9).

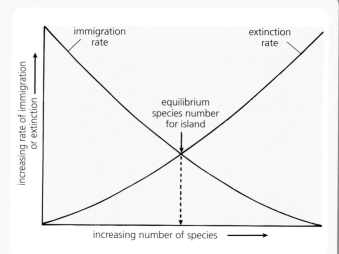

Figure 23.9 Equilibrium species number

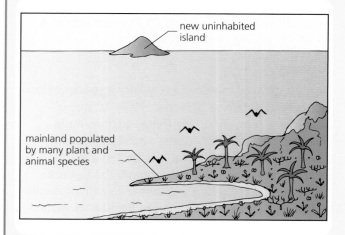

Figure 23.8 Potential colonisation of new island

Effect of isolation on species diversity

The equilibrium species number for two islands of equal size is affected by **distance** from the mainland. The more isolated an island, the smaller the number of immigrants that successfully reach and colonise it (see Figure 23.10).

Effect of area on species diversity

The equilibrium species number for two islands equidistant from the mainland is also affected by the **size** of the island. An island with a large surface

As a result a smaller island has a lower equilibrium species number (in other words, a lower level of species diversity) than a large island (see Figure 23.11). This prediction is supported by evidence from several studies such as the one carried out on diversity of amphibians and reptiles on islands in the West Indies (see Figure 23.12).

Habitat islands

The same factors affect the species diversity of **habitat** islands such as a cold mountain top surrounded by warm lowland, a small pocket of natural forest surrounded by farmland or a lake surrounded by dry land. Island biogeography theory helps to explain the effects of isolation and area on species diversity but it must be kept in mind that island ecosystems are also affected by many other factors such as abiotic disturbances (for example earthquakes).

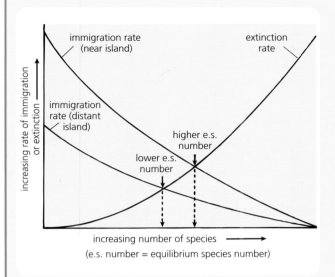

Figure 23.10 Effect of isolation

area has a higher immigration rate because potential colonisers are more likely to discover a larger island than a smaller one. A large island is also likely to have a lower extinction rate than a smaller island. This is because the larger one will tend to possess more resources and a wider range of habitats for use by the immigrants.

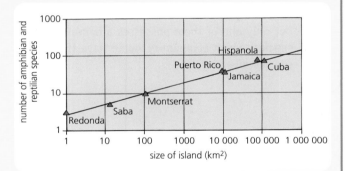

Figure 23.12 Effect of island size on biodiversity

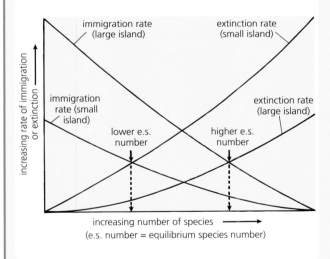

Figure 23.11 Effect of size (area)

Testing Your Knowledge 1

1 a) What is meant by the term *extinction* of a species? (1)

   b) What is the main source of evidence that mass extinction events have occurred in the past? (1)

   c) Explain why a mass extinction event could be caused by an ice age and give an example of the type of animals that might be affected. (2)

   d) Name TWO human activities that are responsible for the current high rate of species extinction. (2)

2 a) Identify TWO components of biodiversity that are measurable. (2)

   b) Why would the loss of population 4 in Figure 23.6 be less serious to the species' chance of survival than the loss of population 1, 2 or 3? (1)

3 a) If two communities are equal in species richness but only one of them possesses a dominant species, which community would have the higher species diversity? (1)

   b) What effect does
      i) increased surface area
      ii) increased isolation have on the species diversity of a habitat island? (2)

4 Decide whether each of the following statements is true or false and then use T or F to indicate your choice. Where a statement is false, give the word that should have been used in place of the word in bold print. (5)

   a) Following a mass extinction event, some surviving taxonomic groups undergo adaptive **radiation**.

   b) The number of different species in an ecosystem is called the species **abundance**.

   c) The proportion of each species in an ecosystem is called the relative **richness**.

   d) Genetic variation in a population is represented by the number and frequency of all the **alleles** possessed by its members.

   e) A larger oceanic island is likely to have a **higher** extinction rate than a smaller island.

24 **Threats to biodiversity**

Threats to biodiversity

Overexploitation

In biology, the expression 'to **exploit** a natural resource' means to make the best use of it. 'To **overexploit** a species' means to remove and use up individuals at a rate that exceeds the species' maximum rate of reproduction.

A common example of overexploitation of species is **overharvesting** (also called **overfishing** in the case of fish, whales and marine invertebrates). This process depletes some species to such a low level that their continued exploitation is no longer sustainable. If the overexploitation is stopped in time the population may be able to recover; if not they may become extinct.

In the past the seas were fished freely without thought for the ability of stocks to replenish themselves. The situation reached a peak with the development of sophisticated sonar techniques to locate shoals and the use of enormous nets (some larger than the size of an Olympic sports stadium) to catch them in. Eventually it was agreed that this overexploitation of fish stocks could not continue unchecked.

Recovery

It is estimated that at present around 70% of the world's marine fishing grounds (fisheries) are fully exploited and that many fish populations have been reduced by 60–95% resulting in lower catches (see Figure 24.1). In recent years attempts have been made to promote the recovery of depleted fish stocks. Strict EU regulations insist that catches must stay within certain **fixed quotas**. Further measures, adopted by many countries, limit fishing by controlling the number of boats, the length of time they spend at sea and the areas where they are allowed to fish.

When these practices are fully supported by the authorities, estimates of some fish populations are found to show **signs of recovery**. In 2010 estimated stocks of cod in the North Sea showed a rise to 54 000 tonnes and reversed the previous downward trend (see Figure 24.2). However, experts claim that

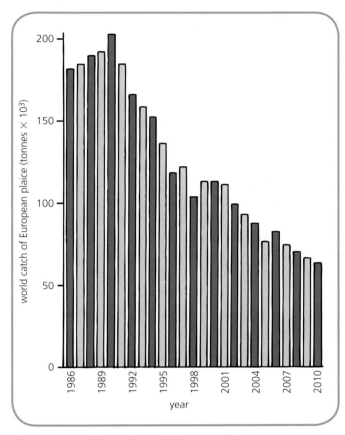

Figure 24.1 Effect of overfishing on plaice

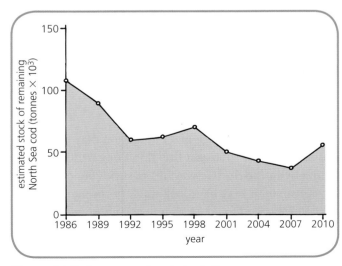

Figure 24.2 Recovery of cod stocks?

stocks of between 70 000 and 150 000 tonnes are needed to indicate a true and lasting recovery.

There is no room for complacency in this matter. If the warning signs are ignored, we risk going the way of the Grandbanks. This cod fishery off the coast of Newfoundland was the richest in the world for 500 years until continuous overexploitation led to its collapse and closure in the 1990s. There is still no evidence of the return of cod to the Grandbanks.

Whales

Although estimates of whale populations tend to be subject to a large margin of error, it is known that their numbers have declined dramatically since the start of commercial whaling.

In 1986 the International Whaling Commission imposed a **moratorium** (suspension of activity) on commercial whaling. However, several countries have ignored the ban or found ways around it (see

Figure 24.3) and about 42 000 whales have been killed since 1986. The downward spiral in whale numbers will only be halted if the moratorium is retained and all countries of the world respect it.

Figure 24.3 Overexploitation of whales?

Related Topic

Use of gel electrophoresis in monitoring harvest species

An enormous, worldwide trade in canned fish and seafood products exists. Some types of fish are of much higher quality than others therefore fraudulent substitution may take place during the canning process. For this reason it is important to be able to check that the contents of a can of fish really match the description on the label.

Several methods of authentication have been developed. In one of these DNA from samples of the

canned fish is amplified using the polymerase chain reaction (see page 22). The DNA is cut up using a restriction enzyme and the fragments separated by gel electrophoresis (see page 12).

When the results are compared with standard species-specific DNA profiles (genetic 'bar codes'), it is possible to tell which one (or more) species was present in the original can of fish. This process is used for harvest species such as tuna and bonito (small tuna-like fish).

Bottleneck effect

A significant percentage of a population may be wiped out by a disaster such as a fire, flood or earthquake acting in an unselective way. If the surviving population is very small, it may have lost much of the genetic variation needed to adapt to future environmental change. Such a population is said to have suffered the **bottleneck effect** as a result of the disaster, which is called the **bottleneck event**.

In Figure 24.4 the bottle containing coloured beads represents **genetic variation** among the members of the original population. The container representing the surviving population is found to possess:

- less genetic variation
- allele frequencies that are different from the original population.

The loss of genetic diversity produces a population

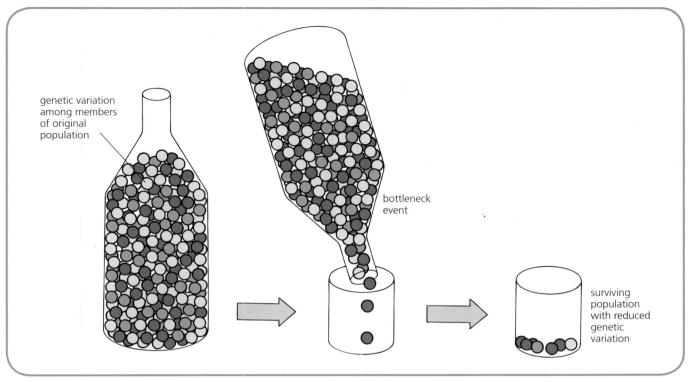

genetic variation among members of original population

bottleneck event

surviving population with reduced genetic variation

Figure 24.4 Bottleneck effect

whose members are so similar that reproduction among them is genetically equivalent to inbreeding. Since inbreeding results in poorer rates of reproduction, the population may become extinct or it may slowly recover (see Figure 24.5) and survive. Some species, such as the northern elephant seal, possess a naturally low level of genetic diversity among their members, yet still manage to remain viable.

Research Topic	Cheetah

There are only a few thousand cheetahs in the world and they are so closely related genetically that a skin graft from one cheetah to another is not rejected. It is thought that extreme climatic change acting as a bottleneck event about 10 000 years ago wiped out all but a handful of cheetahs. Close relatives had no option but to mate with one another and subsequent inbreeding has led to a loss of genetic diversity over the years. In addition, males have a low sperm count and therefore matings often fail to lead to pregnancies.

However, it has been discovered recently that, unlike other big cats, female cheetahs are surprisingly promiscuous and often mate with more than one partner per litter of cubs. The benefit of this behaviour is that the female undergoes **induced ovulation** (release of an egg) each time she mates. She could therefore produce a litter of cubs each with a different father. This process helps to ensure that any traces of genetic diversity survive in the population. It may also serve to protect the cubs from being killed by an adult male cheetah, several of whom are the parents of the litter.

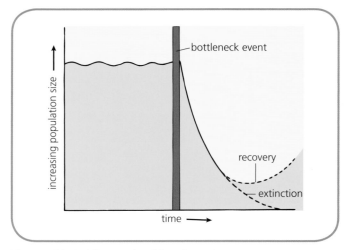

Figure 24.5 Aftermath of bottleneck event

Habitat loss by fragmentation

The process of fragmentation of a habitat (see Figure 24.6) results in the formation of several **habitat fragments** whose total surface area is less than that of the original habitat.

Degradation of the edges of the fragment leads to a further decrease in size of the fragment and loss of habitat. Normally the fragments possess limited resources and are only able to support a lower species richness than that of the original habitat. In addition small fragments can only support small populations and these are more vulnerable to extinction than large populations possessing greater genetic diversity.

Edge to interior ratio

Fragmentation and subsequent degradation of the edges of the fragments result in an **increase in the ratio** of the total length of a fragment's edge to the total surface area of its interior (see Figure 24.7). As a result, species adapted to the original habitat's edge may prosper at the edge of a fragment. However, as their numbers increase, they may be driven to invade the interior of the fragment and compete with the species adapted to the interior. Therefore small fragments do not tend to favour species that need an interior habitat and this results in a loss of biodiversity.

Human causes

Habitat fragmentation often occurs when natural ecosystems such as forests are cleared for agriculture, housing or hydroelectric dams. Often the remaining

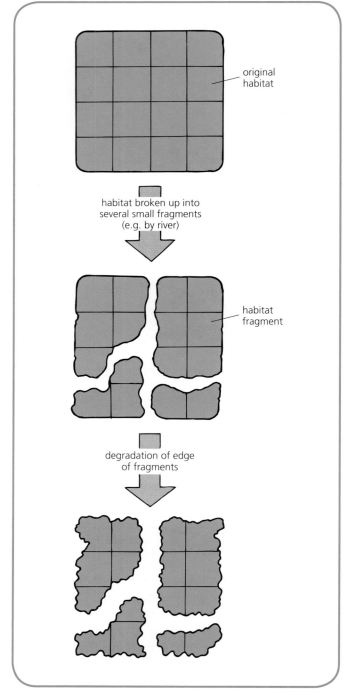

Figure 24.6 Habitat fragmentation

fragments are tiny 'islands' of natural forest isolated from one another by farmland, housing estates or motorways.

Habitat corridors

One possible solution to the problem is to link isolated fragments with **habitat corridors**. A habitat corridor is composed of a narrow strip or a 'stepping-stone'

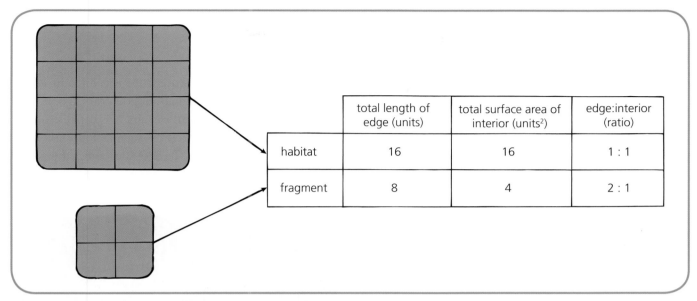

	total length of edge (units)	total surface area of interior (units²)	edge:interior (ratio)
habitat	16	16	1 : 1
fragment	8	4	2 : 1

Figure 24.7 Ratio of edge to interior

series of clumps of quality habitat by which species can move between disconnected fragments of habitat. For example it may take the form of a streamside habitat, a wooded strip between two forest fragments or an underpass beneath a motorway. This would enable the members of a species to feed, mate and recolonise habitats after local extinctions.

It is not yet clear whether the creation of habitat corridors increases biodiversity. They do overcome the problem of isolation but not of loss of interior habitat. Some scientists have suggested that they could even be harmful because they could allow the spread of disease among small vulnerable populations possessing limited genetic diversity.

Habitat corridors for tigers

During the twentieth century, the world's population of tigers was reduced by 95% as a result of hunting and poaching. Three subspecies became extinct and a fourth, the South China tiger, has not been seen for many years. It is estimated that there are about 3000 tigers left in the wild.

To thrive, tigers need large territories containing abundant prey. However, many of these habitats have been cleared by humans for timber, industry, urbanisation and the building of new roads. The remaining tigers in the wild are largely restricted to habitat fragments and nature reserves. Efforts have been made to connect these areas with **habitat corridors** to allow the tigers to find new mates in other regions and **increase genetic variation** among future generations. The presence of a corridor in the far east of Russia, for example, has enabled the Siberian tiger to increase from a population of about 40 to one of around 500.

However, these tigers are so closely related that they are equivalent to just 14 genetically different individuals. Therefore their future remains, at best, uncertain.

Tiger habitat corridors are also present in India but they are not protected legally and exist alongside a dense and fast-growing human population. Some of the corridors have been cut off by dams, highways or urban developments and funds are unavailable for the building of underpasses.

On the positive side, the wild cat conservation group Panthera has set up the Tiger Corridor Initiative and has assessed the potential for a multinational Eastern Himalayan corridor. This would involve several countries including India, Bhutan, Nepal and Thailand. However, the success of any tiger corridor that runs through a region heavily populated by humans depends upon the understanding and acceptance by the local people combined with excellent maintenance and management of the corridor.

Introduced, naturalised and invasive species

The relationship between introduced, naturalised and invasive species is summarised in Figure 24.8. Over the years many foreign species have been introduced to the UK. Only a minority of these non-invasive species have become invasive and have had a negative impact on the local native communities and the economy.

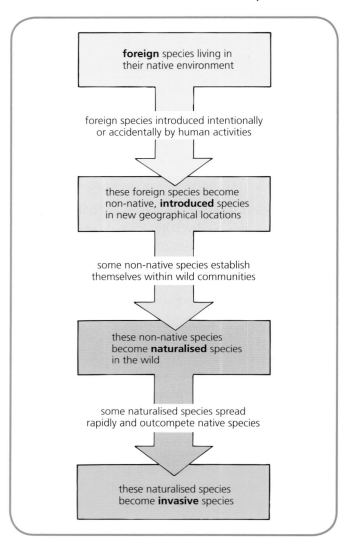

Figure 24.8 Emergence of invasive species

Invasive species

An invasive species normally succeeds because it is able to prey upon or to outcompete the other native members of its adopted community for resources. This is made possible by the fact that the competitors, pathogens, parasites and predators present in its native ecosystem are not present to keep its numbers in check. Therefore it is free to undergo a population explosion.

In some cases invasive species succeed by hybridising with native species.

Economy

Japanese knotweed (see Figure 24.9) was introduced to the UK as a garden plant about 200 years ago. It is now widespread throughout Britain. It is capable of growing through hard structures such as foundations of buildings and car parks. Its activities affect the economy because vast sums of money need to be spent each year to eradicate it.

Figure 24.9 Japanese knotweed

Health

Giant hogweed (see Figure 24.10) was also introduced as a garden plant but it has become invasive. Its sap is poisonous and causes severe burning and blistering of the skin (see Figure 24.11).

Figure 24.10 Giant hogweed

Loss of biodiversity

Many invasive species pose a huge threat to the biodiversity of the region that they invade. In the UK, for example, red squirrels are rapidly facing extinction because they are being outcompeted by their rival, the grey squirrel introduced from North America. Similarly, water voles are being wiped out by American minks (see Case Study below).

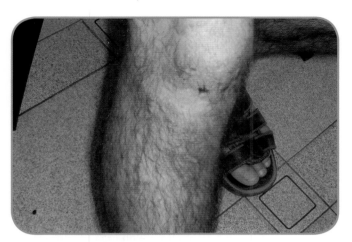

Figure 24.11 Effect of giant hogweed

Greenhouse effect

Carbon dioxide and methane are often referred to as 'greenhouse' gases. This is because they trap infrared radiation (heat) coming from the Earth's surface and reflect it back to Earth, keeping the planet warm (see Figure 24.13). The **greenhouse effect** (so called because the gases play a role similar to the panes of glass in a

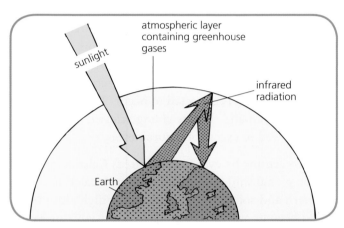

Figure 24.13 Greenhouse effect

Case Study American mink, an invasive species

The **American mink** (see Figure 24.12) is a relative of the stoat and the weasel. It has a rich brown pelt valued by furriers. It was introduced to the UK in 1929 to set up the first of many mink farms. From then on, minks escaped and became established in the wild. Minks hunt in water for fish and frogs and on land for ground-nesting birds and water voles. Like weasels they kill more than they need and may store surplus food in their den.

Figure 24.12 American mink

In recent years the range and number of **water voles** have declined rapidly. Surveys show that these small, herbivorous mammals have disappeared from about 95% of the sites that they used to occupy. Although to a small extent this decrease is due to destruction of their riverside habitats by wash from boats and recreational disturbance, it is largely due to the American mink. It preys on water voles and takes over their burrows. Therefore it has progressed from an intentionally **introduced** species via a **naturalised** species to an **invasive** species.

In the last few years attempts have been made to reverse this process by setting up eradication projects. These have resulted in the removal and humane killing of many mink from North East Scotland. Already water voles are making a comeback in areas where they have not been seen for many years.

greenhouse) is a natural phenomenon. It causes **global warming** which created the conditions necessary for life to evolve on Earth. It continues to be essential; without it, the world would be too cold to support life.

Climate change

As the human population continues to increase, this results in a greater demand for food and other sources of energy. As more countries become developed and industrialised, the average amount of energy consumed per person per year increases. This leads directly and indirectly to an increase in number and concentration of greenhouse gases in the atmosphere. As these form a denser layer, a corresponding increase in the greenhouse effect is expected to occur. This would result in a dramatic **climate change** caused by global warming well in excess of natural levels.

Global warming by even a few degrees Celsius would cause a global shift in climate. Regions located in cold northern and southern latitudes and at high altitudes would become warmer. Regions near the equator would receive less rain. Many experts believe that the process has already begun and are demanding action now.

Impact on biodiversity

There is strong evidence from direct observations that hundreds of species are already **moving their range** in response to a shift in climate. The coniferous forest community in the Northern hemisphere, for example, is invading the region previously occupied exclusively by tundra species. The latter face a possible reduction in biodiversity as a result of increasing competition combined with warming of their natural habitat. Migrant birds that spend part of their annual cycle on tundra are also affected adversely. In addition, it is by no means certain that as the conifer tree line continues to advance northwards, the defrosted tundra soil will support every member of the forest community. So a further loss of biodiversity is likely.

Reduced rainfall in tropical regions will have a drastic effect on any tropical rainforest that has survived future overexploitation by humans. As a result the biodiversity of the rainforest will be decreased further.

As the peaks of mountains warm up, species native to high altitudes such as Alpine flora will face extinction and be replaced by meadow plants from the lower slopes.

Generalists versus specialists

Climate change tends to favour **generalist** species of plants and animals that are able to:

- tolerate a wide range of climatic conditions
- adapt to change rapidly
- extend their range to match climatic shift.

Specialists are species that are highly specialised to life in one specific ecosystem (for example an island). They are unable to move their range or adapt in time to the pace of change, therefore many of them **face extinction**. It is likely that climate change will result in biological communities becoming dominated by generalists at the expense of specialists, leading to an overall **loss of biodiversity**.

Climate change modelling

Much of the information about the possible impact of future climate change on the biodiversity of species and ecosystems is based on bioinformatic data obtained from **computer models** of climate change. A climate change modelling programme uses quantitative methods to **simulate the interaction** between the factors that affect and are affected by climate. It is able to accommodate many input variables such as past, present and projected climate data, physical and chemical structure of the biosphere, types of species, communities, ecosystems and interrelationships.

A programme might, for example, be set the task of forecasting changes to the richness of species that would occur if these species:

- could manage to shift their range at the same pace as projected climatic shift or
- could only manage to shift to a few new areas owing to migration limitation.

Challenge

For appropriate conservation strategies to be developed, accurate forecasts of the impact of climate change on biodiversity are essential. However, climate change modelling has many **limitations** because much of the information fed into the programme is based on speculation. Future levels of the greenhouse gases that drive global warming are unknown. Similarly other related aspects of climate change such as increased global temperature and decreased rainfall remain, at best, 'guestimates'. Therefore caution must be exerted when drawing conclusions.

Despite these limitations, climate modelling does provide us with much useful information about the likely impact of anthropogenic global warming on biodiversity. The real challenge is to find a way to do something about it. Human society discusses endlessly the potential problem and some people even deny its existence. However, little is done on a worldwide scale to bring about a significant reduction in global emissions of greenhouse gases.

Testing Your Knowledge

1 Explain the difference between *exploitation* and *overexploitation* with reference to a named natural resource. (2)

2 a) In what way could a *bottleneck effect* alter the quantity of genetic variation present in a small population of a species? (1)

  b) Why would this decrease the population's chance of survival? (1)

3 a) Copy and complete Table 24.1. (4)

  b) By what means can small populations isolated in habitat fragments be reunited? (1)

4 By what means does an introduced species become:

  a) *naturalised*? (1)

  b) *invasive*? (1)

5 Even with the aid of sophisticated computer modelling, it is impossible to make accurate forecasts about the impact of climate change on biodiversity in the future. Briefly explain why. (1)

	Type of habitat	
	Island fragment	Unfragmented land mass
relative size of habitat (large/small)		
species richness supported (high/low)		
edge : interior (large/small)		
chance of edge species invading interior (high/low)		

Table 24.1

What You Should Know

Chapters 23 and 24

(See Table 24.2 for word bank)

abundance	edge	megafauna
alleles	evolutionary	modelling
bottleneck	extinction	natural
change	fossil	naturalised
climate change	fragmentation	overexploitation
corridors	frequency	radiation
degradation	genetic	remote
diversity	invasive	richness
dominated	island	species

Table 24.2 Word bank for chapters 23 and 24

1 Evidence that several mass extinction events have occurred in the past is indicated by _____ records. Biodiversity slowly recovers after a wave of mass _____ and some of the surviving groups may undergo adaptive _____ and fill ecological niches.

2 The arrival of humans in a new territory was followed by the extinction of many of the large land animals (the _____). The current _____ of ecosystems by humans is escalating at such a rate that it is responsible for a rate of extinction of species at a level many times higher than the _____ rate.

3 Components of biodiversity that can be measured are _____ diversity, species _____ and ecosystem diversity.

4 The genetic diversity of a population consists of the variation shown by the number and _____ of all the _____ of all the genes possessed by its members.

5 _____ diversity of an ecosystem depends on the number of different species present, called the species _____ and the proportion of each species present, called the relative _____. If a community is _____ by one species, it has a lower species diversity than one that is equally rich but not dominated by one species.

6 The smaller and more _____ a habitat _____, the lower the level of its species diversity.

7 Overharvesting is a form of _____ of a population. If the process is brought to a halt, the population may recover. As a result of the _____ effect, a population may be reduced to a small group that lacks the genetic diversity needed to make _____ responses to environmental _____.

8 _____ of a habitat results in the formation of fragments that support a lower level of species richness than the original large area. Species adapted to the _____ of a fragment may invade the interior and outcompete the species living there. Isolated habitat fragments can be linked by _____.

9 When a non-native species is introduced to a new geographical location and establishes itself in the wild, it is said to become _____. When it then spreads rapidly and impacts negatively on native species, it is described as an _____ species.

10 The impact of _____ change on biodiversity can be analysed and forecast using direct observation and climate change _____.

Applying Your Knowledge and Skills

Chapters 17–24

Class of pigment	Name	Principal (P) or accessory (A) pigment	Location
chlorophyll	a	P	all photosynthetic plants
	b	A	higher plants and green algae
	c	A	brown algae
	d	A	some red algae
carotenoid	xanthophyll	A	all photosynthetic plants
	carotene	A	all photosynthetic plants
phycobilin	phycocyanin	A	main phycobilin in blue-green algae
	phycoerythrin	A	main phycobilin in red algae

Table 24.3

Wavelength of light (nm)	Amount of light absorbed/arbitrary units	
	Pigment 1	Pigment 2
400	0.00	0.00
420	0.00	0.00
440	0.00	0.00
460	0.10	0.00
480	0.30	0.05
500	1.00	0.10
520	3.20	0.20
540	4.90	0.30
560	5.00	0.50
580	2.70	0.90
600	0.10	1.70
620	0.05	2.60
640	0.00	2.80
660	0.00	2.20
680	0.00	0.30
700	0.00	0.00

Table 24.4

1 The information in Table 24.3 refers to photosynthetic pigments. The data in Table 24.4 refer to the amount of light absorbed at various wavelengths of light by two of these pigments, each extracted from a different seaweed. All seaweeds belong to a large group of plants called algae.

a) Name ONE principal and THREE accessory pigments found in brown seaweeds. (1)

b) Name a type of plant that would lack all three classes of pigment listed in Table 24.3. (1)

c) Plot the data given in Table 24.4 as two line graphs (curves) to show the absorption spectra of pigments 1 and 2. (3)

d) Refer back to Figure 17.7 on page 230 which shows the spectrum of white (visible) light and devise a way of adding the six colours to one of the axes in your graph. (1)

e) Pigments 1 and 2 are known as the phycobilins.
   i) One of them absorbs orange and red light and appears blue-green to the eye. Identify it by its number and its proper name.
   ii) One of them absorbs green and yellow light and appears red to the eye. Identify it by its number and proper name. (2)

f) Imagine that a sample of each of the phycobilin pigments was placed in turn at point X in the experiment shown in Figure 17.12 on page 233. Make a diagram of the absorption spectrum that you would expect to result in each case. (2)

g) Phycoerythrin is commonly found in seaweeds that live in deep sea water or in dimly-lit rock pools. Suggest how the presence of this pigment helps the plant to survive. (1)

2 The data in Table 24.8 refer to a type of pea plant grown for its edible seeds which make up the plant's economic yield. In addition, much of its vegetation is used as animal fodder.

a) Supply the values missing from boxes X, Y and Z in the table. (3)

b) Which strain of pea plant gives the best seed yield? (1)

c) **i)** Which strain of pea plant most likely generates the highest amount of animal fodder per hectare?
   ii) Explain how you arrived at your answer. (2)

d) Does a high harvest index indicate a relatively high economic yield or a relatively high biological yield for that plant strain? (1)

e) Suggest why many farmers choose to grow strain B despite its relatively low harvest index. (1)

3 The data in Tables 24.6 and 24.7 refer to breeding experiments using maize (*Zea mays*) shown in Figure 24.14.

a) Identify the generation formed by hybridisation. (1)

Strain of pea plant	Biological yield (kg ha^{-1})	Economic yield (kg ha^{-1})	Harvest index (%)
A	2 702	670	[X]
B	3 510	664	19
C	3 100	[Y]	18
D	2 845	686	24
E	[Z]	575	23

Table 24.5

		Number of generations selfed	Mean ear length (mm)	Mean yield (metric tonnes ha^{-1})
Parents	P$_1$	17	84	2.0
	P$_2$	16	107	2.1
Successive generations (resulting from repeated self-fertilisation)	F$_1$	0	162	4.3
	F$_2$	1	141	4.0
	F$_3$	2	147	3.4
	F$_4$	3	121	3.1
	F$_5$	4	94	2.8
	F$_6$	5	99	2.6
	F$_7$	6	110	2.5
	F$_8$	7	107	2.3

Table 24.6

Year	Millions of hectares used for maize planting	Mean yield (metric tonnes ha^{-1})
1932	46	2.4
1946	36	3.4
1957	30	4.1

Table 24.7

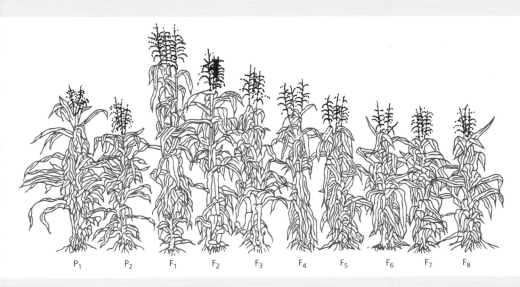

Figure 24.14

b) State THREE pieces of information which provide evidence of hybrid vigour. (3)

c) Which of the following was a true-breeding inbred line: P_1, F_1, F_3, F_5? (1)

d) Using an example from the data to illustrate your answer, explain what is meant by the term *inbreeding depression*. (1)

e) In 1933, American farmers began planting maize grains produced by hybridisation. This practice has continued over the years and has brought about the changes shown in Table 24.7.
   i) State TWO ways in which farmers have benefited by using hybrid maize.
   ii) Explain why farmers must buy expensive hybrid grain every year from supply houses to sow their maize crop instead of simply using grain kept back from the previous year's crop. (3)

4 For successful biological control of red spider mites (M) in a glasshouse, the suppliers of *Phytoseiulus* (P), the predator, recommend the use of 200P to deal with a population of 4000M.

a) Express these data as a simple whole number ratio of P : M. (1)

b) How many P should be ordered to deal with a population of 32 000M? (1)

c) The bar chart shown in Figure 24.15 includes error bars that each represent the 95% confidence level of the mean. (See Appendix 3 for help.) The chart represents the results of an investigation into the numbers of red mite prey (adults and eggs) eaten by *Phytoseiulus*, the predator.
   i) What is the mean number of mite eggs eaten by female predators?
   ii) What can be stated (with a 95% level of confidence) as the minimum number of adult mites that could be eaten per day by male predators?
   iii) Would it be correct to conclude from the data that the number of adult mites eaten by female predators is significantly different from the number eaten by male predators? Explain your answer, with reference to error bars.

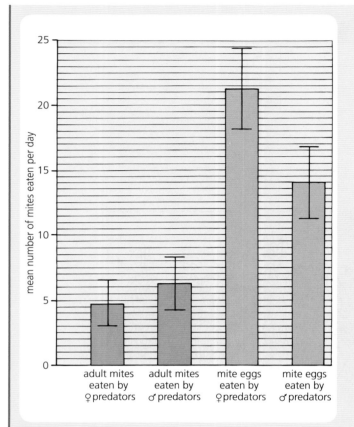

Figure 24.15

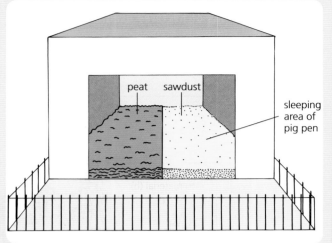

Figure 24.16

c) **i)** What words in the passage mean that the pigs were given time to become acclimatised to their surroundings?
ii) Suggest why this is important. (2)

d) Identify TWO design features of the pig pen in this investigation that must be kept constant. (2)

e) Put the flooring materials (substrates) into descending order of preference according to the results. (1)

iv) Would it be correct to conclude from the data that the number of mite eggs eaten by female predators is significantly different from the number eaten by males? Explain your answer with reference to error bars. (6)

d) Why is this form of biological control not suitable for use on plants grown outside in the open air? (1)

5 An investigation was carried out to discover which flooring material (substrate) was preferred by pigs in their sleeping area. The pens were designed to offer the pigs a choice between two substrates at a time (see Figure 24.16. The eight pigs in each group were left for one week to become habituated to their pen. During the second week, the time spent by the pigs in each substrate was recorded. Three replicas were used for each comparison. The six tables in Figure 24.17 show the results.

a) Why were three replicates of each comparison set up? (1)

b) Why were as many as eight pigs used in each group? (1)

6 Malaria is a debilitating and often fatal disease caused by the unicellular organism *Plasmodium*, a blood parasite. Its life cycle comprises a sexual stage in a mosquito and an asexual stage in a human as shown in Figure 24.18 (see page 338).

a) Why is it wrong to say that 'mosquitoes cause malaria'? (1)

b) In what way is the proboscis of a mosquito very different from the needle of a hypodermic syringe? (1)

c) Suggest why the release of many parasitic spores (merozoites) into the human blood stream is:
i) accompanied by an attack of fever
ii) followed by anaemia. (2)

d) The organism within which the fusion of a parasite's gametes occurs is normally regarded as its primary host. Identify the primary and secondary hosts in the life cycle of *Plasmodium*. (1)

e) Endoparasites live and feed inside their host; ectoparasites live and feed on the outside of their host. Which organism in Figure 24.18 is

pen type 1

mean time spent on material (h)	
P	S
99(+)	69(−)

pen type 2

mean time spent on material (h)	
P	M
82	86

pen type 3

mean time spent on material (h)	
P	W
141(+)	27(−)

pen type 4

mean time spent on material (h)	
M	S
102(+)	66(−)

pen type 5

mean time spent on material (h)	
M	W
138(+)	30(−)

pen type 6

mean time spent on material (h)	
S	W
114(+)	54(−)

key
P = peat
M = mushroom compost
S = sawdust
W = woodbark

+ = result significantly higher than would be expected by chance alone

− = result significantly lower than would be expected by chance alone

Figure 24.17

i) an endoparasite?
ii) an ectoparasite?
iii) Identify the ectoparasite's host. (3)

7 Five male zebra finches, P, Q, R, S and T, were kept together and observed over a period of several days. During this time, a record was kept of the results from 20 confrontations between each pair of birds. The bird which successfully dominated its rival in

each contest was given a score of one point. The results are shown in Table 24.8.

a) Copy and complete the two right-hand columns in the table. (The first example has been done for you.) (1)

b) i) Which bird has the lowest status and is at the bottom of the pecking order?
ii) Explain your choice. (2)

Contest	Score out of 20 points	Winner	Net number of contests won
T v Q	T 17, Q 3	T	14
T v R	T 3, R 17		
P v Q	P 18, Q 2		
Q v R	Q 0, R 20		
Q v S	Q 8, S 12		
R v P	R 13, P 7		
P v T	P 14, T 6		
S v T	S 5, T 15		
R v S	R 19, S 1		
S v P	S 4, P 16		

Table 24.8

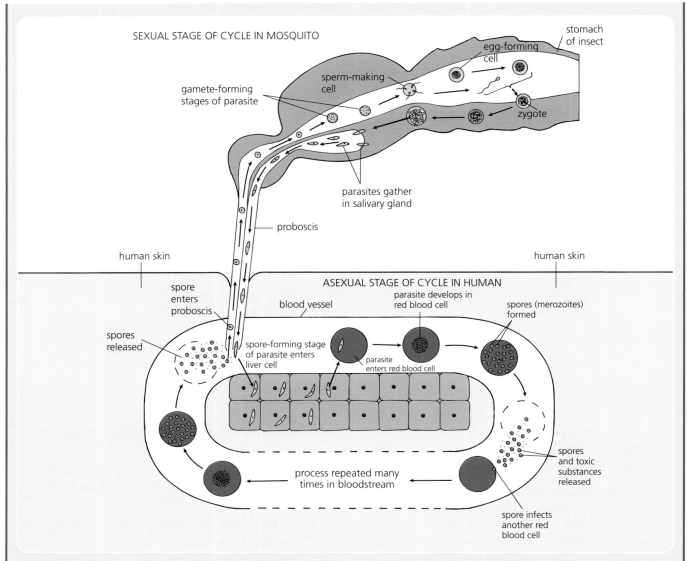

Figure 24.18

c) Give the complete pecking order for the five birds in descending order. (1)

8 Figure 24.19 shows box plots of shell length for three populations of zebra mussel. (See Appendix 2 for help.)

a) What percentage of data is contained in a box in a box plot? (1)

b) i) By what means is the median value of the data indicated in a box plot?
ii) State the median value for each of the populations. (2)

c) i) Which box set shows the widest distribution of values between its median and its upper quartile?

ii) Which box set shows the widest overall distribution of values? (2)

d) Does a whisker represent a 95% level of confidence or an actual value? (1)

e) What was the lowest value recorded? (1)

f) If the data were plotted as a graph of number of individuals against shell length, which population would give a symmetrical bell-shaped curve? (1)

g) Construct an hypothesis to account for the effect of latitude on shell size. (1)

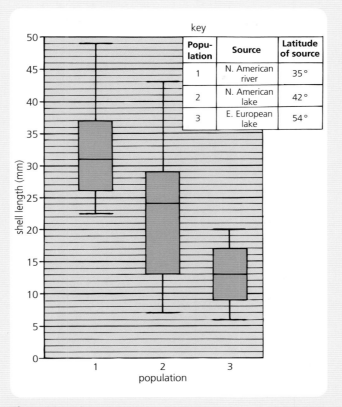

Figure 24.19

Since this group of questions does not include examples of every type of question found in SQA exams, it is recommended that students also make use of past exam papers to aid learning and revision.

Appendix 1

The genetic code

Table Ap1.1 shows DNA's bases grouped into 64 (4^3) triplets of bases.

		second letter of triplet				
first letter of triplet		A	G	T	C	**third letter of triplet**
	A	AAA	AGA	ATA	ACA	A
		AAG	AGG	ATG	ACG	G
		AAT	AGT	ATT	ACT	T
		AAC	AGC	ATC	ACC	C
	G	GAA	GGA	GTA	GCA	A
		GAG	GGG	GTG	GCG	G
		GAT	GGT	GTT	GCT	T
		GAC	GGC	GTC	GCC	C
	T	TAA	TGA	TTA	TCA	A
		TAG	TGG	TTG	TCG	G
		TAT	TGT	TTT	TCT	T
		TAC	TGC	TTC	TCC	C
	C	CAA	CGA	CTA	CCA	A
		CAG	CGG	CTG	CCG	G
		CAT	CGT	CTT	CCT	T
		CAC	CGC	CTC	CCC	C

(A = adenine, G = guanine, T = thymine, C = cytosine)

Table Ap1.1 DNA's bases as 64 triplets

Box plots

The data in Table Ap2.1 refer to three groups of golden delicious apples randomly sampled from orchards A, B and C. It is difficult to compare the variability between the three groups from the data table alone.

Table Ap2.1

Apple number	Mass of apple (g)		
	Group A	Group B	Group C
15	142	131	119
14	130	130	116
13	127	127	115
12	126	125	114
11	122	124	112
10	119	121	110
9	116	120	109
8	110	118	108
7	109	117	106
6	105	115	102
5	100	115	99
4	99	112	96
3	97	110	91
2	96	108	83
1	82	106	76

A **box plot** is a way of presenting information which allows differences between groups, sets, populations etc. to be compared easily. Each box plot shows the **median** which is the **central value** in the series of values when they are arranged in order. A box plot also displays the **upper quartile** (in this case the value 25% above the median) and the **lower quartile** (the value 25% below the median). The maximum and minimum values are called **upper and lower whiskers**. Figure Ap2.1 shows how the data for group A are converted into a box plot.

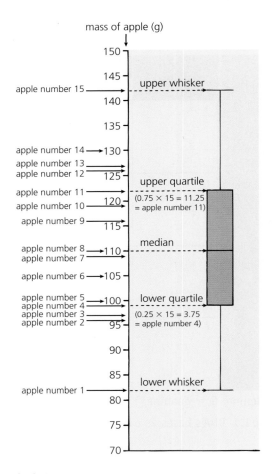

Figure Ap2.1

Figure Ap2.2 shows group A's box plot drawn alongside those for groups B and C. The box plots give a clear visual representation that allows the variability between the three groups to be compared more easily than by studying the table of data.

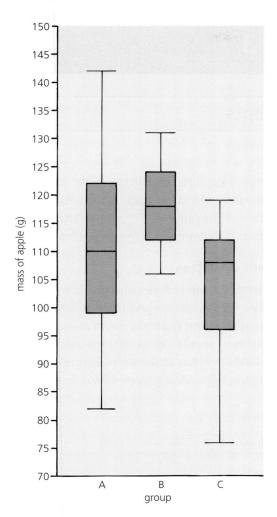

Figure Ap2.2

From these box plots, group B appears to be the best group with respect to mass and uniformity of size. It has a high median value and 50% of the apples are clustered around this value. Although it does not have the highest upper whisker, it contains no apples below a mass of 106 g. Group C appears to be the poorest group with the lowest median and many of its apples featuring in the lower range of mass. It also has the lowest whisker.

Statistical concepts

A scientist needs to organise the data collected as results from an investigation into a manageable form from which conclusions may be drawn.

Mean

The **mean** is often referred to as the average. It is the most widely used measure of the **central tendency** of a set of data. It is found by adding up all the values obtained and dividing them by the total number of values. For example, for the two populations of seedlings shown in the scatter graphs in Figure Ap3.1, the mean for population A = 2100/70 = 30 mm and the mean for population B = 4900/70 = 70 mm.

Range

The **range** is the difference between the two most extreme values in a set of data. For example, for population A the range = 42 − 14 = 28 mm and for population B the range = 92 − 44 = 48 mm.

Standard deviation

Standard deviation is a measure of the spread of individual data values around their mean and shows how much variation from the mean exists. A normal distribution of results can be divided into intervals of standard deviation as shown in Figure Ap3.2. 68% of the values fall within plus or minus one standard

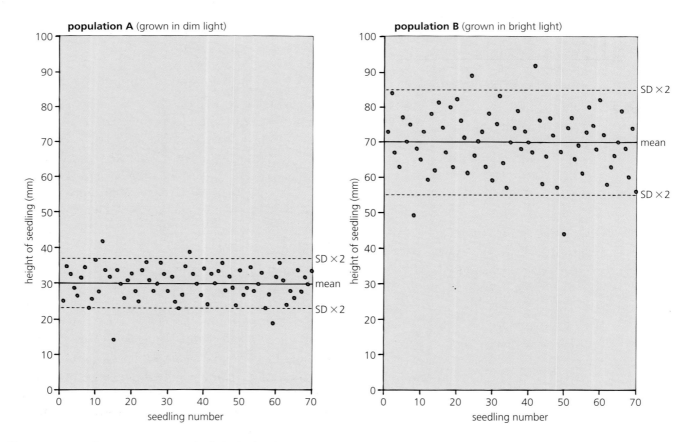

Figure Ap3.1 (SD × 2 = 2 standard deviations)

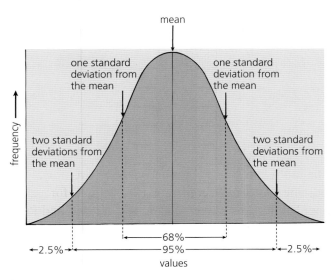

mean

one standard deviation from the mean

one standard deviation from the mean

two standard deviations from the mean

two standard deviations from the mean

frequency

68%

←2.5%→ 95% ←2.5%→

values

Figure Ap3.2

deviation of the mean; 95% of the values fall within plus or minus two standard deviations of the mean.

The standard deviation of a set of data is calculated using a mathematical formula (often with the aid of an appropriate calculator or computer software). The deviation (as two standard deviations above or below the mean) for population A in Figure Ap3.1 equals 7 mm. This low level of deviation reflects the clustering of the values around the mean, with 95% of values lying within the range 23–37 mm. The deviation (as two standard deviations above or below the mean) for population B in Figure Ap3.1 equals 15 mm. This higher level of deviation reflects the wider spread of the values around the mean, with 95% of values lying within the range 55–85 mm.

Quality of data

In a properly designed scientific investigation, several **replicates** of each treatment are set up to allow for experimental error. These replicates produce results with a **central tendency** around the **mean**. A set of results which are **clustered** around the mean indicates data of **high quality**. A comparable set of results (from a replicate of the same treatment) which are widespread are of lower quality.

Significant difference

In biology, an experiment is carried out to test an hypothesis. Once results have been obtained, the scientist needs to know whether these data (which

rarely conform 'exactly to the expected outcome') support the hypothesis or not.

Testing the difference between two means

A **significance test** (a type of statistical analysis) can be used to find out whether the observed differences between two sets of data are statistically significant or simply the result of chance.

The data in Figure 21.30 on page 338, for example, refer to the results of an investigation to find out which flooring material was preferred by pigs in their sleeping area. A **plus sign** after a result indicates that the significance test shows the value to be **significantly higher** than would be expected by chance alone; a **minus sign** after a result indicates a value **significantly lower** than would be expected by chance alone.

In pen type 1, where the pigs spent 99 out of 168 hours on material P and only 69 out of 168 hours on material S, a significant difference is found to exist between the mean times spent on the two materials. Therefore the pigs can be said to prefer material P. In pen type 2, no such significant difference is found to exist between the mean times spent by pigs on materials P and M. Therefore the pigs can be said to show no preference between these two materials.

Finding out if observed values differ from expected values

Results from genetics crosses rarely match the expected ratio exactly. For example, a cross between heterozygous tall pea plants (Tt) and homozygous dwarf pea plants (tt) produced 283 tall and 301 dwarf plants. Statistical analysis using a significance test shows that these data do not differ significantly from 292 tall and 292 dwarf, the expected results for an exact 1:1 ratio.

Error bars

When a bar chart of mean values of data is drawn, it is often important to be able to show variability on the chart. This can be done using **error bars**. These are lines that extend outside and inside each bar and indicate how far from the mean value the true error-free value is likely to be. Error bars can be based on aspects of variability such as 95% level of confidence and standard deviation.

Figure Ap3.3 shows a bar chart of the results from a survey carried out on 10 000 young people in a country to estimate the incidence of asthma. Each bar represents a mean value with a 95% level of confidence whose range is indicated by error bars. Based on the information in the bar chart, health care experts could be 95% confident that the percentage number of asthma cases for the whole population would be 13–21% for 2–4-year-old males, 7–14% for 9–15-year-old females etc.

Significant difference

Error bars also allow a comparison to be made between two means to determine whether they are **significantly different** from one another. If their error bars (based on 95% level of confidence) do not overlap, the difference between the two means is regarded as being significant.

In the example shown in Figure Ap 3.4, it can be said with a 95% level of confidence that in blue light, the rate of photosynthesis did not drop below 10.6 oxygen bubbles min^{-1} and that in orange light, it did not rise above 9.2 bubbles min^{-1}. Therefore the two means are significantly different.

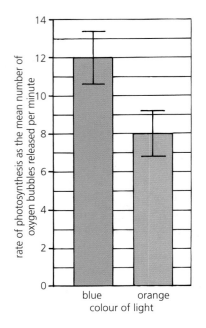

Figure Ap3.4

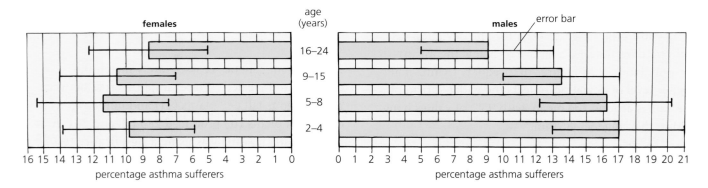

Figure Ap3.3

Appendix 4

Tree of life

Information from DNA and RNA sequences has been used to try to uncover the primary lines of evolutionary history among all organisms on Earth. The **tree of life** shown in Figure Ap4.1 has been constructed using information based on a study of the nucleotide sequence of a type of rRNA possessed by all organisms. Such a study enables scientists to assess the relationships between a wide range of organisms.

Trees of life constructed using data obtained from other nucleotide sequences are found to be very similar though the exact relationships between the three domains and the 'root' of the tree are still under debate.

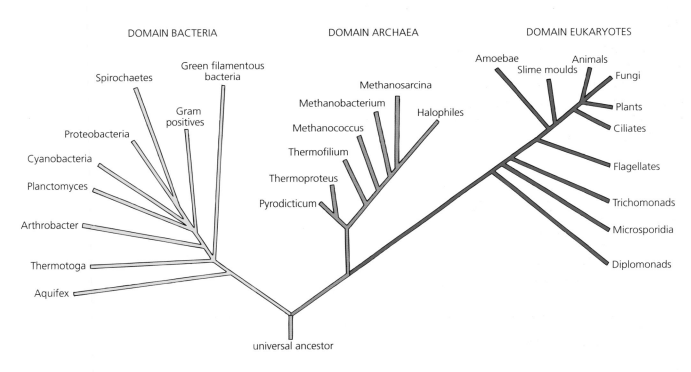

Figure Ap4.1 Tree of life

Testing Your Knowledge Answers

1 Structure of DNA

Testing Your Knowledge

1 a) (i) 4 (ii) adenine (A), thymine (T), guanine (G), cytosine (C) (3)

   b) Hydrogen (1)

   c) Each base can only join up with one other type of base: A with T and G with C. (1)

2 a) (i) and (ii) (2)

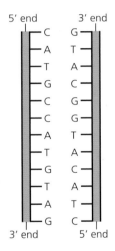

Figure An1.1

   b) Antiparallel (1)

3 a) Double helix (1)

   b) (i) Base pairs (ii) Sugar-phosphate backbones (2)

4 a) (i) Bacterium (ii) Yeast (iii) A tiny ring of DNA. (3)

   b) (i) In a chloroplast (or mitochondrion) of a green plant cell. (ii) In the nucleus of the same green plant cell. (2)

2 Replication of DNA

Testing Your Knowledge

1 a) T (1)

   b) F Cytosine (1)

   c) F Hydrogen (1)

   d) T (1)

   e) T (1)

2 a) 5 (1)

   b) 1 (1)

   c) 4 (1)

   d) 6 (1)

   e) 3 (1)

   f) 2 (1)

3 a) DNA, the four types of nucleotide, appropriate enzymes and an energy supply. (4)

   b) DNA replication ensures that an exact copy of a species' genetic information is passed on from cell to cell during growth and from generation to generation during reproduction. (2)

3 Control of gene expression

Testing Your Knowledge 1

1 a) 20 (1)

   b) Polypeptide (1)

   c) The sequence of bases in DNA. (1)

   d) Arranged in long parallel strands or folded and coiled into a spherical shape. (2)

2 a) F Peptide (1)

   b) F Nitrogen (1)

   c) T (1)

   d) T (1)

   e) F Carbohydrate (1)

Testing Your Knowledge 2

1 A molecule of DNA is double-stranded and contains deoxyribose sugar and the base thymine whereas a molecule of RNA is single-stranded and contains ribose sugar and the base uracil. (3)

2 a) They differ by the sequence of the bases in their DNA. (1)

b) 3 (1)

c) Triplets (1)

3 a) (2)

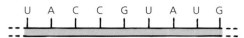

U   A   C   C   G   U   A   U   G

Figure An3.1

b) RNA polymerase (1)

4 (a) An exon is a coding region of DNA; an intron is a non-coding region.

(b) Introns   **(c)** Splicing (3)

Testing Your Knowledge 3

1 a) 1 (1)

b) An amino acid molecule. (1)

2 a) One of many tiny, roughly spherical structures in a cell's cytoplasm (where translation of genetic information into protein occurs). (1)

b) (i) 3   **(ii)** To a codon on mRNA. (2)

c) Peptide (1)

d) It is discharged from the ribosome and reused. (2)

3 (2)

Stage of synthesis	Site in cell
formation of primary transcript of mRNA	nucleus
modification of primary transcript of mRNA	nucleus
collection of amino acid by tRNA	cytoplasm
formation of codon-anticodon links	ribosomes

Table An3.1

4 a) Codons (1)

b) Transcription (1)

c) Intron (1)

d) Cytoplasm (1)

e) Post (1)

f) Phosphate (1)

4 Cellular differentiation

Testing Your Knowledge

1 a) Differentiation is the process by which an unspecialised cell becomes altered and adapted to perform a special function as part of a permanent tissue. (1)

b) A meristem is a group of unspecialised plant cells capable of dividing repeatedly throughout the life of a plant. (1)

2 a) It has cilia which sweep dirt in mucus up and away from the lungs making the cell well suited to its function. (1)

b) During differentiation most genes, including those that code for insulin, were switched off so the goblet cell only expresses the genes left switched on that control the characteristics of that type of cell, such as the secretion of mucus. (2)

3 a) They can reproduce themselves while remaining undifferentiated. They can differentiate into specialised cells when required to do so. (2)

b) (i) Embryonic and tissue (adult) stem cells. **(ii)** Embryonic in a blastocyst; tissue in bone marrow. (4)

c) Embryonic (1)

4 a) (i) Leukemia   **(ii)** Bone marrow (2)

b) Parkinson's disease (1)

c) Because bone marrow cells can only produce more bone marrow cells (and not nerve cells) since many of their genes are switched off. (2)

5 a) Because some people believe that a human embryo, even in its very early stages of development, is already a person and that it is morally wrong that it dies when stem cells are extracted from it. (2)

b) To ensure that the safety procedures carried out are of the highest order and that abuses of the system are prevented. (2)

5 Structure of the genome and 6 Mutations

Testing Your Knowledge 1

1 A mutation is a change in structure or composition of an organism's genome. A mutant is an individual or allele affected by a mutation. (2)

2 a) They occur spontaneously (and at random) but very rarely. (2)

b) (i) No **(ii)** On very rare occasions a mutant allele may confer an advantage on an organism that receives it. (2)

3 a) Substitution, insertion and deletion. (3)

b) (i) Substitution **(ii)** It only affects one amino acid in the protein expressed and does not cause the frameshift effect. (2)

4 a) F Genome (1)

b) T (1)

c) F Eukaryote (1)

d) T (1)

e) F Non-coding (1)

f) F Post (1)

g) T (1)

Testing Your Knowledge 2

1 a) (i) Deletion **(ii)** Harmful **(iii)** Essential genes will be lost. (3)

b) (i) Inversion **(ii)** They become reversed. (2)

2 a) (i) Duplication **(ii)** The extra copies may mutate and produce new useful DNA sequences. (2)

b) (i) Translocation **(ii)** It normally increases the number on one and decreases the number on the other. (2)

3 a) It is a type of mutation which results in a cell receiving one or more extra sets of chromosomes. (1)

b) One parent could have produced a diploid gamete (AA) and the other parent a haploid gamete (B) giving AAB (a type of polyploid called a triploid) at fertilisation. (2)

c) Increased size and vigour. (2)

7 Evolution

Testing Your Knowledge 1

1 (a), (c), (d), (g) and (h) (2)

2 a) It compensated for high rate of gene loss and it led to rapid spread of new genetic sequences. (2)

b) The genetic sequence gained might be harmful. (1)

3 a) (i) Lack of food and overcrowding.

(ii) Natural selection

(iii) Natural selection is the process that results in the increase in *frequency* amongst a *population* of those *genetic sequences* that confer an *advantage* on members of the population. (5)

b) (i) It selects for traits that increase reproductive success and therefore increases the population's chance of survival. **(ii)** Male-to-male competition and female choice. (4)

4 Stabilising selection favours intermediate versions of the trait and acts against the extreme variants. Disruptive selection, on the other hand, favours extreme versions of the trait at the expense of the intermediates. (2)

Testing Your Knowledge 2

1 a) Because the sample of alleles transmitted to the next generation is normally relatively small and often non-representative of the gene pool as a whole. (2)

b) The small group of cattle taken to Iceland acted as a splinter group. They possessed a sample of alleles that did not represent the original population's gene pool. Therefore they developed over a long period of time into a population with frequencies of alleles different from those of the original population. (3)

2 a) (i) No **(ii)** The hybrid is sterile. (2)

b) Speciation is the formation of new biological species by evolutionary change. (1)

c) D, A, C, E, B (1)

3 a) (i) Allopatric **(ii)** Mountain range and river. (2)

b) Sympatric (1)

8 Genomic sequencing

Testing Your Knowledge 1

1 a) The sequence of nucleotide bases in a genome. (1)

b) (i) It is a fusion of molecular biology, statistical analysis and computer technology. **(ii)** They use it to analyse DNA sequences and compare them. (2)

2 a) Yeast and fruit fly. (2)

b) Their genome contains genes equivalent to genes in the human genome that are responsible for diseases. Therefore they may provide understanding of how these genes work. (2)

3 To discover which genetic sequences are only present in the pathogenic strain since some of these will be the ones responsible for disease. (2)

4 a) It means that the same or very similar DNA sequences are present in the genome of a wide range of organisms. (1)

b) Because it codes for an important protein that is needed by almost all plant species. (1)

Testing Your Knowledge 2

1 a) It is the study of evolutionary relatedness amongst different groups of organisms. (1)

b) Molecular information shows how similar or different their genomes are. Structural features, on the other hand, may show no differences although underlying genetic differences are present. (2)

2 Two related groups of organisms known from fossil records to have <u>diverged</u> at a certain point in <u>geological</u> time are chosen. Many genetic <u>sequences</u> for the two groups are compared and the number of nucleotide <u>substitutions</u> by which they differ is determined. The quantity of molecular change in their <u>DNA</u> that has occurred is a measure of how long ago the groups diverged from a common <u>ancestor</u>. The DNA can therefore be used as a molecular <u>clock</u>. (3)

3 a) (i) Bacteria, archaea and eukaryotes. **(ii)** True nucleus bounded by a double membrane and membrane-enclosed organelles. (3)

b)

photosynthetic land plants

↑

multicellular green plants

↑

photosynthetic eukaryotes

↑

photosynthetic prokaryotes

↑

last universal ancestor (2)

4 a) The sequencing and analysis of an individual's genome using bioinformatics. (2)

b) Drug choice and dosage may be customised to suit the individual. The risk of a genetic disease or disorder may be predicted in time to take preventive measures. (2)

9 Metabolic pathways and their control

Testing Your Knowledge 1

1 a) Metabolism is the collective term for the thousands of enzyme-controlled chemical reactions that occur in a living cell. (2)

b) One breaks down complex molecules to simpler ones and normally releases energy; the other builds up simpler molecules into complex ones and consumes energy. (2)

2 a) Membrane (1)

b) (i) So that they can work in an integrated way.

(ii) So that they do not bring about their digestive effect until required. (2)

3 a) A channel-forming protein allows certain molecules to pass through its pore by diffusion which is a passive process requiring no energy.

b) A carrier protein, acting as a pump, actively transports ions across the cell membrane against a concentration gradient and requires energy to do so. (4)

Testing Your Knowledge 2

1 They lower the activation energy needed for the chemical reaction to proceed. They speed up the reaction. They remain unchanged at the end of the reaction. (3)

2 a) The chemical structure of the protein of which the enzyme is made and the bonding between its component amino acids. (1)

b) The chemical attraction between them. (1)

c) Induced fit (1)

d) The shape of the active site ensures that the reactants are correctly <u>orientated</u> so that the reaction can take place. This is made possible by the fact that the enzyme <u>decreases</u> the activation energy needed by the reactants to reach the <u>transition</u> state. (3)

3 a) Quantity of chemical change that occurs per unit time. (1)

b) (i) Initially it causes an increase in rate but at higher concentrations no further increase in rate occurs.
(ii) At low concentrations of substrate there are not enough molecules of substrate to occupy all the active sites on the enzymes. At higher concentrations of substrate, all the active sites on the enzyme molecules are occupied. (4)

Testing Your Knowledge 3

1 a) The regulator gene produces the <u>repressor</u> molecule.

b) The inducer molecule combines with the <u>repressor</u>.

c) When the operator is free, the structural gene is switched <u>on</u>. (3)

2 a) It needs lactose to act as the inducer, combine with the repressor and enable the gene to become switched on.

b) It prevents the wastage of energy and resources. (3)

3 a) Regulator

b) No repressor was being made to keep the structural gene switched off in the absence of lactose. (2)

Testing Your Knowledge 4

1 a) Its molecular shape is similar to that of the substrate. (1)

b) (i) It brings about an increase in the rate of the reaction. (ii) Substrate molecules eventually outnumber those of the competitive inhibitor causing more and more sites on the enzyme molecules to become occupied with substrate rather than inhibitor. (3)

2 a) Activator molecules could bind to allosteric sites making many enzyme molecules adopt their active state and increase the reaction rate.

b) Non-competitive inhibitor molecules could bind to allosteric sites making many enzyme molecules adopt their inactive state and decrease the reaction rate. (2)

3 a) (i) P (ii) Q (2)

b) (i) Q (ii) R (2)

c) Left to right. (1)

d) (i) If a high concentration of R built up some of it would bind to some molecules of enzyme X and slow down the conversion of P to Q. (ii) It keeps the pathway under finely-tuned control. (3)

10 Cellular respiration

Testing Your Knowledge 1

1 a) Adenosine triphosphate (1)

b) ATP has three phosphate groups whereas ADP has two. (1)

c) $ADP + P_i + energy \rightarrow ATP$ (2)

2 a) Two molecules of ATP are used during the energy investment phase so the net gain is only two ATP. (1)

b) As soon as oxaloacetate is formed, it combines with acetyl CoA to form citrate. Therefore there is never very much present at any given moment. (1)

c) ATP is used up at the same rate as it is manufactured. Therefore the quantity remains fairly constant. (2)

3 a) G (1)

b) E (1)

c) C (1)

d) E (1)

e) G (1)

f) G and C (1)

g) C (1)

h) G, C and E (1)

Testing Your Knowledge 2

1 Starch and glycogen (2)

2 1 = protein, 2 = fat, 3 = amino acid, 4 = glycerol, 5 = acetyl coenzyme A. (5)

3 a) (i) glucose → ethanol + carbon dioxide

(ii) glucose → pyruvic acid → lactic acid (2)

b) Equation (ii) (1)

11 Metabolic rate

Testing Your Knowledge

1 a) (i) Metabolic rate is the quantity of energy consumed by an organism per unit time.
(ii) Oxygen consumption per unit time or carbon dioxide production per unit time. (3)

b) BMR is the minimum rate of energy release needed by an endotherm to maintain essential body processes. (1)

2 The heart of a fish contains <u>two</u> chambers. Blood is pumped at <u>high</u> pressure to the gills and then on to the body's capillary beds at <u>low</u> pressure. The heart of a mammal contains <u>four</u> chambers. Blood is pumped to the mammal's lungs at <u>high</u> pressure and to the body's capillary beds at <u>high</u> pressure. (3)

3 A bird's lungs are connected to air sacs that act like bellows keeping air flowing in one direction through channels called parabronchi. This arrangement allows gas

exchange that is more efficient than breathing air in and back out again by the same route. Therefore it enables the bird to obtain the large supply of oxygen needed to generate energy aerobically for flight. (3)

4 a) T (1)

b) F Once (1)

c) F Amphibian/reptile (1)

d) F Higher (1)

e) T (1)

12 Metabolism in conformers and regulators

Testing Your Knowledge

1 (3)

Feature	Conformer	Regulator
ability to control internal environment by physiological means	not able to do so	able to do so
relative metabolic costs of lifestyle	low	high
extent of range of ecological niches that can be exploited	narrow	wide

Table An12.1

2 a) Physiological homeostasis is the maintenance of the body's internal environment within certain tolerable limits despite changes in the body's external environment. (2)

b) (i) When the body's internal environment deviates from its normal level, this change is detected by receptors which communicate with effectors. These trigger responses which return the system to normal. This corrective mechanism is called negative feedback control. **(ii)** It is of advantage to the organism because it provides the stable conditions needed by its body to function efficiently despite wide fluctuations in the external environment. (5)

3 a) Endotherm

b) Human beings are able to maintain constant internal body temperature despite fluctuations in external temperature. (2)

4 a) The hypothalamus has central thermoreceptors which receive nerve impulses from skin thermoreceptors and are sensitive to changes in temperature of blood. (2)

b) Skin and skeletal muscles (2)

13 Metabolism and adverse conditions

Testing Your Knowledge 1

1 Extreme cold and lack of food. (1)

2 a) (i) Decrease of metabolic rate to a minimum. **(ii)** Winter buds present but not growing or absence of leaves. (2)

b) Predictive dormancy means the organism becomes dormant before the adverse conditions arrive whereas consequential dormancy means the organism becomes dormant after the adverse conditions arrive. (2)

c) (i) Predictive **(ii)** They shed their leaves and become dormant in response to decreasing day length before winter arrives. (2)

3 a) (i) They both involve a decrease in metabolic rate. **(ii)** Hibernation is used to survive a period of extreme cold whereas aestivation is used to survive a period of intense heat or drought. (2)

b) Daily torpor as shown by the hummingbird (for example) means that the animal's rate of metabolism becomes greatly reduced for part of each 24-hour cycle during the night. This helps the animal to conserve energy at times when searching for food would be unsuccessful. (2)

Testing Your Knowledge 2

1 a) Migration is the regular movement by the members of a species (e.g. Arctic skua) from one place to another over a relatively long distance and then back again months later. (2)

b) It relocates the bird to a more favourable environment for part of the year enabling it to avoid metabolic adversity. (1)

2 a) Ringing and tagging (2)

b)

transmitter implanted under skin

↓

transmitter gives out signals

↓

signals picked up by receivers on satellites

↓

signals sent to ground station

↓

information relayed to scientists (3)

3 Innate behaviour is inherited and inflexible whereas learned behaviour is gained from experience after birth and is flexible. (2)

4 a) An extremophile is an organism that can live in extreme conditions which would be lethal to most living things. (1)

b) They possess unusual enzymes that function at high temperatures. (1)

14 Environmental control of metabolism

Testing Your Knowledge 1

1 They are easy to cultivate and they grow quickly. (2)

2 a) Nutrient agar is a solid whereas nutrient broth is a liquid. (1)

b) Nutrient broth (1)

3 a) **(i)** For protein synthesis **(ii)** For synthesis of ATP **(iii)** For energy (3)

b) To keep the conditions sterile in order to eliminate contaminants. (1)

4 a) Sensors monitoring temperature, pH and oxygen concentration. (3)

b) 1 = C (acid in), 2 = E (cold water in), 3 = D (oxygen in), 4 = A (products out), 5 = F (cold water out), 6 = B (waste gases out) (6)

c) **(i)** Motor **(ii)** To mix the contents of the fermenter. **(iii)** Stainless steel (3)

Testing Your Knowledge 2

1 Growth is an irreversible gain in dry biomass. Mean generation time is the time needed for population of unicellular organisms to double in number. (2)

2 a) During the lag phase, intense metabolic activity occurs in preparation for cell division. During the stationary phase, on the other hand, metabolism slows down and secondary metabolites are produced. (1)

b) The cells are multiplying at the maximum rate. (1)

c) Lack of nutrients and accumulation of toxic metabolites. (2)

3 a) A primary metabolite (such as an amino acid) is essential for growth whereas a secondary metabolite is not used for growth (and may be toxic). (1)

b) **(i)** Antibiotic **(ii)** It may inhibit the growth of bacteria that would compete with the fungus for resources in the soil ecosystem. (2)

4 Precursor and enzyme inducer (2)

15 Genetic control of metabolism

Testing Your Knowledge 1

1 Genetic stability of Y, ability of Y to grow on low cost nutrients and ability of Y to vastly overproduce the useful product y. (3)

2 a) Mutagenesis is the creation of mutants. (1)

b) Ultra-violet light and mutagenic chemicals. (2)

c) In case a reverse mutation makes them lose their useful characteristic. (1)

3 a) In the absence of outside influences, mutations arise very <u>rarely</u>. (1)

b) An agent that increases the rate of mutagenesis is called a <u>mutagen</u>. (1)

c) Mutagenesis can be used to create a <u>mutant</u> strain that lacks a particular undesirable characteristic. (1)

d) In <u>eukaryotic</u> micro-organisms such as fungi, new genotypes can be produced by <u>sexual</u> reproduction between different strains. (2)

e) Some bacteria can produce new strains by transferring <u>plasmids</u> from one to another. (1)

Testing Your Knowledge 2

1 a) Gene for insulin cut out of the human genome and transferred to and inserted into the genetic material of a bacterium. (2)

b) The insulin produced is the same as the human type. (1)

c) Plasmid (1)

2 a) A restriction endonuclease is an enzyme that cuts open DNA leaving sticky ends whereas a restriction site is a location on a plasmid that gets cut open by an endonuclease. (2)

b) It enables scientists to tell whether or not a host cell has taken up the plasmid vector. (1)

3 C (1)

4 a) Where the protein (or polypeptide) formed needs post-translational modifications done to it to make it function. (1)

b) Yeast (1)

16 Ethical considerations in the use of microorganisms

Testing Your Knowledge

1 A pharmaceutical company would be more likely to develop a new product suitable for treating a common condition found in a developed country because this potentially huge market would be much more profitable than a niche market in a developing country. (2)

2 Yes, in the opinion of the authors, but you have to make up your own mind. Human DNA is neither a novel invention nor an inventive step in a process. These are the basic criteria for deciding if something can be patented or not. (1)

3 Identify the potential hazards.
Construct and apply control measures.
Review effectiveness of control measures and adopt improvements. (3)

17 Food supply, plant growth and productivity

Testing Your Knowledge 1

1 Ability of human population to access food of adequate quantity and quality. (2)

2 Identification of a limiting factor (such as shortage of minerals in the soil) and then increasing the supply of that factor. Replacement of an existing crop strain with a higher-yielding cultivar. (2)

3 Energy loss is reduced therefore more is available to feed humans. (1)

Testing Your Knowledge 2

1 a) By passing a beam of white light through a prism. (1)

b) **(i)** Violet/blue **(ii)** Red (2)

2 a) An absorption spectrum shows the degree of absorption that occurs at each wavelength of visible light by pigment(s). An action spectrum, on the other hand, indicates the effectiveness of each wavelength of visible light at bringing about photosynthesis. (2)

b) Blue and red. (2)

c) Because it absorbs the other colours and gives green back out by transmission and reflection. (2)

3 It extends the range of wavelengths of light that can be used by the plant for photosynthesis. (1)

Testing Your Knowledge 3

1 a) It is transferred to electrons which become excited and raised to a higher energy level. (1)

b) ATP synthase
$$ADP + P_i \xrightarrow{\hspace{3cm}} ATP \text{ (2)}$$

c) The oxygen is released. The hydrogen combines with NADP to form NADPH. (2)

2 a) **(i)** Rubisco **(ii)** ATP and NADPH (3)

b) **(i)** RuBP **(ii)** Sugar (2)

3 a) **(i)** Cellulose **(ii)** Starch (2)

b) Proteins and nucleotides (2)

Testing Your Knowledge 4

1 a) T (1)

b) F Dry (1)

c) F Organic (1)

d) F Productivity (1)

2 Light intensity and carbon dioxide concentration. (2)

3 a) Biological yield means the total biomass of plant material produced whereas economic yield means the biomass of the desired product. (2)

b) Harvest index. (1)

18 Plant and animal breeding

Testing Your Knowledge 1

1 Increase in yield, increase in nutritional value and resistance to pests. (3)

2 a) (i) An inherited characteristic shows discrete variation if it can be used to divide up the members of a species into two or more distinct groups for example round or wrinkled seed shape in peas. **(ii)** An inherited characteristic shows continuous variation when it varies among the members of a species in a smooth, continuous way from one extreme to another such as seed mass in peas. (4)

b) Discrete (1)

c) They refer to the expressions of two different alleles of the same gene. When they are united in the same genotype, the dominant allele is expressed and the recessive allele is masked. (2)

3 It is a cross between an organism whose genotype for a certain trait is unknown and an organism that is homozygous recessive for that trait. It is set up to identify the genotype of the first organism. (2)

4 a) A plot is one of several equal-sized portions of a field whereas a treatment is the way in which one plot is treated compared to other plots with respect to the variable factor being investigated. (2)

b) (2)

Design feature	Reason
randomisation of treatments	to prevent bias existing in the system
selection of treatments involving one variable factor	to ensure that a fair comparison can be made
inclusion of several replicates	to take experimental error (uncontrolled variability) into account

Table An18.1

Testing Your Knowledge 2

1 a) Inbreeding involves the fusion of gametes from close relatives (or both from the one parent in self-pollinating plants). Outbreeding, on the other hand, involves the fusion of gametes from unrelated members of the same species. (2)

b) Homozygous describes a genotype that contains two identical alleles of a particular gene whereas heterozygous refers to a genotype that contains two different alleles of a particular gene. (2)

2 a) T (1)

b) F Heterozygosity (1)

c) T (1)

d) T (1)

e) F Genotype (1)

3 a) Because the harmful alleles have already been weeded out by natural selection. (1)

b) Choose parents that are homozygous for the desired trait but that are heterozygous for other traits. (2)

Testing Your Knowledge 3

1 By crossbreeding it with a different variety. (1)

2 a) Because they inherit desirable characteristics from both parents. (1)

b) (i) Heterozygous **(ii)** Uniform. (2)

c) (i) Varied **(ii)** Some new useful varieties may be obtained from it. (2)

d) They are maintained for the purpose of crossing them with one another to produce crossbreed animals that express hybrid vigour. (1)

3 a) (i) The assembly of overlapping DNA fragments from an organism's genome into a sequence of nucleotide bases. **(ii)** It can be used to identify organisms that possess a particular allele for a desirable characteristic and then use these organisms in a breeding programme. (2)

b) (i) Introduce genetic information from one species into the genome of another. **(ii)** It enables an allele for a desirable characteristic to be inserted into the genome of a crop plant. (2)

19 Crop protection

Testing Your Knowledge 1

1 a) Natural ecosystem (1)

b) (i) Agricultural ecosystem. **(ii)** The pest can feed and reproduce repeatedly without running out of food. (2)

2 Reduction in crop productivity and contamination of grain crop with their seeds. (2)

3 a) Short life cycle and production of many seeds. (2)

b) They are already established and have storage organs that supply food until environmental conditions are favourable for photosynthesis. (2)

4 a) They suck sugar from the plant which is therefore denied some of its energy supply. This affects the crop plant's vigour and yield adversely. (2)

b) Nematode and mollusc. (2)

c) By being airborne or by being carried by vectors. (2)

Testing Your Knowledge 2

1 a) It refers to a traditional non-chemical method that has evolved over time by trial and error. (1)

b) A series of different crop plants are grown in turn on the same piece of ground. If a pest can only attack a certain type of host plant, it is controlled because it cannot survive for years until its host returns. (3)

c) Ploughing and careful choice of time of sowing crop. (2)

2 a) It kills the broad-leaved weeds but not the narrow-leaved cereal crops. (1)

b) The systemic type is absorbed and transported to all plant parts giving overall protection whereas the contact type acts as a protective layer to those plant parts above ground only and may be washed off by rain. (2)

3 a) (1)

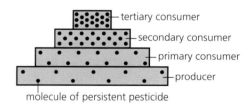

Figure An19.1

b) (i) See Figure An19.1. **(ii)** They are densest at the top because the molecules of persistent chemical accumulate in the food chain and become most concentrated in the tertiary consumer. (3)

4 a) Continued use of pesticide exerts a <u>selection</u> pressure on a population producing a <u>resistant</u> population of pests. (2)

b) The reduction of a <u>pest</u> population by the deliberate introduction of one of its natural enemies is called <u>biological</u> control. (2)

c) The use of a combination of techniques such as chemical and biological control and host plant <u>resistance</u> is called <u>integrated</u> pest management. (2)

d) The form of management referred to in **c)** aims to make <u>minimum</u> use of chemicals on the farm and to <u>control</u> pests. (2)

20 Animal welfare

Testing Your Knowledge

1 a) Contented animals breed more successfully and generate products of higher quality. (1)

b) In their opinion it is wrong to eat meat and eggs from hens that have suffered trimmed beaks and overcrowded conditions. (1)

2 a) (i) B **(ii)** D **(iii)** A **(iv)** C (4)

b) Improve the animals' welfare by enlarging their habitat and including some features present in their natural habitat. (2)

3 a) (i) An ethogram is a list of all the observed behaviours shown by an animal. **(ii)** It may allow an hypothesis to be constructed which, when tested by experiment, may provide information about an animal's welfare needs. (3)

b) It is set up to find out which of two conditions an animal prefers so that the animal's welfare can be enhanced. (2)

c) If it was hungry it would be motivated to find and consume food. If it was thirsty it would be motivated to find and drink water. (2)

21 Symbiosis

Testing Your Knowledge

1 a) Symbiosis is an ecological relationship between organisms of two different species that live in direct contact with one another. (2)

b) (2)

Type of symbiosis	Species 1	Species 2
mutualism	+	+
parasitism	–	+

Table An21.1

2 By direct contact. For example body lice being passed from one person to another.
Released as resistant stages able to survive adverse conditions. For example resistant larvae of cat flea.

Carried by a vector. For example *Plasmodium* carried by mosquitoes. (6)

3 a) It lacks a means of locomotion (and a digestive system). (1)

b) Light needed by its symbiotic partner zooxanthella for photosynthesis does not reach water at depths of 100 metres or more from the surface. (1)

c) It can use the secondary host as a site of asexual reproduction. (1)

22 Social behaviour

Testing Your Knowledge 1

1 a) Head raised, eyes staring, teeth bared, hackles raised. (2)

b) Head lowered, eyes averted, teeth covered, hackles lowered. (2)

c) **(i)** Social hierarchy **(ii)** Real fighting is kept to a minimum. Experienced leadership is guaranteed. (3)

2 All dogs including the subordinate ones obtain food. Large prey can be tackled that would be too big and strong for one dog to overpower. (2)

3 They form a protective group with the cows and calves at its centre and use a combined charge called mobbing to drive off the wolves. (2)

4 a) *Altruism* is 'unselfish' *behaviour* where a *donor* animal behaves in a way that may be *harmful* to itself but *helpful* to another animal, the *recipient*. (3)

b) Reciprocal altruism occurs when one individual at some cost to itself helps another animal in the knowledge that the favour will be returned. (1)

c) Although the individual does not survive, many of its genes will be present in the genomes of its offspring and close relatives. Therefore the genes will survive. (2)

Testing Your Knowledge 2

1 A division of labour exists amongst social insects. Food is gathered by numerous sterile members of the group but reproduction is carried out by a few fertile members only. (2)

2 Pollination of crop plants by insects and pest control by parasitic wasps. (2)

3 a) Recognising danger and foraging for food. (2)

b) It reduces conflict to a minimum enabling the weaker members to live close to the stronger ones. (1)

4 a) F Large (1)

b) F Friendship/cooperation/alliances (1)

c) T (1)

d) F Appeasement/submission (1)

e) T (1)

f) F Alliances (1)

g) T (1)

23 Mass extinction and biodiversity

Testing Your Knowledge

1 a) The complete demise of the species. (1)

b) Fossils (1)

c) If it caused sea levels to drop and vast areas of frozen land to appear then animals (such as certain types of shellfish) that are native to warm sheltered marine waters would perish. (2)

d) Over-hunting and habitat destruction. (2)

2 a) Genetic diversity and species diversity. (2)

b) Because all the alleles that it contains are also found in other populations. (1)

3 a) The one not dominated by one species. (1)

b) **(i)** Increases it **(ii)** Decreases it (2)

4 a) T (1)

b) F Richness (1)

c) F Abundance (1)

d) T (1)

e) F Lower (1)

24 Threats to biodiversity

Testing Your Knowledge 2

1 Exploitation means making the best use of a resource such as fish. Overexploitation means removing individuals such as fish at a rate greater than their maximum rate of reproduction. (2)

2 a) It could reduce it. (1)

b) It would be less able to adapt to environmental change. (1)

3 a) (4)

	Type of habitat	
	island fragment	unfragmented land mass
relative size of habitat (large/small)	small	large
species richness supported (high/low)	low	high
edge : interior (large/small)	large	small
chance of edge species invading interior (high/low)	high	low

Table An24.1

b) By habitat corridors. (1)

4 a) When it survives in the wild. (1)

b) When it outcompetes native species in the wild. (1)

5 Much of the information fed into the programs is based on speculation and guesswork. (1)

Applying Your Knowledge and Skills Answers

Chapters 1–8

1 a) (i) DNAase breaks DNA down into simple molecules. **(ii)** Protease breaks down protein into simple molecules (e.g. peptides). (2)

b) Because the transforming principle is contained in DNA which had been broken down by the enzyme rendering it ineffective. (2)

c) Because the transforming principle is not contained in the protein so it was not destroyed when the protein was broken down by enzyme action. (2)

d) Type of mouse; volume of liquid injected into the mouse. (2)

e) It could be repeated to see if the same results were obtained. (1)

2 (4)

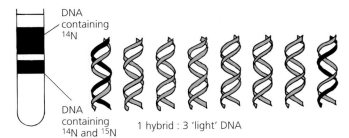

DNA containing ^{14}N

DNA containing ^{14}N and ^{15}N   1 hybrid : 3 'light' DNA

Figure An2.1

3 a) X = U; Y = G (2)

b) 1 (1)

c) UAA, UAG and UGA (3)

d) (i) Phenylalanine **(ii)** Threonine **(iii)** Glycine (3)

e) UUA, UUG, CUU, CUC, CUA and CUG (2)

f) Histidine (1)

4 a) (i) = T, **(ii)** = P, **(iii)** = S, **(iv)** = Q, **(v)** = U, **(vi)** = R (6)

b) B (1)

c) (i) Cow **(ii)** Because it is considered inappropriate to use cells that contain even a tiny amount of cow material to repair human tissue in this way. (2)

5 a) (i) Substitution **(ii)** One of the codons is now GAC instead of AAC. (2)

b) (i) glutamic acid–serine–leucine–threonine **(ii)** As answer to **(i)** (2)

c) (i) Silent **(ii)** The altered codon refers to the same amino acid as the original codon. (2)

d) (i) Missensical **(ii)** It still makes sense but not the original sense because the amino acid has changed to valine and this results in the production of a different type of haemoglobin. (2)

6 a) 3 (1)

b) Isabella and Espanola (2)

c) Santa Cruz (1)

d) X = large seed-eating from Pinta; Y = large cactus-eating from Pinta; Z = medium seed-eating from Culpepper (2)

e) (i) Type X (large seed-eating) **(ii)** One type might become extinct (or two species might survive as small populations living in fierce competition or …?). (2)

7 a) TACTGGTACT (1)

b) ATGACCATGA (1)

8 a) See core text pages 105–106 (and pages 94–95). (4)

b) See core text page 106. (4)

c) See core text page 106. (2)

Chapters 9–16

1 a) (i) Concentration of substrate
(ii) Independent   **(iii)** It caused an increase in reaction rate. (3)

b) Concentration of enzyme (1)

c) (i) A   **(ii)** C   **(iii)** B (3)

d) More enzyme could be added. (1)

2 a) (i) Yellow compound has been formed as a result of the action of ß-galactosidase on ONPG.   **(ii)** Lactose has acted as an inducer and switched on the gene for ß-galactosidase. Yellow compound has been formed as in **(i)**. (2)

b) A very low concentration of lactose was present so its action as an inducer was less pronounced and only a little ONPG was formed. (1)

c) (1)

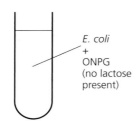

E. coli
+
ONPG
(no lactose present)

Figure An9.1

d) The experiment could be repeated. (1)

e) (i) E would fluoresce; F would not fluoresce.   **(ii)** Cells in E have been transformed therefore they will respond to arabinose acting as an inducer and produce GFP. Cells in F have not been transformed therefore they cannot be induced by arabinose to produce GFP. (3)

3 a) Repeat the experiment with several concentrations of the substrate (succinic acid) as the independent variable factor. (1)

b) If low concentrations give little or no colour change in the presence of malonic acid but higher concentrations do bring about decolourisation of DCPIP, then this shows that malonic acid is less effective at higher concentrations of substrate and is acting as a competitive inhibitor. (2)

4 See core text pages 142–143 and 146–147. (10)

5 a) (i) 10 °C   **(ii)** 30 °C (1)

b) (i) 39 °C   **(ii)** 39 °C (1)

c) (i) Cat   **(ii)** Lizard (1)

d) (i) Lizard   **(ii)** Cat (1)

e) (i) Cat   **(ii)** Physical activity is directly related to metabolic rate which is affected by body temperature. The cat's body temperature remains constantly high therefore it remains potentially active at night making it a better hunter than the lizard whose body temperature falls at night making it slow and poor at catching prey. (3)

6 a) A and B (and D) (1)

b) (i) Only one starling was used.   **(ii)** Repeat the experiment using many starlings. (2)

c) Because no record is left by the bird of its movements. (1)

d) A and B (1)

e) D and F (1)

f) C and E (1)

g) Transparent windows, autumn, overcast sky; mirrored windows, spring, clear sky (2)

7 a) To eliminate experimental error and improve the reliability of the results. (1)

b) This arrangement gives a larger surface area of liquid medium (exposed to air) upon which fungal growth can occur. (1)

c) A (1)

d) (i) As glucose concentration increases so also does dry weight of mycelium.   **(ii)** The more carbohydrate that is available, the more protoplasm the fungus can build.   **(iii)** Sporulation increases to an optimum at 1.0% glucose and then drops at the higher concentration of 10%. (3)

e) (i) They mass produce the vegetative mycelium when they want to obtain the antibiotic and they promote maximum sporulation when they need spores for the next inoculum.   **(ii)** Vegetative = 10%, sporulation = 1%   **(iii)** Repeat the experiment using many more concentrations of glucose e.g. 2%, 3%, 4% etc. (3)

8 a) *Bacillus amyloliquefaciens* (1)

b) *Eco*RI (1)

c) (i) Hind III   **(ii)** Sticky (2)

d) (1)

Figure An15.1

e) (2)

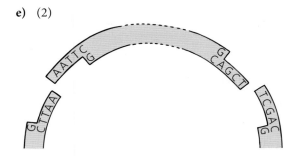

Figure An15.2

Chapters 17–24

1 a) P = chlorophyll a; A = chlorophyll c, xanthophyll and carotene (1)

b) Fungus (1)

c) (3)

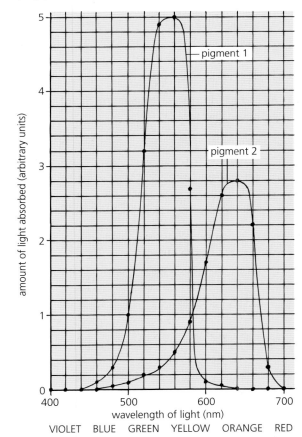

Figure An17.1

d) See *x*-axis of graph in part **c)** (1)

e) **(i)** Pigment 2 = phycocyanin
(ii) Pigment 1 = phycoerythrin (2)

f) (2)

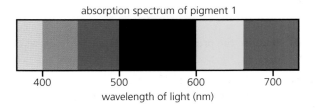

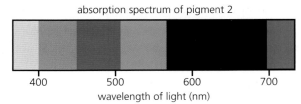

Figure An17.2

g) Since phycoerythrin absorbs green light, this extends the range of wavelengths that can be absorbed beyond those taken in by chlorophyll a and helps the plant to survive in a dimly lit habitat. (1)

2 a) X = 25, Y = 558, Z = 2500 (3)

b) D (1)

c) **(i)** B   **(ii)** This has the highest value per hectare for BY – EY which gives an approximate value for fodder. (2)

d) High economic yield (1)

e) Because they get a reasonable economic yield of peas and a large supply of animal fodder. (1)

3 a) F_1 (1)

b) F_1 is taller, has longer mean ear length and has higher mean yield than either parent. (3)

c) P_1 (1)

d) Inbreeding depression means the decline of a certain characteristic as a result of continuous selfing as shown by plant height in this example. (1)

e) **(i)** The yield has increased dramatically and less land is needed.   **(ii)** By doing so they are guaranteed a bumper F_1 crop whereas grains kept back by themselves would give poorer and poorer plants. (3)

4 a) 1:20 (1)

b) 1600 (1)

c) **(i)** 21.25 **(ii)** 4.25 **(iii)** No, because there is a large overlap between the ranges covered by their error bars. **(iv)** Yes, because there is no overlap between the ranges covered by their error bars. (6)

d) Because the predators would escape and not eat the prey. (1)

5 a) To reduce the effect of experimental error. (1)

b) To increase the reliability of the results. (1)

c) **(i)** 'left for one week to become habituated to their pen'. **(ii)** At the start they might spend more time on a novel substrate out of curiosity but not make it their preferred substrate in the end. (2)

d) Size of pen; mass/volume of substrate used (2)

e) P = M > S > W (1)

6 a) Because the mosquito is only the vector; the disease is caused by *Plasmodium*. (1)

b) The proboscis is a two-way tube. (1)

c) **(i)** Because the toxic substances are also released into the blood stream. **(ii)** Many of the person's red blood cells have been destroyed leaving them anaemic. (2)

d) Primary host = mosquito; secondary host = human (1)

e) **(i)** *Plasmodium* **(ii)** Mosquito **(iii)** Human (3)

7 a) (1)

Winner	Net number of contests won
T	14
R	14
P	16
R	20
S	4
R	6
P	8
T	10
R	18
P	12

Table An22.1

b) **(i)** Q **(ii)** Q was never an overall contest winner against any other bird. (2)

c) R, P, T, S, Q (1)

8 a) 50% (1)

b) **(i)** By a horizontal line inside the box. **(ii)** 1 = 31 mm, 2 = 24 mm, 3 = 13 mm (2)

c) **(i)** 1 **(ii)** 2 (2)

d) An actual value (1)

e) 6 mm (1)

f) 3 (1)

g) As latitude decreases, temperature increases promoting growth. (1)